Katakana

Consonants/semivowels ([y] an... ...els

N	W	R	Y	M	H	N					Vowels
ン	ワ	ラ	ヤ	マ	ハ	ナ					A
		リ		ミ	ヒ	ニ	チ (chi)	シ (shi)	キ	イ	I
		ル	ユ	ム	フ (fu)	ヌ	ツ (tsu)	ス	ク	ウ	U
		レ		メ	ヘ	ネ	テ	セ	ケ	エ	E
	(ヲ)*	ロ	ヨ	モ	ホ	ノ	ト	ソ	コ	オ	O

*ヲ is rarely used in modern Japanese.

Voiceless sounds and voiced/semi-voiced sounds (katakana)

semi-voiced	voiced	voice-less	voiced	voice-less	voiced	voice-less	voiced	voice-less	Vowels
P	B	H	D	T	Z/J	S	G	K	
パ	バ	ハ	ダ	タ	ザ	サ	ガ	カ	A
ピ	ビ	ヒ	(ヂ)*	チ (chi)	ジ (ji)	シ (shi)	ギ	キ	I
プ	ブ	フ (fu)	(ヅ)*	ツ (tsu)	ズ	ス	グ	ク	U
ペ	ベ	ヘ	デ	テ	ゼ	セ	ゲ	ケ	E
ポ	ボ	ホ	ド	ト	ゾ	ソ	ゴ	コ	O

* In standard Japanese, ヂ is pronounced as ジ, and ヅ is pronounced as ズ, so ヂ and ヅ are rarely used in modern spellings.

Contracted sounds (katakana)

R	M	P	B	H	N	T (CH)	Z (J)	S	G	K	[-i] sound character
リ	ミ	ピ	ビ	ヒ	ニ	チ	ジ	シ	ギ	キ	
リャ	ミャ	ピャ	ビャ	ヒャ	ニャ	チャ	ジャ	シャ	ギャ	キャ	small ヤ
リュ	ミュ	ピュ	ビュ	ヒュ	ニュ	チュ	ジュ	シュ	ギュ	キュ	small ユ
リョ	ミョ	ピョ	ビョ	ヒョ	ニョ	チョ	ジョ	ショ	ギョ	キョ	small ヨ

TOBIRA
BEGINNING JAPANESE

初級日本語

とびら

岡まゆみ
Mayumi Oka

近藤純子
Junko Kondo

[文法解説]
筒井通雄
Michio Tsutsui

森祐太
Yuta Mori

奥野智子
Tomoko Okuno

榊原芳美
Yoshimi Sakakibara

曽我部絢香
Ayaka Sogabe

安田昌江
Masae Yasuda

Kurosio Publishers

刊行によせて

　本書は時代にあった新しい初級日本語教科書をお探しの先生方、そして、「これから日本語を始めよう！」「もう一度日本語を勉強したい」と考えている学習者の皆さんに向けて作成しました。合言葉は「日本語学習を通して自分を再発見。世界とつながる」で、初級の日本語教材ながら、知的好奇心を刺激され、学習効果を実感すると同時にワクワク感と達成感が得られる内容となっています。

　本書の主な特徴は以下の通りです。

- 独自の「できるリスト」に基づいた学習到達目標の設定
- デジタル世代にあった言語学習活動
- 日常的な話題・会話と自然な場面設定を通しての言語四技能の習得
- 語彙・漢字・文法・表現・文化の密接な関連づけ
- 現在の日本事情を踏まえた日本文化の紹介
- 反転授業動画を含む充実したオンライン教材の提供

　昨今の情報社会では、初級学習で取り上げられる表層的な文化情報は日本国外でも簡単に得ることができます。よって、本書ではありきたりの文化紹介ではなく、日本の伝統や日本人の習慣など、日本文化の深層部分への気づきを促すような話題も取り入れました。

　図らずも本書はコロナ禍の只中での刊行となりましたが、パンデミックがもたらした「ニューノーマル」という生活様式は教育のあり方にも多大な影響を与え、言語学習も新たな学びの形へと急速に変容しつつあります。本書はこうした新しい言語学習環境に対応することで、世界中のどこにいても日本語が楽しく効率的に学べる教科書を目指しました。

　本書制作にあたり、クリストファー・シャードさんには英語監修と校正に加え、本書の内容に準拠した反転授業用動画を作成していただきました。コロナ禍におけるオンライン教育の広範な普及により、言語教育における動画の有用性とその教育効果が改めて認識されましたが、『初級日本語とびら』はシャードさんの尽力により全課の導入内容に動画を提供することができました。また、平川ワイター永子さんの日英にわたる緻密で的確な校閲・校正には著者一同大いに助けられました。お二人には改めて心よりお礼申し上げます。

　試用版の内容について様々な意見をお寄せくださったイェール大学他の先生方と学生の皆さんにもこの場を借りて感謝の気持ちをお伝えします。そして、毎年試用版を使用して、忌憚のない意見や感想を聞かせてくれたミシガン大学の学生の皆さん、「どうもありがとう！」皆さんのお陰で学習者の視点を十分に取り込んだ教材を完成することができたと感謝しています。

　本書出版の機会を与えてくださったくろしお出版の岡野秀夫社長、忍耐強く編集作業を続けてくださった市川麻里子さんと金髙浩子さん、とびら初級 WEB サイトの構築を担当してくださった堀池晋平さんには深く感謝申し上げます。特に市川さんの秀でた編集能力とプロジェクト遂行力なくしては、本書が今のような完成度に達することはなかったと思います。最後に、日本語教育における本書の重要性を理解し、多大なご援助をくださった国際交流基金ロサンゼルス日本文化センターとミシガン大学日本研究センターにも感謝の意を表します。

　「とびらを開く」というのは何かを新しく始める、未知の世界に目を向けるという意味のメタファーです。書名にある「とびら」という言葉には、「日本という新しい世界へのとびらを開く」という思いを込めました。学習者の皆さんが本書を使って日本語を学ぶことでより広い世界へと視野を広げ、人として成長していくための一助となることを願ってやみません。

2021 年 6 月　著者一同

Preface & Acknowledgments

We created this textbook with you in mind: you, the instructor looking for a beginner-level Japanese textbook suited to our times, and you, the learner excited to begin studying Japanese for the first time or to dive back into Japanese once more. Our touchstone has been the idea that studying Japanese can be both a means of self-rediscovery and a way of connecting to the world, and while this is an introductory text, we have designed it to pique your intellectual curiosity and give you a sense of excitement and achievement throughout the learning process.

Below are some of the distinctive features of this textbook:

- Goal setting based on "*Dekiru* Lists," our original set of learning outcomes
- Language learning activities designed for digital natives
- Acquisition of the four main language skills by addressing and discussing everyday topics in natural settings
- Close linking of vocabulary, kanji, grammar, and culture
- Introduction of Japanese culture through the lens of contemporary Japanese society
- A robust set of online learning materials, including instructional videos suitable for use in a flipped classroom

In this age of information technology, the kind of surface-level cultural information normally introduced in an introductory course in Japanese is easily available from just a cursory internet search. Because of this, in this text we have avoided run-of-the-mill cultural introductions in favor of discussions about Japanese traditions and customs that can lead to deeper discoveries about Japan and its culture.

While this textbook is a work of many years, it is being published in the midst of the COVID-19 pandemic, a global public health emergency that has ushered in a "new normal" with a profound impact on the state of education across the world. Language instruction in particular has had to quickly adapt to new forms of learning, and we have taken great pains to ensure that this textbook is fully compatible with this new language-learning environment so that it can be used anywhere in the world to learn Japanese both enjoyably and efficiently.

There are many people we would like to thank for their help in making this textbook a reality. First is Christopher Schad, who, in addition to editing and proofreading the English in the textbook, has also created the instructional videos mentioned above. The spread of online education during the coronavirus pandemic has shown us just how useful and effective video learning materials can be in language education, and thanks to Chris we have a full panoply of them to provide you with. We would also like to extend our thanks to Eiko Hirakawa Weyter, whose meticulous, precise proofreading in both English and Japanese has been an enormous help. Many thanks to both of you.

We would also like to thank the instructors and students who gave us invaluable feedback on the pilot versions of the text, including those at Yale University. In particular, we would like to express our gratitude to the students at the University of Michigan, who have candidly shared their opinions and impressions with us during every year of development. It is because of you that we have been able to create a textbook that truly incorporates the learner's viewpoint. どうもありがとう (thanks very much)!

Our sincere thanks also go out to our publishing team at Kurosio: President Hideo Okano, who gave us the opportunity to publish this textbook; Mariko Ichikawa and Hiroko Kanetaka, our eternally patient editorial team; and Shinpei Horiike, our website developer. In particular, we have Mariko's superior project management and editorial skills to thank for keeping us organized and adding polish to our work. Finally, we would also like to thank the Japan Foundation Los Angeles and the Center for Japanese Studies at the University of Michigan for providing us with support for the textbook's development.

In Japanese, the phrase *tobira o hiraku* ("to open a door") is used as a metaphor for starting something new or venturing out into the unknown. We chose TOBIRA ("portal; door") as the title for our textbook with this in mind; we hope that it will be a portal for students into the new world of Japan. Moreover, we hope that it can serve as a gateway to a more global mindset and a pathway to personal growth.

June 2021   The authors

CONTENTS

4

Unit 2   まわりとつながる Connecting with others   115

CONTENTS

日本語を
はじめる前に

Before
we begin

『とびらI』の使い方
How to use *TOBIRA I*

📖 An Introduction to the Textbook for Students

◎ The Structure of *TOBIRA I*

- *TOBIRA I* consists of 10 lessons divided into three units, with an additional preparatory lesson to help you participate in classes in Japanese from the very beginning.

- In this textbook, we aim for a comfortable, organic learning experience—it is designed so that you can acquire Japanese just by working through the book, page by page and lesson by lesson.

- The vocabulary, kanji, and grammar points in each lesson are all related to each other, and the activities are structured to allow you to practice speaking, reading, listening, and writing new material while also revisiting and solidifying your grasp on older material.

📖 教師の皆様へ

◎ 『とびらI』の構成

- 『とびらI』は3つのユニットで構成されていて、1課から10課まであります。また、始めから日本語で授業をすることを目指し、準備の課として0課を設けています。

- 本書には「無理のない学習＝各課、各ページの学習を順番に進めていけば知らない間に日本語ができるようになっていること」というねらいがあります。

- 各課の語彙、漢字、文法はお互いに関連性があり、話す・読む・聞く・書くの練習で覚えたことやできるようになったことを積み重ねながら、スパイラルで学んでいくようにデザインしてあります。

各ユニット Each Unit

各課の構成 Structure for Each Lesson

| ユニットの
とびら
Unit
Introduction | → | 各課のとびら
Lesson Introduction | → | 会話
Conversation | → | 単語
Vocabulary | → | 漢字(3課から)
Kanji (L3 onward) |

| 文法
Grammar | → | 話しましょう
Activities | → | 読みましょう
Reading | → | 聞きましょう
Listening | → | ユニットの
チャレンジ
Unit Capstone
Challenge |

| ひらがな：0課 Hiragana: L0 | カタカナ：2課 Katakana: L2 | タイプする：3課 Typing: L3 |

◎ Units

- Each unit consists of three or four lessons, and the theme progresses from the personal and the familiar in the first unit towards larger, more global topics in those that follow.

- At the beginning of each unit is a preparatory "Pre-activity" page that gives you an opportunity to think and talk about topics and themes related to the content of the unit before commencing your study.

- At the end of each unit is a "Challenge" page that introduces opportunities for self-directed study that will deepen the knowledge and further develop the skills you have acquired in the unit. For instance, there are activities such as an online novel, a mascot character contest, and social media posts that provide you with fun, creative ways to further your studies.

◎ ユニットについて

- 1ユニットは3～4課で構成されていて、テーマは個人的なことや身近な話題から始まり、少しずつ外の世界に意識が広がっていくような流れになっています。

- 「ユニット扉」の次頁にある「ユニットXの前に」は、各ユニットに入る前の準備のページです。そのユニットの学習項目と関係するトピックについて、考えたり話し合ったりします。

- 各ユニットの最後には「チャレンジ」があり、そのユニットで学んだことをさらに深く知ったり発展させたりし、自律学習を促します。例えば、オンラインノベル、ゆるキャラコンテスト、SNSに写真を投稿するなど楽しく自主的に日本語が学習できる活動があります。

◉ Lesson 0

- In Lesson 0, you will study Japanese greetings and basic classroom expressions to prepare for the class ahead of you.
- You will also learn about the Japanese sound and writing systems. The textbook itself will mostly focus on reading Japanese characters; writing practice can be found in the workbook.
- The transition to Lesson 1 will be smoother if you master hiragana in Lesson 0 before moving forward, but it is also possible to begin studying material from Lesson 1 as you make your way through Lesson 0.

◉ The Japanese Sound and Writing Systems

- In this section, you will study the sounds of Japanese and the hiragana characters used to write them.
- Pronunciation study modules are available on the *TOBIRA* website. In them, you will find audio files to listen to as you practice your pronunciation.
- You can proceed through the pronunciation study modules in order or pick and choose from them to meet your individual needs. Each module contains exercises for checking your progress at the end.
- Katakana, used most frequently to write foreign words, is introduced in Lesson 2 along with audio clips to help with pronunciation. You will practice reading katakana in the textbook and writing it in the workbook.
- At the end of Lesson 3 you will find instructions for typing in Japanese along with practice exercises.

◉ The Lesson *Tobira* ("Portal") Page

- At the beginning of each lesson is a *Tobira* (or "portal") page, which summarizes the content to be learned in the lesson.
- It also contains a *Dekiru* (or "can do") List that specifies what you will be able to do by the end of the lesson.

◉ ０課について

- ０課では準備として、まず「日本語の挨拶」と「授業で使う基本的な表現」を学びます。
- 次に日本語の音と文字を同時に導入します。本書では主に文字を読む練習を行い、文字を書く練習はワークブックで行います。
- ０課でできるだけひらがなをマスターしておくと、１課からの指導がスムーズに進みますが、０課の途中から１課に入って、ひらがな学習と１課を並行して進めることもできます。

◉ 日本語の音と文字

- ひらがなとひらがなを用いた特殊音などの発音と表記を練習します。
- 発音はモジュール形式の練習が「とびら初級 WEB サイト」にあります。音声ファイルを聞きながら発音の練習ができます。
- 発音の練習は順番通りに進めても、練習したいモジュールを選んで練習してもいいです。また、それぞれのモジュールの最後には、練習したことが身についたかチェックするための課題があります。
- 外国語の言葉を表すカタカナは２課で音声と同時に導入します。カタカナの読み方は本書で練習し、文字を書く練習はワークブックで行います。
- ３課の最後に「日本語のタイプのし方」を練習します。

◉ 各課の扉のページ

- 各課のはじめには「扉」のページがあり、その課で勉強する内容がまとめてあります。
- 「できるリスト」には、その課を終えたら何ができるようになるかが示してあります。

できる I Greet and give a simple self-introduction to people you are meeting for the first time.
初めて会った人に挨拶や簡単な自己紹介をすることができる。 — Entry ☐ Exit ☐

できる II Ask and answer questions about basic information such as people's names, hometowns, etc.
名前や出身などの基本的な情報について、尋ねたり答えたりすることができる。 — Entry ☐ Exit ☐

できる III Briefly talk about things you like.
好きなことやものについて、簡単に話すことができる。 — Entry ☐ Exit ☐

- Before beginning each lesson, you will perform an "Entry Check" to ascertain the lesson's learning objectives. Then, when you finish the lesson, you will perform an "Exit Check" to see what you have learned to do and to make sure you have met those objectives.

- 各課を始める前に、「Entry Check」をして、その課の到達目標を理解します。そして、終わった後で、「Exit Check」をし、「Entry Check」と比べてどんなことができるようになったか、学習成果を確認します。

◎ Conversations

- The conversations in the textbook feature as their main characters a group of students studying Japanese and living in their university's Japan House. These characters will study along with you, and you will improve your Japanese together as you progress through the textbook.

◎ 会話

- 会話の登場人物はジャパンハウスというシェアハウスで日本語を使って生活しています。登場人物たちは日本語のクラスで学んでいて、『とびらⅠ』を通して学習者と共に日本語が話せるようになっていきます。

「とびら」の主な登場人物

MAIN CHARACTERS IN *TOBIRA*

USA

Japan House
ジャパンハウス
Japan Hausu

Keita・けいた Keeta
Ai・アイ Ai
Mark・マーク Maaku
Riemann リーマン Riiman
Nyanta にゃんた Nyanta
Tao タオ Tao

Goble University
ゴーブルだいがく
Gooburu Daigaku

Japan

Jean ジャン Jan

Prof. Kuroda くろだせんせい Kuroda-sensee

- In each lesson there are 3 to 4 conversations and a "Conversation Tips" for more natural speech.
- The conversations align with the lesson's *Dekiru* List, covering each topic on it in order.
- Audio for each conversation is available on the *TOBIRA* website.

- 一課に３つから４つの会話と、自然な話し方をするためのワンポイントアドバイスが入っています。
- 会話の内容は「できるリスト」に順番に対応しています。
- 会話音声は「とびら初級WEBサイト」で聞くことができます。

◎ Vocabulary

- We have chosen around 70 commonly used words as vocabulary to memorize for each lesson; these are presented on both a "Vocabulary with Pictures" page and a "Vocabulary List" page, as seen below.
- On the "Vocabulary with Pictures" page, words are grouped by theme and presented with illustrations to help with memorization.
- In the "Vocabulary List," words are sorted by part of speech and presented along with their English translations, pitch accent, accompanying particles (for verbs), and additional explanation and examples as needed.
- Feel free to use either page, or both, to best fit your learning style and needs.

◎ 単語

- 単語セクションには「絵入り単語」と「品詞別単語リスト」があり、覚える単語として日常生活でよく使う言葉を各課で70程度選んであります。
- 「絵入り単語」はイラスト入りで関連がある単語をまとめています。絵を見ながら覚えることができます。
- 「品詞別単語リスト」は単語を品詞別に並べ、対応する英語、動詞と一緒に使う助詞、ピッチアクセント、誤用を防ぐための補足説明や例が入れてあります。
- 目的や学習スタイルに合わせて２種類の単語ページを使い分けるように指導してください。

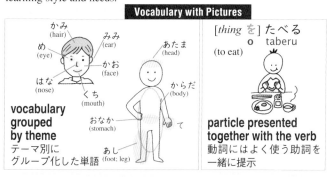

Vocabulary with Pictures

かみ (hair)
みみ (ear)
め (eye)
あたま (head)
かお (face)
はな (nose)
くち (mouth)
からだ (body)
おなか (stomach)
て
あし (foot; leg)

vocabulary grouped by theme
テーマ別にグループ化した単語

[*thing* を] たべる
o taberu
(to eat)

particle presented together with the verb
動詞にはよく使う助詞を一緒に提示

Vocabulary List

NOUNS

1	わたし watashi	I
2	ぼく boku	I [used mainly by men]
3	がくせい gakusee	student
4	だいがくせい daigakusee	university student; college student

pitch accent provided for each word
単語の上にピッチアクセントを提示

- Beginning in Lesson 3, between 14 and 18 new kanji are introduced per lesson, for a total of 139 characters. Whenever possible, we link the new kanji and new vocabulary in each lesson.

- The "Story of Kanji" section introduces important strategies and information that will help you with learning kanji.

- 3課から10課までの各課に、初級レベルの漢字が14-18字、全部で139字紹介してあります。漢字は各課の新出単語とできるだけリンクしています。

- 「かんじのはなし」には、漢字学習の助けになる情報や漢字を覚えるためのストラテジーが紹介してあります。

A Guide to the Kanji Information Chart／漢字基本情報の見方

❶ — 56 — **❸** 見 ｜ ケン **❺** ｜ 意見 opinion   見学する to observe; to visit/tour (a place) [study by observation]
いけん   けんがく

❷ 見   見 **❹** ｜ み（る）**❻** ｜ 見る to see; to watch   （お）花見 cherry-blossom viewing
み   はなみ
み（える）
み（せる）｜ 見える to be visible   見せる to show
み   み **❽**

❼ — to see; to watch **❾** 丨 冂 冂 冃 目 目 見

❶ Index number 通し番号	All the kanji from Lesson 3 through Lesson 10 have index numbers. 第3課から第10課の漢字には通し番号がつけてあります。
❷ Handwritten character 手書き文字	The kanji as it should be written by hand. 手書きの楷書体の文字です。
❸ Mincho font 明朝フォント	One of the most common font styles in Japanese, Mincho is a family of fonts equivalent to Roman alphabet serif fonts such as Times New Roman. 英語の Times New Roman のように、日本語でよく使われるフォントの一つです。
❹ Gothic font ゴシックフォント	Another common Japanese font style, Gothic is a font family that corresponds to Roman alphabet sans-serif fonts such as Arial. 英語の Arial のように、日本語でよく使われるフォントの一つです。
❺ *On*-reading 音読み	A reading borrowed from Chinese; as such, it is written here in katakana. All readings to be memorized for the current lesson are highlighted. カタカナで書いてあります。各課で覚える読み方にはハイライトがしてあります。
❻ *Kun*-reading 訓読み	A reading native to Japanese; as such, it is written here in hiragana. All readings to be memorized for the current lesson are highlighted. ひらがなで書いてあります。各課で覚える読み方にはハイライトがしてあります。
❼ English meaning 英訳	The kanji's basic meaning in English. 漢字の基本的な意味が英語で書いてあります。
❽ Vocabulary list 単語リスト	A list of frequently used words in which the kanji appears. All words to be memorized for the current lesson are highlighted. 漢字を含むよく使われる単語のリストです。各課で覚える単語にはハイライトがしてあります。
❾ Stroke order 書き順	The order in which the strokes that make up the kanji are to be written. Following this order will help you write the character neatly and with good proportions. 漢字を構成している線や点を書く順番が提示してあります。この書き順で書くと漢字がきれいに書けます。

◎ Grammar

- The explanation for each grammar point includes the grammar point's function, an English equivalent or equivalents, the sentence structure it is used in, and example sentences. Each grammar point is also clearly linked to an item on the lesson's *Dekiru* List.

- Grammatical explanations use sentence-structure charts to present grammar concisely. For grammar that is frequently misused, examples of incorrect and correct use are paired, and the incorrect use is also explained.

- The "GID" that appears in grammatical explanations refers to the "Grammar in Depth" supplement provided on the *TOBIRA* website. You can use the QR code in the textbook to jump directly to the section in question. Reading the GID can help you deepen your understanding of particular grammar points and broaden your understanding of Japanese grammar as a whole.

- "Language Notes" also appear in some lessons to highlight important grammatical topics and themes across the various lessons of the textbook.

◎ 文法

- 文法解説は、項目見出し・機能・対応英語・文型・説明・例文からなっています。そして、各文法項目と「できるリスト」のつながりがすぐに分かるようになっています。

- 解説は文型チャートを使い簡潔に説明してあります。誤用が起きやすいものについては、誤用例・正しい文・使えない理由の説明もあります。

- 解説中にある「GID」は Grammar in Depth のことで、文法をより深く理解するための情報が「とびら初級 WEB サイト」で提供されています。本冊から QR コードで直接各項目に飛ぶこともできます。GID で学習者への文法説明を補ったり、自分で読むように指導したりすることで、文法力の強化ができます。また、一つのセクションを通して読むことによって、文法の全体構造が理解しやすくなります。

- 「言語ノート」ではいくつかの重要なトピックを取り上げ、各課の文法解説を補っています。

Abbreviation／略語 Symbol／記号	Meaning／意味	Examples／例
Adj	Adjective／形容詞	おおきい (*I*-adjective); べんり (*Na*-adjective)
Adj(*i*)	*I*-adjective／イ形容詞	おおきい; おもしろい
A(*i*)-stem	Stem of *i*-adjective／イ形容詞の語幹	おおき; おもしろ
Adj(*na*)	*Na*-adjective／ナ形容詞	べんり (な); しずか (な)
Adv	Adverb／副詞	すぐ; ゆっくり
Conj	Conjunction／接続詞	が; から; でも
N	Noun／名詞	がくせい; にほん; バス
Prt	Particle／助詞	は; が; を; に; よ; ね
Q-word	Question word／疑問詞	なに; だれ; どこ
S	Sentence／文	わたしは がくせいです。
V	Verb／動詞	はなす; たべる; くる
V-*masu*	Stem of the *masu*-form of a verb／動詞の「ます形」の語幹	はなします; たべます
V-*nai*	*Nai*-form of a verb minus ない／動詞の「ない形」の動詞から「ない」を取ったもの	はなさない; たべない; こない
V-plain	Plain form of a verb／動詞の普通形	たべる; たべた; たべない; たべなかった
V-*te*	*Te*-form of a verb／動詞のて形	はなして; たべて; きて
Ø	No particle/*da*／助詞や「だ」が不要な場合	まいにち Ø にほんごを はなします。
×	Ungrammatical or unacceptable／非文・不適格文	×わたしは せんこうの にほんごです。
??	Extremely unnatural／非常に不自然	??あめが ふっていません。
GID	Grammar in Depth／より深い文法説明	
⚠	Important note on an frequently misunderstood point／間違いやすいポイントの説明	
FYI	Grammar item that you only need to learn to understand; no exercises are provided／理解するだけでいい文法	

◎ Phonetic Guides

- Romanization (pronunciation guides using the English alphabet) is supplied as follows:
  - ・Lesson 0: all hiragana and katakana (exception: the hiragana section)
  - ・Lesson 1: all hiragana and katakana (exception: the reading section)
  - ・Lesson 2: hiragana in the vocabulary section only; all katakana (exceptions: the katakana section, the reading section)
  - ・Lesson 3: katakana in the vocabulary section only
- Kanji is introduced starting in Lesson 3; from that lesson onward, furigana (hiragana pronunciation guides) are presented along with unlearned kanji and new kanji for the lesson, with two exceptions:
  - ・No furigana are given for new kanji in the kanji practice and reading practice sections.
  - ・Furigana are provided for all kanji in the grammar explanation example sentences so that you can understand the sentences' meaning even if you do not remember the kanji used in them.

◎ Activities

- In this section, you will practice using grammatical items and expressions to fulfill the goals presented in the lesson's *Dekiru* List.
- The exercises will proceed from basic conjugation drills to sentence-building exercises to holistic conversation practice to help you build up your speaking skills naturally and comfortably.
- Exercises focus on natural conversations, simple discussions, and short presentations where the grammar in focus would actually be used. The rich variety in exercise types will keep things fresh and allow you to enjoy practicing.
- The examples for some exercises have parts of them underlined. You can use these examples as the base structure for your answers, substituting in the appropriate words and phrases for the underlined segments.
- Blue text in an example indicates grammar or expressions you should pay particular attention to.
- In Lesson 8, exercises using casual speech also begin to appear; these are marked with a t-shirt icon 👕.

◎ Reading

- There are three sections to each reading practice.
- In the first section, you will practice scanning and skimming to extract information from authentic materials written in Japanese.
- In the second section, you will learn and practice reading strategies to deepen your understanding of Japanese texts by examining sentence structure, word usage, and other aspects of a passage.
- In the final section, you will find fun writing exercises that build on the lesson's readings.

◎ ルビについて

- ローマ字ルビは以下についています。
  - ・0課：すべてのひらがなとカタカナ（例外：ひらがなセクション）
  - ・1課：すべてのひらがなとカタカナ（例外：「よみましょう」のひらがな）
  - ・2課：単語セクションとすべてのカタカナ語（例外：カタカナセクション、「よみましょう」）
  - ・3課：単語セクションのカタカナ語
- 3課から漢字が導入され、3課以降は未習の漢字にはひらがなルビがつきます。
- 新出漢字は、その課の漢字練習と読解練習にはルビがついていません。
- 文法例文に出てくる漢字には全てにルビがつけてあります。学習者が漢字が分からなくて文の意味が取れないことを避けるためです。

◎ 話しましょう

- 「できるリスト」を達成するために必要な文法項目や表現の練習をします。
- 練習は、基本ドリル→文レベル→総合的な練習と段階的になっており、無理なく話す力が身につけられます。
- 習ったことが実際に使える自然な会話、簡単な話し合い、短い発表など変化に富んだ活動で、楽しく練習できます。
- 練習の例に下線がある場合は置き換え練習をするという意味です。
- 青字は注意する助詞や表現を示しています。
- 8課からはカジュアルスピーチも練習します。カジュアルスピーチの練習には👕のマークがついています。

◎ 読みましょう

- 3つのセクションがあります。
- セクション1では生教材などを用いて、スキャニング、スキミングの読み方を使った情報取りの練習をします。
- セクション2では、読解を助ける様々な「読みのストラテジー」を用いて、文構造の把握や語彙の使い方から内容理解まで、より深く正確に読む練習をします。
- セクション3には、読解内容を発展させた楽しい「書く練習」があります。

- The readings themselves are diverse—from blog posts, app screens, and social media comments you are likely to encounter in everyday life to flyers, posters, news articles, folk tales, and essays. Through these texts, you will also have an opportunity to engage with Japan's various cultures.

◎ Listening

- This section provides practice employing a variety of different listening strategies to understand spoken Japanese. These strategies build on each other from lesson to lesson, allowing you to develop your overall listening comprehension abilities as you go.

- You will first do a pre-listening activity and then move on to the main listening practice. There will be words that you have not yet learned in these practices; the goal will be to listen, get the gist of the conversation, and extract the information you need despite the presence of such words.

◎ Instructional Videos

- There are instructional videos for writing, grammar, vocabulary, and expressions on the *TOBIRA* website. You can use these to familiarize yourself with material before class or to review and deepen your understanding afterwards.

◎ The *TOBIRA* Website

- You can access a variety of different supplementary materials on the *TOBIRA* website.

- □ Audio materials: These include audio recordings for the vocabulary, conversation, activities, and listening sections in each lesson. Content for which there is audio available is marked by **◀))LX-X** in the textbook.
- □ Instructional videos: Content for which there are instructional videos available is noted in the textbook.
- □ Grammar in Depth (GID)

In addition, there are links to web content related to each lesson's activities and a corner showcasing student work.

読み物は、ブログ、アプリ、SNSのような学習者が日常的に接するものから、チラシ、ポスター、ニュース記事、昔話、エッセイなど多岐に渡っています。読み物を通して、日本の様々な文化にも触れることができます。

◎ 聞きましょう

- 日本語の聴解に役立つストラテジーを用いて聴く練習をします。ストラテジーを積み上げていくことにより、総合的な聴解力を身につけることが目標です。

- まず、Pre-listening activity の練習をしてから Listening の練習をします。Listening の会話やモノローグには未習の語彙や表現も入っていますが、会話を完全に理解する必要はありません。分からない言葉があってもまずは聞いて、キーワードや会話の要点が把握できるように練習します。

◎ 反転授業 (flipped classroom) 用動画について

- 「とびら初級 WEB サイト」に反転授業 (flipped classroom) 用ビデオがあります (本文内の右アイコン)。文字、漢字、文法の導入、また注意が必要な語彙・表現の指導にご活用ください。反転授業用動画は授業の前に予習として見せることにより、授業ではより実践的、応用的な練習に時間を使うことができます。その他にも、授業内で使用する、自分のクラスの参考にする、学習者が復習や自律学習に使うなど多様な使い方が可能です。特に、オンライン授業やハイブリッド授業に役に立ちます。

◎ 「とびら初級WEBサイト」について

- 「とびら初級 WEB サイト」には、教科書を補助したり、学習を助けたりする各種教材にアクセスできます。

- □ 音声教材：教科書各課の「会話」「単語」「話しましょう」の基本練習、「聞きましょう」などの音声が聞けます。教科書では **◀))LX-X** で示してあります。
- □ 反転授業用ビデオ：教科書ではアイコンで示してあります。
- □ Grammar in Depth (GID)
- □ スケジュール、小テスト、試験、宿題のサンプル
- □ 「聞きましょう」「読み物」の練習問題の模範解答
- □ 「会話」「読み物」の英訳
- □ 「聞きましょう」の音声教材のスクリプト

その他、各課の活動に関連したサイトをまとめたリンク集や学習者の作品を紹介したコーナーなどがあります。

Opening the *tobira* ("door") to Japanese
Japanese basics with Prof. Tobira (Tobira-sensee) and Nyanta

How much do you know about the Japanese language?
When you hear Japanese, what does it sound like?
When you see Japanese text, what does it look like?

Instructional Video
Lesson 0

Your study companions:

にゃんた
Nyanta

とびらせんせい
Tobira-sensee

Let's start studying Japanese together!

Everyday expressions

Q1. How do I greet someone in Japanese?

Here are some examples. Expressions marked with (necktie icon) are used in formal situations, while those marked with (T-shirt icon) are used in casual situations. In Japanese, we switch between different speech styles and levels of formality depending on the situation and the people we are talking to. Do you make similar distinctions in your language, too?

➡ Saying hello and goodbye

 L0-1

❶ おはようございます
Ohayoo gozaimasu
Good morning.

おはよう
Ohayoo
Good morning.

❷ こんにちは
Konnichiwa
Good afternoon.

おはよう
Ohayoo

❸ こんばんは
Konbanwa
Good evening.

❹ さようなら
Sayoonara
Goodbye.

しつれいします
Shitsuree shimasu
Goodbye.
[used when addressing social superiors]

❺ じゃ、また（あした）
Ja, mata (ashita)
See you later;
See you (tomorrow).

➜ Set phrases for specific situations

 Besides greetings, there are some other fixed expressions that Japanese people use whenever a certain situation occurs. These expressions are presented below with illustrations demonstrating their use and additional explanation. Does your language have similar expressions?

⑥ はじめまして
Hajimemashite
どうぞ　よろしく　おねがいします
Doozo　yoroshiku　onegai shimasu
Nice to meet you.
[used when meeting someone for the first time in a formal context]

⑦ しつれいします
Shitsuree shimasu
Excuse me.
[used when entering or leaving a social superior's space]

⑧ おねがいします
Onegai shimasu
Please do me a favor.
[used when asking someone to do something for you]

⑨ （どうも）ありがとうございます
(Doomo) Arigatoo gozaimasu
Thank you (very much).
[used when expressing gratitude]

 Here are some other set phrases, also presented with illustrations demonstrating their use and additional explanation. Do you have expressions like these in your language?

⑩ いってきます
Ittekimasu
I'm going out now.
See you later.

いってらっしゃい
Itterasshai
See you when you get back.

⑪ ただいま
Tadaima
I'm back.

👕 **おかえり**
Okaeri
👔 **おかえりなさい**
Okaeri nasai
Welcome back.

⑫
👕 いただきます
Itadakimasu
Thank you for the meal.
(lit. "[I thankfully]
receive [this food].")
[used before eating]

👕 ごちそうさま
Gochisoosama
👔 ごちそうさまでした
Gochisoosama deshita
That was good.
(lit. "[That] was a treat.")
[used after eating]

⑬ 👕 おやすみ
Oyasumi
👔 おやすみなさい
Oyasumi nasai
Good night.

⑭
あのう、すみません
Anoo,   sumimasen
Um, excuse me.

⑮ 👕 ありがとう
Arigatoo
👔 ありがとうございます
Arigatoo gozaimasu
Thank you.
👔 すみません
Sumimasen
Thank you. (lit. "I'm sorry
[to inconvenience you].")

📢 L0-4

どうぞ
Doozo
Please take this.

👔 どういたしまして
Doo itashimashite
You're welcome.

⑯ 👕 ごめん
Gomen
Sorry.
あ、すみません／ごめんなさい
A,   sumimasen   gomennasai
Oh, I'm sorry.   I'm sorry.

⑰ 👕 おめでとう
Omedetoo
👔 おめでとうございます
Omedetoo gozaimasu
Congratulations!

👕 ありがとう
Arigatoo
👔 ありがとうございます
Arigatoo gozaimasu
Thank you.

Q2.

Are there any words or expressions I should learn to prepare for Japanese class?

That's a good question! Your teacher will often use the following expressions in class. If you learn them ahead of time, you'll be well prepared to participate right from the start!

Addressing each other in class

When you address your teacher, use your teacher's last name plus "sensee," which means "professor" or "teacher."

Ex. Tobira-sensee

When addressing you, your teacher might use your last name plus "san," which is a title like "Mr./Ms./Mx."

Ex. Sumisu-san

⚠ You <u>cannot</u> use "san" to refer to yourself.

⚠ Although there are words in Japanese that roughly translate to the English "you," they are only used in certain specific contexts and can come off as rude if used in other circumstances. It is much more common (and safer in terms of politeness) to address and refer to a conversational partner by their name, as in the example below.

Ex. スミスさんは　なんねんせいですか。
Sumisu-san wa nannensee desu ka.
What year in school are you, Smith-san?

Sumisu-san

Tanaka-san

When in class, you should address your classmates by their last names plus "san" unless directed otherwise.

Exs. Sumisu-san, Tanaka-san

person whose last name is <u>Smith</u>

person whose last name is <u>Tanaka</u>

➡ Classroom instructions

The following are some instructions your teacher might give in the classroom in Japanese.

❶
いってください
Itte kudasai
Please say it.

❷
みてください
Mite kudasai
Please look.

❸
かいてください
Kaite kudasai
Please write.

❹
よんでください
Yonde kudasai
Please read (aloud).

❺
はなしてください
Hanashite kudasai
Please speak.

❻
きいてください
Kiite kudasai
Please listen.

❼
〇〇さんに
san ni
きいてください
kiite kudasai
Please ask 〇〇-san.

❽
もういちど
Moo ichido
one more time

おおきいこえで
Ookii koe de
in a loud(er) voice

いってください
itte kudasai
Please say it ...
[when a teacher gives an instruction to students]

❾
もういちど
Moo ichido
one more time

おおきいこえで
Ookii koe de
in a loud(er) voice

ゆっくり
Yukkuri
(more) slowly

おねがいします
onegai shimasu
Could you please say it ...
[when a student makes a request of a teacher or classmate]

➔ Useful phrases in class

わかりますか。
Wakarimasu ka.
Do you understand?

はい、わかります。
Hai,　wakarimasu.
Yes, I understand.

いいえ、わかりません。
Iie,　wakarimasen.
No, I don't understand.

とびらせんせい、しつもんが　あります。
Tobira-sensee,　shitsumon ga　arimasu.
Prof. Tobira, I have a question.

↑
Sumisu-san

はい、スミスさん。
Hai,　Sumisu-san.
Yes, Mr./Ms./Mx. Smith.

 は　にほんごで　なんですか。
Pencil　wa　nihongo de　nan desu ka.
What is "pencil" in Japanese?

は　にほんごで　えんぴつです。
Pencil　wa　nihongo de　enpitsu desu.
"Pencil" is *enpitsu* in Japanese.

けしゴムは　えいごで　なんですか。
Keshigomu wa eego de　nan desu ka.
What is "*keshigomu*" in English?

けしゴムは　えいごで eraser です。
Keshigomu wa eego de　eraser desu.
"*Keshigomu*" is "eraser" in English.

そうですか。
Soo desu ka.
I see.

わかりました。
Wakarimashita.
I understand (lit. "[I] have understood"); I got it.

The sounds of Japanese

Q3. What kind of sounds does Japanese have?

[a]　[i]　[u]　[e]　[o]

Japanese has five vowels [a], [i], [u], [e], and [o] that can be paired with various consonants such as [k], [s], [t], [m], etc. and semivowels [y] and [w].

[k]　[s]　[t]　[m]　[y]　[w]

"*Inu*" is "dog" in Japanese. As you can see in this word, in general, Japanese words consist of two types of syllables: 1) vowels by themselves (e.g., [i]) and 2) consonant (or semivowel) and vowel combinations (e.g., [nu]).

i　　nu
い　　ぬ

Consonants/semivowels ([y] and [w])											Vowels
N	W	R	Y	M	H	N	T	S	K		
ん	わ	ら	や	ま	は	な	た	さ	か	あ	A
		り		み	ひ	に	ち (chi)	し (shi)	き	い	I
		る	ゆ	む	ふ* (fu)	ぬ	つ (tsu)	す	く	う	U
		れ		め	へ	ね	て	せ	け	え	E
	を** (o)	ろ	よ	も	ほ	の	と	そ	こ	お	O

* See p.22, 4) for more detailed information on the pronunciation of ふ.
** In standard Japanese, "w+o (を)" is generally pronounced as "o."

You can practice the pronunciation of individual hiragana using Pronunciation Module 1 on the *TOBIRA* website!

Pronunciation Module 1-1

Hiragana are phonetic characters—that is, each character has exactly one pronunciation. Each character basically constitutes one syllable and takes the same length of time (i.e., one beat) to say.

Ex.1

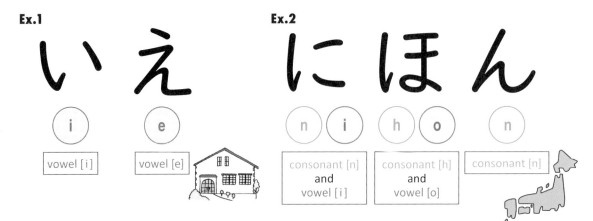

いえ

(i) (e)

vowel [i]   vowel [e]

Ex.2

にほん

(n) (i) (h) (o) (n)

consonant [n] and vowel [i]   consonant [h] and vowel [o]   consonant [n]

The romanization systems for Japanese most widely used today, including those used to type Japanese, are based on one created by an American physician and missionary in the 1800s to help other English speakers learn, read, and write Japanese without having to learn the Japanese writing system. This system of romanization tried to render the sounds of Japanese in a format that would be intuitive to speakers of English, but there are some key differences between how some letters are pronounced in English and Japanese.

---

1) Vowel sounds: There are only five vowels in Japanese. Some vowels might be pronounced differently from the vowels in your language. Japanese "a"（あ）sounds like the "a" in "father" in English, "i"（い）is like the "i" in "machine," "u"（う）is like the "u" in "rude" but with the lips unrounded, "e"（え）is like the "e" in "dress," and "o"（お）is like "o" in "north."

2) [k-], [t-], and [p-] sounds (e.g., "ka," "ki," "ta," "to," "pa" in romanization): These are pronounced as in Spanish or French, with less aspiration (expulsion of breath) than in languages such as English, Chinese, or Korean.

watashi
わたし
(I)

kankoku
かんこく
(South Korea)

---

3) [s-] and [t-] sounds: The consonant changes slightly in some [s-] and [t-] sounds. "s+i"（し）is pronounced as "shi," not "si;" "t+i"（ち）is pronounced as "chi," not "ti;" and "t+u"（つ）is pronounced as "tsu," not "tu."
To reflect these pronunciations, we romanize them as "shi," "chi," and "tsu," respectively.

si → shi（し）

ti → chi（ち）

tu → tsu（つ）

4) "h+u"（ふ）: This is romanized as "fu" and pronounced closer to "fu" than "hu." English "f" is produced with the upper teeth touching the lower lip, but Japanese "f" is created by rounding the lips and pushing air through, as if to blow out a candle.

fu
ふ

---

5) [r-] sounds (e.g., "ra," "ri," "ru," "re," "ro" in romanization): These have traditionally been romanized with an "r," and the consonant [r] in question does in fact sound similar to an [r] in some languages, such as Spanish. It is very different, however, from the English [r], so English speakers should take special care when learning to pronounce this sound.

6) Syllabic [n] sounds: The pronunciation of [n] varies depending on the sounds that precede and follow it, so listen carefully to how you hear [n] pronounced in different positions.

tenpura
てんぷら
(tempura)

gengo
げんご
(language)

kanji
かんじ
(kanji)

hon
ほん
(book)

Q4. How does intonation work in Japanese?

Japanese has a pitch accent rather than the stress accent found in English, so high (**H**) or low (**L**) pitch is given to each sound. Pitch patterns can be used to determine the difference between words that are otherwise pronounced the same.

In this book, the pitch accent of a word is indicated by a line over the segments of the word that are pronounced at a higher pitch, as in the example below (e.g., āme and amē). See Pronunciation Module 4 for additional explanations and exercises.

Ex. ā me / あ め / **H L** (rain)

a mē / あ め / **L H** (candy)

Pronunciation Module 4

The Japanese writing system: Hiragana

Q5. What characters are used to write Japanese?

Hiragana characters
a i u e o
あいうえお

are phonograms—each hiragana represents one sound, and the characters do not have meaning in and of themselves.

Katakana characters
a i u e o
アイウエオ

are also phonograms. Katakana are used to write loanwords, names from foreign countries, names of plants and animals, onomatopoeia, etc.

Kanji characters
kan ji
漢字

are ideograms—each kanji represents an idea or concept.

Q6. When do you use hiragana?

Hiragana can be used to write any Japanese words, but it is usually limited (particularly in formal writing) to grammatical markers and word endings following kanji. Foreign words and loanwords (such as the names of foreign countries and people) are not usually written in hiragana. Although the names of animals and flowers are written in katakana in this book, they can also be written in hiragana if they are native Japanese words.

As you have seen in Q3., there are 46 hiragana characters. Practice reading them aloud with the audio recordings on the *TOBIRA* website.

れんしゅう❶ | **Practice 1 (A-SO)**

Read the following hiragana words aloud. A line over a character indicates that it is pronounced at a higher pitch.

1) あ̅い

(love)

2) す し̅

(sushi)

3) う̅そ

(lie)

4) お̅かし

(snack)

5) え̅き

(train station)

れんしゅう❷ | **Practice 2 (A-HO)**

Read the following hiragana words aloud.

1) な̅に

(what)

2) ふ̅ね

(ship; boat)

3) ひ と̅

(person)

4) ほ̅し

(star)

5) は̅たち

(20 years old)

れんしゅう❸ | **Practice 3 (A-N)**　L0-9

Read the following hiragana words aloud.

1) ゆ̅め

(dream)

2) や̅ま

(mountain)

3) よ̅る

(night)

4) ろ̅く

(six)

5) や す̅み

(break; day off)

れんしゅう❹ | **Practice 4 (N)**　L0-10

Read the following hiragana words aloud, making sure that the "n" (ん) is counted as one beat.

1) さ̅ん (three)　　　　2) よ̅ん (four)　　　　3) に ほ̅ん (Japan)

4) か̅んこく (South Korea)　　5) た く さ̅ん (many; a lot)　　6) な̅んにん (how many people)

■ Writing special sounds (1) : Voiced and semi-voiced sounds

Q7.

What is a voiced sound?
What is a semi-voiced sound?

As shown in the table below,
[g] is the voiced version of [k],
[z] is the voiced version of [s],
[j] is the voiced version of [sh],
[d] is the voiced version of [t], and
[b] is the voiced version of [h].
[p] is the semi-voiced version of [h].

Pronunciation
Module 1-2

Voiced and semi-voiced sounds

semi-voiced	voiced	voice-less	voiced	voice-less	voiced	voice-less	voiced	voice-less	Vowels
P	B	H	D	T	Z/J	S	G	K	
ぱ	ば	は	だ	た	ざ	さ	が	か	A
ぴ	び	ひ	(ぢ)*	ち	じ	し	ぎ	き	I
ぷ	ぶ	ふ	(づ)*	つ	ず	す	ぐ	く	U
ぺ	べ	へ	で	て	ぜ	せ	げ	け	E
ぽ	ぼ	ほ	ど	と	ぞ	そ	ご	こ	O

* In standard Japanese, ぢ is pronounced as じ, and づ is pronounced as ず, so ぢ and づ are rarely used in modern spellings.

れんしゅう❺ | Practice 5 (Voiced and semi-voiced sounds)   L0-11

Read the following hiragana words aloud.

1) ぼく (I [used mainly by men])　　2) じかん (time)　　3) でんわ (telephone)

4) にほんご (Japanese [language])　　5) だいがく (college; university)　　6) ともだち (friend)

■ Writing special sounds (2): Long vowels

Q8.

What are long vowels?
How do you pronounce them?
How do you write them?

When the same vowel appears twice in a row, as in words like *obaasan* (お
ば**あ**さん) and *iie* (い**い**え), this is called a "long vowel." When pronouncing
a long vowel, make sure to extend the vowel and pronounce it as one
sound that lasts for two beats rather than producing two of the same vowel
with a separation in between. See the following example for a comparison
of two words that differ only in vowel length, the first with a short vowel
and the second with a long vowel.

Ex.

One [a] (short vowel): The length of the word is 4 beats in total.

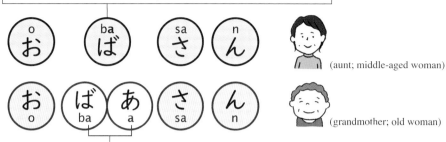

お (o)　ば (ba)　さ (sa)　ん (n)

(aunt; middle-aged woman)

お (o)　ば (ba)　あ (a)　さ (sa)　ん (n)

(grandmother; old woman)

Two consecutive [a]s (long vowel): The length of the word is 5 beats in total.

Long vowels	Words	Long vowels	Words	
aa	おかあさん (mother) okaasan	ee	えいご (English) eego	おねえさん (older sister) oneesan
ii	おにいさん (older brother) oniisan		がくせい (student) gakusee	
uu	すうがく (mathematics) suugaku	oo	ありがとう (Thank you.) arigatoo	おおきい (big) ookii
			おとうさん (father) otoosan	

Words with "-e + い" spellings (e.g., えい, けい, せい, てい, ねい, へい, めい, れい) are also long vowels and are pronounced as [ee] (e.g., えい [ee], けい [kee], せい [see]) instead of [ei].

Exs. 1）えいご (English)　　2）がくせい (student)
　　　　　eego　　　　　　　　gakusee

Words with "-o + う" spellings (e.g., おう, こう, そう, とう, のう, ほう, もう, よう, ろう) are also long vowels and are pronounced as [oo] (e.g., おう [oo], こう [koo], そう [soo]) instead of [ou].

Exs. 1）おうじ (prince)　　2）そうじ (cleaning)
　　　　　ooji　　　　　　　　sooji

Long vowel spellings for [ee] (ええ or えい) and [oo] (おお or おう) are specific to each word; luckily, the spellings えい and おう are much more common than ええ and おお, so you should not have much trouble memorizing the exceptions that use the latter spellings.

れんしゅう❻ Practice 6 (Long vowels)　 L0-12

1)-6) below are some everyday Japanese expressions. Can you write each expression correctly? Choose the correct spelling in hiragana from a.-c. for each, then check your answers with pp.15-17.

1）*Arigatoo*　　a. ありがとお　　　b. ありがとう　　　c. ありがと

2）*Ohayoo*　　a. おはよう　　　　b. おはいよう　　　c. おはよお

3）*Sayoonara*　　a. さよなら　　　　b. さよおなら　　　c. さようなら

4）*Doozo yoroshiku*
　　　a. どぞ　よろしく　　b. どうぞ　よろしく　　c. どおぞ　よろしく

5）*Shitsuree shimasu*
　　　a. しつれいします　　b. しつれします　　c. しつれえします

6）*Gochisoosama deshita*
　　　a. ごちそおさまでした　b. ごちそさまでした　c. ごちそうさまでした

■ Writing special sounds (3): Double consonants (small tsu (つ))

Q9. What are double consonants?
How do you pronounce them?
How do you write them?

You may sometimes hear something that sounds like a pause in the middle of a Japanese word. This special sound is called a "double consonant" and is represented by doubling the consonant in romanization. When writing in hiragana, the first consonant is represented by a small tsu (つ), as in the example below.

Ex.

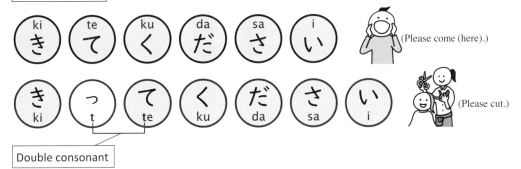

To pronounce the double consonant after [ki], you prepare your mouth for the following consonant (the [t] of [te]) but cut off sound for one beat before moving on.

れんしゅう❼ **Practice 7 (Double consonants)** 🔊 **L0-13**

You learned phrases 1)-5) below in "Everyday expressions" and "Classroom instructions" (pp.15-19). Read each phrase aloud and then match it to its meaning in English from sentences a.-e.

1) いってください •   • a. Please say it.

2) いってきます •   • b. See you when you get back.

3) ゆっくり　いってください •   • c. I am going out now.

4) いってらっしゃい •   • d. Please say it one more time.

5) もういちど　いってください •   • e. Please say it slowly.

■ Writing special sounds (4): Contracted sounds

Q10. What are contracted sounds?
How do you pronounce them?

Contracted sounds are combinations of a consonant with "ya," "yu," or "yo." They are written in hiragana with an [-i] sound character (e.g., き, し, ち, に, ひ, み, and り) and a small [-y] sound character (i.e., や, ゆ, or よ), as in the table below.
Note that these two-character combinations constitute one syllable and last the same length of time (i.e., one beat) as other syllables.

Ex.

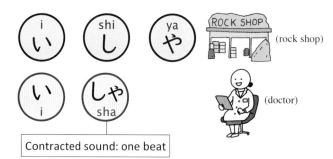

(rock shop)

(doctor)

Contracted sound: one beat

Pronunciation
Module 1-3

Writing contracted sounds

R	M	P	B	H	N	T (CH)	Z (J)	S	G	K	[-i] sound character
り	み	ぴ	び	ひ	に	ち	じ	し	ぎ	き	
りゃ rya	みゃ mya	ぴゃ pya	びゃ bya	ひゃ hya	にゃ nya	ちゃ cha	じゃ ja	しゃ sha	ぎゃ gya	きゃ kya	small や
りゅ ryu	みゅ myu	ぴゅ pyu	びゅ byu	ひゅ hyu	にゅ nyu	ちゅ chu	じゅ ju	しゅ shu	ぎゅ gyu	きゅ kyu	small ゆ
りょ ryo	みょ myo	ぴょ pyo	びょ byo	ひょ hyo	にょ nyo	ちょ cho	じょ jo	しょ sho	ぎょ gyo	きょ kyo	small よ

れんしゅう❽ Practice 8 (Contracted sounds)

 LO-14

Read the following pairs aloud. Can you tell the difference in how they sound?

1) ひやく (leap (forward)) ひゃく (hundred)

2) きやく (rules; terms) きゃく (customer)

3) じゆう (freedom) じゅう (ten)

4) きよう (good with one's hands) きょう (today)

5) びよういん (hair salon) びょういん (hospital)

28

自分を再発見する
<ruby>自<rt>じ</rt></ruby> <ruby>分<rt>ぶん</rt></ruby> <ruby>再<rt>さい</rt></ruby> <ruby>発<rt>はっ</rt></ruby> <ruby>見<rt>けん</rt></ruby>

Rediscovering myself

Lesson 1 | アイです。はじめまして。
I'm Ai. Nice to meet you.

Lesson 2 | しゅうまつになにをしますか。
What are you doing over the weekend?

Lesson 3 | とうきょうでなにをしましたか。
What did you do in Tokyo?

01

Unit1のまえに

1 What aspects of Japan are you interested in? Discuss the topics below with your partner and jot down key words in each balloon.

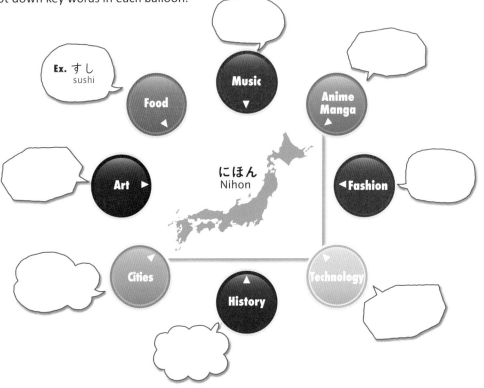

Ex. すし
sushi

Music ▼

Anime Manga ▲

Food ◄

Art ►

にほん
Nihon

◄ Fashion

Cities ◄

History ▲

▲ Technology

2 Below are the main characters of *TOBIRA*. They will be your companions in learning Japanese from here on out. Suppose you are meeting them for the first time—what kind of information would you want to know about them?

MAIN CHARACTERS IN *TOBIRA*

◉ Japan

◉ USA

Japan House
ジャパンハウス
Japan Hausu

Keita・けいた
Keeta

Ai・アイ
Ai

Mark・マーク
Maaku

Riemann
リーマン
Riiman

Nyanta
にゃんた
Nyanta

Tao
タオ
Tao

Jean
ジャン
Jan

Goble University
ゴーブルだいがく
Gooburu Daigaku

Prof. Kuroda
くろだせんせい
Kuroda-sensee

Lesson 1

アイです。 はじめまして。
Ai desu.　　　　　　　Hajimemashite.

I'm Ai. Nice to meet you.

Instructional Video
Lesson 1

DEKIRU List

できるCheck ✓

できる I
Greet and give a simple self-introduction to people you are meeting for the first time.
初めて会った人に挨拶や簡単な自己紹介をすることができる。
Entry ☐　Exit ☐

できる II
Ask and answer questions about basic information such as people's names, hometowns, etc.
名前や出身などの基本的な情報について、尋ねたり答えたりすることができる。
Entry ☐　Exit ☐

できる III
Briefly talk about things you like.
好きなことやものについて、簡単に話すことができる。
Entry ☐　Exit ☐

STRATEGIES

Conversation Tips .... • Active listening with そうですか ↘ (with falling intonation)
　　　　　　　　　　　　　Soo desu ka

Reading .... • Understanding Japanese sentence structure: X は Y です
　　　　　　　　　　　　　　　　　　　　　　　　　　　　　　　　wa　　desu
　　　　　　　　　　　• Sorting information

Listening .... • Picking out keywords in a self-introduction such as a person's name, hometown, etc.

GRAMMAR

① は [Topic marker]　**できる I**
　wa
② X は Y {です／じゃないです} "X {is/is not} Y."　**できる I, II**
　　wa　desu　ja nai desu
③ の [Noun-modifying particle]　**できる I**
　no
④ Questions　**できる II**

　4-1 Yes-no questions

　4-2 Wh-questions

⑤ も [Similarity particle] "too; also; (not) ~ either"　**できる II**
　mo
⑥ と [Noun-listing particle] "and"　**できる III**
　to

かいわ

1 できる I,Ⅱ Ai is visiting Japan for the first time with her family.
Today she is meeting Jean, a friend of her housemate Mark, for the first time in Shibuya, an area in Tokyo. 🔊 L1-1

こちらこそ: me, too
kochirakoso

Ai : あのう、すみません、ジャンさんですか。
Anoo, sumimasen, Jan-san desu ka.

Jean : アイさんですか。
Ai-san desu ka.

Ai : はい、アイです。はじめまして。
Hai, Ai desu. Hajimemashite.

Jean : はじめまして。ジャンです。どうぞ　よろしく！
Hajimemashite. Jan desu. Doozo yoroshiku!

Ai : こちらこそ、どうぞ　よろしく　おねがいします。
Kochirakoso, doozo yoroshiku onegai shimasu.

Jean
いま、しぶやの
スクランブル
こうさてん　　12:00
既読
12:01　わたしも！

2 できる I,Ⅱ Ai and Jean are at a café overlooking Shibuya Scramble Crossing. 🔊 L1-2

パリ: Paris　オハイオ: Ohio
Pari　　　　Ohaio

Ai : ジャンさんの　しゅっしんは　どこですか。
Jan-san no shusshin wa doko desu ka.

Jean : フランスの　パリです。
Furansu no Pari desu.

Ai : そうですか。
Soo desu ka.

わたしの　しゅっしんは　アメリカの　オハイオです。
Watashi no shusshin wa Amerika no Ohaio desu.

Jean : え、「おはよう」ですか。
E, ohayoo desu ka.

Ai : いいえ、「おはよう」じゃないです。オハイオです。
Iie, ohayoo ja nai desu. Ohaio desu.

Jean : ああ、オハイオ。
Aa, Ohaio.

しぶやの　スクランブル　こうさてん
Shibuya no sukuranburu koosaten
Shibuya Scramble Crossing

3 でき̇る̇ II,III Ai and Jean are talking about Mark at the café. 🔊 L1-3

> せんぱい：senior member of a group　ミュージシャン：musician　かっこいい：cool
> senpai　　　　　　　　　　　　myuujishan　　　　　　　　kakkoii

Jean： アイさんは　マークの　だいがくの　がくせいですか。
　　　Ai-san wa　　Maaku no　daigaku no　gakusee desu ka.

Ai ： はい、そうです。わたしも　ゴーブルだいがくの　がくせいです。
　　　Hai,　soo desu.　Watashi mo　Gooburu Daigaku no　gakusee desu.

　　　マークさんは　だいがくの　せんぱいです。
　　　Maaku-san wa　daigaku no　senpai desu.

Jean： そうですか。アイさんの　せんこうは　なんですか。
　　　Soo desu ka.　Ai-san no　senkoo wa　nan desu ka.

Ai ： びじゅつと　にほんごです。いま　にねんせいです。
　　　Bijutsu to　nihongo desu.　Ima　ninensee desu.

　　　ジャンさんの　しごとは　なんですか。
　　　Jan-san no　shigoto wa　nan desu ka.

Jean： ミュージシャンです。
　　　Myuujishan desu.

Ai ： え、ミュージシャン！　かっこいい！
　　　E,　myuujishan!　Kakkoii!

4 でき̇る̇ II,III Ai and Jean continue their conversation at the café. 🔊 L1-4

> クラシック：classical (music)　ロック：rock
> kurashikku　　　　　　　　　　rokku

Jean： アイさんの　しゅみは　なんですか。
　　　Ai-san no　shumi wa　nan desu ka.

Ai ： えっと、おんがくです。クラシックと　J-POP が　すきです。
　　　Etto,　ongaku desu.　Kurashikku to　jeepoppu ga　suki desu.

　　　ジャンさんの　しゅみは？
　　　Jan-san no　shumi wa?

Jean： ぼくの　しゅみも　おんがくです。ロックと　アニソンが　すきです。
　　　Boku no　shumi mo　ongaku desu.　Rokku to　anison ga　suki desu.

Ai ： あのう、アニソンは　なんですか。
　　　Anoo,　anison wa　nan desu ka.

Jean： アニメソングです。
　　　Anime songu desu.

Ai ： あ、アニメソング…　わたしも　アニメの　うたが　だいすきです。
　　　A,　anime songu...　Watashi mo　anime no　uta ga　daisuki desu.

C O N V E R S A T I O N T I P S

Active listening with そうですか↘ (with falling intonation): When you hear new information, you can
　　　　　　　　　　　　Soo desu ka
use そうですか↘ to respond.
　　Soo desu ka

　　A：わたしは　アニメが　すきです。
　　　Watashi wa　anime ga　suki desu.
　　B：そうですか↘。
　　　Soo desu ka.

たんご

● じこしょうかい　Self-introduction

| わたし／ぼく [used mainly by men]
watashi　boku
(I) | なまえ
namae
(name) | おなまえ [used to ask
onamae someone else's name]
(name) | | いま
ima
(now) |

| だいがく
daigaku
(university)
だいがくいん
daigakuin
(graduate school) | いちねんせい
ichinensee
(first-year student)
1st year | にねんせい
ninensee
(second-year student)
2nd year | さんねんせい
sannensee
(third-year student)
3rd year | よねんせい
yonensee
(fourth-year student)
4th year | なんねんせい
nannensee
(what year in
school)
? year |

| せんこう
senkoo
(major) | なに／なん
nani　nan **?**
(what) |

| にほんご
nihongo
(Japanese language)
あいうえお
漢字
アイウエオ | えいご
eego
(English language)
 English | こうがく
koogaku
(engineering)
 | すうがく
suugaku
(mathematics)
 | せいじ
seeji
(politics) | びじゅつ
bijutsu
(art) | コンピュータ
konpyuuta
(computer(s))
 |

| しゅっしん (one's place of origin)
shusshin
 | にほん
Nihon
(Japan)
 | ちゅうごく
Chuugoku
(China)
 | かんこく
Kankoku
(South Korea)
 | マレーシア
Mareeshia
(Malaysia)
 |

| どこ
doko
(where)
 | だれ
dare
(who) **?** | インド
Indo
(India)
 | オーストラリア
Oosutoraria
(Australia)
 | アメリカ
Amerika
(USA)
 | フランス
Furansu
(France)
 |

| Country じん
jin
(... person/people) [nationality] | **Exs.** にほんじん
nihonjin
(Japanese person/people) | アメリカじん
amerikajin
(American person/people) |

| Country ご
go
(... language) | **Exs.** にほんご
nihongo
(Japanese) | ちゅうごくご
chuugokugo
(Chinese) | かんこくご
kankokugo
(Korean) | マレーシアご
mareeshiago
(Malay) | フランスご
furansugo
(French) |

● だいがく　University

| せんせい
sensee
(teacher)
 | がくせい
gakusee
(student)
 | だいがくせい
daigakusee
(college student)
 | だいがくいんせい
daigakuinsee
(graduate student)
 | りゅうがくせい
ryuugakusee
(international student)
 |

| べんきょう
benkyoo
(study)
 | しゅくだい
shukudai
(homework)
Homework | ともだち
tomodachi
(friend)
 | かいしゃいん
kaishain
(company employee) | しごと
shigoto
(job; work) |

● すうじ　Numbers

0	1	2	3	4	5	6	7	8	9	10
ぜろ／ゼロ	いち	に	さん	よん／し	ご	ろく	なな／しち	はち	きゅう／く	じゅう
zero	ichi	ni	san	yon/shi	go	roku	nana/shichi	hachi	kyuu/ku	juu

● ～さい (... years old)

1	2	3	4	5	6	7	8	9	10
いっさい	にさい	さんさい	よんさい	ごさい	ろくさい	ななさい	はっさい	きゅうさい	じ(ゅ)っさい
issai	nisai	sansai	yonsai	gosai	rokusai	nanasai	hassai	kyuusai	jussai

18	19	20	21	24	?
じゅうはっさい	じゅうきゅうさい	はたち	にじゅういっさい	にじゅうよんさい	なんさい
juuhassai	juukyuusai	hatachi	nijuuissai	nijuuyonsai	nansai

● ばんごう (Numbering)

No.1	No.2	No.3	No.4	No.5	No.6	No.7	No.8	No.9	No.10	?
いちばん	にばん	さんばん	よんばん	ごばん	ろくばん	ななばん	はちばん	きゅうばん	じゅうばん	なんばん
ichiban	niban	sanban	yonban	goban	rokuban	nanaban	hachiban	kyuuban	juuban	nanban

でんわ
denwa
(phone)

スマホ
sumaho
(smartphone)

ばんごう (number)
bangoo

でんわばんごう (phone number)
denwa　bangoo

01-346-7893

ぜろいちの　　さんよんろくの　　ななはちきゅうさん
zero ichi no　　san yon roku no　　nana hachi kyuu san

● すきなこと　Favorite things

しゅみ (hobby)
shumi

おんがく (music)
ongaku

うた (song)
uta

ゲーム
geemu
(video game; game)

スポーツ (sports)
supootsu

えいが (movie)
eega

ほん (book)
hon

まんが
manga
(comic book)

アニメ (anime)
anime

ジョギング
jogingu
(jogging)

ダンス (dance)
dansu

● そのほかのひょうげん　Other expressions

X は Y が	
wa　　ga	すきです suki desu (X likes Y.)
	だいすきです daisuki desu (X likes Y a lot; X loves Y.)

はい
hai
(yes)

そうです
soo desu
(That's right.)

いいえ
iie
(no)

そうですか
soo desu ka
(I see.)

35

たんごリスト

🔊 **L1-6**

NOUNS

1	わたし watashi	I
2	ぼく boku	I [used mainly by men]
3	がくせい gakusee	student
4	だいがくせい daigakusee	university student; college student
5	だいがくいんせい daigakuinsee	graduate student
6	りゅうがくせい ryuugakusee	international student
7	せんせい sensee	teacher
8	ともだち tomodachi	friend
9	かいしゃいん kaishain	company employee; office worker
10	しゅくだい shukudai	homework
11	ほん hon	book
12	まんが manga	comic book; manga
13	でんわ denwa	phone
14	なまえ／おなまえ namae　onamae	name [おなまえ (onamae) is used to ask someone else's name.] **Ex.** おなまえは（なんですか）？ 　　Onamae wa (nan desu ka)? What is your name?
15	しゅっしん shusshin	one's place of origin (home-town, home country, etc.)
16	せんこう senkoo	major [field of study]
17	しゅみ shumi	hobby
18	しごと shigoto	job; work
19	うた uta	song
20	えいが eega	movie
21	べんきょう benkyoo	study
22	えいご eego	English language
23	おんがく ongaku	music
24	こうがく koogaku	engineering
25	すうがく suugaku	mathematics
26	せいじ seeji	politics
27	びじゅつ bijutsu	art
28	ばんごう bangoo	number
	でんわばんごう denwa bangoo	phone number
29	だいがく daigaku	university; college
30	だいがくいん daigakuin	graduate school
31	にほん Nihon	Japan
32	ちゅうごく Chuugoku	China
33	かんこく Kankoku	South Korea
34	アメリカ Amerika	USA
35	インド Indo	India
36	オーストラリア Oosutoraria	Australia
37	フランス Furansu	France
38	マレーシア Mareeshia	Malaysia
39	コンピュータ konpyuuta	computer(s)
40	スマホ sumaho	smartphone
41	アニメ anime	anime; animation
42	ゲーム geemu	video game; game
43	スポーツ supootsu	sports

44	ジョギング jogingu	jogging
45	ダンス dansu	dance

ADVERBIAL NOUN

46	いま ima	now

QUESTION WORDS

47	だれ dare	who
48	どこ doko	where
49	なに／なん nani nan	what

NUMBERS

50	ぜろ／ゼロ zero zero	zero
51	いち ichi	one
52	に ni	two [usually elongated as /nii/ when reading out a series of numbers one by one]
53	さん san	three
54	よん／し yon shi	four
55	ご go	five [usually elongated as /goo/ when reading out a series of numbers one by one]
56	ろく roku	six
57	なな／しち nana shichi	seven
58	はち hachi	eight
59	きゅう／く kyuu ku	nine
60	じゅう juu	ten

COUNTERS

61	～さい sai	... years old
	いっさい issai	one year old
	なんさい nansai	how old
62	はたち hatachi	twenty years old

SUFFIXES

63	～ねんせい nensee	...-year student [grade in school]
	いちねんせい ichinensee	first-year student; freshman
	にねんせい ninensee	second-year student; sophomore
	さんねんせい sannensee	third-year student; junior
	よねんせい yonensee	fourth-year student; senior
	なんねんせい nannensee	what year in school
64	～ばん ban	number ...
	いちばん ichiban	number one
	なんばん nanban	what number
65	～ご go	... language
	にほんご nihongo	Japanese language
66	～じん jin	... person/people [nationality]
	にほんじん nihonjin	Japanese person/people

OTHER WORDS AND PHRASES

67	はい hai	yes
68	いいえ iie	no
69	そうです soo desu	That's right; It is so.
70	そうですか soo desu ka	I see. [with falling intonation]
71	XはYがすきです X wa Y ga suki desu	X likes Y.
	XはYがだいすきです X wa Y ga daisuki desu	X likes Y a lot; X loves Y.

Lesson 1

ぶんぽう

1 は [Topic marker]
wa

[1]

Topic		Predicate
わたし Watashi	は wa	たなかです*。 Tanaka desu.
I am Tanaka.		

* See #2 X は Y {です／じゃないです}.
      wa   desu ja nai desu

は (pronounced as /wa/) is what is known as a particle. In general, a particle consists of one or two syllables
wa
and is attached to the end of a noun to indicate the relation of that noun to other parts of the sentence or its

role in the sentence as a whole.

As the name "topic marker" indicates, one of the functions of は is to mark the topic of a sentence. The
                  wa
topic (=X) is what the rest of the sentence is about. The rest of the sentence usually tells what X is or what

X does.

Exs. (1) わたしは　アイです。*I am Ai.*
      Watashi wa Ai desu.

(2) たなかさんは　だいがくせいです。*Tanaka-san is a college student.*
   Tanaka-san wa   daigakusee desu.

(3) リーマンさんは　いちねんせいです。*Riemann is a freshman.*
   Riiman-san wa   ichinensee desu.

2 X は Y {です／じゃないです} "X {is/is not} Y."
wa   desu   ja nai desu

[2]

X (topic)		Y (noun)	
たなかさん Tanaka-san	は wa	じゅうきゅうさい juukyuusai	です。 desu.
Tanaka-san is nineteen years old.			
アイさん Ai-san	は wa	だいがくいんせい daigakuinsee	じゃないです。 ja nai desu.
Ai is not a graduate student.			

You can express the ideas of "X is Y" and "X is not Y" using "X は Y です" and "X は Y じゃないです,"
                                wa desu   wa ja nai desu
respectively. です indicates that the sentence is in present tense and is polite. じゃないです is its negative
      desu   ja nai desu
form. です has another negative form, じゃありません, but this form is less common than じゃないです.
   desu   ja arimasen   ja nai desu

Exs. (1) わたしは　いちねんせいです。*I'm a first-year student.*
      Watashi wa ichinensee desu.

(2) ジャンさんは　ミュージシャンです。*Jean is a musician.*
   Jan-san wa myuujishan desu.

(3) マークさんは　りゅうがくせいじゃないです。*Mark is not an international student.*
   Maaku-san wa ryuugakusee ja nai desu.

3 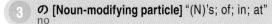 の [Noun-modifying particle] "(N)'s; of; in; at"
no

[3]

N₁	の no	N₂
アイさん Ai-san		せんこう senkoo
Ai's major		

Using の, you can modify a noun (N₂) with another noun (N₁). In N₁ の N₂, N₁ provides information to
no   no
describe or specify N₂. For example, in [3] アイさんの tells whose major the speaker is talking about.
                                          Ai-san no
The meaning relationship between N₁ and N₂ varies according to the meanings of N₁ and N₂. (a)-(d) are

common relationships that N₁ の N₂ represents:
                            no

(a) <u>Possession</u>: N₂ is possessed by N₁; N₂ is an attribute of N₁.

   Exs. わた<u>しの</u>　ほん　*my book(s)*；　アイさ<u>んの</u>　しゅっしん　*Ai's hometown*
        watashi no   hon   Ai-san no   shusshin

(b) <u>Affiliation</u>: N₂ is affiliated with N₁; N₂ {is a member of / belongs to} N₁.

   Exs. きょうとだいがく<u>の</u>　がくせい　*Kyoto University student(s) / student(s) at Kyoto University*
        Kyooto Daigaku no   gakusee

   にほ<u>んの</u>　うた　*song(s) {from / originating in} Japan*
   Nihon no   uta

   レストラ<u>んの</u>　シェフ　*the chef of a restaurant*
   resutoran no   shefu

(c) <u>Existence</u>: N₂ exists in N₁.

   Exs. イギリ<u>すの</u>　ケンブリッジ　*Cambridge, England / the Cambridge in England*
        Igirisu no   Kenburijji

   ホテ<u>るの</u>　へや　*a room in the hotel*
   hoteru no   heya

(d) <u>Inclusion</u>: N₂ is included in N₁.

   Ex. ７３４<u>の</u>２５３<u>の</u>０８１９
        nana san yon no nii goo san no zero hachi ichi kyuu
        [the way to orally provide the phone number (734) 253-0819]

4 Questions

4-1 Yes-no questions

[4-a]

X (topic)		Y (noun)		
たなかさん Tanaka-san	は wa	がくせい gakusee	です desu	か。 ka.
Are you a student, Tanaka-san? / Is Tanaka-san a student? *				

* [Translation 1 / Translation 2] indicates that the sentence in Japanese can be interpreted in two ways in English.

To make a yes-no question, you simply add the question marker か to the end of the sentence.
                                                                ka

Exs.（１）たなかさんの　せんこうは　せいじです<u>か</u>。
        Tanaka-san no   senkoo wa   seeji desu ka.
        Is your major politics, Tanaka-san? / Is Tanaka-san's major politics?

（２）タオさんの　しゅっしんは　アメリカです<u>か</u>。
        Tao-san no   shusshin wa   Amerika desu ka.
        Are you from the US, Tao? (lit. Is your place of origin the US, Tao?) /
        Is Tao from the US? (lit. Is Tao's place of origin the US?)

Yes-no questions are usually responded to with either はい or いいえ.
_{hai} _{iie}

Ex. (3) A: たなかさんは　かいしゃいんです<u>か</u>。
Tanaka-san wa　kaishain desu ka.
Are you a company employee, Tanaka-san? / Is Tanaka-san a company employee?

B1: <u>はい</u>、かいしゃいんです。 *Yes, I am a company employee. / Yes, he is a company employee.*
Hai,　kaishain desu.

B2: <u>はい</u>、そうです。 *Yes, I am. / Yes, he is.*
Hai,　soo desu.

B3: <u>いいえ</u>、かいしゃいんじゃないです。
Iie,　kaishain ja nai desu.
No, I'm not a company employee. / No, he isn't a company employee.

When responding to a yes-no question like (3)-A above, you must include the noun かいしゃいん before
_{kaishain}
です and じゃないです, as in (3)-B1 and (3)-B3, because です and じゃないです cannot be used alone.
_{desu} _{ja nai desu} _{desu} _{ja nai desu}
For a shorter alternative, you can use そう instead of repeating かいしゃいん, as in (3)-B2.
_{soo} _{kaishain}

4-2 **Wh-questions**

[4-b]

X (topic)		は	Y (Q-word)	です	か。
ジャンさんの　しごと Jan-san no　shigoto		は wa	なん* nan	です desu	か。 ka.
What is your occupation, Jean? / What is Jean's occupation?					

*なん is a variation of なに.
_{nan} _{nani}

As seen in [4-b], in wh-questions, you use a Q-word (question word) in the position of Y. The Q-word
changes depending on the topic; e.g., when the topic is a person, you use だれ, as in (1)-A below, and when
_{dare}
the topic is a place, you use どこ, as in (2)-A and (3)-A below.
_{doko}

Exs. (1) A: アイさんの　にほんごの　せんせいは　<u>だれ</u>ですか。
Ai-san no　nihongo no　sensee wa　dare desu ka.
Who's your Japanese teacher, Ai? / Who is Ai's Japanese teacher?

B: くろだせんせいです。 *It's Prof. Kuroda.*
Kuroda-sensee desu.

(2) A: マークさんの　しゅっしんは　<u>どこ</u>ですか。
Maaku-san no　shusshin wa　doko desu ka.
Where are you from, Mark? (lit. Where is your place of origin, Mark?) /
Where is Mark from? (lit. Where is Mark's place of origin?)

B: ボストンです。 *(I'm from / He's from) Boston.*
Bosuton desu.

(3) A: だいがくは　<u>どこ</u>ですか。 *What (lit. What place) is your university?*
Daigaku wa　doko desu ka.

B: ゴーブルだいがくです。 *It's Goble University.*
Gooburu Daigaku desu.

Note that you use どこ rather than なん when you ask what someone's school or company (or favorite
_{doko} _{nan}
sports team, etc.) is, as in (3)-A above.

なん is used before the sounds /d/, /t/, and /n/, as in (4) below, and before counters, as in (5) below. In other
_{nan}
situations, なに is used.
_{nani}

Exs. (4) せんこうは　<u>なん</u>ですか。 *What is your major?*
Senkoo wa　nan desu ka.

(5) <u>なんさい</u> *how old*; <u>なんばん</u> *what number*; <u>なんねんせい</u> *what year in school*
nansai　　　　nanban　　　　　nannensee

5 も [Similarity particle] "too; also; (not) ~ either"
mo

[5]

X (topic)		Y (noun)	
アイさん Ai-san	は wa	だいがくせい daigakusee	です。 desu.
Ai is a college student.			
マークさん Maaku-san	も mo	だいがくせい daigakusee	です。 desu.
Mark is a college student, too.			

You use "X も Y です" to express the idea of "X is also Y," meaning "X, too, is Y." も occurs in the position
　　　　　mo　　desu　　　　　　　　　　　　　　　　　　　　　　　　　　　　　　mo
where は would otherwise occur.
　　 wa

Exs. (1) A: わたしの　せんこうは　こうがくです。*My major is engineering.*
　　　　　　Watashi no　senkoo wa　koogaku desu.

　　　　　B: わたしの　せんこう<u>も</u>　こうがくです。*My major is engineering, too.*
　　　　　　Watashi no　senkoo mo　koogaku desu.

　　　(2) アイさんの　しゅっしんは　アメリカです。*Ai's home country is the US.*
　　　　　Ai-san no　shusshin wa　Amerika desu.

　　　　　マークさんの　しゅっしん<u>も</u>　アメリカです。*Mark's home country is also the US.*
　　　　　Maaku-san no　shusshin mo　Amerika desu.

　　　(3) マークさんは　とうきょうだいがくの　がくせいじゃないです。
　　　　　Maaku-san wa　Tookyoo Daigaku no　gakusee ja nai desu.
　　　　　Mark is not a student at the University of Tokyo.

　　　　　タオさん<u>も</u>　とうきょうだいがくの　がくせいじゃないです。
　　　　　Tao-san mo　Tookyoo Daigaku no　gakusee ja nai desu.
　　　　　Tao is not a student at the University of Tokyo, either.

☞ **GID** (vol.1): B. Particles 2-2. も
　　　　　　　　　　　　　　　　　mo

6 と [Noun-listing particle] "and"
to

[6]

N₁		N₂		
マークさん Maaku-san	と to	タオさん Tao-san	は wa	だいがくせいです。 daigakusee desu.
Mark and Tao are college students.				

You can connect two or more nouns with the particle と to mean "A and B." Note that と can connect only
　　　　　　　　　　　　　　　　　　　　　　　　　　　　to　　　　　　　　　　　　　　　　　　to
nouns.

Exs. (1) ゴーブルだいがくの　がくせいは　タオさん<u>と</u>　リーマンさんです。
　　　　　Gooburu Daigaku no　gakusee wa　Tao-san to　Riiman-san desu.
　　　　　The students at Goble University are Tao and Riemann.

　　　(2) わたしの　しゅみは　スポーツ<u>と</u>　ゲームです。*My hobbies are (playing) sports and games.*
　　　　　Watashi no　shumi wa　supootsu to　geemu desu.

　　　(3) トムさん<u>と</u>　わたしの　せんこうは　こうがくです。
　　　　　Tomu-san to　watashi no　senkoo wa　koogaku desu.
　　　　　Tom and I are majoring in engineering.

Unlike "and" in English, と is not omitted when there are three or more items.
　　　　　　　　　　　　　　to

Ex. (4) アニメ<u>と</u>　まんが<u>と</u>　ゲーム<u>と</u>　おんがく　　*anime, comic books, games, and music*
　　　　　anime to　manga to　geemu to　ongaku

はなしましょう

 できる I Greet and give a simple self-introduction to people you are meeting for the first time.

できるI-A Numbers

Say the following numbers you might come across in your daily life or on a trip. 🔊 **L1-7**

※ See the vocabulary list on p.37 for how to pronounce numbers 2 and 5 when reading numbers in a series.

Ex. さんごなな
san goo nana

357

1)
Room Key
809

2)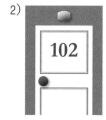
102

3)
国道
246
ROUTE

4)
県道
66
埼玉

5)
110
Police

6)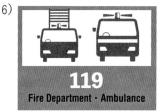
119
Fire Department · Ambulance

7)
CREDIT CARD PLUS
0417 259 6830
GOOD THRU MONTH / YEAR 11 / 23
CARD

できるI-B Age

Say the ages below. 🔊 **L1-8**

Ex. 82 → はちじゅうにさい
hachijuunisai

1) 19 2) 20 3) 31 4) 48 5) 50 6) 94

できるI-C X は Y です
wa desu

Talk about people's biographical information.

Step 1 Look at the following people's profiles and describe them. 🔊 **L1-9**

Ex. ワンさんは　がくせいです。
Wan-san wa　gakusee desu.

Name	ワン Wan	アミーナ Amiina	ゴメス Gomesu	やまだ Yamada 
Profile	**Ex.** student 1) third-year 2) Chinese 3) 21 years old	4) international student 5) second-year 6) Malaysian 7) 20 years old	8) college student 9) fourth-year 10) 22 years old	11) graduate student 12) Japanese 13) 28 years old

Step 2 | Now, talk a little about yourself.

Ex. わたしは　アイ・ブルーノです。（わたしは）　がくせいです。
Watashi wa　Ai Buruuno desu.　（Watashi wa）　gakusee desu.

（わたしは）にねんせいです。<Continue>
（Watashi wa）　ninensee desu.

1) name　　　2) occupation　　　3) school year (if applicable)　　　4) additional information

---

できるI-D　**Noun-modifying particle の**
no

1 Modify a noun with another noun to show possession.

Step 1 | Create phrases in the form N₁ の N₂ based on the pictures below.
no

Ex. ほん → アイさんの　ほん
hon　　Ai-san no　　hon

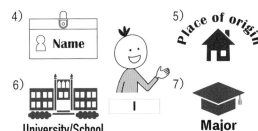

Step 2 | Now, make sentences about yourself using phrases 4)-7) from Step 1.

Ex. わたしの　なまえは　ダニエル・キムです。
Watashi no　namae wa　Danieru Kimu desu.

2 Modify a noun with another noun to add a description.

Step 1 | Describe each of the nouns pictured below by modifying it with another noun.

Ex. ほん → えいごの　ほん
hon　　eego no　　hon

Step 2 | Choose some items around you and describe them as shown in the example below.

Ex. にほんごの　ほん
nihongo no　　hon

3 Modify a noun with another noun to show affiliation.

[Step 1] Make noun phrases based on the cues provided.

Ex. <u>ゴーブルだいがくの</u>　<u>がくせい</u>
Gooburu Daigaku no 　gakusee

Ex. Goble University

1) Tobira University

2) your own

3)

4)

5) your own

[Step 2] Now, make sentences about yourself using phrases 2) and 5) from Step 1.

Ex. わたしは　ゴーブルだいがくの　がくせいです。
Watashi wa 　Gooburu Daigaku no 　gakusee desu.

4 Modify a noun with another noun to show location.

[Step 1] How much do you know about world geography? Create phrases in the form N$_1$ の N$_2$ with each of the following countries and its capital city. 🔊 **L1-12**

Ex. <u>インドの</u>　<u>ニューデリー</u>
Indo no 　Nyuuderii

Ex.

1)

2)

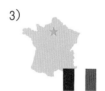
3)

4)

your own

[Step 2] Make a sentence specifying your place of origin.

Ex. わたしの　しゅっしんは　インドの　ニューデリーです。
Watashi no 　shusshin wa 　Indo no 　Nyuuderii desu.

5 Create noun phrases based on the cues below. Pay attention to the word order to make sure the phrases make sense.

Ex. ゲーム／ともだち → ともだちの　ゲーム
geemu 　tomodachi 　tomodachi no 　geemu

1) せんせい／へや (room)
sensee 　heya

2) えいが／フランス
eega 　Furansu

3) にほん／きょうと
Nihon 　Kyooto

4) こうがく／せんせい
koogaku 　sensee

5) インド／ダンス
Indo 　dansu

6) よねんせい／だいがく
yonensee 　daigaku

6 Try talking about phone numbers in Japanese.

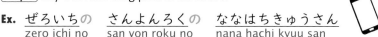

Step 1 Say the following phone numbers.

Ex. <u>ぜろいちの</u>　<u>さんよんろくの</u>　<u>ななはちきゅうさん</u>
zero ichi no　　san yon roku no　　nana hachi kyuu san

Ex. 01-346-7893　　1) 06-6012-5634　2) 734-555-0198　　3) your own

Step 2 Make sentences telling someone the phone numbers of the people/institutions below.

Ex. ともだちの　でんわばんごうは
Tomodachi no　denwa bangoo wa

ぜろいちの　さんよんろくの　ななはちきゅうさんです。
zero ichi no　san yon roku no　　nana hachi kyuu san desu.

Ex. ともだち　　1) わたし　　2) だいがく　　3) your own
tomodachi　　　watashi　　　　daigaku

7 Talk about yourself, including each of the topics below.

Ex. わたしの　せんこうは　せいじです。（わたしの）しゅっしんは…　<Continue>
Watashi no　senkoo wa　seeji desu.　（Watashi no）shusshin wa...

Ex. major　　1) place of origin　　2) phone number　　3) hobby

8 Suppose the following people are your friends. Introduce them to your classmates in Japanese.

Ex. レオさんは　だいがくせいです。（レオさんは）じゅうきゅうさいです。
Reo-san wa　daigakusee desu.　（Reo-san wa）　juukyuusai desu.

レオさんの　しゅっしんは　オーストラリアの　シドニーです。
Reo-san no　shusshin wa　Oosutoraria no　Shidonii desu.

Ex. レオ（Leo） Reo • college student • 19 years old • place of origin: Sydney, Australia	1) アレックス（Alex） Arekkusu • student at Goble University • fourth-year student • Ai's friend
2) チェン（Chen） Chen • place of origin: Shanghai, China • major: English • hobby: games	3) ゆか（Yuka） Yuka • first-year student at Kyoto University • major: engineering • place of origin: Osaka, Japan

9 Introduce yourself to your partner following the example below.

> **Useful expression** まだ　わかりません：undecided (*lit.* don't know yet)
> Mada　wakarimasen

> **Ex.** はじめまして。
> Hajimemashite.
> 1) [Name] わたしは　キムです。
> Watashi wa　Kimu desu.
> 2) [Affiliation / School year]
> オーストラリアだいがくの　いちねんせいです。
> Oosutoraria Daigaku no　　　　ichinensee desu.
> 3) [Major] わたしの　せんこうは　せいじです。
> Watashi no　senkoo wa　　seeji desu.
> 4) [Place of origin] （わたしの）　しゅっしんは　かんこくの　ソウル (Seoul) です。
> (Watashi no)　shusshin wa　　Kankoku no　Sooru desu.
> 5) [Hobby] （わたしの）　しゅみは　ゲームです。
> (Watashi no)　shumi wa　　geemu desu.
> どうぞ　よろしく　おねがいします。
> Doozo　yoroshiku　onegai shimasu.

 Ask and answer questions about basic information such as people's names, hometowns, etc.

できるⅡ-A │ **Question marker か and negative sentences**
　　　　　　　　　　　　　　ka

1 Take turns asking and answering questions about people with your partner.

[Step 1] Ask each other questions about the Japan House members based on the cues provided, and answer based on the information in the table below.　🔊 **L1-14**

※ Ai's two majors should be connected with と.
　　　　　　　　　　　　　　　　　　　　　to

Name	School status	Major	Place of origin
アイ・ブルーノ （19） Ai Buruuno	student at Goble University	art and Japanese	Ohio, USA
マーク・シルバ （22） Maaku Shiruba	fourth-year student at Goble University	politics	Boston, USA
タオ・ホワン （20） Tao Howan	international student at Goble University	engineering	Penang, Malaysia
リーマン・ゴルド （17） Riiman Gorudo	first-year student at Goble University	mathematics	New Delhi, India

Ex.1 アイさん／じゅうきゅうさい
　　　　Ai-san　　juukyuusai

　A: アイさんは　じゅうきゅうさいですか。
　　　Ai-san wa　　juukyuusai desu ka.

　B: はい、じゅうきゅうさいです。or はい、そうです。
　　　Hai,　juukyuusai desu.　　　　Hai,　soo desu.

Ex.2 アイさん／にじゅういっさい
　　　　Ai-san　　nijuuissai

　A: アイさんは　にじゅういっさいですか。
　　　Ai-san wa　　nijuuissai desu ka.

　B: いいえ、にじゅういっさいじゃないです。じゅうきゅうさいです。
　　　Iie,　nijuuissai ja nai desu.　　Juukyuusai desu.

1）アイさんの　せんこう／こうがく
Ai-san no　　senkoo　　koogaku

2）アイさんの　しゅっしん／アメリカの　オハイオ
Ai-san no　　shusshin　　Amerika no　　Ohaio

3）マークさん／にじゅうにさい
Maaku-san　　nijuunisai

4）マークさん／さんねんせい
Maaku-san　　sannensee

5）タオさん／りゅうがくせい
Tao-san　　ryuugakusee

6）タオさんの　せんこう／せいじ
Tao-san no　　senkoo　　seeji

7）リーマンさん／いちねんせい
Riiman-san　　ichinensee

8）リーマンさんの　しゅっしん／アメリカ
Riiman-san no　　shusshin　　Amerika

Step 2 Now, pair up with someone you haven't spoken with before, or someone you have spoken very little with. Guess their year in school, major, place of origin, etc. and ask questions based on your guesses. How much can you guess correctly?

Ex. A: ○○さんは　いちねんせいですか。
　　　　　san wa　　ichinensee desu ka.

　　　B: はい、いちねんせいです。or いいえ、いちねんせいじゃないです。<Continue>
　　　　　Hai,　ichinensee desu.　　　　　Iie,　　　ichinensee ja nai desu.

2 Practice using Japanese question words.

Step 1 What question words do you need to ask these questions? Fill in ＿＿ with the appropriate question words. 🔊 **L1-15**

Ex. おなまえは　なんですか。
Onamae wa　nan desu ka.

1）がっこう (school) は　＿＿＿＿＿＿＿ですか。
　Gakkoo wa　　　　　　　　　　desu ka.

2）＿＿＿＿＿＿ねんせいですか。
　　　　　　　　nensee desu ka.

3）せんこうは　＿＿＿＿＿＿ですか。
　Senkoo wa　　　　　　　　desu ka.

4）しゅっしんは　＿＿＿＿＿＿ですか。
　Shusshin wa　　　　　　　　desu ka.

5）にほんごの　せんせいは　＿＿＿＿＿＿ですか。
　Nihongo no　　sensee wa　　　　　　　　desu ka.

6）でんわばんごうは　＿＿＿＿＿＿ですか。
　Denwa bangoo wa　　　　　　　desu ka.

7）しゅみは　＿＿＿＿＿＿ですか。
　Shumi wa　　　　　　　desu ka.

Step 2 Ask some of questions 1)-4) from Step 1 about the Japan House members and answer based on their profiles on p.46.

Ex. A: アイさんは　なんさいですか。
　　　　　Ai-san wa　　nansai desu ka.

　　　B: じゅうきゅうさいです。
　　　　　Juukyuusai desu.

Group Work

Step 3 Practice asking and answering some of the questions from Step 1 with as many classmates as possible. (You do not have to ask all the questions.)

1 You are talking about Li-san and Zhao-san. Look at the information about them in the box and describe their similarities in relation to the cues below.

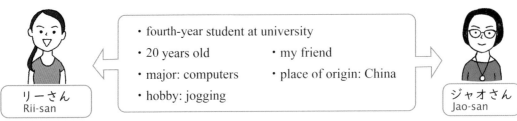

🔊 L1-16

リーさん
Rii-san

・ fourth-year student at university

・ 20 years old   ・ my friend

・ major: computers   ・ place of origin: China

・ hobby: jogging

ジャオさん
Jao-san

Ex.1   university student

→ リーさんは　だいがくせいです。ジャオさんも　だいがくせいです。
Rii-san wa　daigakusee desu.　Jao-san mo　daigakusee desu.

Ex.2   place of origin: South Korea

→ リーさんの　しゅっしんは　かんこくじゃないです。
Rii-san no　shusshin wa　Kankoku ja nai desu.

ジャオさんの　しゅっしんも　かんこくじゃないです。
Jao-san no　shusshin mo　Kankoku ja nai desu.

1) fourth-year student at university   2) 18 years old   3) my friend   4) major: politics

5) place of origin: China   6) hobby: movies

2 Describe your similarities with the Japan House members, referring to the information provided about them in できるⅡ-A-1 on p.46 as needed.

Ex. アイさんは　だいがくせいです。わたしも　だいがくせいです。
Ai-san wa　daigakusee desu.　Watashi mo　daigakusee desu.

アイさんは　はたちじゃないです。わたしも　はたちじゃないです。
Ai-san wa　hatachi ja nai desu.　Watashi mo　hatachi ja nai desu.

3 Find similarities and differences.

Step 1 Ask your classmates' names, statuses, school years, majors, and places of origin.

Ex. A: はじめまして。あのう、おなまえは　なんですか。
Hajimemashite.　Anoo,　onamae wa　nan desu ka.

B: スミスです。
Sumisu desu.

A: スミスさんは　だいがくせいですか。
Sumisu-san wa　daigakusee desu ka.

B: いいえ、だいがくせいじゃないです。だいがくいんせいです。
Iie,　daigakusee ja nai desu.　Daigakuinsee desu.

A: わたしも　だいがくいんせいです。せんこうは　なんですか。<Continue>
Watashi mo　daigakuinsee desu.　Senkoo wa　nan desu ka.

Step 2 Present the similarities and differences you found between you and your classmates. Who did you have the most in common with?

Ex. スミスさんは　だいがくいんせいです。わたしも　だいがくいんせいです。
Sumisu-san wa　daigakuinsee desu.　Watashi mo　daigakuinsee desu.

スミスさんの　せんこうは　せいじです。わたしの　せんこうは　こうがくです。
Sumisu-san no　senkoo wa　seeji desu.　Watashi no　senkoo wa　koogaku desu.

できる
III **Briefly talk about things you like.**

できるⅢ-A **Noun-listing particle と**
to

1 Practice describing the things you like.

Step 1 Circle the things you like.

おんがく スポーツ アニメ／ べんきょう えいが ほん ゲーム ダンス
ongaku supootsu anime benkyoo eega hon geemu dansu
まんが
manga

Step 2 Describe what you like using the things listed in Step 1. You can connect nouns with と.
to

Ex. わたしは　おんがくと　えいがが　すきです。
Watashi wa ongaku to eega ga suki desu.

2 Using the cues from the previous exercise, talk about the things you like with your partner.

Ex. A: ○○さんの　しゅみは　なんですか。
san no shumi wa nan desu ka.

B: スポーツです。バスケットボールと　サッカーが　すきです。
Supootsu desu. Basukettobooru to sakkaa ga suki desu.

A: そうですか。わたしも　サッカーが　だいすきです。
Soo desu ka. Watashi mo sakkaa ga daisuki desu.

バスケットボール
basukettobooru

サッカー
sakkaa

Review

Now you can introduce yourself and have a short conversation in Japanese.

Step 1 Pair up with a classmate and briefly introduce yourselves to each other, then ask follow-up questions to get to know each other better. Use できるⅡ-B-③ Step 1 on p.48 as a model.

Step 2 After your conversation, introduce your partner to your classmates in three or more sentences.

Opening	**Ex.** こちら (this person) は　たなかさんです。
	Kochira wa Tanaka-san desu.
Details	たなかさんは　ゴーブルだいがくの　よねんせいです。
(school year, place of	Tanaka-san wa Gooburu Daigaku no yonensee desu.
origin, things they like,	しゅっしんは　にほんの　おきなわです。
etc.)	Shusshin wa Nihon no Okinawa desu.
	たなかさんは　えいがと　スポーツが　すきです。
	Tanaka-san wa eega to supootsu ga suki desu.

よみましょう

1 How many expressions do you remember from L0? Can you recognize them in hiragana? Match the following pictures 1)-11) with the expressions a.-n. in the center box. Write the letter corresponding to the appropriate expression in each bubble.

あるがくせいの　いちにち（A day in one student's life）

Center box:
a. こんばんは　　b. いただきます　　c. いってきます
d. おかえりなさい　e. ごちそうさま　　f. じゃ、また
g. おはようございます　　h. いってらっしゃい
i. ただいま　　j. こんにちは　　k. しつれいします
l. おやすみなさい　m. おはよう　　n. ありがとう

2 Do you like word searches?

Step 1 Find **13 words** that you have learned in L1. (You can include the example in this number.) The words appear both horizontally (from right to left or left to right) and vertically (from top to bottom).

し	な	に	だ	れ
ゆ	ん (Ex.)	ほ	い	ま
く	お	ん	が	く
だ	や	ご	く	ぼ
い	と	も	だ	ち
な	ま	え	い	が

Step 2 After you find all 13 words, choose **9** of them. Write those words in hiragana and then write their meanings.

	Word in hiragana	Meaning
1	**Ex.** ほん	book
2		
3		
4		
5		
6		
7		
8		
9		
10		

3 In order to get to know the Japan House (JH) members better, read their member profiles on the JH Bulletin Board. Words we have not studied yet are marked with a dotted underline in the text and defined in the gray-shaded area.

りょこう：trip　ニューデリー：New Delhi　かんじ：kanji
　　　　　　　Nyuuderii

はじめまして。わたしは　マーク・シルバです。
　　　　　　　　　　　　　Maaku　　Shiruba
ゴーブルだいがくの　よねんせいです。せんこうは　せいじです。
Gooburu
しゅみは　りょこうです。どうぞ　よろしく。

はじめまして。ぼくは　リーマン・ゴルドです。ゴーブルだいが
　　　　　　　　　　　Riiman　　Gorudo　　　　Gooburu
くの　いちねんせいです。じゅうななさいです。しゅっしんは
インドの　ニューデリーです。せんこうは　すうがくです。すうが
Indo　　　　Nyuuderii
くと　かんじが　すきです。よろしく　おねがいします。

はじめまして。わたしは　タオ・ホワン
　　　　　　　　　　　　　Tao　Howan
です。はたちです。しゅっしんは
マレーシアです。にねんせいです。せん
Mareeshia
こうは　こうがくです。しゅ
みは　おんがくです。よろ
しく　おねがいします。

はじめまして。アイ・ブルーノです。
　　　　　　　　Ai　　Buruuno
いま、だいがくの　にねんせいです。
せんこうは　びじゅつと　にほんご
です。ネコが　だいすき
　　　　neko
です。どうぞ　よろしく
おねがいします。
ネコ
neko

Understanding Japanese sentence structure: X は Y です

1） In the profiles above, circle the particles は and の and underline です.

Ex. わたし⬭は　マーク・シルバです。ゴーブルだいがく⬭の　よねんせいです。
　　　　　　　Maaku　Shiruba　　　　Gooburu

Sorting information

2） Fill in the table below with the information you've learned about the JH members, inserting ✕ if no information is available. Then, fill in the rightmost column with your own information.

Info ＼ なまえ	マーク・シルバ Maaku　Shiruba	リーマン・ゴルド Riiman　Gorudo	タオ・ホワン Tao　Howan	アイ・ブルーノ Ai　Buruuno	your own
なんねんせい					
せんこう					
なんさい					
しゅっしん					
すきなもの／こと (favorite thing)					

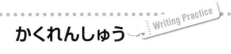

かくれんしゅう

Based on your information in the table above, write your own self-introduction.

ききましょう

>>>>> リスニング・ストラテジー : Listening strategy <<<<

Picking out keywords in a self-introduction such as a person's name, hometown, etc.
Since you've just started learning Japanese, it is only natural that there will be many words and expressions you don't know when you encounter Japanese outside of the classroom. In this section, we'll practice listening to realistic, natural conversations in Japanese and picking out keywords. You don't need to understand everything you hear to get the gist of what's being said. Don't worry about any unknown words and expressions—just focus on keywords.

1 **Pre-listening activity:** When you meet someone for the first time, what kind of information do you normally exchange with each other? Check all the boxes below that apply, and make sure you can say the words for all of these topics in Japanese.

☐ family（かぞく）
　　kazoku
☐ work

☐ hobbies

☐ hometown

☐ name

☐ school year

 L1-17

2 **Listening:** You are studying abroad in Japan and are attending a welcome party for international students. You meet the following two people at the party. Listen to their self-introductions and find out their hometowns and the names of their colleges. Then, fill in the table below. You may write the answers in either your language or in Japanese.

	なまえ namae	しゅっしん shusshin	だいがく daigaku
1)	スミス Sumisu		
2)	ソフィ Sofi		

L1-18

3 **Listening:** Read statements 1) and 2) below. Then, listen to the conversations at a welcome party and mark ○ if the statement is true and × if it is false.

	Statement	○ or ×
1)	Their majors are the same.	
2)	The man likes "Dragon Ball" and "One Piece."	

 Exit Check ☑

Now it's time to go back to the DEKIRU List for this chapter (p.31) and do the exit check to see what new things you can do now that you've completed the lesson.

しゅうまつになにをしますか。
What are you doing over the weekend?

Instructional Video
Lesson 2

DEKIRU List

できるCheck ✓

できる I

Tell someone about your daily life and what you plan to do.
日常生活や予定などについて、簡単に話すことができる。

Entry ☐ Exit ☐

できる II

Expand conversations about familiar topics by adding follow-up questions.
身近な話題について、質問をして話題を広げることができる。

Entry ☐ Exit ☐

できる III

Talk about the frequency of actions in daily life.
日常生活ですることの頻度について、尋ねたり答えたりすることができる。

Entry ☐ Exit ☐

STRATEGIES

Conversation Tips .... ・ Japanese fillers あの（う）and えっと
・ じゃ "If that's the case"

Reading .... ・ Getting information from event flyers
・ Understanding Japanese sentence structure: Verb sentences
・ Compare and contrast

Listening .... ・ Picking out keywords for expanding a conversation

GRAMMAR

1 *Masu*-forms [Polite forms of verbs] できる I

2 Case particles (1) できる I

2-1 を [Direct object marker]

2-2 に [Time marker]

2-3 に [Destination marker]

2-4 で [Location marker]

2-5 Word order in verb sentences

3 Verb sentence questions and answers できる I

4 は [Topic marker] できる II

5 Adverbs of frequency できる III

かいわ

1 できる I　Ai and Jean continue talking at the café.　🔊 L2-1

> おかし：snack

Jean：あの、アイさんは　あした　どこに　いきますか。
　　　　　　Ai

Ai　：あしたですか。えっと、あさ　10じごろ

　　　とうきょうスカイツリーに　いきます。
　　　　　　Sukaitsurii

Jean：スカイツリーですか。いいですね。
　　　Sukaitsurii

Ai　：スカイツリーの　あとで、あきはばらに　いきます。
　　　Sukaitsurii

Jean：そうですか。あきはばらで　なにを　しますか。

Ai　：まんがを　たくさん　かいます。

　　　にほんの　おかしも　ちょっと　かいます。

とうきょうスカイツリー
Sukaitsurii

ふじさん
(Mt. Fuji)

あきはばら

2 できる I, II　Ai and Jean continue talking at the café.　🔊 L2-2

> まいしゅう：every week　ライブ：live show
> 　　　　　　　　　　　　raibu

Ai　：あの、ジャンさんは　まいしゅう　しゅうまつに　なにを　しますか。
　　　　　　Jan

Jean：えっと、どようびに　ジムに　いきます。
　　　　　　　　　　　jimu

　　　それから、にちようびに　しごとを　します。

Ai　：そうですか。しごとは　なにを　しますか。

Jean：ライブを　します。
　　　raibu

Ai　：え、ライブ？
　　　　　raibu

Jean：ええ、ぼくは　ミュージシャンです。
　　　　　　　　　myuujishan

　　　だから、まいしゅう　にちようびに　SNSで　ライブを　します。
　　　　　　　　　　　　　　　　　esuenuesu　raibu

Ai　：そうですか。じゃ、わたしは　アメリカで　ジャンさんの　ライブを　みます。
　　　　　　　　　　　　　　　　　Amerika　　Jan　　　　　raibu

Jean：ありがとう。

3 できる Ⅱ,Ⅲ **Ai and Jean continue talking at the café.**  L2-3

SF: Sci-Fi　ホラー：horror　ざんねんです：I am sorry.
esuefu　　 horaa

Jean：あのう、アイさんは　よく　えいがを　みますか。
　　　　　　Ai

Ai　：はい、よく　みます。

Jean：そうですか。えいがは　なにが　すきですか。

Ai　：アニメが　すきです。SFも　ときどき　みます。でも、ホラーは　ちょっと…
　　　anime　　　　　　　esuefu　　　　　　　　　　　　　　horaa

Jean：そうですか。ぼくも　あまり　ホラーを　みません。
　　　　　　　　　　　　　　horaa

　　　あのう、アイさんは　こんしゅうの　どようびに　なにを　しますか。
　　　　　　　　Ai

Ai　：どようび？　わたしは　どようびに　アメリカに　かえります。
　　　　　　　　　　　　　　　　　　　　Amerika

Jean：そうですか。ざんねんです。

CONVERSATION **TIPS**　　ワンポイント　 L2-4

1. Japanese fillers あの（う）**and** えっと：Both are fillers like "uh..." and "um..." in English. You will sound more natural if you can use one of these fillers instead of defaulting to those from your language or leaving silent pauses while you think.

A：あのう、しゅみは　なんですか。

B：えっと、ゲームと　スポーツです。
　　　　　geemu　　supootsu

2. じゃ **"If that's the case":** You can use じゃ before you state a decision or make a suggestion.

A：アイさんは　あした　パーティーに　いきますか。
　　Ai　　　　　　　paatii

B：はい、いきます。

A：じゃ、わたしも　いきます。

55

たんご

▶ **The words written in gray** are supplemental vocabulary.

● まいにちのせいかつ　Daily life

あさ
asa
(morning)

ひる
hiru
(daytime; midday)

よる
yoru
(night; evening)

きょう
kyoo
(today)

あした
ashita
(tomorrow)

やすみ
yasumi
(break; day off)

おきる
okiru
(to get up; to wake up)

ねる
neru
(to sleep; to go to bed)

[thing を] のむ
o nomu
(to drink)

おちゃ
ocha
((green) tea)

みず
mizu
(water)

コーヒー
koohii
(coffee)

[thing を] たべる
o taberu
(to eat)

ごはん
gohan
(meal; cooked rice)

あさごはん
asagohan
(breakfast)

ひるごはん
hirugohan
(lunch)

ばんごはん
bangohan
(dinner)

[thing を] きく
o kiku
(to listen to)

[person に*] きく
ni kiku
(to ask)

[thing を] みる
o miru
(to look at; to watch)

[thing を] よむ
o yomu
(to read)

[thing を] かう
o kau
(to buy)

テレビ
terebi
(TV)

ニュース
nyuusu
(news)

インターネット／
intaanetto
ネット
netto
(internet)

SNS
esuenuesu
(social media)

[thing を]
o
する
suru
(to do)

しゅくだいを
shukudai o
する
suru
(to do homework)

ゲームをする
geemu o suru
(to play a game)

スポーツをする
supootsu o suru
(to play sports)

べんきょう(を)
benkyoo o
する
suru
(to study)

アルバイトをする
arubaito o suru
(to work part-time)

アルバイトにいく
arubaito ni iku
(to go to a part-time job)

アルバイト／バイト
arubaito baito
(part-time job)

[place に] いく
ni iku
(to go)

[place に] くる
ni kuru
(to come)

[one's home base に]
ni
かえる
kaeru
(to return)

かいものにいく
kaimono ni iku
(to go shopping)

かいもの
kaimono
(shopping)

コンサート／パーティー
konsaato paatii
にいく
ni iku
(to go to a concert/party)

がっこうにいく
gakkoo ni iku
(to go to school)

うちにかえる
uchi ni kaeru
(to go home)

コンサート
konsaato
(concert)

パーティー
paatii
(party)

* This に marks the indirect object.

じかんのひょうげん　Time expressions

～じ (... o'clock)

1	2	3	4	5	6	
いちじ	にじ	さんじ	よじ	ごじ	ろくじ	
ichiji	niji	sanji	yoji	goji	rokuji	
7	**8**	**9**	**10**	**11**	**12**	**?**
しちじ	はちじ	くじ	じゅうじ	じゅういちじ	じゅうにじ	なんじ
shichiji	hachiji	kuji	juuji	juuichiji	juuniji	nanji

ごぜん
gozen
(AM)

ごご
gogo
(PM; afternoon)

～ごろ
goro
(around; about)

Ex. いちじごろ (around one o'clock)
ichijigoro

～はん
han
(half (past))

Ex. にじはん (half past two)
nijihan

いつ
itsu
(when)

～ようび (...day)

Mon	Tue	Wed	Thu	Fri	Sat	Sun	?
げつようび	かようび	すいようび	もくようび	きんようび	どようび	にちようび	なんようび
getsuyoobi	kayoobi	suiyoobi	mokuyoobi	kin'yoobi	doyoobi	nichiyoobi	nan'yoobi

こんしゅう (this week)
konshuu

らいしゅう (next week)
raishuu

しゅうまつ (weekend)
shuumatsu

Frequency expressions

0% ─── 100%

ぜんぜん
zenzen
(never)

あまり
amari
(not very often)

ときどき
tokidoki
(sometimes)

よく
yoku
(often)

まいにち
mainichi
(every day)

ばしょ　Places

いえ／うち
ie　　uchi
(house; home)

がっこう
gakkoo
(school)

しょくどう
shokudoo
(cafeteria; dining hall)

としょかん
toshokan
(library)

へや
heya
(room)

りょう
ryoo
(dormitory)

アパート
apaato
(apartment)

カフェ
kafe
(café)

クラス
kurasu
(class)

ジム
jimu
(gym)

レストラン
resutoran
(restaurant)

そのほかのひょうげん　Other expressions

それから sorekara (and (then))	だから dakara (therefore)	でも demo (however)	たくさん takusan (many; a lot)	ちょっと chotto (a little)	ええ ee (yes [casual]; uh-huh [while listening])	じゃ ja (well; if that's the case)

いいですね
ii desu ne
(That's good; Nice!)

Noun の あとで
　　　　no ato de
(after Noun)
Ex. クラス の あとで
　　kurasu　no ato de
　　(after class)

おんがくが すきです
Ongaku ga suki desu
(I like music.)

おんがくは なにが すきですか
Ongaku wa nani ga suki desu ka
(When it comes to music, what do you like?)

～は ちょっと...
　wa　chotto
(I don't particularly care for ...)

たんごリスト

L2-5

RU-VERBS

1	おきる okiru	to get up; to wake up
2	ねる neru	to sleep; to go to bed
3	たべる taberu	to eat [thing を]
4	みる miru	to look at; to watch; to see [thing を]

U-VERBS

5	いく iku	to go [place に]
6	かえる kaeru	to return [one's home base に]; to go home
7	かう kau	to buy [thing を]
8	きく kiku	to listen to; to hear [thing を]; to ask [person に*]
9	のむ nomu	to drink [thing を]
10	よむ yomu	to read [thing を]

IRREGULAR VERBS

11	くる kuru	to come [place に]
12	する suru	to do [thing を]

SURU-VERBS

13	べんきょう(を)する benkyoo o suru	to study [thing を]
14	アルバイト(を)する arubaito o suru バイト(を)する baito o suru	to work part-time

NOUNS

15	ごはん gohan	meal; cooked rice
16	あさごはん asagohan	breakfast
17	ひるごはん hirugohan	lunch
18	ばんごはん bangohan	dinner; supper

19	おちゃ ocha	(green) tea
20	みず mizu	water
21	ごぜん gozen	AM
22	ごご gogo	PM; afternoon
23	やすみ yasumi	break; day off
24	いえ／うち ie uchi	house; home
25	がっこう gakkoo	school
26	しょくどう shokudoo	cafeteria; dining hall
27	としょかん toshokan	library
28	へや heya	room
29	りょう ryoo	dormitory
30	かいもの kaimono	shopping
31	コーヒー koohii	coffee
32	テレビ terebi	TV
33	ニュース nyuusu	news
34	インターネット／ intaanetto ネット netto	internet
35	SNS （エスエヌエス） esuenuesu	social media
36	アパート apaato	apartment
37	カフェ kafe	café
38	ジム jimu	gym
39	レストラン resutoran	restaurant
40	クラス kurasu	class; course

* This に marks the indirect object.

41	コンサート konsaato	concert
42	パーティー paatii	party

ADVERBIAL NOUNS

43	あさ asa	morning
44	ひる hiru	daytime; midday
45	よる yoru	night; evening
46	きょう kyoo	today
47	あした ashita	tomorrow
48	こんしゅう konshuu	this week
49	らいしゅう raishuu	next week
50	しゅうまつ shuumatsu	weekend
51	まいにち mainichi	every day

ADVERBS

52	よく yoku	often
53	ときどき tokidoki	sometimes
54	あまり（〜ません） amari　　masen	(not) ... very often; (not) ... very much
55	ぜんぜん（〜ません） zenzen　　masen	(not) ... at all; never
56	たくさん takusan	many; a lot
57	ちょっと chotto	a little

QUESTION WORD

58	いつ itsu	when

CONJUNCTIONS

59	それから sorekara	and (then); in addition
60	だから dakara	therefore; so
61	でも demo	however; but
62	じゃ ja	well; if that's the case

SUFFIXES

63	〜じ ji	... o'clock
	いちじ ichiji	one o'clock
	なんじ nanji	what time
64	〜ようび yoobi	...day
	げつようび getsuyoobi	Monday
	かようび kayoobi	Tuesday
	すいようび suiyoobi	Wednesday
	もくようび mokuyoobi	Thursday
	きんようび kin'yoobi	Friday
	どようび doyoobi	Saturday
	にちようび nichiyoobi	Sunday
	なんようび nan'yoobi	what day of the week
65	〜ごろ goro	around; about [time]
	いちじごろ ichijigoro	around one o'clock
66	〜はん han	half (past)
	にじはん nijihan	half past two [time]

OTHER WORDS AND PHRASES

67	ええ ee	yes [casual]; uh-huh [while listening]
68	いいですね ii desu ne	That's good; Nice!
69	Noun の あとで no　ato de	after Noun
70	Topic は なにが すきですか Topic wa　nani ga suki desu ka	When it comes to [the topic], what do you like?
71	Noun は ちょっと… wa　chotto	I don't particularly care for ...; ... isn't good for me. [indirect rejection]

ぶんぽう

1 Masu-forms [Polite forms of verbs]

In this lesson, you will learn how to use verbs in Japanese to talk about actions performed by you and others. [1] provides an example.

[1]

		V (masu-form)
わたしは	まいにち	およぎます。
I swim everyday.		

Verbs are used in a variety of forms. Here, you will learn the *masu*-forms, which are used when you talk about a person's action politely. The way to make the *masu*-form of a verb differs depending on what kind of verb it is.

Japanese verbs can be categorized into three groups according to the way they conjugate (i.e., the way they change their forms): *ru*-verbs, *u*-verbs, and irregular verbs. The dictionary forms (i.e., the basic forms that appear in dictionary entries) of *ru*-verbs all end in る, while the dictionary forms of *u*-verbs can end in a variety of syllables with the /u/ sound, including う、く、す、つ、ぬ、ぶ、む、and る.

The rules for making the *masu*-forms from the dictionary forms for each group of verbs are as follows:

a) *Ru*-verbs

Dictionary form	たべる taberu	みる miru	おきる okiru	ねる neru
Masu-form	たべます tabemasu	みます mimasu	おきます okimasu	ねます nemasu

How to make the *masu*-form from the dictionary form:

Drop the final る and add ます. **Ex.** たべる + ます → たべます

b) *U*-verbs

N	W	R	Y	M	H	N	T	S	K		
ん	わ	ら	や	ま	は	な	た	さ	か	あ	A
		り		み	ひ	に	ち	し	き	い	i
		る	ゆ	む	ふ	ぬ	つ	す	く	う	U
		れ		め	へ	ね	て	せ	け	え	E
	を	ろ	よ	も	ほ	の	と	そ	こ	お	O

← Endings before ます

← Endings of the dictionary forms

Dictionary form	のむ nomu	いく iku	かえる kaeru
Masu-form	のみます nomimasu	いきます ikimasu	かえります kaerimasu

How to make the *masu*-form from the dictionary form:

Step 1 Change the final character to the corresponding character in the *i*-row of the hiragana table.
Exs. のむ → のみ; いく → いき

Step 2 Add ます.
Exs. のみ + ます → のみます; いき + ます → いきます

c) Irregular verbs

There are only two irregular verbs in Japanese, くる and する, and their conjugations are not rule-based and must simply be memorized.

Dictionary form	くる kuru	する* suru
Masu-form	きます kimasu	します shimasu

* *Suru*-verbs like べんきょうする are also irregular verbs. (See Language Note: *Suru*-verbs (p.84).)

The dictionary forms of *ru*-verbs always end with either *–iru* or *–eru* (e.g., *miru*, *taberu*), which means that a verb is an *u*-verb if its dictionary form ends with *-aru*, *-uru*, or *-oru*. However, even if the dictionary form of a verb ends with *–iru* or *–eru*, you cannot automatically determine that it is a *ru*-verb because there are a handful of *u*-verbs whose dictionary forms also end with *–iru* or *–eru*. For example, かえる "to return" ends with *-eru*, but it is an *u*-verb because its *masu*-form is not かえます but かえります. *U*-verbs whose dictionary forms end with *–iru* include はいる "to enter," きる "to cut," しる "to get to know," and はしる "to run."

The polite ending ます indicates that the verb tense is non-past. The negative form of ます is ません.

Dictionary form	*Masu*-form (non-past)	
	Affirmative	Negative
たべる	たべます	たべません
のむ	のみます	のみません
くる	きます	きません

By using the non-past *masu*-forms of verbs, you can talk about future actions and present habitual actions.

2 Case particles (1)

Here you will learn some case particles. Case is a grammatical term used to refer to the role of a word (particularly a noun) in a sentence, and case particles indicate the grammatical relations between the nouns they mark and the verbs that follow.

☞ **GID** (vol.1): B. Particles 1. Case particles

2-1 を [Direct object marker]

[2-a]

		N (direct object)		V (transitive)	
A:	あした	なに	を	します	か。
	What are you going to do tomorrow?				
B:		テニス tenisu	を	します。	
	I'm going to play tennis.				

In verb sentences (i.e., sentences that contain a verb), the verb is placed at the end of the sentence, and if the verb is a transitive verb (i.e., a verb that requires a direct object), the direct object is marked by the particle を (pronounced as /o/) and is generally placed right before the verb. The question word なに "what" takes the same position and is not brought to the beginning of the sentence as it would be in English, as in [2-a]-A above.

Lesson 2

Exs. (1) わたしは　まいにち　コーヒーを　のみます。*I drink coffee every day.*
koohii

(2) わたしは　スポーツを　しません。*I don't play sports.*
supootsu

(3) タオ：アイさんは　にほんごの　クラスの　あとで　なにを　しますか。
Tao　　Ai　　　　　　　　　　　kurasu
What are you doing after Japanese class, Ai?

アイ：ひるごはんを　たべます。*I'm eating lunch.*
Ai

Note that before を, なに is used rather than なん. (Compare Tao's line in (3) above with L1 #4-2.)

2-2 に [Time marker] "at; on; in"

[2-b]

	N (time)		
わたしは　まいにち	6 じ	に	おきます。
I get up at six every day.			

You use the particle に to mark the time of an action.

Exs. (1) まいにち　7 じに　あさごはんを　たべます。*I eat breakfast at seven every day.*

(2) げつようびと　もくようびに　アルバイトを　します。
arubaito
I work part-time on Mondays and Thursdays.

(3) A: まいにち　なんじに　ねますか。*What time do you go to bed every day?*

B: （まいにち）　12 じに　ねます。*I go to bed at twelve (every day).*

Certain kinds of time nouns do not take に. Those nouns include:

(a) Relative-time nouns (i.e., nouns that specify a time only in relation to the time that they are used and thus have no fixed referent): Exs. きょう, あした, こんしゅう, らいしゅう

(b) Periodical-time nouns (i.e., nouns that contain まい "every"): Exs. まいにち, まいしゅう

Exs. (4) A: いつ　パーティーを　しますか。*When are you throwing a party?*
paatii

B: あした ø* （パーティーを）　します。*I'm throwing (a party) tomorrow.*
paatii
(*ø means that nothing is used in this position.)

(5) まいにち ø　にほんごを　はなします。*I speak Japanese every day.*

に after あさ, ひる, よる, しゅうまつ, and ～ごろ is optional.

Exs. (6) わたしは　まいにち　あさ（に）　コーヒーを　のみます。
I drink coffee in the morning every day. koohii

(7) タオさんは　しゅうまつ（に）　えいがを　みます。*Tao watches movies on weekends.*
Tao

(8) A: まいにち　なんじに　おきますか。*What time do you get up every day?*

B: 9 じごろ（に）　おきます。*I get up around nine.*

2-3 に [Destination marker] "to"

[2-c]

	N (destination)		V (motion)
わたしは　きょう	としょかん	に	いきます。
I will go to the library today.			

You also use the particle に to mark the destination of a movement. The verbs that occur with "N (destination) に" include いく, くる, and かえる. Although に is more common, へ (pronounced as /e/) can also be used to mark the destination of a movement.

Exs. (1) わたしは　きょう　うち<u>に</u>　かえりません。 *I'm not going back home today.*

(2) みかさんは　8じに　がっこう<u>に</u>　きます。
Mika comes to school at eight o'clock.

(3) A: あ、トムさん、どこ<u>に</u>　いきますか。 *Oh, (hi) Tom, where are you going?*
Tomu

B: レストラン<u>に</u>　いきます。ばんごはんを　たべます。
resutoran
I'm going to a restaurant. I'm eating dinner (there).

As an extended use, the particle に can also mark events (e.g., コンサート "concert," パーティー "party,"
konsaato   paatii
etc.) and activities (e.g., かいもの "shopping," アルバイト "part-time job," etc.), as in (4) and (5).
arubaito

Exs. (4) たなかさんは　にちようびに　コンサート<u>に</u>　いきます。
konsaato
Tanaka-san is going to a concert on Sunday.

(5) やまださんは　きょう　かいもの<u>に</u>　いきます。
Yamada-san is going shopping today.

☞ **GID** (vol.1): B. Particles 1-3. に and 1-4. へ

2-4 で [Location marker] "at; in"

[2-d]

わたしは	N (location)		V (action)
わたしは	としょかん	で	べんきょうします。
I study at the library.			

You use the particle で to mark the location of an action.

Exs. (1) わたしは　あした　レストラン<u>で</u>　アルバイトを　します。
resutoran   arubaito
I'm working (my part-time job) at the restaurant tomorrow.

(2) しゅうまつ　へや<u>で</u>　えいがを　みます。
I'm going to watch a movie in my room on the weekend.

(3) A: きょう　どこ<u>で</u>　ひるごはんを　たべますか。 *Where are you eating lunch today?*

B: うち<u>で</u>　（ひるごはんを）　たべます。 *I am eating (lunch) at home.*

2-5 Word order in verb sentences

In verb sentences, the verb usually occurs at the end of the sentence, and if there is a topic, it comes at the beginning. The general word order for verb sentences is as follows:

Topic – Time – Location – Direct Object – Verb (action)

Ex. (1) みかさんは　どようびに　レストランで　アルバイトを　します。
resutoran   arubaito
Mika works a part-time job at a restaurant on Saturdays.

Topic – Time – Destination – Verb (motion)

Ex. (2) みかさんは　きんようびに　ジムに　いきます。
jimu
Mika goes to the gym on Fridays.

3 Verb sentence questions and answers

As you learned in Lesson 1, yes-no questions can be made simply by adding the question marker か to the end of a sentence. In response to yes-no questions, the verb is repeated in either the affirmative or the negative form.

Ex. (1)　A： きょう　ゲームを　しますか。 *Are you going to play games today?*
　　　　　　　　　　geemu

　　　　B1：はい、（ゲームを）　します。 *Yes, I am.*
　　　　　　　　　　　geemu

　　　　B2：いいえ、（ゲームを）　しません。 *No, I'm not.*
　　　　　　　　　　　　geemu

As seen in (1), ゲームを is not repeated in B1 or B2 because it is understood without being said. しま
　　　　　　　geemu
す cannot be omitted, however, because a complete sentence requires an element that provides tense and politeness information, such as a verb or "Noun + です." (For more about omitting sentence elements, see

GID (vol.1): I. Ellipsis.)

(2) and (3) provide more examples of verb sentence questions and the responses to them.

Exs. (2)　A： きんようびに　がっこうに　いきますか。

　　　　　　　Are you going to school on Friday? / Do you go to school on Fridays?

　　　　B1：はい、（きんようびに　がっこうに）　いきます。 *Yes, I am. / Yes, I do.*

　　　　B2：いいえ、（きんようびに　がっこうに）　いきません。 *No, I'm not. / No, I don't.*

　　(3)　A： きょう　としょかんで　にほんごを　べんきょうしますか。

　　　　　　　Are you going to study Japanese in the library today?

　　　　B1：はい、（きょう　としょかんで　にほんごを　べんきょう）　します。 *Yes, I am.*

　　　　B2：いいえ、（きょう　としょかんで　にほんごを　べんきょう）　しません。

　　　　　　　No, I'm not.

Note that in (2)-B1 and (2)-B2, きんようびに and がっこうに are omitted, and in (3)-B1 and (3)-B2, きょう, としょかんで, にほんごを, and べんきょう are omitted.

4 は [Topic marker] "As for; Speaking of"

[4-a]

A:	わたしは　おんがくが　すきです。		
	I like music.		
B:	Topic		
	おんがく	は	なにを　ききますか。
	What kind of music do you listen to? (lit. As for music, what do you listen to?)		

[4-b]

A:	わたしの　しゅみは　スポーツです。		
		supootsu	
	My hobby is (playing) sports.		
B:	Topic		
	スポーツ	は	なにを　しますか。
	supootsu		
	What kind of sports do you play? (lit. As for sports, what do you play?)		

You can expand a conversation using the topic marker は, as seen in [4-a] and [4-b]. For example, in [4-a], Speaker A mentions おんがく and Speaker B wants to know more about that, while in [4-b], Speaker A mentions スポーツ and Speaker B asks for more specific information about that. In such situations, Speaker
supootsu
B first presents the topic with は and then asks a specific question in the following part of the sentence.

Exs. (1) A: わたしは　まいにち　ゲームを　します。 *I play games every day.*
geemu

B: ゲームは　なにを　しますか。
geemu
What games do you play? (lit. As for games, what do you play?)

(2) A: わたしは　まいにち　コーヒーを　のみます。 *I drink coffee every day.*
koohii

B: コーヒーは　どこで　かいますか。
koohii
Where do you buy your coffee? (lit. As for coffee, where do you buy it?)

(3) A: きょう　かいものに　いきます。 *I'm going shopping today.*

B: そうですか。かいものは　どこに　いきますか。
I see. Where are you going shopping? (lit. As for shopping, where are you going?)

5 Adverbs of frequency

[5]

	Adverb of frequency		Verb (affirmative)
わたしは	よく	としょかんで	べんきょうします。
I often study at the library.			
			Verb (negative)
わたしは	あまり	ゲームを geemu	しません。
I don't play games very often.			

You can express how often someone does something or something happens using frequency adverbs such as よく, ときどき, あまり, and ぜんぜん. Frequency adverbs usually occur before verb phrases (i.e., Noun + Particle + Verb). Note that some frequency adverbs are always used with the affirmative forms of verbs (e.g., よく, ときどき) and some are always used with the negative forms of verbs (e.g., あまり, ぜんぜん).

Exs. (1) アイさんは　ときどき　カフェで　あさごはんを　たべます。
Ai　　　　　　　　　　kafe
Ai sometimes eats breakfast at a café.

(2) リーマンさんは　ぜんぜん　パーティーに　いきません。
Riiman　　　　　　　　　　paatii
Riemann never goes to parties.

(3) A: よく　えいがを　みますか。 *Do you watch movies often?*

B1: はい、よく　みます。 *Yes, I often do (watch movies).*

B2: いいえ、あまり　みません。 *No, I don't watch (movies) very much.*

はなしましょう

でき
る
I Tell someone about your daily life and what you plan to do.

できるI-A Time expressions

1 Let's practice forming time expressions in Japanese. L2-6

Ex. 8 AM → ごぜん　はちじ

1) 9 AM
2) 10 AM
3) 11:30 AM
4) 12:30 PM

5) 4 PM
6) around 5 PM
7) around 6:30 PM
8) around 7:30 AM

2 You are asked what time it is. Say the time in Japanese.

Ex. 7:00

A: すみません。いま、なんじですか。

B: しちじです。

A: しちじですか。ありがとうございます。

B: どういたしまして。

1) 9:00
2) 2:00
3) 12:00
4) 3:30
5) 4:30
6) 5:30

3 First, say the days of the week in Japanese. Then, answer the following questions.

1) きょうは　なんようびですか。

2) あしたは　なんようびですか。

3) がっこうの　やすみは　なんようびですか。

4 Look at the pictures below and talk about the days the places are closed and the people have off.

Ex. Tue A: レストランの　やすみは　なんようびですか。 L2-7
resutoran
B: かようびです。

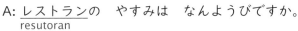

1) Wed
2) Thu
3) Mon
4) Fri & Sun
5) Sat & Sun

くろだせんせい
アルバイト
arubaito

5 Do you know the time difference between Japan and other countries? Let's find out. Look at the map below and check the time in the various places across different time zones.

Ex. にほん → A: <u>にほん</u>は　いま　なんじですか。

B: <u>にちようびの　ごぜん　くじ</u>です。

Lesson
2

1) スペイン　　　2) ケニア　　　3) ペルー　　　4) アメリカ／シアトル
　Supein　　　　　 Kenia　　　　　Peruu　　　　　Amerika　　Shiatoru

5) オーストラリア／シドニー　　　6) インドネシア／ジャカルタ
　Oosutoraria　　　　Shidonii　　　　Indoneshia　　　Jakaruta

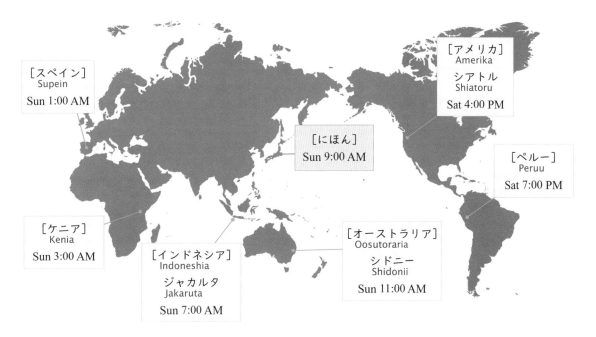

［スペイン］
Supein
Sun 1:00 AM

［アメリカ］
Amerika
シアトル
Shiatoru
Sat 4:00 PM

［にほん］
Sun 9:00 AM

［ペルー］
Peruu
Sat 7:00 PM

［ケニア］
Kenia
Sun 3:00 AM

［インドネシア］
Indoneshia
ジャカルタ
Jakaruta
Sun 7:00 AM

［オーストラリア］
Oosutoraria
シドニー
Shidonii
Sun 11:00 AM

6 (Information gap) You and your partner each have a partial evening TV schedule—Student A's version is below, while Student B's can be found on p.75. Ask each other for the information missing from your schedules.

Ex. えいが → A: えいがは　なんようびの　なんじですか。

B: にちようびの　はちじです。

1) うた　　2) スポーツ　　3) アニメ　　4) ドラマ (drama)　　5) にほんの　あさごはん
　　　　　　　supootsu　　　anime　　　　dorama

Student A

TVにほん						
	Sun	**Mon**	**Tue**	**Wed**	**Thu**	**Fri**	**Sat**
8 PM	Ex. えいが		にほんご	びじゅつ	にほんの　いま		
9 PM		ニュース nyuusu				ニュース nyuusu	コンサート konsaato

Student B ➡p.75

1 Let's practice conjugating verbs into the *masu*-forms used when speaking politely. L2-8

Ex. ねる → ねます → ねません

1) おきる　　2) みる　　3) たべる　　4) いく　　5) のむ　　6) よむ

7) きく　　8) かえる　　9) かう　　10) する　　11) くる

2 Talk about daily activities.

Step 1 Look at the activity row of the table below and make sentences. Wang-san does all the activities listed while Gómez-san does not. L2-9

Ex. ワンさんは　あさごはんを　たべます。
　　　　Wan

　　　ゴメスさんは　あさごはんを　たべません。
　　　　Gomesu

	Ex.	1)	2)	3)	4)	5)	6)
Activity							
Time	7:30	around 9:30	Monday	today	this week	every day	night

Step 2 Expand the sentences you made in Step 1 by adding the time expressions provided. Pay attention to the time marker particle as certain time expressions do not take に. L2-10

Ex. ワンさんは　しちじはんに　あさごはんを　たべます。
　　　　Wan

Step 3 Make questions about some of the activities above and ask them to your partner. When asked, include time expressions in your answers if possible.

Ex. A: ○○さんは　あさごはんを　たべますか。

　　　B: はい、まいにち　はちじごろ(に)　たべます。or いいえ、たべません。

3 Make sentences about where you go and what you do there based on the cues provided. Pay attention to the motion verbs and particles you use. L2-11

Ex. しょくどうに　いきます。しょくどうで　あさごはんを　たべます。

	Ex.	1)	2)	3)	4)	5)
Place					friend's house	home
Activity	eat breakfast	buy coffee	study Japanese	work part-time	play a game	do homework

4 Look at the table below and talk about Ai's week. Expand the sentences step by step by adding time expressions and places.

Ex. ❶ アイさんは　べんきょうします。 `+ time`
　　　　 Ai

　　　 ❷ （アイさんは）　にちようびに　べんきょうします。 `+ place`
　　　　　 Ai

　　　 ❸ （アイさんは）　にちようびに　ともだちの　へやで　べんきょうします。
　　　　　 Ai

Ai's week	Ex.	1)	2)	3)	4)	5)
❶ Activity	study	movie	read a book	part-time job	dance	listen to songs
❷ Time	Sunday	Monday	Wednesday around 4 PM	Thursday 5 PM	Friday around 7 AM	Saturday 3:30 PM
❸ Place	friend's room	Japan House	library	dorm's cafeteria	gym	café

5 Expand your conversation using various question words.

Step 1 What should be inserted to appropriately complete the following exchanges? Fill in
　　　 ＿＿＿ with the appropriate question words. 🔊 **L2-12**

Ex. A: まいにち　なんじごろ（に）　だいがくに　いきますか。

　　　 B: じゅうじごろ　いきます。

1) A: ＿＿＿＿＿に　おきますか。　　　　　　B: しちじはんに　おきます。

2) A: あさ　＿＿＿＿＿を　たべますか。　　　 B: ベーグル (bagel) を　たべます。
　　　　　　　　　　　　　　　　　　　　　　　 beeguru

3) A: ＿＿＿＿＿で　しゅくだいを　しますか　 B: としょかんで　します。

4) A: ＿＿＿＿＿に　アルバイトを　しますか。 B: すいようびと　もくようびに　します。
　　　　　　　　 arubaito

5) A: どようびに　＿＿＿＿＿に　いきますか。 B: ともだちの　うちに　いきます。

6) A: ＿＿＿＿＿　かいものに　いきますか。　 B: しゅうまつに　いきます。

Step 2 Is your partner's daily routine the same as yours? Ask questions and find out.

> **Possible topics**　あさごはん　　にほんご　　ジム　　コーヒー　　ニュース
> 　　　　　　　　　　　　　　　　　　　　　 jimu　　 koohii　　 nyuusu

Ex.　A: ○○さんは　まいにち　あさごはんを　たべますか。

Yes	No
B: はい、たべます。	B: いいえ、たべません。
A: なんじごろ　たべますか。	A: そうですか。わたしも　たべません。
B: はちじごろ　たべます。	B: そうですか。
A: そうですか。わたしも　あさ　はちじごろ	
たべます。どこで　たべますか。	
B: りょうの　しょくどうで　たべます。	

6 Do you have an interesting daily routine? Pick a day of the week and fill in the chart with what you typically do. Describe your routine in detail.

Ex. わたしの　もくようびの　スケジュール (schedule) です。
sukejuuru

あさ　しちじはんごろ　おきます。

それから、SNSを　みます。
esuenuesu

あさごはんを　たべません。

はちじはんに　がっこうに　いきます。

だいがくで… <Continue>

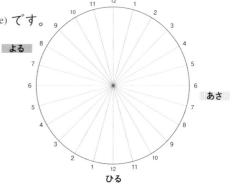

Expand conversations about familiar topics by adding follow-up questions.

できるII-A **Topic marker は**

1 Expand conversations about the topics in the box below for Dialogue 1 and the actions listed for Dialogue 2 by adding follow-up questions using the topic marker は, as shown in the examples.

Dialogue 1

Possible topics	おんがく	えいが	ほん	スポーツ	ゲーム	アニメ
				supootsu	geemu	anime

クラシック: classical music　ベートーベン: Beethoven
kurashikku　　　　　　　　Beetooben

Ex. A: わたしは　おんがく が　すきです。

B: そうですか。おんがく は　なにが　すきですか。(← Follow-up question)

A: {クラシック／ベートーベン}が　すきです。
kurashikku　　Beetooben

Dialogue 2

Ex. しゅくだい を　する

A: クラスの　あとで　しゅくだい を　します。
kurasu

B: そうですか。しゅくだい は　どこで　しますか。(← Follow-up question)

or しゅくだい は　なにを　しますか。

A: がっこうの　としょかんで　します。

or カタカナの　しゅくだいを　します。
katakana

1) ひるごはんを　たべる　　2) えいがを　みる　　3) カフェに　いく
kafe

4) アルバイトを　する　　5) your own
arubaito

2 Ask your classmates what their hobbies are and then ask follow-up questions to gain more information.

Ex. A: ○○さんの　しゅみは　なんですか。

B:（わたしの　しゅみは）　えいがです。

A: そうですか。えいがは　なにが　すきですか。

B: ホラー (horror) が　すきです。△△さんも　ホラーが　すきですか。
　　horaa　　　　　　　　　　　　　　　　　　　　　　horaa

A: いいえ、ホラーは　ちょっと…
　　　　　horaa

Group Work

3 Talk about pop culture.

[Step 1] Interview your classmates and find out what pop culture they like. Choose a topic from the options below. Ask as many classmates as possible.

ゲーム	アニメ	まんが	J‐POP
geemu	anime		jeepoppu

Ex. A: ○○さんは　アニメを　みますか。
　　　　　　　　　　　anime

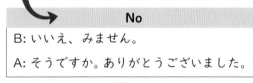

Yes	No
B: はい、みます。	B: いいえ、みません。
A: そうですか。	A: そうですか。ありがとうございました。
アニメは　なにを　みますか。 　anime	
B: \<name of anime\>と　\<name of anime\>を 　みます。	
A: そうですか。ありがとうございました。	

[Step 2] Now, tell the rest of the class what you found out about the people you interviewed.

Ex. ○○さんと　△△さんは　アニメを　みます。
　　　　　　　　　　　　　　　anime

アニメは　\<name of anime\>を　みます。
anime

1 Let's practice using the three conjunctions from this lesson.

Step 1 Select a conjunction to complete each sentence below: それから, でも, or だから. 🔊 L2-13

1) わたしは　まいにち　7じごろ　おきます。＿＿＿＿＿、あさごはんを　たべます。

2) わたしは　ほんが　だいすきです。＿＿＿＿＿、まいにち　としょかんに　いきます。

3) わたしは　ごぜん　2じごろ　ねます。＿＿＿＿＿、しゅうまつは　12じに　ねます。

4) わたしは　テレビの　ニュースを　みません。＿＿＿＿＿、ネットの　ニュースを　みます。
　　　　　　　　terebi　　　nyuusu　　　　　　　　　　　　　netto　　　　　nyuusu

5) わたしは　よる　ほんを　よみます。＿＿＿＿＿、ねます。

6) きょうは　にちようびです。＿＿＿＿＿、クラスに　いきません。
　　　　　　　　　　　　　　　　　　　　　　kurasu

Step 2 Personalize the sentences in Step 1 by adding your own information.

1) わたしは　まいにち　＿＿＿じごろ　おきます。それから、＿＿＿＿＿＿＿＿＿＿＿＿。

2) わたしは　＿＿＿＿＿＿＿が　だいすきです。だから、まいにち　＿＿＿＿＿＿＿＿＿＿＿＿。

3) わたしは　＿＿＿じごろ　＿＿＿＿＿＿ます。でも、しゅうまつは　＿＿＿じに　＿＿＿＿＿＿ます。

4) わたしは　＿＿＿＿＿＿＿＿＿＿＿ません。でも、＿＿＿＿＿＿＿＿＿＿＿ます。

5) わたしは　よる　＿＿＿＿＿＿＿＿＿＿ます。それから、ねます。

6) きょうは　にちようびです。だから、＿＿＿＿＿＿＿＿＿＿＿。

2 Tell your partner about yourself in three sentences.

Step 1 Look at the pictures below and make sentences.

1)

わたしは　ブログを　＿＿＿＿ます。
　　　　burogu
それから、ツイート (tweet) を　＿＿＿＿ます。
　　　　　tsuiito
でも、ニュースを　＿＿＿＿ません。
　　　　nyuusu

2)

わたしは　＿＿＿＿が　すきです。
それから、＿＿＿＿が　すきです。
だから、＿＿＿＿を　＿＿＿＿ます。

3)

every day　　　✕ a lot

わたしは　＿＿＿＿が　だいすきです。
だから、＿＿＿＿＿＿＿＿ます。
でも、＿＿＿＿＿＿＿＿ません。

Step 2 Now, talk about yourself using the patterns below.

1) わたしは _____ます。それから、_____ます。でも、_____ません。

2) わたしは _____が すきです。それから、_____が すきです。だから、_____ます。

3) わたしは _____が だいすきです。だから、_____。でも、_____。

できる
Ⅲ **Talk about the frequency of actions in daily life.**

できるⅢ-A **Adverbs of frequency**

1 Talk about how often you and your classmates do the following things.

Step 1 First, say how often Smith-san does the following things using the given frequency words. 🔊 L2-14

Ex.1 スミスさんは まいにち うちで にほんごを はなします (to speak)。
Sumisu

Ex.2 スミスさんは あまり ジムに いきません。
Sumisu　　　　　　　 jimu

0 ぜんぜん	★ あまり	★★ ときどき	★★★ よく	★★★★ まいにち

Ex.1 ★★★★ speak Japanese at home	1) ★★★★ listen to music	2) ★★★ drink coffee	3) ★★★ go to a party	4) ★★ go to bed around 1 AM	5) ★★ eat dinner at a restaurant
Ex.2 ★ go to the gym	6) 0 read manga	7) ★ watch a movie	8) 0 go to his friend's house	9) ★ work at his part-time job	10) ★ go to stay at his parents' house （うちに かえる）

Step 2 Now, talk with your partner about how often you do the things in Step 1.

Ex. A: ○○さんは よく うちで にほんごを はなしますか (to speak)。

B: はい、まいにち はなします。

A: そうですか。わたしも まいにち はなします。

or わたしは あまり はなしません。

2 Can you live without a smartphone?

Step 1 Ask your partner the following questions. Answer using frequency words.

スマホ チェック
sumaho chekku

Smartphone Usage Checklist	ぜんぜん 0	あまり ★	ときどき ★★	よく ★★★	まいにち ★★★★
1) ネットの ビデオ (video) を みる netto bideo					
2) ネットの ゲームを する netto geemu					
3) SNS を よむ esuenuesu					
4) SNS で コメント (comment) を する esuenuesu komento					
5) クラスで スマホを みる kurasu sumaho					

Step 2 Calculate your partner's point total and tell your partner the result.

ぜんぜん　　　　あまり　　　　ときどき　　　　よく　　　　　まいにち
0 pt. ×____ + 1 pt. ×____ + 2 pts. ×____ + 3 pts. ×____ + 4 pts. ×____ = _____ pts.

16-20 pts.	6-15 pts.	0-5 pts.
Do you think you might be using your smartphone too much? Be careful about how often and how long you use your phone.	You may have become a bit dependent on your smartphone. Try to spend some time each day without your device.	You are at low risk of smartphone addiction.

Group Work

3 What are your criteria for choosing a housemate? Suppose you are living in the Japan House and there is a vacant room. You are going to interview two candidates who want to live there.

Step 1 Ask your interview questions to the two candidates. Answer using frequency words.

0 ぜんぜん ｜ ★ あまり ｜ ★★ ときどき ｜ ★★★ よく ｜ ★★★★ まいにち

しつもん (question)	Candidate 1: さん	Candidate 2: さん
1) しゅうまつ いえで パーティーを しますか。 paatii		
2) ともだちは へやに きますか。		
3) アニメを みますか。 anime		
4) your own		
5) your own		

Step 2 Who will you choose to be your housemate? Decide which person is a good match for you and explain your reason(s).

Ex.　ハウスメートは　〇〇さんです。△△さんは　ぜんぜん　アニメを　みません。
　　　hausumeeto　　　　　　　　　　　　　　　　　　　　　　　anime

でも、〇〇さんは　よく　アニメを　みます。
　　　　　　　　　　　　　anime

わたしも　よく　アニメを　みます。だから、〇〇さんです。
　　　　　　　　　anime

Review

Now you can expand conversations about daily life by adding follow-up questions.

ROLE PLAY Is there anyone you admire who you would like to meet and talk with in real life?

Role A Play the role of the person you admire and answer B's questions.

Role B Play the role of a fan of the person that A admires. Ask three questions.

Self-introduction	Ex. A: はじめまして。わたしは　かしゅ (singer) の　〇〇です。

B: はじめまして。アイ・ブルーノです。
　　　　　　　　　Ai　　Buruuno
　わたしは　〇〇さんの　ファン (fan) です。
　　　　　　　　　　　　　　fan

A: ありがとうございます。

Q&A
• Ask three questions

B: あの、〇〇さんの　しゅみは　なんですか。

A: しゅみは　おんがくです。

　だから、まいにち　おんがくを　ききます。

B: そうですか。わたしも　おんがくが　すきです。

　あの、おんがくは　よく　なにを　ききますか。

A: J-POP を　よく　ききます。
　　jeepoppu
　　<Continue>

できるI-A 6

Ex.　えいが → A: えいがは　なんようびの　なんじですか。

　　　　　　　B: にちようびの　はちじです。

1) にほんご　　2) コンサート　　3) にほんの　いま　　4) ニュース　　5) びじゅつ
　　　　　　　　　konsaato　　　　　　　　　　　　　　　　　　nyuusu

Student B

TVにほん							
	Sun	**Mon**	**Tue**	**Wed**	**Thu**	**Fri**	**Sat**
8 PM	Ex. えいが	にほんの あさごはん				ドラマ dorama (drama)	ドラマ dorama (drama)
9 PM			うた	スポーツ supootsu	アニメ anime		

よみましょう

Getting information from event flyers

1 The following events will be held in your area this weekend.

1）Choose an appropriate description of each event from the box below and write the corresponding number in [ ]. Guess the meanings of the underlined words from the pictures and other contextual clues.

(1) にほんのえいが	(2) にほんのフェスティバル	(3) けんどうのしあい
(4) ラーメンコンテスト	(5) ティーセレモニーのクラス	

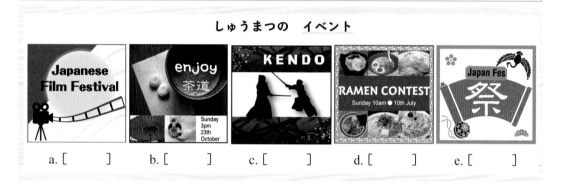

しゅうまつの イベント

a. [   ]   b. [   ]   c. [   ]   d. [   ]   e. [   ]

2）Talk with your classmates about which event you will go to and why.

Ex. わたしは スポーツが だいすきです。だから、けんどうの しあいに いきます。

2 Read the passage below about Haru's weekly schedule and answer the questions that follow.

　わたしは　はるです。にほんの　だいがくの　３ねんせいです。せんこうは　けんちくがくです。それから、だいがくの　えいごクラブの　メンバーです。

　わたしは　まいにち　8じはんに　おきます。あさ　うちでコーヒーを　のみます。それから、えいごの　ニュースを　ききます。ぜんぜん　あさごはんを　たべません。

　げつようびと　かようびと　もくようびと　きんようびは　だいがくで　べんきょうします。9じはんに　クラスに　いきます。12じごろ　しょくどうで　ひるごはんを　たべます。ごごもクラスで　べんきょうします。かようびと　もくようびは　えいごクラブに　いきます。クラブで　えいごを　はなします。8じごろうちに　かえります。すいようびと　しゅうまつは　だいがくにいきません。だから、ペットショップで　アルバイトを　します。

けんちくがく：
architecture

クラブ：club

メンバー：member

はなします：
to speak

ペットショップ：
pet shop

76

ばんごはんは　ルームメートと　うちで　たべます。あまり　レストランに　いきません。でも、ときどき　コンビニで　ばんごはんを　かいます。ばんごはんの　あとで、クラスの　ほんを　よみます。しゅくだいも　たくさん　します。まいにち　SNS を　みます。あまり　テレビを　みません。ごぜん　１じごろ　ねます。まいにち　いそがしいです。でも、たのしいです。

ルームメートと：
with [my] roommate

コンビニ：
convenience store

いそがしいです：
I'm busy.

たのしいです：
It's fun.

Understanding Japanese sentence structure: Verb sentences

1) In each sentence with a verb in the passage, underline the verb and circle the time/place/object particles used with it.

Ex.　８じはん(に)　おきます。あさ　うち(で)　コーヒー(を)　のみます。

Compare and contrast

2) First, find out when Haru does the following activities, then **compare** your daily activities with Haru's. **Choose your busiest day of the week** for the comparison.

	a. get up	b. go to first class	c. eat lunch	d. go home	e. go to bed	f. work part-time
When Haru does each activity	8:30 AM					
When you do it	____ AM					

Comprehension check

3) Mark ○ if the statement about Haru is true and × if it is false.

（　　）あさ　うちで　コーヒーを　のみます。

（　　）まいにち　だいがくに　いきます。

（　　）かようびと　もくようびに　クラブで　えいごを　はなします。

（　　）ルームメートと　よく　レストランで　ばんごはんを　たべます。

（　　）あまり　クラスの　べんきょうを　しません。

（　　）ときどき　SNS と　テレビを　みます。

- -

かくれんしゅう　*Writing Practice*

Using the information from "When you do it" in ②-2) above, write about your daily life under the title「わたしの　いちにち (A day in my life)」.

- -

ききましょう

Picking out keywords for expanding a conversation

In your native language, you probably use follow-up questions to expand a conversation without giving it much thought. In the same way, you can also expand a conversation in Japanese by picking up on any interesting information you hear and asking questions to follow up. We'll practice using this strategy here.

1 **Pre-listening activity:** Imagine you are having a conversation and the person you are talking with says the statements in 1) and 2) below. How would you expand the conversation by using the question words listed on the right below? Choose one or two question words and create follow-up questions.

1)

にほんの　レストランに　いきます。
resutoran

Your follow-up question: _____

- ☐ when
- ☐ where
- ☐ what
- ☐ what time
- ☐ what day

2)

しゅうまつ　よく　スポーツを　します。
supootsu

Your follow-up question: _____

- ☐ where
- ☐ what
- ☐ what time
- ☐ what day

 L2-15

2 **Listening:** Listen to the conversations between friends and write down any keywords you hear that you might be able to ask follow-up questions about. Then, identify which of these keywords you think will be most helpful in expanding the conversation, circle them, and write follow-up questions you could ask about them. You may write your answers in either your language or in Japanese.

Keywords (Exs. topic, when, where, what, etc.) / possible follow-up questions
1)
2)
3)

 Exit Check ☑

Now it's time to go back to the **DEKIRU List** for this chapter (p.53) and do the exit check to see what new things you can do now that you've completed the lesson.

The Japanese writing system: Katakana

In this section, we'll learn how to read katakana. You can practice how to write katakana in the workbook.

🔟 Introduction

Q1. When do you use katakana?

Katakana is typically used to write loanwords such as the names of foreign countries and people. It is also frequently used for the names of animals and flowers, particularly in academic writing, and we will follow that practice in this textbook as well. Onomatopoeia (words that imitate the sounds made by animals, humans, machines, etc., and words that seek to express actions, conditions, or states as sounds) are also generally written in katakana. Examples of each of these uses can be found below.

Due to cultural influence from the United States and other foreign countries, the number of foreign loanwords in Japanese is on the rise. In fact, it is said that more than 60% of new words added to Japanese dictionaries nowadays are katakana words. For this reason, mastery of katakana is just as important as mastery of hiragana and kanji for learners of Japanese.

2️⃣ Basic characters

In many ways, katakana is similar to hiragana—there are 46 characters in total, and each represents exactly one sound. You may note that some katakana characters look similar to their hiragana counterparts—can you tell which ones?

Consonants/semivowels ([y] and [w])											Vowels
N	W	R	Y	M	H	N	T	S	K		
ン	ワ	ラ	ヤ	マ	ハ	ナ	タ	サ	カ	ア	A
		リ		ミ	ヒ	ニ	チ	シ	キ	イ	I
		ル	ユ	ム	フ	ヌ	ツ	ス	ク	ウ	U
		レ		メ	ヘ	ネ	テ	セ	ケ	エ	E
	(ヲ)*	ロ	ヨ	モ	ホ	ノ	ト	ソ	コ	オ	O

* ヲ is rarely used in modern Japanese.

3 Voiced and semi-voiced sounds

The rule for writing voiced sounds is the same as the one for hiragana.

semi-voiced	voiced	voice-less	voiced	voice-less	voiced	voice-less	voiced	voice-less	Vowels
P	B	H	D	T	Z/J	S	G	K	
パ	バ	ハ	ダ	タ	ザ	サ	ガ	カ	A
ピ	ビ	ヒ	(ヂ)*	チ	ジ	シ	ギ	キ	I
プ	ブ	フ	(ヅ)*	ツ	ズ	ス	グ	ク	U
ペ	ベ	ヘ	デ	テ	ゼ	セ	ゲ	ケ	E
ポ	ボ	ホ	ド	ト	ゾ	ソ	ゴ	コ	O

* In standard Japanese, ヂ is pronounced as ジ, and ヅ is pronounced as ズ, so ヂ and ヅ are rarely used in modern spellings.

れんしゅう❶ Practice 1 (A-SO and the corresponding voiced sounds) L2-16

Read the following katakana words aloud and match them to the pictures below.

1) アイス (　　)　2) キス (　　)　3) ココア (　　)　4) ガス (　　)　5) アジア (　　)

a. 　b. 　c. 　d. 　e.

れんしゅう❷ Practice 2 (A-HO and the corresponding voiced sounds) L2-17

Read the following katakana words aloud and match them to the pictures below.

1) バナナ (　　)　2) テスト (　　)　3) バス (　　)　4) テニス (　　)　5) ドア (　　)

a. 　b. 　c. 　d. 　e.

れんしゅう❸ Practice 3 (A-N and the corresponding voiced sounds) L2-18

Read the following katakana words aloud and match them to the pictures below.

1) コアラ (　　)　2) パンダ (　　)　3) ライオン (　　)　4) ペンギン (　　)　5) スカンク (　　)

a. 　b. 　c. 　d. 　e.

4 Double consonants

The rule for double consonants is also the same as the one for hiragana: just add a small tsu (ッ).

れんしゅう❹　Practice 4 (Katakana words with double consonants)　L2-19

Read the following katakana words aloud and match them to the pictures below.

1) ベッド（　　）2) チケット（　　）3) ナッツ（　　）4) ロボット（　　）5) オリンピック（　　）

a. 　b. 　c. 　d. 　e.

5 Contracted sounds

The rule for contracted sounds is also the same as the one for hiragana.

R	M	P	B	H	N	T (CH)	Z (J)	S	G	K	[-i] sound character
リ	ミ	ピ	ビ	ヒ	ニ	チ	ジ	シ	ギ	キ	
リャ	ミャ	ピャ	ビャ	ヒャ	ニャ	チャ	ジャ	シャ	ギャ	キャ	small ヤ
リュ	ミュ	ピュ	ビュ	ヒュ	ニュ	チュ	ジュ	シュ	ギュ	キュ	small ユ
リョ	ミョ	ピョ	ビョ	ヒョ	ニョ	チョ	ジョ	ショ	ギョ	キョ	small ヨ

れんしゅう❺　Practice 5 (Contracted sounds)　L2-20

Read the following katakana words aloud and match them to the pictures below.

1) ジョギング（　　）　2) ハッシュタグ（　　）　3) キャンプ（　　）　4) シャツ（　　）

a. 　b. 　c. 　d.

hashtag

6 Special characteristics of katakana writing

Q2. What are the characteristics of katakana writing?

While there are many similarities to hiragana writing, there are also some important differences you should be aware of.
In this section, we'll learn two aspects of Japanese writing unique to katakana. You can learn more details and other special uses of katakana in the workbook.

81

⦿ Special characteristics of katakana writing (1): Long vowels

Long vowels are represented differently in hiragana and katakana.

For instance, when the doctor says "Say 'ah!'" in English, this is transcribed as a long vowel in Japanese. How this long vowel is written, however, differs between hiragana (Ex.1) and katakana (Ex.2).

Say "ah!"

Ex.1 ああ！
(a a)

Ex.2 アー！
(a a)

🔊 **L2-21**

In katakana, a dash (ー) is used to represent long vowels. When katakana is written vertically, the long vowel marker is also written vertically, as in the example in the speech bubble on the right below.

ああ！
アー！

ア　あ
｜　あ
！　！

For example, the English sounds -er, -or, and -ar are all written as the long vowel [aa] in Japanese. Long vowels and diphthongs (i.e., compound vowels) like [ei] and [ou] in English are also written as long vowels in Japanese.

🔊 **L2-22**

> **Exs.** シアター　theater　　ドクター　doctor　　スター　star
>
> ケーキ　cake　　ホーム　home

⦿ Special characteristics of katakana writing (2): Small アイウエオ and the [v] sound

In addition to using small ヤユヨ to write the contracted sounds you learned in the hiragana section, small アイウエオ can also be used in katakana to more accurately transcribe the pronunciation of a loanword as it is pronounced in its language of origin. The following are some examples of katakana "small アイウエオ" combinations that are commonly used in loanwords:

🔊 **L2-23**

> **Exs.** ファミリー　family　　パーティー　party　　フォーク　fork or folk

In 1991, the use of "ヴ" with small vowels was encouraged for transcribing the [v] sound. For example, the spelling of "violin" was changed from バイオリン to ヴァイオリン. In practice, however, バビブベボ remain more common in katakana transcriptions of foreign words containing the [v] sound.

Because of transcription options like this, there are often several ways of spelling certain loanwords using katakana. (See the workbook for more information.)

🔊 **L2-24**

> **Ex.** ヴァイオリン or バイオリン　violin

⦿ Substitution of sounds that don't exist in Japanese (1): English [th] sound

As there is no [th] sound in Japanese, the voiceless [th] in English (as in "think" and "third") is rendered as [s], and the voiced [th] (as in "that" or "mother") is rendered as [z].

🔊 **L2-25**

> **Exs.** シンク　can be read as "think" or "sink"
>
> スミス　Smith　　ブラザー　brother

◉ Substitution of sounds that don't exist in Japanese (2): English [l] and [r] sounds

As there is no distinction between [l] and [r] in Japanese, the English [l] and [r] are both rendered in Japanese as ラリルレロ sounds.

Exs. ライト　　can be read as "light" or "right"

リーダー　can be read as "leader" or "reader"

ロビー　　can be read as "lobby" or "Robby"

れんしゅう❻ **Practice 6 (Sports)**

Do you play any sports? What is your favorite sport? The following katakana words all represent types of sports. Read the words aloud and match them to their English equivalents.

Japanese		English
1) ホッケー	•	• a. basketball
2) サッカー	•	• b. soccer
3) バスケットボール	•	• c. figure skating
4) ビーチバレー	•	• d. beach volleyball
5) フィギュアスケート	•	• e. hockey

れんしゅう❼ **Practice 7 (Country names)** L2-28

The following are the names of countries from all over the world. Read each word aloud, guess which country it is, and then write the appropriate letter a.-i. in each (　) for the country's location on the map.

Country names in katakana

1) アメリカ　　（　）　2) オーストラリア　（　）　3) ブラジル　　（　）

4) フランス　　（　）　5) インド　　　　（　）　6) ケニア　　　（　）

7) マレーシア　（　）　8) メキシコ　　　（　）　9) ロシア　　　（　）

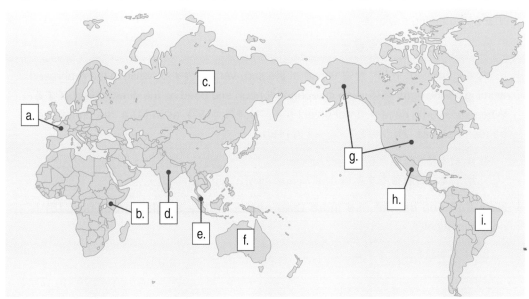

Writing special sounds in katakana

Below are some of the most commonly used character combinations for writing special sounds in katakana.

	W	V	F	D	DY	T	TS	CH	J	SH	KW	
		ヴァ	ファ				ツァ					A
	ウィ	ヴィ	フィ	ディ		ティ						I
		ヴ		ドゥ	デュ	トゥ						U
	ウェ	ヴェ	フェ				ツェ	チェ	ジェ	シェ		E
	ウォ	ヴォ	フォ				ツォ				クォ	O

Suru-verbs

Verbs like 勉強する are called *suru*-verbs. A *suru*-verb consists of a noun and the verb *suru* that follows it. In most *suru*-verbs, the noun portion is either a kanji-compound word or an English-origin word. Here are more examples of *suru*-verbs, some of which appear in Lesson 3:

(1) kanji-compound *suru*-verbs: 掃除する (to clean), 料理する (to cook), 旅行する (to travel)

(2) English-origin *suru*-verbs: アルバイトする (to work part-time), arubaito
デートする (to date), メールする (to email)
deeto meeru

Suru-verbs can be rephrased by turning the noun portion into the object of the verb する and marking it with を, as in (3).

(3) 勉強する (to study) → 勉強をする (lit. to do studying)

In the original verb in (3), 勉強 is part of the *suru*-verb 勉強する, while in the rephrased wording on the right, 勉強 is an independent noun and used as the direct object of する. When *suru*-verbs have a direct object (i.e., "N_1をN_2する"), as in (4)-a, the phrase can be rephrased as "N_1のN_2をする," as in (4)-b.

(4) a. 日本語を勉強する (to study Japanese)
b. 日本語の勉強をする (lit. to do Japanese study)

Note that you cannot use more than one を with a single verb. Thus, (5) is ungrammatical.

(5) × 日本語を勉強をする

DEKIRU List

できるCheck ✔

できる I

Ask and answer simple questions about family structure.
家族の構成や人数について、簡単に尋ねたり答えたりすることができる。

Entry ☐　Exit ☐

できる II

Ask and answer questions about things someone did in the past.
過去にしたことについて、尋ねたり答えたりすることができる。

Entry ☐　Exit ☐

できる III

Invite your friends to an event and decide on the details.
友達をイベントや活動に誘って、時間や場所などを決めることができる。

Entry ☐　Exit ☐

STRATEGIES

Conversation Tips .... ・ Showing your surprise and interest with へえ

Reading .... ・ Getting information from a family introduction
・ Identifying the subject and verb of a sentence
・ Recognizing sequence

Listening .... ・ Understanding omitted words

GRAMMAR

① Past *masu*-forms of verbs `できるII`

② と [Accompaniment marker] "with" `できるII`

③ は [Contrast marker] `できるII`

④ が [Contrast conjunction] "but" `できるII`

⑤ や [Noun-listing particle (non-exhaustive)] "and" `できるII`

⑥ 〜ませんか and 〜ましょう `できるIII`

　6-1 〜ませんか [Invitation]

　6-2 〜ましょう [Proposition]

⑦ 〜ましょうか [Suggestion] `できるIII`

かいわ

1 ^{できる} Summer break has just ended. Mark and Tao are talking together at the Japan House. 🔊 **L3-1**

> ふたご: twins　シンガポール: Singapore　シェフ: chef

Mark： タオさんは　なんにんかぞくですか。

Tao ： ろくにんかぞくです。りょうしんと　ふたごのきょうだいと　あねと

　　　　おとうとです。ふたごのなまえは　メイです。

Mark： へえ、ふたごですか。メイさんも　だいがくせいですか。

Tao ： はい、メイは　シンガポールだいがくのがくせいです。

Mark： そうですか。ごりょうしんのしごとは　なんですか。

Tao ： ちちは　レストランのシェフです。ははは　えいごのせんせいです。

Mark： へえ、そうですか。

<Ai arrives back at the Japan House.>

2 ^{できる} Ai has just returned to the Japan House from her trip to Japan. She starts talking with Mark and Tao about her trip. 🔊 **L3-2**

> おいしい: delicious

Tao ： アイさん、とうきょうで　なにを　しましたか。

Ai ： しぶやや　とうきょうスカイツリーや　あきはばらに　いきました。

　　　　しゃしんを　たくさん　とりましたよ。

Tao ： そうですか。

Ai ： それから、にほんのたべものも　たくさん　たべました。

Mark： すしや　ラーメンを　たべましたか。

Ai ： えっと、すしは　たべましたが、ラーメンは　たべませんでした。

Mark： そうですか。にほんのラーメンは　おいしいですよ。

　　　　あ、ジャンさんに　あいましたか。

ラーメン (ramen)

Ai ： はい、あいました。ジャンさんと　たくさん　はなしました。

3 Mark, Tao, and Ai continue to talk about their summer break. L3-3

> フィンランド: Finland　サウナ: sauna　ムーミンワールド: Moomin World　キャラクター: character

Lesson
3

Ai ：マークさんは　ことしのなつやすみに　なにを　しましたか。

Mark：7がつに　かぞくと　フィンランドに　いきました。

Ai ：フィンランドですか！　いいですね。フィンランドで　なにを　しましたか。

Mark：えっと、サウナに　はいりました。それから、うみで　およぎました。

Ai ：へえ、いいですね。

Mark：あ、それから、ムーミンワールドで　ムーミンに　あいました。

Ai ：ムーミン？

Mark：ええ、ムーミンは　フィンランドのほんのキャラクターです。

　　　こどものとき、わたしは　よく　ムーミンのほんを　よみました。

Ai ：へえ、そうですか。

 4 The three continue their conversation. L3-4

> おみやげ: something brought back from a trip

Ai ：マークさん、タオさん、おみやげのおかしです。どうぞ。

Mark：え、にほんのおかしですか。

Tao ：わたしは　にほんのおかしが　だいすきです。

　　　いま　いっしょに　たべませんか。

Mark：ええ、そうしましょう。

Tao ：のみものは　なにを　のみましょうか。

Mark：コーヒーは　どうですか。

Tao ：あの、コーヒーは　ちょっと…　あさ　たくさん　のみました。

Ai ：じゃ、にほんのおちゃは　どうですか。

Tao ：え、にほんのおちゃ！　いいですね。

 L3-5

CONVERSATION TIPS

Showing your surprise and interest with へえ: You might have heard native speakers of Japanese say へえ in response to something they have heard. It is often followed by そうですか, いいですね, or ほんとうですか (Really?) and is used in combination with these expressions to convey the speaker's interest in and/or surprise at what has been said.

　　A：わたしのあには　うちゅうひこうし (astronaut) です。

　　B：へえ、ほんとうですか。すごい (amazing) ですね。

たんご

▶ **The words written in gray** are supplemental vocabulary.

● まいにちのせいかつ Daily life

[person に／と]
あう
(to meet; to run into)

ひと
(person)

[person/animal と]
あそぶ
(to play; to have fun)

[language を]
はなす
(to speak)

しゃしんをとる
(to take a picture)

しゃしん
(picture)

うんどうする
(to (get) exercise;
to work out)

[thing を] かく
(to write)

てがみ
(letter [correspondence])

メール
meeru
(email)

たんご
(vocabulary; word)

かんじ
(kanji;
Chinese character)

[transportation/thing に] のる
(to get on; to ride)

じてんしゃ
(bicycle; bike)

[place に] りょこうする
(to travel to)

[place を] りょこうする
(to travel in/around)

[place に] はいる
(to enter)

おふろにはいる
(to take a bath)

（お）ふろ
(bath)

シャワーをあびる
shawaa
(to take a shower)

シャワー
shawaa
(shower)

[person と]
デートする
deeto
(to go out on a date)

[place で] およぐ (to swim)

うみ (sea; ocean)

こうえん (park)

[place を]
そうじする
(to clean)

[thing を]
せんたくする
(to do the laundry)

[thing を]
りょうりする
(to cook)

[thing を]
つくる
(to make)

（お）すし
(sushi)

にほんりょうり
(Japanese cuisine)

サラダ
sarada
(salad)

ピザ
piza
(pizza)

イタリアりょうり
itaria
(Italian cuisine)

たべもの (food)

のみもの (drink; bevarage)

にく
(meat)

さかな
(fish)

やさい
(vegetable)

おかし
(snack; sweet;
confection)

パン
pan
(bread)

ケーキ
keeki
(cake)

ビール
biiru
(beer)

（お）さけ
(alcohol;
Japanese sake)

コーラ
koora
(cola)

● じかんのひょうげん Time expressions

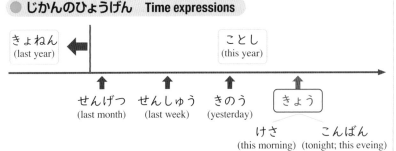

きょねん
(last year)

ことし
(this year)

せんげつ
(last month)

せんしゅう
(last week)

きのう
(yesterday)

きょう

けさ
(this morning)

こんばん
(tonight; this eveing)

なつやすみ
(summer vacation/break/holiday)

あさ ひる ばん
(night; evening)

● かぞく　Family

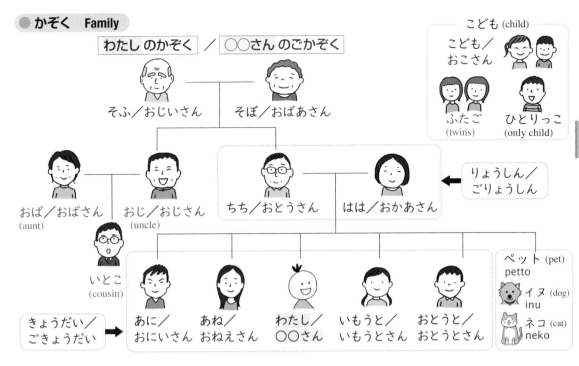

わたし のかぞく　/　○○さん のごかぞく

こども (child)

こども／
おこさん

ふたご
(twins)

ひとりっこ
(only child)

そふ／おじいさん　　　そぼ／おばあさん

りょうしん／
ごりょうしん

おば／おばさん
(aunt)

おじ／おじさん
(uncle)

ちち／おとうさん　　　はは／おかあさん

いとこ
(cousin)

ペット (pet)
petto

イヌ (dog)
inu

ネコ (cat)
neko

きょうだい／
ごきょうだい

あに／
おにいさん

あね／
おねえさん

わたし／
○○さん

いもうと／
いもうとさん

おとうと／
おとうとさん

● ～にん (Counter for people)

1	2	3	4	5	6
ひとり	ふたり	さんにん	よにん	ごにん	ろくにん
7	**8**	**9**	**10**	**11**	**?**
しちにん	はちにん	きゅうにん	じゅうにん	じゅういちにん	なんにん

● ～がつ (the ...th month of the year)

January	February	March	April	May	June	July
いちがつ	にがつ	さんがつ	しがつ	ごがつ	ろくがつ	しちがつ
August	**September**	**October**	**November**	**December**		**?**
はちがつ	くがつ	じゅうがつ	じゅういちがつ	じゅうにがつ		なんがつ

● そのほかのひょうげん　Other expressions

ひとりで (alone; by oneself)	そして (and (then); also)

Noun の とき
(at the time of Noun; when (someone) was Noun)

こども
(child)

こうこう
(high school)

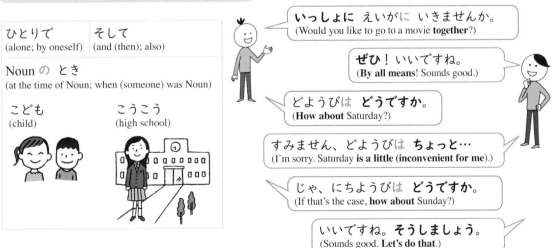

いっしょに えいがに いきませんか。
(Would you like to go to a movie **together**?)

ぜひ！ いいですね。
(**By all means**! Sounds good.)

どようびは どうですか。
(**How about** Saturday?)

すみません、どようびは ちょっと…
(I'm sorry. Saturday **is a little (inconvenient for me)**.)

じゃ、にちようびは どうですか。
(If that's the case, **how about** Sunday?)

いいですね。 そうしましょう。
(Sounds good. **Let's do that**.)

たんごリスト

🔊 **L3-6**

RU-VERB PHRASE

1	シャワーをあびる shawaa	to take a shower

U-VERBS / U-VERB PHRASES

2	あう	to meet; to run into [person に／と]
3	あそぶ	to play; to have fun [person/animal と]
4	およぐ	to swim [place で]
5	かく	to write [thing を]
6	つくる	to make [thing を]
7	のる	to get on; to ride [transportation/thing に]
8	はなす	to speak [language を]
9	はいる	to enter [place に]
10	おふろにはいる	to take a bath
11	しゃしんをとる	to take a picture

SURU-VERBS

12	せんたくする	to do the laundry; to wash (in the laundry) [thing を]
13	そうじする	to clean [place を]
14	りょうりする	to cook [thing を]
15	うんどうする	to (get) exercise; to work out
16	りょこうする	to travel to [place に]; to travel in/around [place を]
17	デートする deeto	to go out on a date [person と]

NOUNS

18	ごかぞく	(someone else's) family
	かぞく	my family; family [general term]
19	おじいさん	(someone else's) grandfather
	そふ	my grandfather
20	おばあさん	(someone else's) grandmother
	そぼ	my grandmother

21	ごりょうしん	(someone else's) parents
	りょうしん	my parents
22	おとうさん	(someone else's) father
	ちち	my father
23	おかあさん	(someone else's) mother
	はは	my mother
24	ごきょうだい	(someone else's) sibling
	きょうだい	my sibling; sibling [general term]
25	おにいさん	(someone else's) older brother
	あに	my older brother
26	おねえさん	(someone else's) older sister
	あね	my older sister
27	いもうとさん	(someone else's) younger sister
	いもうと	my younger sister
28	おとうとさん	(someone else's) younger brother
	おとうと	my younger brother
29	おこさん	(someone else's) child
	こども	my child; child [general term]
30	ひとりっこ	only child
31	ひと	person
32	たべもの	food
33	さかな	fish
34	にく	meat
35	やさい	vegetable
36	すし／おすし	sushi
37	おかし	snack; sweet; confection
38	のみもの	drink; beverage
39	さけ／おさけ	alcohol; Japanese sake
40	かんじ	kanji; Chinese character

41	たんご	vocabulary; word
42	てがみ	letter [correspondence]
43	じてんしゃ	bicycle; bike
44	うみ	sea; ocean
45	こうえん	park
46	こうこう	high school
47	なつやすみ	summer vacation/break/holiday
48	イヌ inu	dog
49	ネコ neko	cat
50	ペット petto	pet
51	サラダ sarada	salad
52	パン pan	bread
53	ピザ piza	pizza
54	ケーキ keeki	cake
55	コーラ koora	cola
56	ビール biiru	beer
57	メール meeru	email

ADVERBIAL NOUNS

58	きょねん	last year
59	ことし	this year
60	せんげつ	last month
61	せんしゅう	last week
62	きのう	yesterday
63	けさ	this morning
64	ばん	night; evening
65	こんばん	tonight; this evening

CONJUNCTION

66	そして	and (then); also

COUNTER

67	～にん	[counter for people]
	ひとり	one person
	ふたり	two people
	さんにん	three people
	よにん	four people
	なんにん	how many people

SUFFIX

68	～がつ	the ...th month of the year
	いちがつ	January
	にがつ	February
	さんがつ	March
	しがつ	April
	ごがつ	May
	ろくがつ	June
	しちがつ	July
	はちがつ	August
	くがつ	September
	じゅうがつ	October
	じゅういちがつ	November
	じゅうにがつ	December
	なんがつ	what month

OTHER WORDS AND PHRASES

69	ぜひ	by all means
70	いっしょに	together (with)
71	Noun は どうですか	How about Noun?
72	Noun は ちょっと…	Noun is a little (inconvenient for me). [used to reject a suggestion or invitation indirectly] [see L6 Conversation Tips]
73	そうしましょう	Let's do that.; Let's do so.
74	ひとりで	alone; by oneself
75	Noun の とき	at the time of Noun; when (someone) was Noun

かんじ

▶ The **highlighted words** below are the vocabulary you will need to learn to read and write in kanji in this chapter.
▶ ✳**Special reading:** A special reading is assigned to a kanji compound word as a whole; in this case, it is impossible to assign each kanji in the compound a particular part of the reading.

1	一	イチ イッ	一 one いち	一月 January いちがつ	一時 one o'clock いちじ	一日 one day いちにち
	一		一年 one year いちねん	一歳 one year old いっさい	一ぴき one small animal いっ	一分 one minute いっぷん
		ひと	一人 ✳ one person ひとり	一人っ子 ✳ only child ひとり こ	一人で ✳ alone; by oneself ひとり	
			一つ one; one object ひと	一日 ✳ the first day of the month ついたち		
one	一					

2	二	ニ	二 two に	二月 February にがつ	二年生 second-year student にねんせい	二分 two minutes にふん
	二	ふた	二人 ✳ two people ふたり	二日 ✳ two days; the second day of the month ふつか		
			二つ two; two objects ふた			
			二十日 ✳ the twentieth day of the month はつか	二十歳 ✳ twenty years old はたち		
two	二 二					

3	三	サン	三 three さん	三月 March さんがつ	三人 three people さんにん	三時 three o'clock さんじ
	三		三千 three thousand さんぜん	三百 three hundred さんびゃく	三分 three minutes さんぷん	
		みっ	三日 three days; the third day of the month みっか		三つ three; three objects みっ	
three	三 三 三					

4	四	シ	四月 April しがつ	四／四 four し よん	四人 four people よにん	四年生 fourth-year student よねんせい
	四	よん よ／よっ	四時 four o'clock よじ	四分 four minutes よんぷん		
			四日 four days; the fourth day of the month よっか		四つ four; four objects よっ	
four	丨 冂 丣 四 四					

5	五	ゴ	五 five ご	五月 May ごがつ	五人 five people ごにん	五時 five o'clock ごじ
	五		五百 five hundred ごひゃく	五分 five minutes ごふん		
		いつ	五つ five; five objects いつ	五日 five days; the fifth day of the month いつか		
five	丆 丆 五 五					

6	六	ロク ロッ	六 six ろく	六月 June ろくがつ	六人 six people ろくにん	六時 six o'clock ろくじ
	六		六千 six thousand ろくせん	六百 six hundred ろっぴゃく	六分 six minutes ろっぷん	
		むい むっ	六日 six days; the sixth day of the month むいか		六つ six; six objects むっ	
six	亠 六 六 六					

7	七	シチ	七月 July しちがつ	七人／七人 seven people しちにん ななにん		七時 seven o'clock しちじ
	七		七年／七年 seven years しちねん ななねん			
		なな なの	七 seven なな	七つ seven; seven objects なな	七日 seven days; the seventh day of the month なのか	
seven	七 七					

8	八八	ハチ ハッ やっ よう	八 eight はち	八月 August はちがつ	八人 eight people はちにん	八時 eight o'clock はちじ
			八歳 eight years old はっさい	八百 eight hundred はっぴゃく	八分 eight minutes はっぷん	
			八つ eight; eight objects やっ		八日 eight days; the eighth day of the month ようか	
eight		ノ 八				

9	九九	キュウ ク ここの	九／九 nine きゅう く	九人 nine people きゅうにん	九千 nine thousand きゅうせん
			九月 September くがつ	九時 nine o'clock くじ	
			九日 nine days; the ninth day of the month ここのか	九つ nine; nine objects ここの	
nine		ノ 九			

10	十十	ジュウ ジュッ ジッ とお	十 ten じゅう	十月 October じゅうがつ	十人 ten people じゅうにん	十年 ten years じゅうねん
			十歳／十歳 ten years old じゅっさい じっさい		十分／十分 ten minutes じゅっぷん じっぷん	
			十 ten; ten objects とお	十日 ten days; the tenth day of the month とおか		
ten		一 十				

11	月月	ガツ ゲツ	～月 the ...th month of the year (Ex. 一月 January, 十二月 December, がつ いちがつ じゅうにがつ
			何月 what month) お正月 New Year's holidays 月曜日 Monday なんがつ しょうがつ げつようび
			～か月 ... months [duration] (Exs. 一か月 one month, 三か月 three months) げつ いっ げつ さん げつ
		つき	今月 this month 先月 last month 来月 next month 月 moon こんげつ せんげつ らいげつ つき
moon; month		ノ 几 月 月	

12	私私	シ	私立 private [school, etc.] しりつ
		わたし わたくし	私 I 私 I [polite and formal] 私達 we わたし わたくし わたしたち
I; private		ノ 二 千 矛 禾 私 私	

13	子子	シ	女子 girl; woman 男子 boy; man じょし だんし
		こ	子ども my child; child お子さん (someone else's) child こ こ
			一人っ子 * only child 男の子 boy 女の子 girl ひとり こ おとこ こ おんな こ
child		マ 了 子	

14	人人	ジン ニン	～人 ... people [nationality] (Exs. アメリカ人 American, 日本人 Japanese) じん じん にほんじん
			～人 ... people [counter for people] (Exs. 三人 three people, 四人 four people, にん さんにん よにん
			一人 * one person, 二人 * two people) 一人っ子 * only child 一人で * alone ひとり ふたり ひとり こ ひとり
		ひと	人 a person 男の人 man 女の人 woman ひと おとこ ひと おんな ひと
person		ノ 人	

1 Look at Yamada-san's business card on the right and answer the questions below.

　1) 山田さんの電話番号は何番ですか。
　　　やまだ　　　でんわばんごう　なんばん

　2) 山田さんのファックス (FAX) の番号は何番ですか。
　　　やまだ　　　　　　　　　　　　　ばんごう　なんばん

　3) 山田さんのビルの部屋番号は何番ですか。
　　　やまだ　　　　　　　　　　へ　やばんごう　なんばん

2 The picture below is a map showing predictions for when the cherry blossoms will bloom in Japan.

Step 1 Write the readings for the following months a.-l.

a. 十月 _____ 　　b. 五月 _____ 　　c. 三月 _____ 　　d. 十一月 _____

e. 四月 _____ 　　f. 一月 _____ 　　g. 八月 _____ 　　h. 九月 _____

i. 十二月 _____ 　　j. 六月 _____ 　　k. 二月 _____ 　　l. 七月 _____

Step 2 Choose the month a.-l. in which you can see cherry blossoms in each city shown on the map.

Ex. 福岡 3/23 (March 23ʳᵈ)　→　(　c.　)
　　ふくおか

1) 東京　　(　　　　)
　　とうきょう

2) 札幌　　(　　　　)
　　さっぽろ

3) 仙台　　(　　　　)
　　せんだい

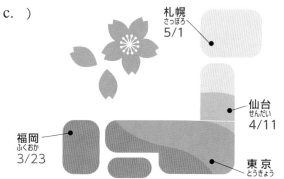

札幌
さっぽろ
5/1

仙台
せんだい
4/11

福岡
ふくおか
3/23

東京
とうきょう
3/27

3 Look at the picture of Ben's family. (He is on the far left.) Write the reading of the kanji compounds a.-j., then choose the correct answers from the list for questions 1) and 2).

a. 一人 _____ 　　b. 二人 _____ 　　c. 三人 _____ 　　d. 四人 _____

e. 五人 _____ 　　f. 六人 _____ 　　g. 七人 _____ 　　h. 八人 _____

i. 九人 _____ 　　j. 十人 _____

1) ベンさんは何人家族ですか。　　(　　　　)
　　　　　　　なん　か ぞく

2) ベンさんの子どもは何人ですか。　　(　　　　)
　　　　　　　　　　　なん

ベンさん

■ The history of Japanese writing systems

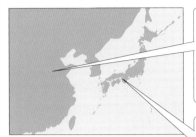

Around 3000 years ago, kanji were invented in China.

山 "mountain"   川 "river"   日 "sun"

Around 1500 years ago, in the mid-6th century, Buddhism was first introduced to Japan via Korea. Because kanji were used to write the Buddhist scriptures, they were also introduced and began to be used in Japan at this time.

In **8th and 9th centuries**,

Hiragana were invented, and women in the imperial court began to use them to write letters and poems.

Kanji		Hiragana
安 ➡	安 ➡	あ
以 ➡	ゐ ➡	い
宇 ➡	宇 ➡	う

* Hiragana were created from the shapes of kanji.

court lady

Katakana were also invented to make Buddhist scriptures in Chinese easier to read and understand.

Kanji	Katakana	Kanji	Katakana
阿 ➡	ア	宇 ➡	ウ
伊 ➡	イ	江 ➡	エ

* Katakana were created from parts of kanji (the red parts in the examples above).

Buddhist monk

In **the 12th century**, authors began to employ a mixture of kanji and kana (hiragana and/or katakana) in their literature that is the basis for the Japanese writing system today. They wrote vertically (top to bottom and right to left).

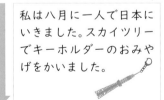

私は八月に一人で日本にいきました。スカイツリーでキーホルダーのおみやげをかいました。

オーストラリア

Katakana for non-Japanese words

After 1945, the writing system was reformed, and certain conventions were established, including writing horizontally (left to right), using katakana to write foreign words, and designating a certain list of kanji for everyday use.

ぶんぽう

1 Past *masu*-forms of verbs

[1]

		V (past)
きょねん	ハワイに	いきました。
I went to Hawaii last year.		

When you talk about an action in the past, you use the verb ending 〜ました instead of 〜ます. The past negative ending is 〜ませんでした. The following table shows how the ます part conjugates:

	Affirmative	Negative
Non-past	（たべ）ます	（たべ）ません
Past	（たべ）ました	（たべ）ませんでした

Exs. (1) ジャパンハウスで　ばんごはんを　たべました。 *I had dinner at the Japan House.*

(2) A: きのう、ジムに　いきましたか。 *Did you go to the gym yesterday?*

B: いいえ、いきませんでした。 *No, I didn't.*

(3) A: しゅうまつ　なにを　しましたか。 *What did you do over the weekend?*

B: アルバイトを　しました。 *I worked part-time.*

2 と [Accompaniment marker] "with"

[2]

		N		
A:	きのう	だれ	と	べんきょうしましたか。
	Who did you study with yesterday?			
B:		アイさん	と	べんきょうしました。
	I studied with Ai.			

You can express the idea of "with" as in "to study with someone" using と.

Exs. (1) アイさんは　ときどき　マークさんと　いっしょに　あさごはんを　たべます。
Ai sometimes has breakfast together with Mark.

(2) マークさんは　かぞくと　フィンランドに　いきました。
Mark went to Finland with his family.

(3) わたしは　しゅうまつ　ともだちと　いっしょに　としょかんで　にほんごを　べんきょうしました。
I studied Japanese with my friend at the library over the weekend.

ほあ **GID** (vol.1): B. Particles 1-6. と

3 は [Contrast marker]

[3]

S₁		S₂
わたしは　まいにち　おちゃ{は／を}　のみます。	でも、	コーヒーは　のみません。
I drink tea every day. However, I do not drink coffee.		

In addition to functioning as a topic marker, は can also be used as a contrast marker. In [3], tea and coffee are contrasted in terms of which beverage the speaker habitually drinks. Note that は replaces the direct object marker を when it marks direct objects.

In S₁, you can also use を to mark おちゃ. In this case, the contrastive meaning is represented only by S₂.

Exs. (1) わたしは　ロック{は／を}　ききます。でも、ヒップホップは　ききません。
I listen to rock music. I do not, however, listen to hip-hop.

(2) けんさんは　がくせいです。みかさんも　がくせいです。でも、トムさんは
がくせいじゃないです。*Ken is a student. Mika is also a student. However, Tom is not a student.*

(3) リサさんは　テニスを　します。サッカーも　します。でも、ゴルフは　しません。
Lisa plays tennis. She also plays soccer. However, she doesn't play golf.

In (3), the direct object in the second sentence (= サッカー) is marked by も. As this example shows, when も marks direct objects, it replaces the direct object marker を.

☞ **GID** (vol.1): B. Particles　1-8. Absence of が and を

4 が [Contrast conjunction] "but"

[4]

S₁		S₂
きのう　うみに　いきました	が、	およぎませんでした。
I went to the beach yesterday, but I did not swim.		

You can connect two sentences using が. The meaning of が differs depending on what the sentences before and after が (i.e., S₁ and S₂) represent. If S₁ and S₂ represent contrastive ideas, or if S₂ is not what is commonly expected from S₁, が is interpreted as "but" in English. As seen in (1) below, when S₁ and S₂ share the same topic, that topic is not repeated in S₂. Note that in Japanese, が and many other conjunctions are placed <u>at the end</u> of a sentence and usually followed by a comma.

Exs. (1) わたしは　やさいは　たべますが、にくは　たべません。
I eat vegetables, but I don't eat meat.

(2) こどものときは　よくテレビを　みましたが、いまは　あまり　みません。
I often watched TV when I was a child, but I don't watch it much now.

(3) あしたは　にちようびですが、わたしは　がっこうに　いきます。
Tomorrow is Sunday, but I'm going to school.

でも also means "but." However, でも always occurs in the sentence-initial position, as in (4).

Ex. (4) あしたは　にちようびです。<u>でも、</u>わたしは　がっこうに　いきます。
Tomorrow is Sunday. However, I'm going to school.

5 や [Noun-listing particle (non-exhaustive)] "and"

[5]

N₁		N₂		
たなかさん	や	スミスさん	と	パーティーに いきました。
I went to a party with Tanaka-san and Smith-san (among others).				

You can list nouns using や. Unlike the noun-listing particle と (see L1 #6), however, や indicates that the list is not exhaustive—that is, it communicates that only a few representative examples are being listed and that there are more being left unsaid. For example, [5] above indicates that the list of people the speaker went to the party with includes more than just Tanaka-san and Smith-san.

Exs. (1) しゅうまつ うんどうや ゲームを しました。
I exercised and played games (among other things) over the weekend.

(2) わたしは どようびに パンや おかしを つくりました。
I made bread, sweets, etc. on Saturday.

(3) まいにち だいがくで にほんごや すうがくを べんきょうします。
I study Japanese, mathematics, etc. at college every day.

☞ **GID** (vol.1): B. Particles 4-1.と vs. や

6 ～ませんか and ～ましょう

6-1 ～ませんか [Invitation] "Would you like to ~?"

[6-a]

	V (negative)	
しゅうまつ わたしのいえに	きません	か。
Would you like to come to my house this weekend?		
(lit. Won't you come to my house this weekend?)		

You can invite the listener to do something using the negative question ～ませんか.

Exs. (1) あした パーティーを しませんか。*Would you like to have a party tomorrow?*

(2) カフェで コーヒーを のみませんか。*Would you like to drink some coffee at a café?*

(3) しゅうまつ いっしょに こうえんに いきませんか。
Would you like to go to the park together this weekend?

Note that the topic marker は is not used when addressing the listener with ～ませんか.

× トムさんは わたしのうちに きませんか。
→ トムさん、わたしのうちに きませんか。*Would you like to come to my house, Tom?*

6-2 ～ましょう [Proposition] "Let's ~."

[6-b]

	V (polite volitional form)
どようびに	あいましょう。
Let's meet on Saturday.	

You can propose doing something together with the listener by using ～ましょう. (For the difference between ～ましょう and ～ませんか, see **GID** (vol.1): H. Important sentence patterns 2. ～ませんか vs. ～ましょう.)

Exs. (1) すしを　つくり<u>ましょう</u>。*Let's make sushi.*

(2) きょう　いっしょに　としょかんで　にほんごを　べんきょうし<u>ましょう</u>。
Let's study Japanese together at the library today.

You can also use this form in response to an invitation with 〜ませんか, as in (3) below.

Ex. (3) A: あした　いっしょに　ばんごはんを　たべませんか。
Would you like to have dinner together tomorrow?

B: ええ、たべ<u>ましょう</u>。*Yes, let's.*

---

7 〜ましょうか [Suggestion] "Shall we ~?"

[7]

こんしゅう　パーティーを	V (polite volitional form) しましょう	か。
Why don't (lit. Shall) we have a party this week?		

You can suggest something to do with the listener using 〜ましょうか, as in [7] and (1).

Ex. (1) きょうのごご、いっしょに　ジムに　いき<u>ましょうか</u>。
Why don't (lit. Shall) we go to the gym together this afternoon?

You can also combine 〜ましょうか with question words to solicit suggestions from the listener about the details of plans, as in (2) and (3) below.

Exs. (2) A: いっしょに　ばんごはんを　たべませんか。*Would you like to have dinner together?*

B: いいですね。どこで　たべ<u>ましょうか</u>。
That sounds good. Where should (lit. shall) we eat?

A: 「ロメオ」は　どうですか。*How about "Romeo?"*

(3) A: いっしょに　えいがを　みませんか。*Would you like to watch a movie together?*

B: いいですね。なにを　み<u>ましょうか</u>。
That sounds good. What should (lit. shall) we watch?

〜ましょうか in (2) and (3) above is usually pronounced with falling intonation, while in (1) and [7], it can be pronounced with either rising intonation or falling intonation.

Note that 〜ましょうか is a suggestion expression and that it is not appropriate to use when you want to make an invitation. For example, the following sentence is not appropriate to start a conversation with an invitation to have coffee together. In this situation, 〜ませんか is used instead.

✕ けんさん、きょう　いっしょに　コーヒーを　のみ<u>ましょうか</u>。
Ken, shall we have coffee together today?

→ けんさん、きょう　いっしょに　コーヒーを　のみ<u>ませんか</u>。
Ken, would you like to have coffee together today?

はなしましょう

 Ask and answer simple questions about family structure.

できるI-A Counter for people 〜にん

1 Do you know how many players there are on a team in the following sports? 🔊 **L3-7**

Ex. サッカー

A: サッカーのチーム (team) は　なんにんですか。

B: じゅういちにんです。 or わかりません。 (I don't know)

1) やきゅう　　　2) バレーボール　　3) ラグビー　　　4) バスケットボール

5) クリケット　　　6) your own

2 How many people are there in the families below? 🔊 **L3-8**

Ex. A: なんにんかぞくですか。

B: さんにんかぞくです。

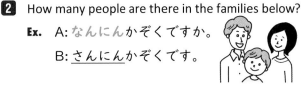

1)　　　　　　　　2)　　　　　　　　3)　　　　　　　　4) your own

できるI-B Kinship terms

1 First, read かいわ1 on p.86 from this lesson. Using the dialogue as a model, ask about your classmates' families and fill in the table below. If you don't want to talk about your own family, you can talk about an imaginary family.

しつもん (question)	さん	さん
1) なんにんかぞく？		
2) かぞくのメンバー (member) は だれ？		
3) Other info (job, age, etc.)		

2 Are there any families from anime/manga/dramas/movies/books that you like? Make a presentation of around five sentences about the family you have chosen, and your listener(s) will ask follow-up questions.

Ex.

Introduction	わたしは　アニメの『おひさまかぞく』が　すきです。
Family structure	おひさまさんは　よにんかぞくです。
Members	おひさまさんと　おとうさんと　おかあさんと
	いもうとさんです。
	それから、ペットのイヌです。
Job(s)	おとうさんは　かいしゃいんです。
Additional info	おとうさんは　まいにち　ビールを　のみます。

 Ask and answer questions about things someone did in the past.

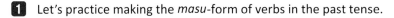 できるⅡ-A　**Past *masu*-forms of verbs**

1 Let's practice making the *masu*-form of verbs in the past tense.　 L3-9

Ex.　たべる → たべました → たべませんでした

1) おきる　　2) みる　　3) いく　　4) のむ　　5) はなす　　6) かえる

7) あう　　8) かく　　9) のる　　10) およぐ　　11) くる　　12) うんどうする

2 Tell your partner whether or not you did the following activities yesterday or this morning.

Ex.　にほんごを　べんきょうする

→ わたしは　{きのう／けさ}　にほんごを　べんきょうしました

or べんきょうしませんでした。

1) あさごはんを　たべる　　2) コーヒーを　のむ　　3) おふろに　はいる

4) にほんごを　はなす　　5) こうえんに　いく　　6) てがみを　かく

7) かぞくに　あう　　8) デートする　　9) せんたくする

3 Describe what アクティブ (active) さん and レイジー (lazy) さん did/didn't do last week based on the cues provided.

Ex. せんしゅう　アクティブさんは　あさのクラスに　いきました。

でも、レイジーさんは　あさのクラスに　いきませんでした。

アクティブ (active) さん	レイジー (lazy) さん
Ex. あさのクラス／いく	Ex. あさのクラス／×いく
1) まいにち／７じはんごろ／おきる	1) まいにち／９じごろ／おきる
2) まいにち／ジム／うんどうする	2) あまり／ジム／×うんどうする
3) しゅうまつ／としょかん／しゅくだい／する	3) しゅうまつ／あまり／しゅくだい／×する
4) デートのまえに (before) ／シャワー／あびる	4) デートのまえに／シャワー／×あびる
5) レストラン／ともだち／にくとサラダ／たべる	5) いえ／ひとりで／おかし／たべる

4 Are you more like アクティブさん or レイジーさん? Describe what you did/didn't do last week and say which type of person you are.

Ex. せんしゅう　わたしは　あまり　べんきょうしませんでした。

それから、しゅうまつ　うちで　ゲームを　たくさん　しました。

だから、わたしは　ちょっと　レイジーさんです。

できるⅡ-B 　**Contrast marker は, conjunction が, and non-exhaustive listing particle や**

1 Talk about the things people did/didn't do yesterday.

Step 1 Make sentences about what Tao did/didn't do yesterday based on the cues provided.

Ex. きのう　タオさんは　<u>コーラ</u>を　<u>のみ</u>ました。<u>おちゃ</u>も　<u>のみ</u>ました。　L3-10

でも、<u>おさけ</u>は　<u>のみ</u>ませんでした。

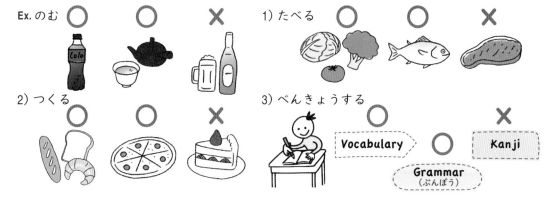

Step 2 Using the same verbs as in Step 1, create your own sentences.

Ex. きのう　わたしは　みずを　のみました。おちゃも　のみました。

でも、ビールは　のみませんでした。

2 Connect the sentences that you made in できるII-A-③ on p.102 into one sentence.

Ex. せんしゅう　アクティブさんは　あさのクラスに　いきました。

でも、レイジーさんは　あさのクラスに　いきませんでした。

→ せんしゅう　アクティブさんは　あさのクラスに　いきましたが、

レイジーさんは　あさのクラスに　いきませんでした。

3 Let's play a bingo game that will let you learn more about your classmates' lives in high school.

Step 1 Before starting, check the vocabulary in 1)-8) in the table below and create question sentences to ask your classmates if they performed each activity frequently in high school.

Step 2 Ask your classmates the questions you created in Step 1. Write down the name of the person you asked in each box and circle "Yes" or "No" based on their answer. The first person who completes a horizontal, vertical, or diagonal line with all "Yes" or all "No" answers wins!

Ex. A: こうこうのとき、よく　スポーツを　しましたか。

B: はい、ときどき　しました。or いいえ、あまり　しませんでした。

Ex. sports / play Yes · No _____さん	1) J-POP / listen Yes · No _____さん	2) room / clean Yes · No _____さん
3) travel Yes · No _____さん	4) your own Yes · No _____さん	5) picture / take Yes · No _____さん
6) email / write Yes · No _____さん	7) bicycle / ride Yes · No _____さん	8) cook Yes · No _____さん

Step 3 Choose one piece of information you learned about your classmates and share it with the class, comparing and contrasting with yourself.

Ex.1 ○○さんは　こうこうのとき　よく　りょうりを　しました。

わたしも　よく　りょうりを　しました。

Ex.2 △△さんは　ごかぞくと　よく　りょこうしましたが、

わたしは　あまり　しませんでした。

4 Let's talk about your childhood.

Step 1 Brainstorming: When you were a child, what was popular among your friends? List more than three titles or items in each box below.

えいが		ゲーム	
おんがく		おかし	

Step 2 Choose one category from the table in Step 1 and talk about it, giving two specific examples. Ask follow-up questions using question words from the box below.

> **Useful follow-up questions**　なに？　　いつ？　　どこ？　　だれ？　　なんさいのとき？

Ex.　A: わたしは　こどものとき　よく　マリオや　ポケモンのゲームを　しました。

　　　B: へえ、そうですか。よく　だれと　ゲームを　しましたか。 <Continue>

できる Ⅲ　**Invite your friends to an event and decide on the details.**

できるⅢ-A　**Invitations with ～ませんか and propositions with ～ましょう**

Try inviting your classmates to an event or activity.

Step 1 Let's practice using ～ませんか. First, make an invitation sentence based on each set of cues below.　🔊L3-12

Ex.　<u>しゅうまつ</u>　いっしょに　<u>ゲームを</u>　<u>し</u>ませんか。

Ex. weekend / game　　1) weekend / movie　　2) tomorrow night / have fun　　3) Saturday afternoon / go to a cat café

4) after class / study at the library　　5) tonight / make dinner at my house　　6) next Sunday / the sea　　7) your own

Step 2 Next, make invitations to your classmate using the same cues as in Step 1 above.

Ex.　A: ○○さん、しゅうまつ　いっしょに　ゲームを　しませんか。

　　　B: ☺ いいですね。ぜひ、しましょう。

　　　　☹ すみません。{しゅうまつ／ゲーム}は　ちょっと…

できるⅢ-B **Suggestions with 〜ましょうか**

1 Let's practice using 〜ましょうか. You are going to hang out with your friend this coming weekend and you need to decide on the details of your plan. Make questions to solicit suggestions from your friend. 🔊 **L3-13**

Ex. なんじ／あう → なんじに　あいましょうか。

1) なに／する 　　2) どこ／いく 　　3) どこ／あう

4) えいが／なに／みる 　5) ばんごはん／なに／たべる 　6) your own

2 Invite your friend to an activity that you would like to do over the weekend. Decide on the details such as time and location.

Ex. A: 〇〇さん、しゅうまつ　いっしょに　えいがを　みませんか。

B: いいですね。みましょう。

A: なにを　みましょうか。

B: ホラー (horror) は　どうですか。

A: ホラーですか。ホラーは　ちょっと…　コメディ (comedy) は　どうですか。

B: いいですね。そうしましょう。どこで　みましょうか。

<Decide on the details: time, location, etc.>

A: じゃ、7じに　とびらシアター (theater) で　あいましょう。

B: はい。じゃ、また。

3 Invite your partner to an activity that is popular right now.

Step 1 What is currently popular in your city/country in each category below?

1) えいが： _____ 　2) レストラン： _____

3) おんがく： _____ 　4) your own： _____

Step 2 Ask if your partner has already done the activities you listed in Step 1, then make an invitation if they have not.

Ex. A: 〇〇さん、『トイワールド』を　みましたか。

Yes	No
B: ええ、みました。 A: そうですか。 　いつ　みましたか。(← Follow-up) B: せんしゅうのしゅうまつに　みました。 A: そうですか。 <Continue>	B: いいえ、まだです (not yet)。 A: そうですか。じゃ、しゅうまつ 　いっしょに　みませんか。(← Invite) B: いいですね。 　みましょう／そうしましょう。(← Accept) 　いつ　あいましょうか。(← Decide on the details) <Continue>

Review

Now you can both talk about what you did in the past and invite someone to do an activity with you.

Step 1 First, ask what your partner did over the weekend and see if there is any activity that you two can do together for fun. Then, invite your partner to the activity and decide on details for meeting up.

"What did you do over the weekend?"	**Ex.** A: ○○さん、せんしゅうのしゅうまつ　なにを　しましたか。 B: ともだちと　レストランに　いきました。
Ask follow-up questions	A: そうですか。レストランは　どこに　いきましたか。 B: インドりょうりのレストランに　いきました。 A: へえ、いいですね。わたしも　インドりょうりが　すきです。
Invite	B: じゃ、こんしゅうのしゅうまつ　いっしょに　インドりょうりのレストランに　いきませんか。
Decide on the details (time, location, etc.)	A: はい、ぜひ！　いつ　いきましょうか。 B: そうですね。どようびの７じごろは　どうですか。 A: どようびの７じですか。いいですよ。 B: どこで　あいましょうか。 A: そうですね。わたしのりょうは　どうですか。
Confirm	B: ええ、そうしましょう。じゃ、どようびの７じに　△△さんのりょうで　あいましょう。

Step 2 Report your plan as well as your meeting time and location to your classmates.

Ex.　わたしと　△△さんは　どようびの７じに　△△さんのりょうで　あいます。
それから、インドりょうりのレストランで　ばんごはんを　たべます。

よみましょう

Getting information from a family introduction

1 Read the passage below and fill in ( ) with the appropriate words and numbers.

モナ（48）
ぼくの（　　　　）です。
イタリアりょうりの（　　　　）です。

はるき（50）
ぼくの（　　　　）です。
しごとは（　　　　）です。

ゆう（23）
ぼくの（　　　　）です。
だいがくいんせいです。
しゅみは（　　　　）です。

ぼく（　　）
はは は（　　　　）人です。
しゅみは（　　　　）と（　　　　）です。

ハッピー（2）
（　　　　）が だいすきです。

> ぼくのなまえは　あきらです。19さいです。だいがく二ねんせいです。ぼくのかぞくは
> 四人かぞくです。りょうしんと　あねと　ぼくです。ペットは　イヌのハッピーです。は
> はのなまえは　モナです。しゅっしんは　イタリアのミラノです。イタリアりょうりのせ
> んせいです。ちちは　にほんじんです。カメラマンです。あねは　だいがくいんせいです。
> しゅみは　ダンスです。ぼくのしゅみは　アニメと　eスポーツです。ぼくは　まいにち
> こうえんで　ハッピーと　あそびます。ハッピーは　こうえんが　だいすきです。

2 Ai wrote a composition about her summer break for her Japanese class and posted it on the course website. Read her composition and answer the questions that follow.

いちばのツアー♪

　　きょねんの五月に　かぞくと　きょうとに　いきました。私は　に
ほんのたべものが　だいすきです。だから、きょうとで　一人で　た
べもののいちばのツアーに　いきました。　えいごのツアーです。　で
も、ツアーの<u>ガイドの人</u>は　えいごと　にほんごを　はなしました。
だから、私は　ガイドの人と　にほんごを　はなしました。えいごを
はなしませんでした。

　　いちばで　さかなや　やさいや　<u>おみやげの</u>
<u>みせ</u>を　みました。そして、しゃしんを　とり
ました。<u>みんな</u>は　おみやげを　たくさん　か
いましたが、私は　あまり　かいませんでした。
でも、にほんのおかしの<u>サンプル</u>を　たくさん
たべました。

協力：京都錦市場商店街

　　ツアーのあとで、<u>わがし</u>のみせで　かぞくと　あいました。そして、
いっしょに　わがしを　つくりました。<u>おもしろかったです</u>。<u>こんど</u>
私と　いっしょに　わがしを　つくりませんか。

いちば：market
ツアー：tour

ガイドの人：guide

おみやげ：souvenir
みせ：store; shop
みんな：everyone

サンプル：sample
わがし：traditional
　Japanese sweets
おもしろかったです：
　It was interesting.
こんど：near future

1） Find each sentence with a past tense verb in Ai's composition and underline the verb. Then, choose who did each action from the box below.

▶Check Point: In Japanese, it is common to omit any information that could be understood without being explicitly stated.

Ai (**A**)　　tour guide (**G**)　　tour participants (**P**)　　Ai's family (**F**)　　readers (**R**)

Exs. きょうとに　<u>いきました</u>。（A）　　おみやげのみせを　<u>みました</u>。（A）と（P）

Recognizing sequence

2） Insert the letters for activities a.-f. below into (　) to match the order in which Ai did these activities on her trip.

（　a　）→（　　　）→（　　　）→（　　　）→（　　　）→（　　　）

a. went on a market tour	b. went to a *wagashi* shop	c. ate various Japanese snacks
d. made *wagashi*	e. took photos	f. met her family

Comprehension check

3） Mark ○ if the statement is true and × if it is false.

（　　）アイさんは　がっこうのともだちと　きょうとに　いきました。

（　　）ツアーのガイドの人は　にほんごを　はなしました。だから、アイさんは　えいごを　はなしませんでした。

（　　）アイさんは　いちばで　しゃしんを　とりました。

（　　）アイさんは　いちばで　にほんのたべものを　たくさん　かいました。

（　　）アイさんは　わがしを　つくりましたが、かぞくは　つくりませんでした。

かくれんしゅう　*Writing Practice*

Write a blog post in Japanese about a memorable trip you have gone on. Share your favorite photos as well.

Useful vocabulary　よかったです (It was good.)　きれいでした (It was beautiful/clean.)
おもしろかったです (It was interesting.)

ききましょう

>>>>> リスニング・ストラテジー : Listening strategy <<<<<

Understanding omitted words

In Japanese, many things are not explicitly restated when they have already been introduced into the conversation or when they are understood from the context. Omitted words can include both the topic and other parts of the sentence that are the same as what has been previously stated. To avoid miscommunication, it is important to pay careful attention to what information has been omitted.

1 **Pre-listening activity:** Look at the transcripts of the three conversations below and figure out what has been omitted.

わたしは

Ex. たなか：はじめまして。たなかです。あの、おなまえは　なんですか。

すずき：すずきです。

わたしのなまえは

1）たなか：あしたは　J-POP のコンサートですよ。

すずき：え、J-POP のコンサートですか。なんじですか。

2）やまだ：たなかさんは　なんにんかぞくですか。

たなか：ごにんかぞくです。やまださんは？

やまだ：よにんかぞくです。

3）キム　：きのう　わたしは　あさ　6じに　うんどうしました。アイさんは？

アイ　：9じに　しました。

2 **Listening:** Listen to the conversations. Each conversation will be interrupted by a chime, and the audio will then present three choices for how it might continue. Listen to choices a.-c., then circle the letter corresponding to the most appropriate continuation.

1）a.　　b.　　c.

2）a.　　b.　　c.

3）a.　　b.　　c.

Exit Check ☑

Now it's time to go back to the **DEKIRU** List for this chapter (p.85) and do the exit check to see what new things you can do now that you've completed the lesson.

Unit1 チャレンジ

1 Find useful learning resources

Try finding some self-learning applications to help you study Japanese (e.g., hiragana/katakana, kanji, vocabulary). If you find any good ones, please share them with your classmates!

2 「おもいでのしゃしんコンテスト」Nostalgic photo contest

Step 1 Choose your favorite photo you took on a trip or during some fun activity you did.

Step 2 Show the photo to your classmates and describe it to them.

> **Useful follow-up questions** いつ？ なんさいのとき？ だれと？ どこに？ どこで？ なにを？

Ex. わたしは きょねんのはちがつに かぞくと ハワイ (Hawaii) に いきました。
うみで あにと サーフィン (surfing) を しました。 <Continue>

Step 3 Upload the photo on social media or your Japanese course website with a brief description in Japanese. Write some short comments on your classmates' photos.

kuro_40

#ハワイ #うみにいきました

hana いいですね！

Nya-ko わたしもハワイがすきです♡

3 Online Novel

Now you can start reading our original online novel titled "Hello, Japan!"

タイプする　Typing in Japanese

❶ Introduction

Typing on the computer and other electronic devices has become an essential part of modern life, and this is just as true for Japanese as it is for other major world languages.

❷ Typing hiragana on a computer

> How do you type in Japanese?
> I can't seem to get the characters I want to type to appear...

It is common to use Roman character input when typing, which generates hiragana by combining the vowels and consonants of the Roman alphabet. To do this, first enable Japanese input on your device (not covered here), then switch your input method to hiragana mode.

Mac

Choose "Hiragana" from the input menu that appears on the right-hand side of the menu bar, or cycle through the language input options by pressing the "Command" key and spacebar. Once in hiragana mode, you should also turn off "Live Conversion" in the input menu to keep your hiragana from automatically converting to kanji.

Windows

Select the language abbreviation for Japanese on the far right of the taskbar, or select the language by pressing the "Alt" and "Shift" keys. Then, press the "Alt" and "~" keys to choose "Hiragana" or "Half-width Alphanumeric" (Roman alphabet).

When you type, you will see hiragana first, but this can then be converted to katakana or kanji if desired. Hit the spacebar to convert the character(s) currently underlined.

Ex. Type "na" → な → Space → ナ → Enter → ナ

Special sounds

	How to type	Examples
1) Particle は	Type "ha" as it is spelled in hiragana.	わたしはくろだです。 = watashihakurodadesu.
2) [n] sound (ん)	Type "nn." (Type "n" twice.)	ほん = honn おんがく = onngaku おんなのひと = onnnanohito
3) Small *tsu* (っ) (double consonant)	Type the subsequent consonant twice.	きって = kitte いっぽん = ipponn
4) Long vowels	Type as spelled in hiragana.	おかあさん = okaasann えいご = eigo ばんごう = banngou
5) Contracted sounds	Type as in the examples on the right.	きゃ = kya しゅ = shu or syu じゅ = ju, jyu, or zyu ちょ = cho or tyo

れんしゅう❶ Practice 1 (Typing regular hiragana words)

Practice typing the words 1)-15) below from LL1-3.

1) こんにちは	2) さようなら	3) おはよう	4) えいが	5) こうこう
6) おじいさん	7) せいじ	8) せんこう	9) いっさい	10) がっこう
11) としょかん	12) べんきょう	13) ちょっと	14) りょこう	15) じてんしゃ

③ Typing katakana on a computer

There are two ways to type katakana: 1) type in hiragana and convert the input to katakana, or 2) use the katakana mode and type directly in katakana.

How you type the special sounds is the same as for hiragana, except for long vowels (explained below). How to type the special combinations which appear only in katakana will be explained in the next section.

Long vowels in katakana:

Press [-] (the key to the right of [0] (zero))

Ex. アパート = apa-to

れんしゅう❷ Practice 2 (Typing katakana words)

Practice typing the katakana words 1)-10) below from LL1-3.

1) カタカナ	2) アメリカ	3) レストラン	4) アルバイト	5) ゲーム
6) コンサート	7) スポーツ	8) インターネット	9) ニュース	10) コンピュータ

④ Special combinations that only appear in katakana words

Special combinations

ウィ	ウェ	ウォ	シェ	ジェ	チェ	ティ	ディ	デュ
WI	WE	UXO	SHE	JE	CHE	THI	DHI	DHU
ファ	フィ	フェ	フォ	ヴァ	ヴィ	ヴ	ヴェ	ヴォ
FA	FI	FE	FO	VA	VI	VU	VE	VO

* See "Writing special sounds in katakana" (p.84) for more combinations.

れんしゅう❸ Practice 3 (Typing katakana words with special combinations)

Type the katakana words in 1)-8) below. Some of them are vocabulary from LL1-3 with special character combinations.

1) カフェ 2) パーティー 3) ファイト 4) メロディー

5) ウェブ 6) シェフ 7) アルファベット 8) エヴァンゲリオン

⑤ Typing your name in katakana on a computer

わたしはアイ・ブルーノです。

Non-Japanese names generally feature a middle dot (" ・ " なかてん) between the given name and the family name to make it clear where one ends and the other begins. Press the "/" key in hiragana mode, then hit the spacebar to convert to " ・ " if necessary.

れんしゅう❹ Practice 4 (Typing your name in katakana)

Type your name in katakana.

⑥ Typing kanji on a computer

You can type kanji on a computer in two steps: 1) type the word in hiragana, and 2) hit the spacebar to convert it to the correct kanji.

Ex. にほん → [Space] → 二本 → [Space] → 日本 → [Enter] → 日本

れんしゅう❺ Practice 5 (Typing kanji)

Type some words and sentences with kanji. First, type the text in 1)-4) in hiragana and then hit the spacebar. Did the characters in the right column appear?

Hit the space bar after each particle for the most accurate conversion. Don't type the whole sentence at once without hitting the spacebar!

Type these words/phrases:	See if the following kanji appear:
1) だいがく	大学
2) りゅうがくせい	留学生
3) わたしは　だいがくせいです	私は　大学生です
4) スミスさんは　かいしゃいんです	スミスさんは　会社員です

7 Typing punctuation/symbols

Punctuation/symbols

	Symbols	How to type	Examples
1) Comma	、（てん）	Press the **comma key** in hiragana mode.	いま、なんじですか。
2) Period	。（まる）	Press the **period key** in hiragana mode.	
3) Dot	・（なかてん）	Press the "**/**" **key** in hiragana mode, then hit the spacebar to convert if necessary.	アイ・ブルーノ
4) Parentheses	（　）（かっこ）	Shift+9, Shift+0 (Type "( )" in hiragana mode.)	一月（いちがつ）
5) Corner brackets (Japanese quotation marks)	「　」 （かぎかっこ）	In either hiragana or katakana modes, press the "[" (next to "P") and "]" keys.	「ハウル」というえいがを みました。

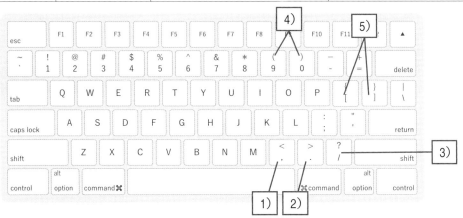

れんしゅう⑥ **Practice 6 (Typing hiragana, katakana, and kanji)**

Suppose you have an online conversation partner and want to introduce yourself briefly. Type up a self-introduction email, making sure to include your name, the name of your school, your school year, hometown, age, etc.

Ex.

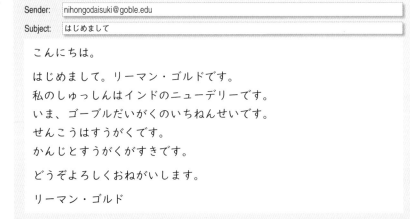

Sender:	nihongodaisuki@goble.edu
Subject:	はじめまして

こんにちは。

はじめまして。リーマン・ゴルドです。
私のしゅっしんはインドのニューデリーです。
いま、ゴーブルだいがくのいちねんせいです。
せんこうはすうがくです。
かんじとすうがくがすきです。

どうぞよろしくおねがいします。

リーマン・ゴルド

まわりとつながる

Connecting with others

02

Unit2のまえに

The theme of this unit is "Connecting with others." To start, look at the map of Japan below to see some of the famous places and festivals there, then discuss Q1.-Q4. with your classmates. You can use either Japanese or your own language in your discussion.

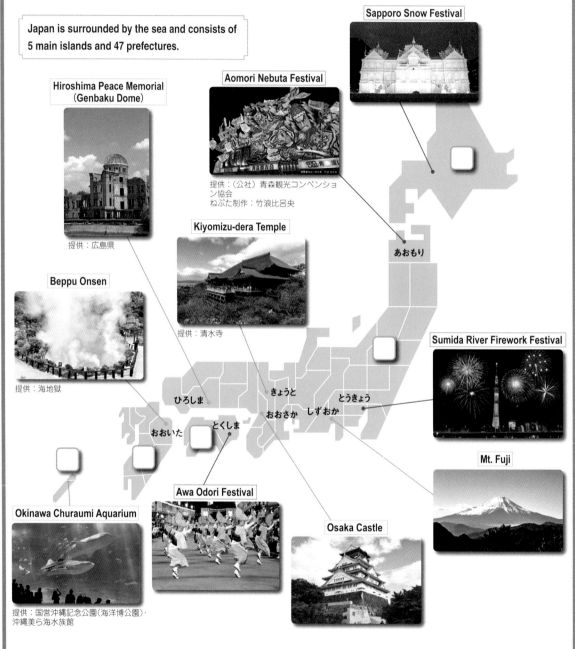

Japan is surrounded by the sea and consists of 5 main islands and 47 prefectures.

Sapporo Snow Festival

Aomori Nebuta Festival

提供：（公社）青森観光コンベンション協会
ねぶた制作：竹浪比呂央

Hiroshima Peace Memorial (Genbaku Dome)

提供：広島県

Kiyomizu-dera Temple

提供：清水寺

Beppu Onsen

提供：海地獄

Sumida River Firework Festival

Mt. Fuji

あおもり

ひろしま　きょうと　とうきょう
おおさか　しずおか
おおいた　とくしま

Awa Odori Festival

Okinawa Churaumi Aquarium

提供：国営沖縄記念公園（海洋博公園）・
沖縄美ら海水族館

Osaka Castle

Q1. The names of the five main islands of Japan are: [a. ほっかいどう b. ほんしゅう c. きゅうしゅう d. しこく e. おきなわ]. Put the appropriate letter for the island name into each ☐ on the map.

Q2. Do you know the names of any prefectures? Can you locate them on the map?

Q3. Have you ever been anywhere in Japan? If you were to go to Japan, which of the famous places and festivals on the map above would you want to see?

Q4. Introduce some famous places, events, etc. from your place of origin to your classmates. Do you have any good recommendations?

私もたこ焼きを一つください。
や　　　　　　　ひと
One *takoyaki* for me too, please!

STRATEGIES

Conversation Tips ....・Showing agreement and filling pauses with そうですね
Reading ....・Getting information from a music app and a flyer
　　　　　　　　　　・Understanding Japanese sentence structure: Adjective sentences
　　　　　　　　　　・Identifying the logical connection between sentences
　　　　　　　　　　・Identifying omitted words
Listening ....・Listening to longer sentences and picking out necessary information

GRAMMAR

❶ Demonstratives 　できる I
　1-1 これ・それ・あれ・どれ [Demonstrative pronouns]
　1-2 このN・そのN・あのN・どのN [Demonstrative adjectives]
❷ Numbers and counters 　できる I
❸ Adjective + Noun 　できる II
❹ Adjectives and nouns used as predicates 　できる II,III
　4-1 *I*-adjectives used as predicates
　4-2 *Na*-adjectives used as predicates
　4-3 Nouns used as predicates

❺ Case particles (2) 　できる IV
　5-1 で [Means marker]
　5-2 から [Starting point marker]
　5-3 まで [Ending point marker]

かいわ

1 できる I Ai, Tao, and Riemann are shopping online. 🔊 L4-1

> オフ：off [discount]　セント：cent　すごい：amazing　意味：meaning

タオ　　：このＴシャツはとてもいいですね。

アイ　　：そうですね。それはいくらですか。

タオ　　：780円の15％オフです。えっと、あのう…

リーマン：663円ですよ、タオさん。

　　　　　今日、663円は6ドル29セントです。

タオ　　：すごい、リーマンさん！

アイ　　：みんなでいっしょにＴシャツを買いませんか。

タオ　　：ええ、そうしましょう！　アイさんはどれにしますか。

アイ　　：そうですね…　あ、私はこれにします。

リーマン：アイさん、そのＴシャツの漢字は「愛」です。意味は「love」ですよ。

アイ　　：え、本当ですか。私の名前のＴシャツ！！

2 できる I,II The members of the Japan House are at a party for international students where they meet a Japanese student. 🔊 L4-2

> こちらこそ：me, too

けいた　：初めまして、赤井圭太です。出身は日本の大阪です。どうぞよろしく。

リーマン：こちらこそ、よろしくお願いします。あのう、大阪はどんな町ですか。

けいた　：そうですね…　にぎやかな町ですよ。それから、おもしろい町です。

　　　　　これはたこ焼きです。大阪の食べ物です。

アイ　　：たこ焼きですか。あのう、熱いですか。

けいた　：いいえ、あまり熱くないですよ。どうぞ。

アイ　　：いただきます。とてもおいしいです！

リーマン：あのう、私もたこ焼きを一つください。あ、熱い！

3 できる III, IV　The party is coming to an end.　🔊 L4-3

> カラオケ：karaoke　ここ：here　もちろん：of course　ファン：fan

マーク　：今から、みんなでカラオケに行きませんか。

けいた　：いいですね。どこに行きましょうか。

マーク　：えっと、カラオケ「とびら」はどうですか。

けいた　：ここから「とびら」まで、どうやって行きますか。

マーク　：歩いて行きましょう！　十分ぐらいですよ。

リーマン：あのう、ぼくはカラオケはちょっと…

<The next day>

リーマン：アイさん、カラオケはどうでしたか。

アイ　　：楽しかったですよ。

リーマン：そうですか。よかったですね。

　　　　　アイさんはどんな歌を歌いましたか。

アイ　　：私はアニソンを歌いました！

リーマン：へえ、アニソンは何を歌いましたか。

アイ　　：ポケモンを歌いました。

リーマン：えっ、日本語で歌いましたか。

アイ　　：はい、もちろん！

リーマン：そうですか。子どもの時、ポケモンはとても有名でしたね。

アイ　　：ええ、そうですね。とてもおもしろかったですね。

　　　　　私はピカチュウのファンでした。

ポケモン、ゲットだぜ〜

C O N V E R S A T I O N T I P S　ワンポイント　🔊 L4-4

Showing agreement and filling pauses with そうですね：そうですね can be used: 1) to agree with someone's statement and 2) while thinking, as an equivalent to "let me see/hmm." Make sure you can clearly distinguish the difference between そうですね and そうですか↘ and use each expression correctly. (See L1 Conversation Tips for more on そうですか↘.)

　　　　<At a café>

　　　　A：あのう、何にしますか。

　　　　B：うーん、そうですね…　えっと、私は野菜のケーキにします。

　　　　A：そうですか。じゃ、私も野菜のケーキにします。

　　　　A：このケーキはおいしいですね。

　　　　B：そうですね。

Lesson **4**

たんご

▶ **The words written in gray** are supplemental vocabulary.

● まいにちのせいかつ　Daily life

● コメントする (Expressing impressions)

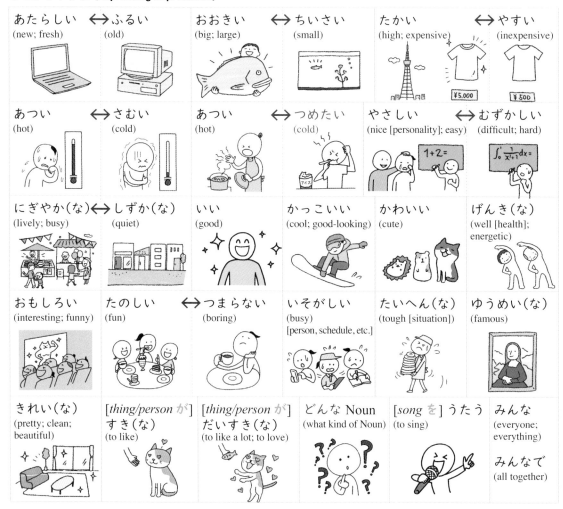

あたらしい ⟷ ふるい
(new; fresh)　(old)

おおきい ⟷ ちいさい
(big; large)　(small)

たかい ⟷ やすい
(high; expensive)　(inexpensive)

あつい ⟷ さむい
(hot)　(cold)

あつい ⟷ つめたい
(hot)　(cold)

やさしい ⟷ むずかしい
(nice [personality]; easy)　(difficult; hard)

にぎやか(な) ⟷ しずか(な)
(lively; busy)　(quiet)

いい
(good)

かっこいい
(cool; good-looking)

かわいい
(cute)

げんき(な)
(well [health]; energetic)

おもしろい
(interesting; funny)

たのしい ⟷ つまらない
(fun)　(boring)

いそがしい
(busy)
[person, schedule, etc.]

たいへん(な)
(tough [situation])

ゆうめい(な)
(famous)

きれい(な)
(pretty; clean; beautiful)

[*thing/person* が] すき(な)
(to like)

[*thing/person* が] だいすき(な)
(to like a lot; to love)

どんな Noun
(what kind of Noun)

[*song* を] うたう
(to sing)

みんな
(everyone; everything)

みんなで
(all together)

● かいもの (Shopping)

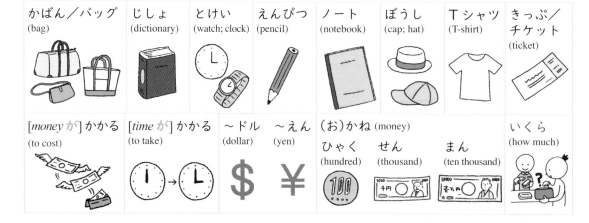

かばん／バッグ
(bag)

じしょ
(dictionary)

とけい
(watch; clock)

えんぴつ
(pencil)

ノート
(notebook)

ぼうし
(cap; hat)

Tシャツ
(T-shirt)

きっぷ／チケット
(ticket)

[*money* が] かかる
(to cost)

[*time* が] かかる
(to take)

～ドル
(dollar)

～えん
(yen)

(お)かね (money)

ひゃく
(hundred)

せん
(thousand)

まん
(ten thousand)

いくら
(how much)

● Demonstratives

これ (this (one)) 　　それ (that (one)) 　　あれ (that (one over there)) 　　どれ (which (one)) 　どの Noun (which Noun)　だれの Noun (whose Noun)

この Noun (this Noun)　　その Noun (that Noun)　　あの Noun (that Noun (over there))

● たべる (Dining)

おいしい (delicous; tasty)　　まあまあ(な) (okay; so-so)　　おすすめ (recommendation)

（お）はし (chopsticks)　ナイフ (knife)　フォーク (fork)　スプーン (spoon)　て (hand)

[Noun に] する (to decide on Noun)

Noun にします (I'll have Noun.)

どう (how; how about)

なにで／なんで (how; by what means)

どうやって (how; in what way; by what means)

● のりもの (Transportation)

くるま (car)　バス (bus)　でんしゃ (train)　ちかてつ (subway)　まち (town; city)　バスてい (bus stop)

ひこうき (airplane)　タクシー (taxi)　あるいて (on foot)

なにで／なんで (how; by what means) どうやって (how; in what way; by what means)

どのくらい／どのぐらい (how far [distance]; how long [time])

〜くらい／〜ぐらい (approximately; about [quantity])

● かぞえる　Counting

● 〜じかん (... hours)

1	いちじかん	7	ななじかん ／ しちじかん
2	にじかん	8	はちじかん
3	さんじかん	9	くじかん
4	よじかん	10	じゅうじかん
5	ごじかん	1.5	いちじかんはん
6	ろくじかん	?	なんじかん

● 〜ふん (... minutes)

1	いっぷん	7	ななふん
2	にふん	8	はちふん ／ はっぷん
3	さんぷん	9	きゅうふん
4	よんぷん	10	じ（ゅ）っぷん
5	ごふん	30	さんじ（ゅ）っぷん
6	ろっぷん	?	なんぷん

● 〜つ (General counter for things without a specific counter)

1	ひとつ	5	いつつ	8	やっつ
2	ふたつ	6	むっつ	9	ここのつ
3	みっつ	7	ななつ	10	とお
4	よっつ	?	いくつ		

● そのほかのひょうげん　Other expressions

 たこやきは **とても**おいしいです。 (*Takoyaki* is **very** delicious.)

たいてい (usually; generally)

ほんとうですか。 (**Really?**; **Is that true?**)

Lesson 4

たんごリスト

🔊 L4-5

U-VERBS

1	うたう	歌う	to sing [*song* を]
2	かかる		to cost [*money* が]; to take [*time* が] **Ex.1** じかんがかかる to take time **Ex.2**１じかんかかる to take one hour

I-ADJECTIVES

3	あたらしい	新しい	new; fresh
4	ふるい	古い	old [thing (not used for people)]
5	おおきい	大きい	big; large
6	ちいさい	小さい	small
7	たかい	高い	high; expensive
8	やすい	安い	inexpensive; cheap [price]
9	あつい	暑い／熱い	hot [air temperature]; hot [to the touch]
10	さむい	寒い	cold [air temperature]
11	おいしい		delicious; tasty
12	いい		good
13	かっこいい		cool; good-looking [appearance]
14	かわいい		cute
15	おもしろい		interesting; funny
16	たのしい	楽しい	fun
17	つまらない		boring
18	いそがしい	忙しい	busy [person, schedule, etc.; not place]
19	やさしい		nice [personality]; easy
20	むずかしい	難しい	difficult; hard

NA-ADJECTIVES

21	きれい		pretty; clean; beautiful
22	しずか	静か	quiet
23	にぎやか		lively; busy [place]; boisterous [person]
24	げんき	元気	well [health]; energetic
25	たいへん	大変	tough [situation]
26	まあまあ		okay; so-so
27	ゆうめい	有名	famous
28	すき	好き	to like [*thing/person* が]
29	だいすき	大好き	to like a lot; to love [*thing/person* が]

NOUNS

30	みんな		everyone; everything
31	かね／おかね	（お）金	money
32	くるま	車	car
33	ちかてつ	地下鉄	subway
34	でんしゃ	電車	train
35	ひこうき	飛行機	airplane
36	はし／おはし	（お）箸	chopsticks
37	て	手	hand
38	えんぴつ		pencil
39	かばん／バッグ		bag
40	きっぷ／チケット		ticket
41	じしょ	辞書	dictionary
42	とけい	時計	watch; clock
43	ぼうし		cap; hat
44	まち	町	town; city
45	おすすめ		recommendation **Ex.1** わたしのおすすめ my recommendation **Ex.2** おすすめの Noun Noun that (one) recommends
46	タクシー		taxi
47	バス		bus
48	バスてい	バス停	bus stop

| 49 | Ｔシャツ
（ティーシャツ） | | T-shirt |
| 50 | ノート | | notebook |

DEMONSTRATIVES

51	これ		this (one)
52	それ		that (one)
53	あれ		that (one over there)
54	この Noun		this Noun
55	その Noun		that Noun
56	あの Noun		that Noun (over there)

ADVERBS

| 57 | たいてい | | usually; generally;
almost always |
| 58 | とても | | very |

QUESTION WORDS

59	いくら		how much
60	だれの Noun	誰の	whose Noun
61	どう		how; how about
62	どうやって		how; in what way; by what means
63	どの Noun		which Noun
64	どのくらい／ どのぐらい		how far [distance]; how long [time]; how many; how much
65	どれ		which (one)
66	どんな Noun		what kind of Noun
67	なにで／なんで	何で	how; by what means

NUMBERS *

68	ひゃく	百	hundred
69	せん	千	thousand
70	まん	万	ten thousand

COUNTERS

71	～えん	～円	yen [currency in Japan]
72	～ドル		dollar
73	～ふん	～分	... minute(s)

	いっぷん	一分	one minute
	にふん	二分	two minutes
	さんぷん	三分	three minutes
	なんぷん	何分	how many minutes
74	～じかん	～時間	... hour(s)
	いちじかん	一時間	one hour
	にじかん	二時間	two hours
	さんじかん	三時間	three hours
	いちじかん はん	一時間半	one hour and a half
	なんじかん	何時間	how many hours
75	～つ		[general counter for things without a specific counter]
	ひとつ	一つ	one; one object
	ふたつ	二つ	two; two objects
	みっつ	三つ	three; three objects
	いくつ		how many

SUFFIX

| 76 | ～くらい／
～ぐらい | | approximately; about
[quantity]
Ex.1 いちじかんぐらい
about one hour
Ex.2 いちじかんはん
ぐらい
about one hour and a
half |

OTHER WORDS AND PHRASES

77	あるいて	歩いて	on foot **Ex.** あるいていく to go on foot
78	Noun にする		to decide on Noun **Ex.** Noun にします I'll have Noun; I'll go with Noun. [ordering things]
79	ほんとうですか	本当 ですか	Really?; Is that true?
80	みんなで		all together

* See additional information about these numbers on
p.133.

かんじ

▶ **The highlighted words** below are the vocabulary you will need to learn to read and write in kanji in this chapter.
▶ ✲**Special reading:** A special reading is assigned to a kanji compound word as a whole; in this case, it is impossible to assign each kanji in the compound a particular part of the reading.

| 15 百 百 百 | ヒャク ビャク ピャク ヒャッ | 百 one hundred ひゃく　　三 百 three hundred さんびゃく　　六 百 six hundred ろっぴゃく 八 百 eight hundred はっぴゃく　　百 人 one hundred people ひゃくにん 百 本 one hundred (long, cylindrical) objects ひゃっぽん |
| hundred | | 一 ァ ァ 百 百 百 |

| 16 千 千 千 | セン ゼン | 千 one thousand せん　　三 千 three thousand さんぜん　　八 千 eight thousand はっせん 千 円 one thousand yen せんえん　　千 人 one thousand people せんにん |
| thousand | | ノ ニ 千 |

| 17 万 万 万 | マン バン | 一 万 ten thousand いちまん　　十 万 one hundred thousand じゅうまん 百 万 one million ひゃくまん　　万 里 の 長 城 The Great Wall of China ばんり　　ちょうじょう |
| ten thousand | | 一 フ 万 |

| 18 円 円 円 | エン | 円 yen [currency in Japan]; circle えん　　百 円 one hundred yen ひゃくえん 円 高 strong yen [exchange rate] えんだか　　円 安 weak yen [exchange rate] えんやす |
| yen [currency in Japan]; circle | | l 冂 冂 円 |

| 19 曜 曜 曜 | ヨウ | 日 曜 日 Sunday にちようび　　月 曜 日 Monday げつようび　　火 曜 日 Tuesday かようび 水 曜 日 Wednesday すいようび　　木 曜 日 Thursday もくようび　　金 曜 日 Friday きんようび 土 曜 日 Saturday どようび　　何 曜 日 what day of the week なんようび |
| day of the week | | l 冂 冂 日 日ˈ 日゠ 日ᵓ 日ᵕ 日ᵕ 日ᵕᵕ 曜 曜 曜 曜 曜 曜 曜 曜 |

20 日 日 日	ニチ ニ カ ジツ	日 曜 日 Sunday にちようび　　一 日 one day いちにち　　毎 日 every day まいにち　　日 本 Japan にほん 一 日 ✲ the first day of the month ついたち　　二 日 ✲ the second day of the month ふつか 三 日 the third day of the month みっか　　休 日 holiday; day off きゅうじつ
	び ひ	明 日 ✲ tomorrow あした　　今 日 ✲ today きょう　　いい 日 good day ひ
sun; day		l 冂 月 日

21 火 火 火	カ	火 曜 日 Tuesday かようび　　火 山 volcano かざん　　火 事 fire [destructive] かじ　　火 星 Mars かせい
	ひ び	火 fire ひ　　花 火 fireworks はなび
fire		火 火 少 火

| 22 水 水水 water | スイ / みず | 水曜日 Wednesday すいようび　　水泳 swimming すいえい
水 water みず　　水着 swimming suit みずぎ |
| | 丿 刁 才 水 | |

| 23 木 木木 tree | モク / き | 木曜日 Thursday もくようび　　木星 Jupiter もくせい
木 tree き　　木下さん Kinoshita-san [last name] きのした |
| | 一 十 オ 木 | |

| 24 金 金金 gold; money | キン / かね | 金曜日 Friday きんようび　　現金 cash げんきん　　奨学金 scholarship しょうがくきん　　税金 tax ぜいきん
お金 money かね　　お金持ち rich person かねも |
| | 丿 人 今 今 全 余 金 金 | |

| 25 土 土土 soil; ground; earth | ド ト / つち | 土曜日 Saturday どようび　　土星 Saturn どせい　　土地 ground; land とち
土 soil; earth つち |
| | 一 十 土 | |

| 26 学 学学 learning | ガク ガッ / まな(ぶ) | 大学 university; college だいがく　　大学生 college student だいがくせい　　学生 student がくせい
学校 school がっこう　　学期 semester がっき　　学会 academic conference がっかい
学ぶ to study; to learn まな |
| | ⺍ ⺍ ⺍ ⺍ 学 学 学 | |

| 27 生 生生 life; birth | セイ ショウ / い(きる) う(まれる) | 学生 student がくせい　　先生 teacher せんせい　　生活 life せいかつ
一生 one's whole life (from birth to death) いっしょう
生きる to live い　　生まれる to be born う |
| | 丿 ト 牛 生 生 | |

| 28 先 先先 ahead; previous | セン / さき | 先生 teacher せんせい　　先月 last month せんげつ　　先学期 last semester せんがっき　　先週 last week せんしゅう
先輩 senior member of a group せんぱい
先に ahead さき |
| | 丿 ⺊ 生 先 先 先 | |

| 29 年 年年 year | ネン / とし | ～年生 ...-year student [grade in school] (Ex. 一年生 first-year student) ねんせい　　いちねんせい
去年 last year きょねん　　来年 next year らいねん
今年 * this year ことし　　年 year; age とし |
| | 丿 年 午 午 年 年 | |

30	大 / 大 / 大	ダイ タイ	大学 university; college　　大学生 college student　　大人 * adult だいがく　　　　　　　　だいがくせい　　　　　　　　おとな
			大好き(な) to like a lot; to love　　大切(な) important だいす　　　　　　　　　　　たいせつ
			大変(な) tough [situation] たいへん
		おお(きい)	大きい big; large おお
big; large		一 ナ 大	
31	小 / 小 / 小	ショウ	小学生 elementary school student　　小学校 elementary school しょうがくせい　　　　　　　　　　しょうがっこう
		ちい(さい) お こ	小さい small　　小川さん Ogawa-san [last name] ちい　　　　　おがわ
			小包 package; parcel　　小鳥 small bird こづつみ　　　　　　　　ことり
small		⌐ 小 小	

● あたらしいよみかた　New readings

The following are new readings for kanji that you have already learned. Read each word aloud.

1) 一つ　　2) 二つ　　3) 三つ　　4) 四つ　　5) 五つ　　6) 六つ　　7) 七つ
　ひと　　　　ふた　　　　みっ　　　　よっ　　　　いつ　　　　むっ　　　　なな

8) 八つ　　9) 九つ　　10) 十　　11) 六百　　12) 八百　　13) 月曜日　　14) 先月
　やっ　　　ここの　　　とお　　　ろっぴゃく　　はっぴゃく　　げつようび　　せんげつ

● れんしゅう　Practice

1　In Japan, many restaurants have daily lunch specials. Look at the restaurant menu below. Which special would you like to eat for lunch at this restaurant? Which day would you need to go there in order to get that special? How much is it?

2　Below is a social media post that Ogawa-san has written about her college life. Read the post aloud, then write the readings for the underlined words.

私は今、大学一年生です。月曜日から金曜日まで大学の図書館でアルバイトをします。
　　いま　　　　　　　　　　　　　　　　　　　　　としょかん

月曜日と水曜日と木曜日は十二時から三時までです。火曜日と金曜日は四時から七時まで
　　　　　　　　　　　　　　　　　じ　　　　　じ　　　　　　　　　　　　　　　　　　　　じ　　　　　じ

です。学生がたくさん来ます。ときどき先生も来ます。土曜日と日曜日は、アルバイトを
　　　　　　　　　　　　き　　　　　　　　　　　き

しませんが、たいてい午後に図書館で勉強します。
　　　　　　　　　ごご　　としょかん　べんきょう

■音読みと訓読み (Imported Chinese-style readings and native Japanese readings)

The Japanese did not have a writing system until kanji was introduced from China. In the mid-6th century, Japanese people initially assigned readings to the characters based on their pronunciations in Chinese. These are called *on-yomi*, or "sound readings." They also, however, began to apply kanji to native Japanese words based on their meanings. That is the origin of *kun-yomi*, or "interpretive readings."

For example, when words using the kanji 人, meaning "person," were first introduced into Japanese, the character was given the readings にん and じん based on the Chinese pronunciation of the imported words, and these are the *on-yomi* of this kanji today. (The reason there are two different *on-yomi* for 人 is because different words using the character 人 were imported from different areas of China at different times, and thus brought with them different Chinese pronunciations.) Meanwhile, ひと is the original Japanese word for "person," so it also became associated with the kanji 人 and went on to become the *kun-yomi* for this character.

When you see one kanji alone, it is most likely read with its *kun-yomi*, whereas when you see two or more kanji together, they are most likely read with their *on-yomi*. For example, the word 三人 means "three people," and the reading of 人 is にん. Japanese people imported the reading さんにん along with the word 三人 from Chinese, so にん in this word is an *on-yomi*.

くんよみ (kun-yomi)

· Japanese-origin reading
· For native Japanese words
· When you see one kanji alone, it is most likely read with its *kun-yomi*.

おんよみ (on-yomi)

· Chinese-origin reading
· Mostly for words borrowed from Chinese
· When you see two or more kanji together, they are most likely read with their *on-yomi*.

れんしゅう Practice

Read each of the following words 1)-6) aloud, and then guess whether the underlined part is an *on-yomi* or a *kun-yomi*.

1) <u>大</u>きい	おんよみ くんよみ	2) <u>大</u>学	おんよみ くんよみ
3) <u>水</u>をのみます	おんよみ くんよみ	4) <u>水</u>曜日	おんよみ くんよみ
5) <u>百</u>円	おんよみ くんよみ	6) お<u>金</u>	おんよみ くんよみ

ぶんぽう

1 Demonstratives

Demonstratives are a group of words that are used to point out something you want to refer to and distinguish it from other things.

1-1 これ・それ・あれ・どれ [Demonstrative pronouns] "this; that; that one over there; which one"

[1-a]

Demonstrative pronoun		
これ／それ／あれ	は	私 の自転車です。
{This/That/That one over there} is my bicycle.		

You can refer to something close to the speaker using これ, something close to the listener using それ, and something distant from both the speaker and the listener using あれ. どれ is used to ask which one a certain thing is.

Exs. (1) A: <u>それ</u>は何ですか。*What is that?*

B: <u>これ</u>はたこ焼きです。日本の食べ物です。*This is* takoyaki. *It's a Japanese food.*

(2) <At a bakery>

A: <u>これ</u>は何ですか。*What is this?*

B: <u>それ</u>ですか。<u>それ</u>はとうふのケーキです。*(You mean) that one? That's tofu cake.*

(3) <At a bicycle shed>

田中　：スミスさんの自転車は<u>どれ</u>ですか。*Which one is your bicycle, Smith-san?*

スミス：<u>あれ</u>です。*That one over there is.*

どれ cannot be marked by は because an unknown thing cannot be a topic. (See Language Note: 「は」と「が」 (pp.185-186).)

× <u>どれ</u>はワンさんの飲み物ですか。 → ワンさんの飲み物は<u>どれ</u>ですか。
Which one is Wang-san's drink?

1-2 このN・そのN・あのN・どのN [Demonstrative adjectives] "this N; that N; that N over there; which N"

[1-b]

Demonstrative adjective	N		
この／その／あの	本 ほん	は	だれの本ですか。 ほん
Whose book is {this book/that book/that book over there}?			

To say "this N," "that N," "that N over there," and "which N," you use このN, そのN, あのN, and どのN, respectively. Like どれ, "どのN" cannot be used with は.

Exs. (1) A: そのアニメは日本のアニメですか。
に ほん

Is that a Japanese anime? (lit. Is that anime a Japanese anime?)

B: はい。いっしょに見ませんか。*Yes. Would you like to watch it together?*
み

(2) \<At a party>

A: 田中さんはどの人ですか。（× 田中さんはどれですか。）
た なか ひと た なか

Which person is Tanaka-san?

B: あの人です。*That person over there.*
ひと

(3) スミス ：このバスは図書館に行きますか。*Does this bus go to the library?*
と しょかん い

運転手 (driver)：はい、行きます。*Yes, it does.*
うんてんしゅ い

⚠ Because この, その, あの, and どの are a kind of adjectives, you must use them with nouns. The following sentences on the left below are ungrammatical and must be rephrased as shown on the right.

× <u>この</u>は私のアパートです。 → <u>これ</u>は私のアパートです。*This is my apartment.*
わたし わたし

× 私の水は<u>この</u>です。 → 私の水は<u>これ</u>です。*My water is this one (lit. this).*
わたし みず わたし みず

2 Numbers and counters

[2]

N	Prt	Number	Counter	
オレンジ	を	三 みっ	つ	ください。
Give me three oranges.				

When you say things like "three oranges," "six pieces of bread," and "two glasses of water" in Japanese, you use the number and the appropriate counter for the object, as seen in [2]. Note that the number and the counter occur after the noun and the particle. Thus, the following sentences are ungrammatical:

× <u>三つ</u>オレンジをください。
みっ

× オレンジ<u>三つ</u>をください。
みっ

Exs. (1) 今日、ケーキを<u>四つ</u>買いました。*I bought four cakes today.*
きょう よっ か

(2) ジムで<u>一時間</u>運動しました。*I exercised for one hour at the gym.*
いち じ かんうんどう

(3) \<At a fast food restaurant>

ハンバーガーを<u>二つ</u>とコーラを<u>一つ</u>ください。
ふた ひと

Give me two hamburgers and one cola, please.

3 Adjective + Noun

Adjectives are a group of words that are used to describe the characteristics of objects, people, animals, etc. In this lesson, you will learn about Japanese adjectives and how they are used.

[3-a]

	I-adjective	N	
昨日 きのう	おもしろい	映画 えいが	を見ました。 み
I watched an interesting movie yesterday.			

[3-b]

Na-adjective		N	
にぎやか	な	町 まち	ですね。
This is a lively town, isn't it?			

You can describe an object, person, etc. by using an adjective as a noun-modifier. There are two major groups of adjectives in Japanese: *i*-adjectives and *na*-adjectives. They are so called because their noun-modifying forms end with い and な respectively, as in [3-a] and [3-b].

Exs. (1) 先週、新しい時計を買いました。とてもかわいい時計です。
せんしゅう　あたら　　とけい　か　　　　　　　　　　　　　とけい

I bought a new clock last week. It's a very cute clock.

(2) きれいな音楽ですね。*It's a beautiful piece of music, isn't it?*
おんがく

(3) A: 山川さんはどんな人ですか。*What kind of person is Yamakawa-san?*
やまかわ　　　　　ひと

B: 楽しい人ですよ。*He is a fun person (to be with).*
たの　ひと

4 Adjectives and nouns used as predicates

4-1 *I*-adjectives used as predicates

[4-a]

Topic	Predicate*	
		I-adjective
この（お）すしは	とても	おいしいです。
This sushi is very delicious.		

* The predicate is the portion of a sentence following the topic or subject that tells what the topic or subject is or does.

You can also describe a thing, person, etc. by using an adjective as a predicate.

I-adjectives conjugate in predicate position as follows (です is a polite ending):

	Affirmative (polite)	Negative (polite)
Non-past	（たか）いです *	（たか）くないです
Past	（たか）かったです	（たか）くなかったです

* Non-past affirmative forms without です (e.g., たかい) are referred to as dictionary forms because they are the forms that appear in dictionary entries.

いい is an irregular *i*-adjective; its stem (= the portion that does not conjugate) is よ, but its non-past affirmative form is いい rather than よい.

	Affirmative (polite)	Negative (polite)
Non-past	いいです	よくないです
Past	よかったです	よくなかったです

かっこいい is a compound adjective consisting of かっこ "looks" and いい. Thus, the same conjugation rules apply to かっこいい, i.e., かっこいいです, かっこよくないです, etc. Note that かわいい is not a compound adjective.

Exs. (1) A: そのケーキはおいしいですか。*Is that cake delicious?*

B: いいえ、ぜんぜんおいしくないです。*No, it's not delicious at all.*

(2) 昨日のテストは難しくなかったです。*Yesterday's test wasn't difficult.*
　　きのう　　　　　　むずか

(3) <Looking at a movie list>
A: この映画はどうでしたか。*How was this movie?*
　　えいが
B: あまりよくなかったです。*It wasn't very good.*

4-2 *Na*-adjectives used as predicates

[4-b]

Topic	Predicate	
	Na-adjective	
このレストランは	有名 ゆうめい	です。
This restaurant is famous.		

When you use a *na*-adjective as a predicate, you must add です or a variation of it to the adjective in order to indicate a tense, a politeness level, and whether the predicate is affirmative or negative. The table below shows the negative and past forms of です.

	Affirmative (polite)	Negative (polite)
Non-past	（静か）です しず	（静か）じゃないです しず
Past	（静か）でした しず	（静か）じゃなかったです しず

Exs. (1) 友達の寮はきれいです。でも、私の寮はきれいじゃないです。
　　　　ともだち　りょう　　　　　　　　　わたし　りょう

My friend's dorm is clean, but my dorm is not.

(2) 昨日の宿題は大変でした。*Yesterday's homework was tough.*
　　きのう　しゅくだい　たいへん

(3) A: パーティーはどうでしたか。*How was the party?*

B: まあまあでした。あまりにぎやかじゃなかったです。

It was so-so. It wasn't very lively.

Nouns used as predicates

[4-c]

Topic	Predicate		
		N	
マークさんは	去年 きょねん	三年生 さんねんせい	でした。
Mark was a third-year student last year.			

When you use a noun as a predicate, you must add です or a variation of it to the noun, as shown in the table below, in order to indicate a tense, a politeness level, and whether the predicate is affirmative or negative.

	Affirmative (polite)	Negative (polite)
Non-past	（学生）です がくせい	（学生）じゃないです がくせい
Past	（学生）でした がくせい	（学生）じゃなかったです がくせい

Exs. (1)　このペンは１００円でした。*This pen was 100 yen.*
えん

　　　(2)　大学の時、父と母はクラスメートでした。
だいがく　とき　ちち　はは
My father and mother were classmates in their college years.

　　　(3)　去年のルームメートはあまりいい人じゃなかったです。
きょねん　　　　　　　　　　　　　　　ひと
My roommate last year was not a very nice person.

5　Case particles (2)

で [Means marker] "by; with; using; in"

[5-a]

	N		
毎日 まいにち	バス	で	学校に行きます。 がっこう　い
I go to school by bus every day.			

You can express a means of doing something using Noun + で. The noun before で typically refers to a mode of transportation, a tool, a language, etc.

Exs. (1)　A: {なんで／なにで／どうやって} 図書館に行きますか。
としょかん　い
How (lit. By what) are you going to go to the library?

　　　　　B: 自転車で行きます。*I'm going there by bicycle.*
じてんしゃ　い

　　　(2)　A: どうやって（お）すしを食べますか。*How do you eat sushi?*
た

　　　　　B: 箸で食べます。*I eat it with chopsticks.*
はし　た

　　　　　C: 私は手で食べます。*I eat it with my hands.*
わたし　て　た

　　　(3)　パーティーでけいたさんと日本語で話しました。
にほんご　はな
I talked with Keita in Japanese at the party.

なんで can also mean "how come; why," so in (1) you can use なにで instead of なんで to avoid ambiguity.

5-2 から **[Starting point marker]** "from; (starting) at"

[5-b]

N		
シドニー	から	日本_{にほん}に行_いきます。
I'm going to Japan from Sydney.		

You can indicate the starting point of a moving action using から. から can also be used for a starting point in time.

Exs. (1) 初_{はじ}めまして。けいたです。日本_{にほん}から来_きました。

Nice to meet you. I'm Keita. I'm from Japan. (lit. I came from Japan.)

(2) 明日_{あした}６時_じからパーティーをします。来_きませんか。

We are going to have a party starting at six o'clock. Would you like to come?

5-3 まで **[Ending point marker]** "to; till"

[5-c]

		N		
寮_{りょう}	から	大学_{だいがく}	まで	自転車_{じてんしゃ}で15分_{ふん}ぐらいかかります。
It takes about fifteen minutes by bike from my dorm to the university.				

You can indicate the ending point of a moving action using まで. まで can also be used for an ending point in time.

Exs. (1) 京都_{きょうと}から東京_{とうきょう}まで自転車_{じてんしゃ}で旅行_{りょこう}しました。大変_{たいへん}でしたが、楽_{たの}しかったです。

I traveled from Kyoto to Tokyo by bike. It was hard, but it was fun.

(2) 毎日_{まいにち}２時_じから４時_じまで日本語_{にほんご}を勉強_{べんきょう}します。*I study Japanese from two to four every day.*

☞ **GID** (vol.1): B. Particles 1. Case particles

● **すうじ Numbers**

		10 ～じゅう	100 ～ひゃく	1,000 ～せん	10,000 ～まん
1	いち	10 じゅう	100 ひゃく	1,000 せん	10,000 いちまん
2	に	20 にじゅう	200 にひゃく	2,000 にせん	20,000 にまん
3	さん	30 さんじゅう	300 さん**びゃく**　sanbyaku	3,000 さん**ぜん**　sanzen	30,000 さんまん
4	よん／し	40 よんじゅう	400 よんひゃく	4,000 よんせん	40,000 よんまん
5	ご	50 ごじゅう	500 ごひゃく	5,000 ごせん	50,000 ごまん
6	ろく	60 ろくじゅう	600 ろっ**ぴゃく**　roppyaku	6,000 ろくせん	60,000 ろくまん
7	なな／しち	70 ななじゅう	700 ななひゃく	7,000 ななせん	70,000 ななまん
8	はち	80 はちじゅう	800 はっ**ぴゃく**　happyaku	8,000 はっ**せん**　hassen	80,000 はちまん
9	きゅう／く	90 きゅうじゅう	900 きゅうひゃく	9,000 きゅうせん	90,000 きゅうまん

Lesson **4**

はなしましょう

できる I Do your shopping and order food by referring to things around you.

できる I-A Demonstrative pronouns これ・それ・あれ・どれ

1 Point at things near your partner and ask what those things are called in Japanese.

Ex. A: それは日本語で何ですか。
　　　 B: これですか。時計です。
　　　 or これですか。分かりません。先生に聞きましょう。

2 Point at things near you and ask what those things are called in Japanese.

Ex. A: これは日本語で何ですか。
　　　 B: それですか。ノートです。
　　　 or それですか。分かりません。先生に聞きましょう。

3 Point at things far from both you and your partner and ask what those things are called in Japanese.

Ex. A: あれは日本語で何ですか。
　　　 B: どれですか。
　　　 A: あれです。<Point clearly at the object.>
　　　 B: ああ、あれは時計です。

4 Now, point at things in a variety of different locations and ask your partner what those things are called in Japanese.

できる I-B Demonstrative adjectives このN・そのN・あのN・どのN

1 Make sentences using この, その, or あの based on the cues provided.　🔊 L4-6

Ex. あの人は田中さんです。

Ex. 人／田中さん

1) 辞書／フランス語の辞書

2) 時計／日本の時計

3) 飲み物／お酒

4) 人／私の友達

5) ネコの名前／にゃんた

Group Work

2 In a group, place one small item you have (e.g., a pen) into a bag. Then, take turns and try to identify the owner of each item.

[Step 1] Pick out an item that is not yours and try to determine whose it is within two guesses.

Ex. A: このペン (pen) は〇〇さんのペンですか。

B: いいえ、私のペンじゃないです。or はい、私のペンです。

[Step 2] If you cannot identify the item's owner within two guesses, ask your groupmates whose item it is.

Ex. A: このペンはだれのペンですか。

B: 私のペンです。

Lesson 4

3 (Information gap) You are at a bakery in Japan. Ask what kind of bread is in the various locations around the shop.

Ex. C= Customer, S= Store attendant

C: すみません。

それは何のパンですか。

S: {このパン／これ} ですか。

フルーツ (fruits) のパンです。

C: ああ、そうですか。

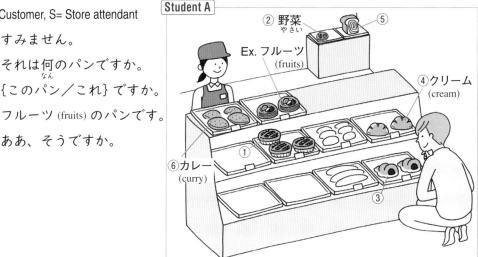

Student A

② 野菜
やさい

⑤

Ex. フルーツ
(fruits)

④クリーム
(cream)

①

⑥カレー
(curry)

③

Student B ➡p.145

できるI-C **Numbers and counters**

1 Let's practice saying large numbers in Japanese. Take turns with your partner asking for the price and answering according to the price tag. For 9)-12), give the prices in the currency you most often use in your everyday life. 🔊 L4-7

Ex. A: いくらですか。

B: 820 円です。
えん

¥820

ユーロ(€) : euro ポンド(£) : pound

1) ¥130

2) $650

3) €710

4) £880

5) $1,300

6) ¥3,740

7) £1,210

8) €8,420

9) 16,900

10) 72,100

11) 84,500

12) 99,999

2 You and your friend are shopping online for a clock and a T-shirt to give to your classmate.

$\boxed{\text{Step 1}}$ First, ask each other how much each item is. Use sentence-final particles as appropriate.
(See Language Note on p.150 for more information.)

Ex. A: すしの時計_{とけい}はいくらですか。

B: えっと、9,300 円_{えん}ですよ。

A: 9,300 円_{えん}ですか。高_{たか}いですね。

B: そうですね。

Ex. | ¥9,300 | | ¥4,850 | | ¥21,300 | | ¥16,000 |

| ¥1,600 | | ¥10,800 | | ¥3,800 | | ¥1,530 |

$\boxed{\text{Step 2}}$ Discuss which clock and T-shirt you will buy for your classmate.

Ex. A: どの時計_{とけい}にしますか。

B: すしの時計_{とけい}はどうですか。

A: すしの時計_{とけい}はちょっと高_{たか}いですね。

B: でも、〇〇さんはすしが大好_{だいす}きですよ。

A: 本当_{ほんとう}ですか。じゃ、すしの時計_{とけい}にしましょう。

3 You are shopping at a Japanese flea market.

$\boxed{\text{Step 1}}$ You are now looking to buy a hat or bag. Ask the prices of the various hats or bags for sale and buy the one you like most. When you finish, switch roles with your partner.

Ex. A: あのう、すみません。そのぼうしはいくらですか。

B: {このぼうし／これ} ですか。3,800 円です。

A: そうですか。じゃ、このぼうしはいくらですか。

B: そのぼうしは 2,500 円_{えん}です。

A: じゃ、このぼうしをください。

B: はい、ありがとうございます。

136

Step 2 Now, create your own flea market booth and sell your items.

Role A You are a vender. Prepare physical items or pictures of items to sell and make up prices.

Role B You are a customer. Ask about the prices of the items for sale. Buy the item you like most.

4 Have you ever seen a menu from a Japanese restaurant?

Step 1 First, look at the Tobira Restaurant menu below and see what kind of food and drinks it has on it. Next, practice phrases to order the various menu items.

うどん：udon (thick wheat noodles)

Ex.1 肉うどんを二つください。
　　　にく　　　　ふた

Ex.2 お茶を一つとコーヒーを二つください。
　　　ちゃ　　ひと　　　　　　　　ふた

Step 2 You are now at the Tobira Restaurant to eat lunch. Decide what to eat with your partner and order.

Ex. A: ○○さんは何にしますか。
　　　　　　　　　　なに

B: 私はランチセットにします。

　　 380円ですよ。安いですね。
　　　　　えん　　　　　やす
　　 △△さんは？

A: 私は肉が大好きです。
　　　　にく　だい す
　　 だから、肉うどんにします。
　　　　　　　にく

B: 飲み物は何にしますか。
　　のみ　もの　なに

\<Decide what to order\>

A: すみません。ランチセットを一つ
　　　　　　　　　　　　　　　　　ひと
　　 と肉うどんを一つとお茶を二つ
　　　にく　　　　ひと　　　ちゃ　ふた
　　 ください。

Step 3 Search for menus from Japanese fast food chains online. Do the same activities in Step 1 and Step 2 with the menus you find.

できる Ⅱ　Briefly describe the things around you.

できるⅡ-A　Adjective + Noun

1 Comment on each of the pictures below in a sentence using a noun-modifying adjective based on the cue provided.　(L4-8)

Ex.　A: どんな魚ですか。
　　　　　さかな

　　　B: 大きい魚です。
　　　　　おお　さかな

Ex. big	1) small	2) new	3) old	4) inexpensive	5) expensive

6) lively	7) quiet	8) interesting	9) boring	10) easy	11) difficult

2 Ask each other about the following topics and what kind of places/people they are.

Ex.　出身／どこ
　　　しゅっしん
　　　A: ○○さんの出身はどこですか。
　　　　　　　　しゅっしん
　　　B: オーストラリアのシドニー (Sydney) です。
　　　A: そうですか。シドニーはどんな町ですか。
　　　　　　　　　　　　　　　　　　まち
　　　B: にぎやかな町です。それから、おもしろい町です。
　　　　　　　　　まち　　　　　　　　　　　　まち

1) 出身／どこ　　2) 高校／どこ　　3) 親友 (best friend) ／だれ　　4) your own
　　しゅっしん　　　　こうこう　　　　しんゆう

3 What are your favorites from the following categories? Ask your classmate what their favorites are, then expand the conversation by asking follow-up questions.

Ex.　町
　　　まち
　　　A: ○○さんの好きな町はどこですか。
　　　　　　　　　す　　まち
　　　B: ロンドンです。
　　　A: ロンドンはどんな町ですか。
　　　　　　　　　　　　　　まち
　　　B: とても楽しい町ですよ。それから、きれいな町です。
　　　　　　　たの　まち　　　　　　　　　　　　　まち
　　　A: そうですか。<Expand>

1) カフェ　　2) 映画　　3) 歌手 (singer)　　4) クラス　　5) your own
　　　　　　　えいが　　　　かしゅ

できるⅡ-B　Adjectives used as predicates (Non-past)

1 Let's practice making the non-past affirmative and negative forms of adjectives.　🔊 L4-9

Ex.1 ちいさい → ちいさいです → ちいさくないです

Ex.2 たいへん → たいへんです → たいへんじゃないです

1) たのしい　　　2) おいしい　　　3) さむい　　　4) あつい　　　5) かわいい　　6) いい

7) かっこいい　　8) げんき　　　9) ゆうめい　　　10) きれい　　11) しずか　　12) にぎやか

2 Look at the pictures in できるⅡ-A-**1** and describe them again with the adjectives as predicates.

Ex. この <ruby>魚<rt>さかな</rt></ruby> は <ruby>大<rt>おお</rt></ruby>きいです。　🔊 L4-10

<ruby>小<rt>ちい</rt></ruby>さくないです。

3 Let's talk about your university!

Role A　You are a prospective student from Japan visiting your partner's university. Ask your partner, who works in the admissions office, for information about the school.

Role B　You are working at your university's admissions office, where your partner is visiting as a prospective student. Answer their questions about the school.

Step 1　Ask the following yes-no questions about the university. Switch roles once you've asked all the questions.

Ex.　this university / big?

A: この <ruby>大学<rt>だいがく</rt></ruby> は <ruby>大<rt>おお</rt></ruby>きいですか。

B: はい、とても <ruby>大<rt>おお</rt></ruby>きいです。 or いいえ、あまり <ruby>大<rt>おお</rt></ruby>きくないです。

1) campus (キャンパス) / pretty?　　2) dorm food / delicious?　　3) dorm rooms / big?

4) winter (冬) / cold?　　5) study / tough?　　6) your own

Step 2　Ask how the following topics are in order to learn more about the university.

Ex. クラス　A: この <ruby>大学<rt>だいがく</rt></ruby> のクラスはどうですか。

B: そうですね…。ちょっと <ruby>難<rt>むずか</rt></ruby>しいですが、とても <ruby>楽<rt>たの</rt></ruby>しいですよ。

or あまり <ruby>難<rt>むずか</rt></ruby>しくないです。それから、とても <ruby>楽<rt>たの</rt></ruby>しいですよ。

1) クラス　　2) <ruby>生活<rt>せいかつ</rt></ruby> (life)　　3) <ruby>町<rt>まち</rt></ruby>　　4) your own

4 Do you have any restaurant recommendations? Take turns with your partner describing your favorite restaurant and asking follow-up questions.

Ex. 私のおすすめのレストランは「ボーノ」です。<ruby>大<rt>おお</rt></ruby>きいレストランです。

ちょっと <ruby>高<rt>たか</rt></ruby>いですが、とてもおいしいです。私の <ruby>好<rt>す</rt></ruby>きな <ruby>料理<rt>りょうり</rt></ruby> は

トマトパスタ (tomato pasta) です。<ruby>来週<rt>らいしゅう</rt></ruby>、いっしょに <ruby>行<rt>い</rt></ruby>きませんか。

できる III Share impressions about things you have done.

 できる III-A **Adjectives and nouns used as predicates (Past)**

1 Let's practice *i*-adjective conjugations and です conjugations with *na*-adjectives/nouns. 🔊 L4-11

Ex.1

	non-past	
	おおきいです	おおきくないです
affirmative		negative
	おおきかったです	おおきくなかったです
	past	

Ex.2

	non-past	
	しずかです	しずかじゃないです
affirmative		negative
	しずかでした	しずかじゃなかったです
	past	

Ex.3

	non-past	
	がくせいです	がくせいじゃないです
affirmative		negative
	がくせいでした	がくせいじゃなかったです
	past	

1) やさしい   2) おもしろい   3) いそがしい   4) むずかしい   5) あつい

6) いい   7) かっこいい   8) たいへん   9) げんき   10) にぎやか

11) きれい   12) せんせい   13) おさけ

2 Let's play a guessing game! Choose one of the items below and suppose you received the item as a birthday present（プレゼント）yesterday. Have your partner guess what you got until they figure it out, as in the example.

Ex. A: プレゼントはまんがでしたか。

B: はい、まんがでした。or いいえ、まんがじゃなかったです。

3 Ask and answer questions about how each of the following topics was based on the cues provided.

Ex. yesterday / very busy 🔊 L4-12

A: 昨日はどうでしたか。
　　きのう

B: とても忙しかったです。
　　　いそが

Yesterday?	1) very tough	2) not very busy	3) your own
Yesterday morning?	4) a bit hot	5) not very cold	6) your own
High school teacher?	7) very cool	8) not nice at all	9) your own
Japanese test（テスト）?	10) so-so	11) not good at all	12) your own

4 Talk about the following periods of time in the past. Expand the conversation by asking at least three follow-up questions.

Ex. 先週の週末
せんしゅう　しゅうまつ

A: ○○さん、先週の週末はどうでしたか。(← How?)
せんしゅう　しゅうまつ

B: とてもよかったです。

A: そうですか。何をしましたか。(← What?)
なに

B: 友達とうちでゲームをしました。
ともだち

A: へえ、いいですね。どんなゲームをしましたか。(← More follow-up questions)

B: カードゲームをしました。とてもおもしろかったです。<Continue>

1) 先週の週末　　2) 去年の夏休み　　3) 高校の生活 (life)　　4) your own
　せんしゅう　しゅうまつ　　　きょねん　なつやす　　　こうこう　せいかつ

Lesson
4

5 Do you like traveling?

Step 1 Suppose your partner went to ski in Hokkaido in Japan last year. Ask for details about the trip.
🔊 L4-13

Ex.1　スキー (ski)　😊 not very difficult　😊 fun

Ex.2　スキー (ski)　🙁 a little difficult　😊 fun

Ex.　A: スキーはどうでしたか。

B: Ex.1 あまり難しくなかったです。それから、楽しかったです。
むずか　　　　　　　　　　　たの

Ex.2 ちょっと難しかったですが、楽しかったです。
むずか　　　　　　　　　たの

1) 町　　　　　　　　　🙁 not very big　　😊 lively
まち

2) ホテル (hotel)　　　😊 very big　　　　🙁 not clean

3) 山 (mountain)　　　🙁 very cold　　　　😊 pretty
やま

4) 温泉 (hot springs)　😊 good　　　　　　😊 clean
おんせん

5) 食べ物　　　　　　　😊 not very expensive　😊 very tasty
た　もの

Step 2 Now, talk about trips you've taken and ask each other for details.

Ex.　A: 私は先月、友達とハワイ (Hawaii) に行きました。
せんげつ　ともだち　　　　　　　　い

B: へえ、いいですね。ハワイ (Hawaii) はどうでしたか。

A: ちょっと暑かったですが、とてもきれいでした。<Continue>
あつ

できる IV　Talk about how to do something.

できる IV-A　Means marker で

1　Look at the pictures below and state how Ai does the following activities. **L4-14**

Ex.　アイさんは箸でご飯を食べます。
はし　　はん　た

　　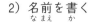　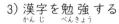

Ex. ご飯を食べる　1) 写真をとる　2) 名前を書く　3) 漢字を勉強する
はん　た　　　しゃしん　　　なまえ　か　　　かんじ　べんきょう

4) 日本語の宿題をする　　5) タオさんと話す
にほんご　しゅくだい　　　　　はな

2　Ask your partner if they often do the following things. If they do, ask what they use to do them.

Ex.　写真をとる
しゃしん

A: ○○さんはよく写真をとりますか。
しゃしん

B: はい、よくとりますよ。

A: {何で／どうやって} とりますか。
なに

B: スマホでとります。

A: そうですか。私はカメラ (camera) でとります。or 私もスマホでとります。

1) 音楽を聞く　　2) 映画を見る　　3) ○○を食べる　　4) your own
おんがく　き　　　えいが　み　　　　　　　た

3　Take turns describing your favorite food. When you present, show a picture of the food. Your partner will ask follow-up questions.

| **Useful vocabulary**　甘い: sweet　からい: spicy; hot　すっぱい: sour　冷たい: cold |
| あま　　　　　　　　　　　　　　　　　　　　　　　つめ |
| スプーン: spoon　フォーク: fork　ナイフ: knife |

Ex.　A: 私の好きな中国の食べ物はショーロンポーです。
す　ちゅうごく　た　もの

英語で "soup dumpling" です。熱いですが、とてもおいしいですよ。
えいご　　　　　　　　　あつ

B: そうですか。ショーロンポーは {何で／どうやって} 食べますか。
なに　　　　　　た

A: たいていスプーンと箸で食べます。<Continue>
はし　た

1 Did you have a fulfilling weekend last weekend?

$\boxed{\text{Step 1}}$ Describe what Ai did last Saturday.　　　　　　　　　　　🔊 **L4-15**

Ex.1 slept / 2 AM - 12 PM　　アイさんは<u>午前２時</u>から<u>午後１２時</u>まで<u>寝ました</u>。
　　　　　　　　　　　　　　　　　ごぜん　じ　　　　ごご　　じ　　　　　ね

Ex.2 slept / 10 hours　　　　　アイさんは<u>１０時間</u>寝ました。
　　　　　　　　　　　　　　　　　　　　じかん　ね

1) played with the cat / 1 PM - around 2:30 PM　　2) went on foot / from home to a pretty park

3) read a new book / from page 1 (１ページ) to page 35　　4) studied at a quiet library / 3 hours

5) sang at karaoke (カラオケ) / 2.5 hours　　　　6) cleaned her room / around 1.5 hours

$\boxed{\text{Step 2}}$ Talk about your last Saturday afternoon with your partner.

Ex.　A: 先週の土曜日の午後は何をしましたか。
　　　　　せんしゅう　どようび　ごご　なに

　　　　B: えっと、土曜日は午後１時から３時ごろまでジムで運動しました。
　　　　　　　　どようび　ごご　じ　　　じ　　　　　　うんどう

　　　　　それから、３時間ぐらい勉強しました。
　　　　　　　　　じかん　　べんきょう

　　　　A: そうですか。運動は何をしましたか。<Continue>
　　　　　　　　　うんどう　なに

2 Let's go to the Tokyo Skytree!

$\boxed{\text{Step 1}}$ First, make a sentence with each transportation method to review the vocabulary you will need.　　　　🔊 **L4-16**

Ex.　<u>車</u>で行きます。
　　　くるま　い

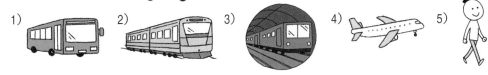

1)　　　　2)　　　　3)　　　　4)　　　　5)

$\boxed{\text{Step 2}}$ Now, look at the pictures below and explain what mode of transportation is used for each step and how long it takes.　　🔊 **L4-17**

Ex.　大学からバス停まで歩いて行きます。歩いて１５分かかります。
　　　だいがく　　　てい　　ある　い　　　ある　　　ふん

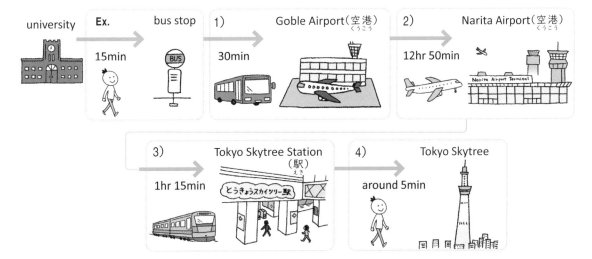

3 Ask your partner how they get from one place to another and how long it takes.

Ex. ここ (here) → うち

A: ○○さんのうちはどこですか

B: キャンパス (campus) の近く (nearby) です。

A: そうですか。ここからうちまで {何で／どうやって} 帰りますか。(← How?)

B: たいてい自転車で帰ります。

A: 自転車で {どのくらい／どのぐらい} かかりますか。(← How long?)

B: そうですね。15分 {くらい／ぐらい} かかります。

A: そうですか。○○さんのうちはどんなうちですか。(← Follow-up question)

B: とても小さいアパートです。

1）ここ (here) → うち　　2）この町 → 出身の町／国 (country)　　3）好きな○○

4 Suppose you are in Tokyo now and have decided to go to another city to see more of Japan.

Step 1 | Decide on a destination. You can choose a city from the map or suggest any other Japanese cities that you know.

Ex. A: ○○さん、明日はどこに行きましょうか。

B: そうですね。大阪はどうですか。

A: 大阪はどんな町ですか。

B: にぎやかな町です。

それから、とてもおもしろいですよ。

A: いいですね。じゃ、大阪にしましょう。

Nara: old and pretty

Nagano: quiet but pretty

Yokohama: big and fun

Ex. **Osaka**: lively and very interesting

Step 2 | Go on the internet to look up and compare different transportation methods you could use to get to the destination you've chosen and decide on the best way to get there.

Useful vocabulary　速い: fast　遅い: slow

Ex. A: 東京から大阪までどうやって行きましょうか。

B: えっと、新幹線 (bullet train) で行きませんか。

A: 新幹線でどのぐらいかかりますか。

B: 2時間30分ぐらいかかります。チケットは1万4千円ぐらいですよ。

A: そうですか。速いですが、ちょっと高いですね。

B: じゃ、バスで行きましょうか。<Continue>

Review

Now you can describe your favorite city and food in detail. Share your favorite city you have been to recently with your classmates!

タイ：Thailand　バンコク：Bangkok　マーケット：market

Lesson 4

| Favorite city? | **Ex.** | A: ○○さんの好きな町はどこですか。 |

Favorite city?

How did you get there?/How long did it take?

What kind of city is it?

What did you do there?

How was X?
(food, people, etc.)

More follow-up Qs!

Ex.

A: ○○さんの好きな町はどこですか。

B: タイのバンコクです。去年の夏休みに友達と行きました。

A: ここからタイまでどのぐらいかかりましたか。

B: 飛行機で12時間ぐらいかかりました。

A: バンコクはどんな町ですか。

B: にぎやかな町です。ちょっと暑かったですが、楽しかったです。

A: そうですか。バンコクで何をしましたか。

B: たくさんタイの食べ物を食べました。それから、マーケットで買い物しました。

A: そうですか。タイの食べ物はどうでしたか。

B: とてもおいしかったですよ。あまり高くなかったです。

<Continue>

できるⅠ-B　3

Ex.　C= Customer, S= Store attendant

C: すみません。

　それは何のパンですか。

S: {このパン／これ} ですか。

　フルーツ (fruits) のパンです。

C: ああ、そうですか。

Student B

②　⑤お茶

Ex. フルーツ (fruits)

④

①肉

⑥

③コーヒー

よみましょう

1 What kind of music do you like? In Japanese, many music genres are written in katakana.

Step 1 What are music genres ①-⑬ below called in your language?

Step 2 Match music genres ①④⑥⑦⑨⑩⑪⑬ with the corresponding pictures a.-h.

Step 3 Choose two music genres and talk about your favorite performers or groups from them.

Ex. 私の好きな音楽はJ-POPです。好きな歌手 (singer) は東京 RINGO です。

　　す　　おんがく　　　　　　　　　す　　かしゅ　　　　　とうきょう

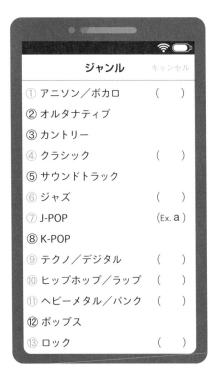

2 You are going to a Japanese *taiko* drumming performance by the Wadaiko Band. Look at the flyer below and answer the questions that follow in Japanese. Guess the meaning of the words you do not know.

1) 和太鼓バンドのライブは何曜日で

　わ だい こ　　　　　　　　なんようび

すか。どこでしますか。

2) 何時から何時までですか。何時間

　なんじ　　なんじ　　　　　　なんじかん

ですか。

3) 四人で (as a group of four) アリーナシー

ト で見ます。全部で (in total) いくら

　　み　　　ぜんぶ

ですか。

4) どうやってチケットを買いますか。

　　　　　　　　　　　　　　か

146

3 ゴーブル大学は先週から休みです。だから、マークさんは家族といっしょに日本に旅行しました。
Read his restaurant review and answer the questions that follow in Japanese.

> コンサートホール: concert hall　〜セット: 〜 combo　二人で: the two of us together　まっちゃ：green tea

日本語でグルメレポート by マーク

1　昨日は土曜日でした。ちょっと忙しかったですが、楽しかったです。家族といっしょに太鼓のコンサートに行きました。□□□、みんなで有名な日本のレストランに行きました。レストランの名前は「さくら」です。コンサートホールから

5　さくらまで歩いて15分ぐらいかかりました。
　　さくらで父はとんかつを食べました。母はそばが好きです。□□□、天ぷらそばセットにしました。私と弟は二人ですき焼きを一つ食べました。すき焼きは肉と野菜の料理です。ちょっと熱かったですが、とてもおいしかったです。デ

10　ザートも食べました。父と弟はまっちゃアイスクリームにしました。母と私はさくらもちにしました。さくらもちはたいてい手で食べます。□□□、母は箸で食べました。さくらもちはまあまあでした。
　　さくらは大きいレストランでした。そして、きれいでした。

15　ちょっと高かったですが、とてもおいしかったです。このレストランの私のおすすめは、すき焼きです！

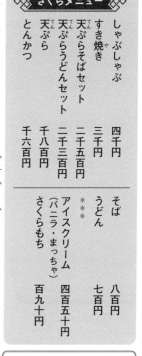

さくらメニュー

しゃぶしゃぶ	四千円
すき焼き	三千円
天ぷらそばうどんセット	二千五百円
天ぷら	二千三百円
とんかつ	千八百円
	千六百円

そば	八百円
うどん	七百円
アイスクリーム（バニラ・まっちゃ）	四百五十円
さくらもち	百九十円
***	

私のレビュー ★★★★☆
おすすめ→すき焼き！

1) Who ate what? Write the person who ate each item in ( ) under its picture.

すき焼き　　　　天ぷらそばセット　　　とんかつ　　　　さくらもち
(rice cake filled with sweet bean paste and wrapped in a cherry leaf)

(　　　　　)　　(　　　　　)　　(　　　　　)　　(　　　　　)

Understanding Japanese sentence structure: Adjective sentences

2) Including the example below, there are 10 adjectives (*I*-adj. and *Na*-adj.) conjugated in various ways in Mark's review. Underline the other nine. (If the same adjective appears multiple times, you should count it only once towards the total of nine.)

Ex. (l.1)　忙しかったですが、

3) Write the letter for the most appropriate conjunction from the box below into each ☐ in Mark's review to make it more cohesive.

> a. でも　　b. それから　　c. だから

4) **Step 1** Circle each topic marker は in Mark's review and underline the topic of the sentence.

Ex. 昨日(は)土曜日でした。
きのう

Step 2 Sentences a.-c. below from Mark's review do not have topics explicitly stated. Insert the missing topics in [　].

▶Check Point : In Japanese, it's common to omit information that has already been mentioned and/or can be easily understood without being explicitly stated.

Ex. (ll.2-3)　[　　私　　は] 家族といっしょに太鼓のコンサートに行きました。
かぞく　　　　　　たいこ　　　　　　　　　　　　い

a. (l.7)　[　　　　　は] 天ぷらそばセットにしました。
てん

b. (l.9)　[　　　　　は] ちょっと熱かったですが、とてもおいしかったです。
あつ

c. (l.15)　[　　　　　は] ちょっと高かったですが、とてもおいしかったです。
たか

5) Mark ◯ if the statement is true and ✕ if it is false.

（　　　）　マークさんは日曜日に日本のレストランに行きました。
にほん　　　　　　い

（　　　）　レストランは小さかったです。でも、きれいでした。

（　　　）　マークさんはこのレストランのすき焼きが好きです。
や　　　　す

6) Answer the questions below in Japanese.

a. コンサートホールからレストランまで、どのぐらいかかりましたか。

b. マークさんの家族のご飯は、全部で (in total) いくらでしたか。
かぞく　　はん　ぜんぶ

c. マークさんのお母さんは、さくらもちを何で食べましたか。
かあ　　　　　　　　　　なに　た

d. 「このレストラン」(ll.15-16) の名前は何ですか。
なまえ　なん

・・・

かくれんしゅう　*Writing Practice*

Write a review of a restaurant where you have eaten recently.

・・・

ききましょう

 リスニング・ストラテジー : Listening strategy

Listening to longer sentences and picking out necessary information
When conversing in a foreign language, it is important to be able to extract the essential information you need from what others are saying. In this lesson, we will practice picking out keywords and essential information from longer sentences while ignoring any unnecessary information.

Lesson 4

1 **Pre-listening activity:** Tao wants to go to a restaurant in town with inexpensive but tasty food. She's asking Mark if he has any recommendations.

1) What kind of adjectives do you think Tao needs to listen for? List them below. How do you say these words in Japanese?

 L4-18

2) Listen to Mark, keeping in mind the adjectives you listed above. Based on what you hear, which restaurant do you think Tao will go to?

Circle the restaurant you think Tao is likely to go to: わかば／しゃらく

 L4-19

2 **Listening:** You want to treat your roommate to a meal on his birthday (たんじょうび), so you asked three of your friends about their favorite restaurants. Take notes in the table below while listening to their answers, then decide on a restaurant to go to.

Your roommate has the following preferences:

1. Highly rated
2. Not too expensive
3. Likes meat & vegetables
4. Doesn't like fish

Name of the restaurant	ほし (stars)	Price	Food	Choice
1) ナマステ	☆ ☆ ☆ ☆ ☆	low / moderate / high	fish / meat / vegetable	
2) あやか	☆ ☆ ☆ ☆ ☆	low / moderate / high	fish / meat / vegetable	
3) ソウル	☆ ☆ ☆ ☆ ☆	low / moderate / high	fish / meat / vegetable	

 **Exit Check** ☑

Now it's time to go back to the DEKIRU List for this chapter (p.117) and do the exit check to see what new things you can do now that you've completed the lesson.

「ね」と「よ」

The sentence-final particle ね is used to ask for and to give agreement. Its function is similar to that of tag questions in English (e.g., "..., isn't it?," "..., is it?," etc.).

(1) A: このTシャツはかわいいですね。 <a step up in pitch: asking for agreement>
   This T-shirt is cute, isn't it?

   B: ええ、とてもかわいいですね。 <a step up in pitch: giving agreement>
   Yes, it's very cute.

ね is also used to ask for confirmation, but not to give confirmation.

(2) A: テストは明日ですね。 <rising intonation: asking for confirmation>
   The test is tomorrow, right?

   B: はい、そうです。 *Yes, that's right.*

The sentence-final particle よ is used when 1) the speaker believes that the listener does not have a piece of information that the speaker has, and 2) the speaker believes that the listener needs or should have that piece of information.

(3) A: 京都はどんな町ですか。 *What is the city of Kyoto like?*
   B: とても古い町です。それから、とてもきれいですよ。
   It's a very old city. It's also very beautiful.

In (3), B (the speaker) is giving A (the listener) information that B believes A doesn't have. Note that if you overuse よ, it can sound rude or aggressive, so try to use it in moderation. Note also that ね and よ are not used in written language except for informal correspondences (e.g., personal emails, texts, messages on social media, etc.). For this reason, you should avoid using these particles in compositions and academic papers.

DEKIRU List

できるCheck ✓

できる I

Describe who or what is in a place that you are familiar with.
身近な場所に何があるか、だれがいるかについて、話すことができる。

Entry ☐ Exit ☐

できる II

Describe in detail a place that the listener does not know well.
相手が知らない場所について、詳しく説明することができる。

Entry ☐ Exit ☐

できる III

Ask and answer questions about the locations of things and people.
物や人の位置について、尋ねたり答えたりすることができる。

Entry ☐ Exit ☐

できる IV

Ask and answer questions about possessions and events.
持っている物やイベントについて、尋ねたり答えたりすることができる。

Entry ☐ Exit ☐

STRATEGIES

Conversation Tips .... • Japanese interjections あ（あ）and え（っ）

Reading .... • Getting information from photos posted on a website
　　　　　　　　　　　 • Visualizing
　　　　　　　　　　　 • Clarifying

Listening .... • Predicting: Context clues

GRAMMAR

1 X (place) にYがあります・います [Existence] できるI

2 Location nouns できるI

3 XというY "Y called/named/titled X" できるII

4 〜から [Reason conjunction] できるII

5 Particle + も・は [Double particles] できるII

　5-1 Particle + も

　5-2 Particle + Contrast marker は

　5-3 Particle + Topic marker は

6 XはY (place) にあります・います
[Whereabouts] できるIII

7 ここ・そこ・あそこ・どこ
[Demonstrative pronouns of location] できるIII

8 XはYがあります・います [Possession] できるIV

9 X (place) でY (event) があります
[Event location] できるIV

かいわ

1 できる I,II Keita is visiting the Japan House and Ai is showing him around. 🔊 **L5-1**

桜の木（さくら き）: cherry tree　咲く（さ）く: to bloom　お花見（はなみ）: cherry blossom viewing

アイ　　　：けいたさん、この部屋（へや）はリビングです。

けいた　　：あ、リビングに大きい窓（まど）がありますね。

アイ　　　：ええ。この窓（まど）から桜（さくら）の木（き）が見（み）えますよ。

　　　　　　毎年四月（まいとし）に桜（さくら）が咲（さ）きますから、みんなで木（き）の下（した）でお花見（はなみ）をします。

けいた　　：そうですか。いいですね。

　　　　　　ジャパンハウスにはメンバーが何人（なんにん）いますか。

アイ　　　：えっと… 四人…

にゃんた　：ニャー

けいた　　：あ、テーブルの下（した）にネコがいますね。

アイ　　　：あ、あれは「にゃんた」というネコです。

　　　　　　ジャパンハウスにはメンバーが全部（ぜんぶ）で四人とネコが一（いっ）ぴきいます。

2 できる II,III Ai and Keita continue talking together in the living room. 🔊 **L5-2**

剣道（けんどう）: kendo [a fencing-like sport based on Japanese swordmanship]

けいた　　：あ、あそこにもネコがいますよ。

アイ　　　：え、どこですか。

けいた　　：桜（さくら）の木（き）の下（した）です。

アイ　　　：ああ、あれはにゃんたの友達（ともだち）です。「ミロ」というネコです。

けいた　　：そうですか。にゃんたは人気（にんき）がありますね。

　　　　　　あの、アイさん、来週（らいしゅう）の日曜日（にちようび）は忙（いそが）しいですか。

アイ　　　：日曜日ですか。午後（ごご）は忙（いそが）しくないです。

けいた　　：よかったら、剣道（けんどう）の試合（しあい）に来（き）ませんか。

アイ　　　：え、剣道（けんどう）の試合（しあい）？

けいた　　：ええ、ぼくは日曜日にポートセンターで剣道（けんどう）の試合（しあい）をします。

アイ　　　：え、本当（ほんとう）ですか。はい、行（い）きます！　あの、ポートセンターはどこにありますか。

けいた　　：美術館（びじゅつかん）のとなりにあります。ここから歩（ある）いて20分（ぷん）ぐらいですよ。

アイ　　　：そうですか。

けいた ：ポートセンターにはおいしいレストランや映画館もありますから、
　　　　楽しいですよ。これは剣道の試合のチケットです。どうぞ。

アイ 　：ありがとうございます。

 3 できる IV　After Keita has left, Mark and Ai are looking around for something.　 L5-3

探す：to look for

マーク ：ああ、いません。

アイ 　：ああ、ありません。

マーク ：え、ありません？

アイ 　：え、いません？　マークさん、何がいませんか。

マーク ：にゃんたです。アイさん、家の中ににゃんたがいませんよ。

アイ 　：えっ、本当ですか。

マーク ：ええ、リビングにもいません！　キッチンにもいません！

アイ 　：にゃんた！　どこ？

マーク ：あの、アイさんは何がありませんか。

アイ 　：剣道のチケットがありません。日曜日にポートセンターで
　　　　けいたさんの剣道の試合があります。

マーク ：アイさん、今、時間がありますか。
　　　　いっしょににゃんたとチケットを探しましょう。

アイ 　：ええ、そうしましょう。私のにゃんた！　私のチケット！

CONVERSATION TIPS　ワンポイント L5-4

Japanese interjections あ（あ）**and** え（っ）: Both of these are interjections that express the speaker's surprise. They differ in what the speaker's surprise is directed toward.

・あ（あ）: Used when the speaker is surprised by something they have discovered, realized, or remembered.

・え（っ）: Used when the speaker is surprised by or cannot believe something they have heard.

　A：ああ、財布 (wallet) がありません。

　B：え、財布？

　A：ええ、財布の中に十万円ありました。

　B：えっ、十万円！

　A：あ、すみません。かばんの下にありました！

たんご

● まいにちのせいかつ　Daily life

◎ しぜん (Nature)

| かわ (river) | き (tree) | やま (mountain) | とり (bird) | はな (flower) | [thing/person が] みえる (to be visible) | おと (sound) | こえ (voice) (singing/chirping) | [sound/voice が] きこえる (to be audible) |

◎ まち (Town)

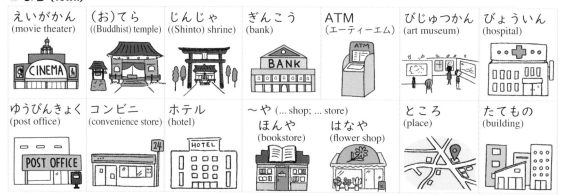

えいがかん (movie theater)　（お）てら ((Buddhist) temple)　じんじゃ ((Shinto) shrine)　ぎんこう (bank)　ATM (エーティーエム)　びじゅつかん (art museum)　びょういん (hospital)

ゆうびんきょく (post office)　コンビニ (convenience store)　ホテル (hotel)　～や (... shop; ... store)　ほんや (bookstore)　はなや (flower shop)　ところ (place)　たてもの (building)

◎ いえ／うち (House)

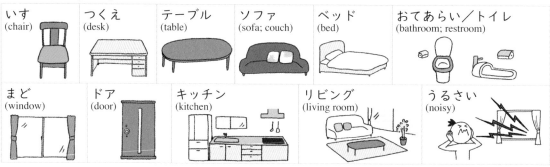

いす (chair)　つくえ (desk)　テーブル (table)　ソファ (sofa; couch)　ベッド (bed)　おてあらい／トイレ (bathroom; restroom)

まど (window)　ドア (door)　キッチン (kitchen)　リビング (living room)　うるさい (noisy)

◎ いち (Location words)

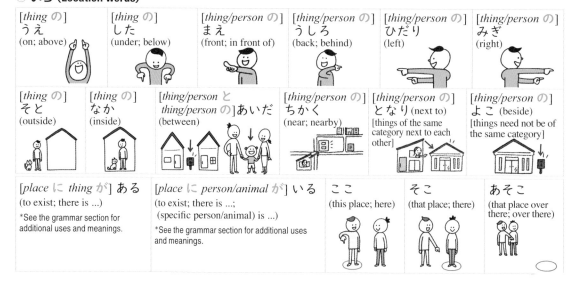

[thing の] うえ (on; above)　[thing の] した (under; below)　[thing/person の] まえ (front; in front of)　[thing/person の] うしろ (back; behind)　[thing/person の] ひだり (left)　[thing/person の] みぎ (right)

[thing の] そと (outside)　[thing の] なか (inside)　[thing/person と thing/person の] あいだ (between)　[thing/person の] ちかく (near; nearby)　[thing/person の] となり (next to) [things of the same category next to each other]　[thing/person の] よこ (beside) [things need not be of the same category]

[place に thing が] ある (to exist; there is ...) *See the grammar section for additional uses and meanings.　[place に person/animal が] いる (to exist; there is ...; (specific person/animal) is ...) *See the grammar section for additional uses and meanings.　ここ (this place; here)　そこ (that place; there)　あそこ (that place over there; over there)

● かつどうとイベント　Activities and events

[place を] かんこうする (to sightsee)	にんきがある (to be popular)	イベント (event)	しあい (game; match [competition])	たんじょうび (birthday)

● じかん　Time

じかん (time)	こんげつ (this month)	らいげつ (next month)	まいとし (every year)	〜ねん (the year ...)	Exs. 2030 ねん　にせんさんじゅうねん　　1995 ねん　せんきゅうひゃくきゅうじゅうごねん	なんねん (what year)

     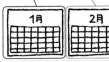

Lesson 5

◉ 〜にち (the ...th day of the month)

月	火	水	木	金	土	日
1 ついたち	2 ふつか	3 みっか	4 よっか	5 いつか	6 むいか	7 なのか
8 ようか	9 ここのか	10 とおか	11 じゅういちにち	12 じゅうににち	13 じゅうさんにち	14 じゅうよっか
15 じゅうごにち	16 じゅうろくにち	17 じゅうななにち／じゅうしちにち	18 じゅうはちにち	19 じゅうくにち	20 はつか	21 にじゅういちにち
22	23	24 にじゅうよっか	25	26	27 にじゅうななにち／にじゅうしちにち	28
29 にじゅうくにち	30 さんじゅうにち	31				? なんにち

● かぞえる　Counting

◉ 〜まい (Counter for flat objects)

1	いちまい	7	ななまい
2	にまい	8	はちまい
3	さんまい	9	きゅうまい
4	よんまい	10	じゅうまい
5	ごまい	11	じゅういちまい
6	ろくまい	?	なんまい

◉ 〜ひき (Counter for small animals/insects)

1	いっぴき	7	ななひき
2	にひき	8	はっぴき
3	さんびき	9	きゅうひき
4	よんひき	10	じ(ゅ)っぴき
5	ごひき	11	じゅういっぴき
6	ろっぴき	?	なんびき

◉ 〜かい (Counter for floors)

1	いっかい	7	ななかい
2	にかい	8	はっかい／はちかい
3	さんがい／さんかい	9	きゅうかい
4	よんかい	10	じ(ゅ)っかい
5	ごかい	B	ちか (basement)
6	ろっかい	?	なんかい

● そのほかのひょうげん Other expressions

ぜんぶ (all)	ぜんぶで (in total; in all)

よかったら
(if you like; if possible)

ざんねん（な）
(unfortunate; regrettable; disappointing)

ざんねんですね。
(That's too bad; It's disappointing.)

155

たんごリスト

🔊 L5-5

RU-VERBS

1	いる		to exist; there is ...; (specific person/animal) is ... [*place* に *person/animal* が]
			to be/stay (in a location) [*person/animal* は *place* に]
			to have [*person/animal* は *related person/ pet animal* が]
2	きこえる	聞こえる	to be audible [*sound/voice* が] **Ex.** おとがきこえます The sound is audible.
3	みえる	見える	to be visible [*thing/person* が] **Ex.** やまがみえます The mountain is visible.

U-VERB / U-VERB PHRASE

4	ある		to exist; there is ... [*place* に *thing* が]
			to be (in a location) [*thing* は *place* に]
			to have [*person* は *thing* が]
			there is ... [*place* で *event/activity* が]
5	にんきがある	人気がある	to be popular

SURU-VERB

6	かんこうする	観光する	to sightsee [*place* を]

I-ADJECTIVE

7	うるさい		noisy; (annoyingly) loud

NA-ADJECTIVE

8	ざんねん	残念	unfortunate; regrettable; disappointing

NOUNS

9	たんじょうび	誕生日	birthday
10	たてもの	建物	building
11	ちか	地下	basement; underground
12	おてあらい／ トイレ	お手洗い	bathroom; restroom; toilet
13	ところ	所	place

14	えいがかん	映画館	movie theater
15	てら／おてら	（お）寺	(Buddhist) temple
16	じんじゃ	神社	(Shinto) shrine
17	ぎんこう	銀行	bank
18	びじゅつかん	美術館	art museum
19	びょういん	病院	hospital
20	ゆうびんきょく	郵便局	post office
21	かわ	川	river
22	き	木	tree
23	やま	山	mountain
24	とり	鳥	bird
25	はな	花	flower
26	おと	音	sound
27	こえ	声	voice; singing/chirping (of a bird/insect)
28	いす		chair
29	つくえ	机	desk
30	まど	窓	window
31	しあい	試合	game; match [competition]
32	じかん	時間	time
33	ATM （エーティーエム）		ATM
34	コンビニ		convenience store
35	ホテル		hotel
36	キッチン		kitchen
37	リビング		living room
38	ソファ		sofa; couch
39	テーブル		table
40	ベッド		bed
41	ドア		door
42	イベント		event

LOCATION NOUNS

43	うえ	上	on; above; on top of* [*thing* の]
44	した	下	under; below* [*thing* の]
45	まえ	前	front; in front of* [*thing/person* の]
46	うしろ	後ろ	back; behind* [*thing/person* の]
47	ひだり	左	left [*thing/person* の]
48	みぎ	右	right [*thing/person* の]
49	そと	外	outside [*thing* の]
50	なか	中	inside [*thing* の]
51	あいだ	間	between* [*thing/person* と *thing/person* の]
52	ちかく	近く	near; nearby* [*thing/person* の]
53	となり		next to* [*thing/person* の] [Things described as next to each other must be of the same category: a person next to a person, a building next to a building, etc.]
54	よこ	横	beside* [*thing/person* の] [Things need not be of the same category.]

DEMONSTRATIVES

55	ここ		this place; here
56	そこ		that place; there
57	あそこ		that place over there; over there

ADVERBIAL NOUNS

58	こんげつ	今月	this month
59	らいげつ	来月	next month
60	まいとし	毎年	every year
61	ぜんぶ	全部	all

COUNTERS

62	～かい	～階	[counter for floors]
	いっかい	一階	first floor
	なんかい	何階	what floor

63	～ひき		[counter for small animals/insects]
	いっぴき	一ぴき	one (small animal)
	なんびき	何びき	how many (small animals)
64	～まい	～枚	[counter for flat objects]
	いちまい	一枚	one (flat object)
	なんまい	何枚	how many (flat objects)

SUFFIXES

65	～や	～屋	... shop; ... store
	ほんや	本屋	bookstore
	はなや	花屋	flower shop
66	～にち	～日	[the ...th day of the month]
	ついたち	一日	the first day of the month
	ふつか	二日	the second day
	みっか	三日	the third day
	よっか	四日	the fourth day
	いつか	五日	the fifth day
	むいか	六日	the sixth day
	なのか	七日	the seventh day
	ようか	八日	the eighth day
	ここのか	九日	the ninth day
	とおか	十日	the tenth day
	はつか	二十日	the twentieth day
	なんにち	何日	what day of the month
67	～ねん	～年	the year ...
	なんねん	何年	what year

OTHER WORDS AND PHRASES

| 68 | ぜんぶで | 全部で | in total; in all |
| 69 | よかったら | | if you like; if possible |

* To be accurate, うえ means "the space on top of [*thing*]," した "the space under [*thing*]," etc. as explained in the grammar section.

かんじ

▶ **The highlighted words** below are the vocabulary you will need to learn to read and write in kanji in this chapter.
▶ **＊Special reading:** A special reading is assigned to a kanji compound word as a whole; in this case, it is impossible to assign each kanji in the compound a particular part of the reading.

32 上 上 上	ジョウ	上手(な) ＊ to be good at じょうず
	うえ あ(がる) かみ	上 on; above; on top of　　上田さん Ueda-san [last name]　　上がる to go up; to rise うえ　　　　　　　　　　　　うえだ　　　　　　　　　　　　あ 川上さん Kawakami-san [last name] かわかみ
up; above	丨 上 上	

33 下 下 下	カ	地下 underground　　　地下鉄 subway ちか　　　　　　　　ちかてつ
	した くだ(さる) さ(がる)	下 under; below　　山下さん Yamashita-san [last name] した　　　　　　　　やました 下さる to give (me)　　下がる to go down　　下手(な) ＊ to be bad at くだ　　　　　　　　さ　　　　　　　　　へた
down; below	一 丅 下	

34 中 中 中	ジュウ チュウ	～中／～中 throughout; in the middle of (**Exs.** 一年中 all year round, じゅう　ちゅう　　　　　　　　　　　　　　　　　いちねんじゅう 日本中 throughout Japan, 勉強中 in the middle of studying) にほんじゅう　　　　　　　べんきょうちゅう
	なか	中国 China　　　中学生 middle school student　　中 inside ちゅうごく　　　　ちゅうがくせい　　　　　　　　　なか
middle; inside	丨 口 口 中	

35 外 外 外	ガイ	海外 overseas; abroad　　外国 foreign country かいがい　　　　　　　　がいこく 外国語 foreign language　　外国人 foreigner がいこくご　　　　　　　　がいこくじん
	そと	外 outside そと
outside	ノ ク タ タ 外 外	

36 右 右 右	ユウ	左右 left and right さゆう
	みぎ	右 right　　右足 right leg　　右手 right hand　　右側 right side みぎ　　　みぎあし　　　　　みぎて　　　　　　みぎがわ
right	ノ ナ ナ 右 右	

37 左 左 左	サ	左右 left and right さゆう
	ひだり	左 left　　左足 left leg　　左手 left hand　　左側 left side ひだり　　ひだりあし　　　ひだりて　　　　　ひだりがわ
left	一 ナ ナ 左 左	

38 山 山 山	サン ザン	富士山 Mt. Fuji　　火山 volcano ふじさん　　　　　かざん
	やま	山 mountain　　中山さん Nakayama-san [last name] やま　　　　　　なかやま 山川さん Yamakawa-san [last name]　　山下さん Yamashita-san [last name] やまかわ　　　　　　　　　　　　　　　やました
mountain	丨 山 山	

39 川 下	かわ／がわ	川 river かわ 　山川さん Yamakawa-san [last name] やまかわ
		川田／川田さん Kawada/Kawata-san [last name] かわだ　かわた
		天の川 the Milky Way あま　がわ 　小川さん Ogawa-san [last name] おがわ
river		ノ　ノ　川

40 寺 寺 寺	ジ	寺院 temple じいん 　東大寺 Todai-ji [a temple in Nara] とうだいじ
	てら／でら	寺／お寺 temple てら　てら 　清水寺 Kiyomizu-dera [a temple in Kyoto] きよみずでら
Buddhist temple		一　十　土　生　寺　寺

（Lesson 5）

41 何 何 何	なに／なん	何／何 what なに　なん 　何月 what month なんがつ 　何日 what date; how many days なんにち
		何曜日 what day of the week なんようび 　何時 what time なんじ 　何時間 how many hours なんじかん
		何人 how many people なんにん 　何年 what year なんねん 　何年生 what year in school なんねんせい
what		ノ　イ　イ　个　佢　佢　何

42 時 時 時	ジ	～時 ... o'clock (Exs. 一時 one o'clock, 四時 four o'clock, 何時 what time) じ　いちじ　よじ　なんじ
		時間 time じかん 　～時間 ... hours (Exs. 四時間 four hours, 何時間 how many hours) じかん　よじかん　なんじかん
	とき	子どもの時 in childhood こ　とき 　時計 * clock; watch とけい
time		丨　冂　日　日　旷　旷　旷　旷　時　時

43 間 間 間	カン／ゲン	時間 time じかん 　～時間 ... hours (Ex. 四時間 four hours) じかん　よじかん
		～日間 ... days (Ex. 三日間 three days) かかん　みっかかん 　～週間 ... weeks (Ex. 一週間 one week) しゅうかん　いっしゅうかん
		～年間 ... years (Ex. 一年間 one year) ねんかん　いちねんかん 　人間 human being にんげん
	あいだ／ま	間 between あいだ 　仲間 companion; friend なかま 　間違い mistake まちが
between		丨　冂　冋　冋　門　門　門　門　間　間　間

44 毎 毎 毎	マイ	毎年／毎年 every year まいとし　まいねん 　毎日 every day まいにち 　毎朝 every morning まいあさ
		毎晩 every night まいばん 　毎週 every week まいしゅう 　毎月 every month まいつき
every; each		一　仁　仁　夲　毎　毎

45 明 明 明	メイ	明日 * tomorrow あした 　説明する to explain せつめい 　発明する to invent はつめい 　文明 civilization ぶんめい
	あか（るい）／あ（ける）	明るい bright あか 　夜明け dawn よあ
bright		丨　冂　日　日　町　明　明　明

46 今 今 今	コン	今月 this month こんげつ 　今年 * this year ことし 　今週 this week こんしゅう
		今学期 this semester こんがっき 　今度 next time こんど 　今晩 tonight こんばん
	いま	今 now いま 　今日 * today きょう 　今朝 * this morning けさ
now		ノ　人　今　今

47	田 田	た だ	上田さん Ueda-san [last name] うえだ	川田／川田さん Kawada/Kawata-san [last name] かわだ　　かわた
			田中さん Tanaka-san [last name] たなか	寺田さん Terada-san [last name] てらだ
			山田さん Yamada-san [last name] やまだ	中田／中田さん Nakada/Nakata-san [last name] なかだ　　なかた
			本田さん Honda-san [last name] ほんだ	田舎 * countryside; rural area いなか
rice field			丨 冂 冂 田 田	

48	町 町	チョウ	町長 the mayor of a town ちょうちょう	
			〜町 the town of ... (Ex. 山川町 the town of Yamakawa) ちょう　　　　　やまかわちょう	
		まち	町 town まち　　田舎町 country town いなかまち　　港町 port city/town みなとまち	
town			丨 冂 冂 田 田 田丁 町	

49	花 花	カ	花粉症 hay fever; seasonal allergies かふんしょう	生花 fresh flower せいか
		はな ばな	花 flower はな　　花火 fireworks はなび	（お）花見 cherry-blossom viewing はなみ
			花屋 flower shop はなや	生け花 flower arrangement いばな
flower			一 花 艹 花 花 花 花	

● あたらしいよみかた　New readings

The following are new readings for kanji that you have already learned. Read each word aloud. (*Indicates words with special readings.)

1) 一日 * ついたち　2) 二日 * ふつか　3) 三日 みっか　4) 四日 よっか　5) 五日 いつか　6) 六日 むいか　7) 七日 なのか　8) 八日 ようか　9) 九日 ここのか
10) 十日 とおか　11) 二十日 * はつか　12) 一ぴき いっ　13) 十ぴき／十ぴき じゅっ　じっ　14) 木 き　15) 今年 * ことし　16) 毎年 まいとし

● れんしゅう　Practice

1 In Japan, seal stamps are widely used instead of signatures. There are many kinds of these stamps, as you can see on the right—most feature names written in kanji, but there are also stamps written in hiragana, katakana, or the Roman alphabet. While not generally used for official purposes, some stamps even include illustrations.

The stamps on the right feature some common Japanese last names in kanji. Can you read them?

2 A lot of cats have come to your house! First, write the readings for the underlined kanji in a.-e. Then, look at the picture below and choose the correct cat from 1)-6) for each description a.-e.

Ex. 家の外 いえ　　　6)

a. クッションの上　_____

b. 箱 (box) の中 はこ　_____

c. 箱 (box) の下 はこ　_____

d. 黒い (black) ネコの右 くろ　_____

e. グレーのネコの左　_____

3 Below is a passage Kawada-san has written about Sakura Park in her town. Read the passage aloud, then write the readings for the underlined words. Finally, answer the two questions at the end of the passage.

私の<u>町</u>に「さくら<u>公園</u>」という公園があります。さくら公園にはきれいな<u>花</u>がたくさ
<small>こうえん</small>　　　　　　<small>こうえん</small>　　　　　　　　　<small>こうえん</small>

んあります。<u>公園</u>の<u>近</u>くには<u>お寺</u>もあります。<u>毎日</u>この公園には人がたくさん<u>来</u>ます。
<small>こうえん　ちか</small>　　　　　　　　　　　<small>こうえん</small>　　　　　　　　<small>き</small>

日曜日は<u>朝</u><u>七時</u>から大きいフリーマーケットがあります。
<small>あさ</small>

とても<u>楽</u>しい<u>公園</u>です。<u>明日</u>はさくら公園で<u>花見</u>のイベントがあります。
<small>たの　　こうえん</small>　　　　　　　　　　　　<small>はな み</small>

私は<u>山川</u>さんといっしょに<u>桜</u>を<u>見</u>ます。イベントは<u>二時間</u>ぐらいです。
<small>さくら　み</small>

みなさんの<u>町</u>には公園がありますか。<u>公園</u>でよく<u>何</u>をしますか。
<small>こうえん</small>　　　　　　　<small>こうえん</small>

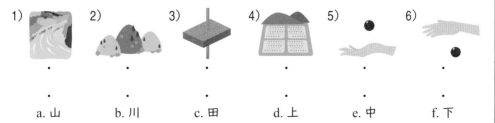

Lesson 5

かんじのはなし　The Story of Kanji

■ The origins of kanji

Pictographic kanji: Pictographs are characters based on the shapes of the physical objects they represent, as illustrated by the two examples below. Many pictographic kanji relate to nature. The people who first invented kanji lived closely connected to mountains and rivers. They created the first kanji by copying the shapes they saw in nature.

There are many kanji characters that combine two pictographic kanji, such as 明 (bright), a combination of 日 and 月.

Ideographic kanji: Ideographs, on the other hand, represent abstract ideas or concepts, as seen in the examples below. People initially used a combination of simple lines and dots to describe abstract concepts, and these evolved into some very basic kanji we still use today.

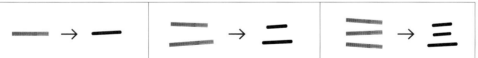

れんしゅう　Practice

Try matching each picture from 1)-6) below with the appropriate kanji from a.-f.

1)　2)　3)　4)　5)　6)

a. 山　　b. 川　　c. 田　　d. 上　　e. 中　　f. 下

In the practice above, 山, 川, and 田 are pictographic, while 上, 下, and 中 are ideographic.

ぶんぽう

1 **X (place) にYがあります・います [Existence]** "There is Y in/at X (place)."

[1-a]

X (place)		Y (subject)		
この建物 たてもの	に	いいレストラン	が	あります。
There is a good restaurant in this building.				

You can express the idea that there is something/someone somewhere using 〜があります・います. が here is a particle that marks the sentence's subject. あります is used for inanimate things, including plants, and います is used for humans and living things other than plants. In this sentence pattern, に is used to mark the place of existence.

Exs. (1) あ、公園に大きいイヌがいますよ。*Look! There's a large dog in the park.*
こうえん　おお

(2) 去年は図書館にカフェがありましたが、今はありません。
きょねん　としょかん　　　　　　　　　　　　いま
There was a café in the library last year, but it's gone (lit. there isn't) now.

[1-b]

	X (place)		Y (subject)		
A:	この美術館 びじゅつかん	に	何 なに	が	ありますか。
	What is in this art museum?				
B:	（この美術館 びじゅつかん	に）	ピカソの絵 え	が	あります。
	There {is a painting / are paintings} by Picasso (in this art museum).				

You can use this sentence pattern when you want to ask who or what is in a particular place.

Ex. (3) <Wang-san is talking on the phone to Smith-san, who is in his dorm room.>

ワン　：今、スミスさんの部屋にだれがいますか。*Who is in your room now?*
　　　　いま　　　　　　　　へや

スミス：山田さんと田中さんがいますよ。*Yamada-san and Tanaka-san are (here).*
　　　　やまだ　　たなか

Information about how many or how much of something there is comes after the subject marker が. (See L4 #2.)

Exs. (4) 公園に子どもがたくさんいます。（✕ 子どもたくさんがいます。）
こうえん　こ　　　　　　　　　　　　　こ
There are many children in the park.

(5) 山田さんの家にネコが12ひきいます。（✕ ネコ12ひきがいます。）
やまだ　　　いえ
There are twelve cats in Yamada-san's house.

2 Location nouns

[2]

X (reference point)		Y (location noun)
レストラン	の	前 まえ
(the space) in front of the restaurant		

In Japanese, relative locations — that is, locations expressed in terms of something or someone (e.g., in front of X, next to X, under X, etc.) — are expressed using the structure XのY, where Y is a location noun that represents a relative location in terms of X. There are many location nouns. Common location nouns include: 前 "the space in front of X," 後ろ "the space behind X," 上 "the space on top of/above X," 下 "the space under X," 間 "the space between X₁ and X₂," 横 "the space beside X," となり "the space next to X," and 近く "the space near X."

Exs. (1) テーブルの上 *(the space) {on top of / over} the table*

(2) 図書館のとなり *(the space) next to the library*

(3) 銀行とホテルの 間 *(the space) between the bank and the hotel*

Note that XのY is a noun phrase and can be used in the same way all other nouns are used, as in (4)-(6).

Exs. (4) 机 の上に田中さんの本があります。*On top of the desk is Tanaka-san's book.*

(5) 明日、図書館の前で会いませんか。*Would you like to meet in front of the library tomorrow?*

(6) 家の近くの公園にとても大きいイヌがいました。
There was a very large dog in the park near my house.

3 XというY "Y called/named/titled X"

[3]

X (name)		Y (generic noun)	
『となりのトトロ』	という	映画 えいが	を見ました。
I saw a movie called "My Neighbor Totoro."			

You can express the idea of "Y called/named/titled X" using という. In XというY, Y is always a generic noun and X is often the name of someone or something. Using this structure, you can specify a particular member of the group of people or things that Y refers to. You can use XというY when you assume that the listener doesn't know who or what X is.

Exs. (1) 私 の町に「さくら」というカフェがあります。*There's a café named Sakura in my town.*

(2) このすし屋に「ドラゴンロール」というすしがあります。とてもおいしいですよ。
There's a sushi roll called the Dragon Roll at this restaurant. It's really tasty.

(3) 昨日、山田さんという人に会いました。*I met a person named Yamada yesterday.*

4 ～から **[Reason conjunction]** "because; so"

[4]

S₁ (reason)		S₂
今日は忙しいです きょう　いそが	から、	パーティーに行きません。 い
Because I am busy today, I'm not going to the party. (= I am busy today, so I'm not going to the party.)		

You can express the reason that someone does something or something happens using から. "S₁から、S₂" is identical to "S₁。だから、S₂" in meaning.

In this sentence structure, a comma is commonly placed after から for readability.

Exs. (1) この映画はおもしろいですから、人気があります。 *This movie is interesting, so it is popular.*
えいが　　　　　　　　　　　　　にんき

(2) 勉強しませんでしたから、テストはよくなかったです。
べんきょう

I didn't study, so my test (grade) wasn't good.

(3) 今日は寒いですから、買い物に行きません。 *It is cold today, so I'm not going shopping.*
きょう　さむ　　　　　　　か　もの　い

⚠ Note that から is attached to the end of the reason sentence. The following sentence is nonsensical because the reason sentence and the result sentence are in the wrong positions.

× 買い物に行きませんから、今日は寒いです。 *lit. I'm not going shopping, so it is cold today.*
か　もの　い　　　　　　　　きょう　さむ

---

5 Particle + も・は **[Double particles]**

5-1 Particle + も

[5-a]

		Double particle	
去年、東京に行きました。 きょねん　とうきょう　い	それから、京都 きょうと	にも	行きました。 い
Last year I went to Tokyo, and I went to Kyoto, too.			

When you want to express similarity with a noun that already has a particle attached, the particle of similarity も is attached to the end of that "Noun + Particle" combination, resulting in a double particle, as in [5-a].

Exs. (1) お寺で写真をとりました。神社でもとりました。
てら　しゃしん　　　　　　じんじゃ

I took pictures at a temple. I took pictures at a shrine, too.

(2) 週末、友達と会いませんでした。家族とも会いませんでした。
しゅうまつ　ともだち　あ　　　　　　　かぞく　あ

I didn't see (lit. meet) my friends over the weekend. I didn't see (lit. meet) my family, either.

Remember that when you express similarity with a topic, subject or direct object, no double particle occurs because も replaces は, が, and を.

5-2 Particle + Contrast marker は

[5-b]

	Double particle			Double particle	
東京 とうきょう	に（は）	行きましたが、京都 い　　　　　　　　　きょうと		には	行きませんでした。 い
I went to Tokyo, but not to Kyoto.					

Double particles also occur when contrastive elements are marked by the contrast marker は. For example, in [5-b], 東京に and 京都に are contrasted using は, yielding double particles. Here, the first は is optional. Without は after 東京に, the first sentence carries no contrastive meaning.

Exs. (1) 私の町に（は）大きい映画館がありますが、となりの町にはありません。
わたし　まち　　　　　　おお　　えいがかん　　　　　　　　　　　　　　　　まち

There is a big movie theater in my city, but not in the neighboring city.

(2) 図書館で（は）勉強しますが、カフェではしません。
と しょかん　　　　べんきょう

I study at the library, but not at a café.

(3) 昨日、黒田先生と（は）話しました。でも、ブラウン先生とは話しませんでした。
きのう　くろだせんせい　　　　はな　　　　　　　　　　　　　せんせい　　　　はな

Yesterday I talked to Prof. Kuroda. However, I didn't talk to Prof. Brown.

Note that when the subject or the direct object is contrasted, a double particle does not occur because が and を are replaced by は.

5-3 Particle + Topic marker は

[5-c]

	New topic	Double particle	
私の出身はシカゴです。 わたし　しゅっしん	シカゴ	には	いいレストランがたくさんあります。
I'm from Chicago. There are many good restaurants in Chicago.			

When a location of existence is presented as the topic of the sentence, the topic marker は is attached to the location particle of existence に, as in [5-c], yielding a double particle. This often happens when the speaker picks up a noun from the preceding sentence and talks about it (i.e., presents it as the new topic). As another example, in (1) below, は is attached to で, which is the location particle of action.

Exs. (1) 去年、広島に行きました。広島では原爆ドームを見ました。
きょねん　ひろしま　い　　　　　ひろしま　　げんばく　　　　　み

I went to Hiroshima last year. There (lit. in Hiroshima), I saw the Atomic Bomb Dome.

(2) 田中 ：スミスさんの家の近くに「ルパン」という新しいパン屋がありますね。
たなか　　　　　　　　　　いえ　ちか　　　　　　　　　　　　　あたら　　　　　や

There is a new bakery named Lupin near your house, right?

スミス：ええ、ルパンにはとてもおいしいフランスパンがありますよ。

Yes, they sell very tasty baguettes there (lit. at Lupin).

Note that when the subject or the direct object is presented as the topic, the subject marker が and the direct object marker を are replaced by は, in which case no double particle occurs.

6 XはY (place) にあります・います [Whereabouts] "X is in/at Y."

[6-a]

X (topic / subject)		Y (place)		
セントラルパーク	は	ニューヨーク	に	あります。
Central Park is in New York.				

You can use あります・います to tell where someone or something is. In sentence pattern [6-a], the focus is on the location of the person or thing you are talking about. In other words, this sentence pattern is used when the existence or presence of X is already established and you want to say or ask where X is. The sentence pattern introduced in #1 (i.e., Placeに Xが あります・います), on the other hand, is used to say or ask who or what is in a particular place.

Exs. (1) リーマンさんは今、リビングに います。 *Riemann is in the living room now.*

(2) 私の兄は去年、東京に いましたが、今、大阪に います。
My elder brother was in Tokyo last year, but he's in Osaka now.

[6-b]

	X (topic / subject)		Y (place)		
A:	にゃんた	は	どこ	に	いますか。
	Where is Nyanta?				
B:	（にゃんた	は）	アイさんの部屋	に	います。
	He's in Ai's room.				

You can use sentence pattern [6-b] when you want to ask where someone or something is.

Ex. (3) <At a restaurant>

A: あの、すみません。トイレはどこに ありますか。
Uh, excuse me. Where is the restroom (located)?

B: 地下に ありますよ。 *It's in the basement.*

In the sentence pattern "Xは Placeに あります・います," if the context is clear, です may be used instead of にあります・います, as in (4).

Ex. (4) A: すみません。ATM はどこですか。（＝ ATM はどこに ありますか。）
Excuse me. Where can I find an ATM?

B: あの銀行の前です。（＝ あの銀行の前に あります。）*There's one in front of that bank.*

☞ **GID** (vol.1): H. Important sentence patterns 1. ある／いる sentences

☞ Language Note:「は」と「が」(pp.185-186)

7 ここ・そこ・あそこ・どこ [Demonstrative pronouns of location] "here; there; over there; where"

You can refer to a place close to the speaker by using ここ, a place close to the listener by using そこ, and a place distant from both the speaker and the listener by using あそこ (Fig. 1). When the speaker is standing close to the listener, そこ is used to refer to a place at a small distance from them, while あそこ is used to refer to a place farther away (Fig. 2).

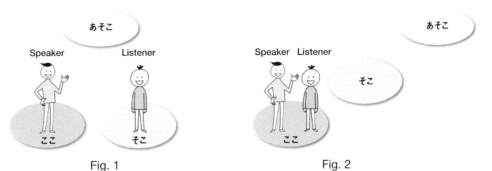

Fig. 1　　　　　　　　　　　Fig. 2

You can ask where someone or something is using どこ.

Exs. (1) アイ：にゃんたは<u>どこ</u>にいますか。*Where is Nyanta?*

タオ：<u>ここ</u>にいますよ。*He's here.*

(2) スミス　　：トイレは<u>どこ</u>にありますか。
Where is the restroom?

ウェイター：<u>あそこ</u>にあります。*It's over there.*

(3) スミス　　：ドリンクバーは<u>どこ</u>ですか。
Where is the drink bar?

ウェイター：<u>そこ</u>です。*It's there.*

8 XはYがあります・います [Possession] "X has Y."

[8]

X (possessor)		Y (possessed object)		
アイさん	は	かわいいネコ	が	います。
Ai has a cute cat.				

You can express the idea that someone has something or someone using 〜があります・います. In this case, you present the possessor with は and what is possessed with が.

Exs. (1) 私 はお金が全然ありません。でも、友達がたくさんいます。
　　　わたし　　かね　ぜんぜん　　　　　　　　　　ともだち
I don't have any money, but I have many friends.

(2) 私 は 車 が ありませんから、自転車で学校に行きます。
　　わたし　くるま　　　　　　　　　じてんしゃ　がっこう　い
I don't have a car, so I go to school by bicycle.

The possessor is omitted when it is understood from the context.

Ex. (3) 私は今週とても忙しいです。(私は)時間がありません。
       わたし　こんしゅう　　　　いそが　　　　　　　わたし　　じ かん
       I'm very busy this week. I have no time.

Number or amount information comes after Yが.

Exs. (4) ワン：田中さんはご兄弟が何人いますか。*How many siblings do you have, Tanaka-san?*
         　　た なか　　　　きょうだい　なんにん

         田中： 弟が二人います。*I have two little brothers.*
         た なか　おとうと　ふ た り

    (5) 私はネコが２ひきとイヌが１ぴきいます。*I have two cats and one dog.*
       わたし

---

9 **X (place) で Y (event) があります [Event location] "There is Y at X."**

[9]

	X (place)		Y (event)		
明日 あした	私の寮 わたし　りょう	で	パーティー	が	あります。
There is a party at my dorm tomorrow.						

You can also express the idea that there is an event somewhere using 〜があります. In this case, you use で to mark the location of the event instead of に, which is used for a location of existence.

Exs. (1) 来週、私の町でコンサートがあります。*There's a concert in my town next week.*
       らいしゅう　わたし　まち

    (2) A: 明日サッカーの試合があります。いっしょに行きませんか。
          あした　　　　　　し あい　　　　　　　　　　　　　い
         There is a soccer game tomorrow. Would you like to go together?

         B: 試合はどこでありますか。*(As for the game) where is it?*
          し あい

         A: となりの町であります。*It's in the neighboring city.*
          　　　　まち

    (3) 去年、私の学校で日本のアニメのイベントがありましたが、今年はありません。
       きょねん　わたし　がっこう　に ほん　　　　　　　　　　　　　　　　　　ことし
       There was a Japanese anime event at my school last year, but there isn't one this year.

☞ **GID** (vol.1): B. Particles 1-5. で

Activities

はなしましょう

できる I Describe who or what is in a place that you are familiar with.

できる I-A Existence　X (Place) に Y があります・います

1 Which should you use for each of the nouns below, あります or います?　 L5-6

Ex. 学生 → います

1) 山
やま
2) 鳥
とり
3) 神社
じんじゃ
4) 子ども
5) 花
はな
6) 魚
さかな

7) 焼き魚 (grilled fish)
や　ざかな
8) ゾンビ (zombie)
9) トイレ

2 What type of things and people are there in your city, university, and room?

Step 1 Describe what the city, university, and room below have.　L5-7

Ex. <u>私の町</u>に<u>きれいな公園</u>が<u>あります</u>。
まち　　　　　　こうえん

Ex. きれいな公園
こうえん
1) 大きい病院
びょういん
2) 有名なホテル
ゆうめい

私の町
まち

3) 大きい図書館
としょかん
4) おいしいカフェ
5) 留学生
りゅうがくせい

私の大学
だいがく

6) かっこいいソファ
7) おおきい窓
まど
8) かわいいネコ

私の部屋
へや

Step 2 Describe your actual city, university, and room using the cues from Step 1.

Ex. 私の町にきれいな公園があります。 or 私の町にきれいな公園がありません。
まち　　　　　こうえん　　　　　　　　　　　まち　　　　　こうえん

3 What can be found in a city? Let's practice describing some cities, including what they have in them.

Step 1 Describe characteristics of cities in Japan with your partner based on the cues provided.

Ex. A: ○○さんの好きな町はどこですか。
す　まち

B: 仙台です。
せんだい

A: そうですか。あのう、仙台に何がありますか。
せんだい　なに

B: 自然がたくさんあります。いい所ですよ。
しぜん　　　　　　　　　　ところ

1) Nagano
2) Kyoto
Ex. Sendai
3) Osaka

City name	What exists there	What it is like
Ex. Sendai	a lot of nature（自然）しぜん	nice
1) Nagano	a lot of high mountains, big rivers, etc.	pretty
2) Kyoto	a lot of old temples, shrines, etc.	interesting
3) Osaka	a lot of delicious food / a lot of funny people	fun

Step 2 Talk about a city you like (any city in the world) using the dialogue in Step 1 as a model.

169

1 Getting your body involved can help you master the Japanese location words. Listen carefully to the location words your instructor says and make an appropriate gesture to indicate each one.

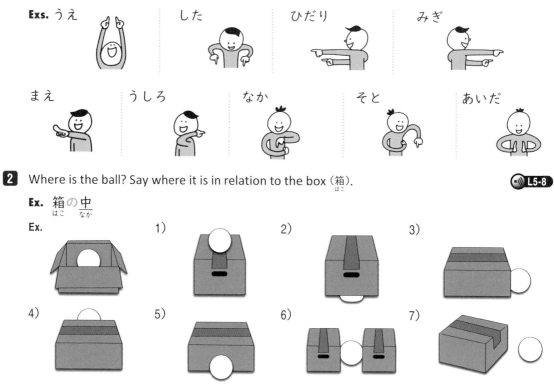

2 Where is the ball? Say where it is in relation to the box（箱）. 🔊 **L5-8**

Ex. 箱 の 中
はこ　　なか

Ex.　　　1)　　　2)　　　3)

4)　　　5)　　　6)　　　7)

3 You are going to meet up with your friends. Let's practice using location nouns to talk about meeting places.

Step 1 Make a noun phrase for each location provided in the cues below. 🔊 **L5-9**

Ex. 映画館の前
えいがかん　まえ

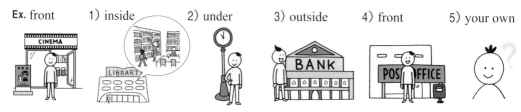

Ex. front　1) inside　2) under　3) outside　4) front　5) your own

Step 2 Suppose you would like to get together with your partner this weekend to do something fun. Invite your partner to an activity of your choice, and then decide where to meet.

Ex. A: ○○さん、金曜日にいっしょに映画を見ませんか。
えいが　み

B: いいですね。見ましょう。どこで会いましょうか。
み　　　　　あ

A: 映画館の前はどうですか。
えいがかん　まえ

B: 映画館の前ですね。分かりました。
えいがかん　まえ　　　わ

4 Ask each other what is in each location in the picture below. L5-10

Ex. 窓の外／ある
まど そと

A: 窓の外に何がありますか。
まど そと なに

B: 大きい木がたくさんあります。
き

1) テーブルの上／ある
うえ

2) 冷蔵庫 (refrigerator) の上／いる
れいぞうこ うえ

3) いすの上／ある
うえ

4) いすの下／ある
した

5) テーブルの下／いる
した

6) 窓の横／ある
まど よこ

Lesson
5

5 Show a picture you have taken or drawn of your room to your partner and describe three things in it.

かべ: wall　ポスター: poster

Ex. A: これは私の部屋です。
へや

① かべにゲームのポスターがあります。私は毎日このゲームをします。
まいにち

② それから、机の上に写真がたくさんあります。私の家族や友達の写真です。
つくえ うえ しゃしん かぞく ともだち しゃしん

③ そして、ベッドの上にネコがいます。私のペットです。
うえ

B: いい部屋ですね。私もこのゲームをします。どのキャラクターが好きですか。
へや す

(↑ Comment & Follow-up question)

Describe in detail a place that the listener does not know well.

できるⅡ-A　XというY

1 Let's practice describing things by their names.

Step 1 First, identify the things and places below with their names and general categories.

Ex. 「ひのくにや」という本屋 L5-11
ほんや

Ex. on campus

1) near university

2) in front of the library

3) next to my school

おとがわ

4) near my house

なかだけ

5) in my city

Step 2 Next, describe where each of the places and things in Step 1 exists. L5-12

Ex. 大学のキャンパスに「ひのくにや」という本屋があります。
ほんや

2 Do you have any favorite places nearby that your classmates may not know about? Talk about them in detail.

> **Possible topics**　〇〇屋
> や
> 　　レストラン　　山　　川　　公園　　スーパー (supermarket)
> 　　　　　　　　　　　　やま　　かわ　　こうえん

Ex.　A: 私の家の近くに「ルパン」というパン屋があります。
　　　　　　いえ　ちか　　　　　　　　　　　　　　や
　　　　このパン屋はおすすめです。
　　　　　　　　や
　　　　B: そうですか。どんなパンをよく買いますか。(← Follow-up question)
　　　　　　　　　　　　　　　　　　　か
　　　　<Continue>

できるⅡ-B　Reason 〜から

1 Match each reason in the left column with the corresponding consequence in the right column, then connect them with から to form one complete sentence.　🔊 **L5-13**

Ex. 私はピザが好きですから、よく食べます。
　　　　　　　す　　　　　　　　た

Ex. 私はピザが好きです。 　　　　　　　す	・ 人気があります。 　　　　にんき
1) にゃんたはかわいいです。	・ よく食べます。 　　　た
2) 今月はアルバイトをたくさんしました。 　　こんげつ	・ うるさかったです。
3) 昨日ルームメートがパーティーをしました。 　きのう	・ 忙しかったです。 　　いそが
4) 私の部屋の前に大きい木があります。 　　　へや　まえ　　　　き	・ 来年も行きます。 　　らいねん　い
5) ハワイ (Hawaii) の旅行は楽しかったです。 　　　　　　　りょこう　たの	・ よく鳥の声が聞こえます。 　　　　とり　こえ　き

2 Add a reason to the following sentences in order to provide more details.

Ex. よく勉強します → 私は日本語が好きですから、よく勉強します。
　　　　べんきょう　　　　にほんご　　す　　　　　　　べんきょう
1) 〇〇は人気があります　　　　2) 〇〇が好きです
　　　　にんき　　　　　　　　　　　　　　す
3)「〇〇」という {レストラン／カフェ etc.} によく行きます
　　　　　　　　　　　　　　　　　　　　　　　　い
4) 残念です or 残念でした　　　　5) 楽しかったです　　　　6) your own
　　ざんねん　　ざんねん　　　　　　　たの

3 Recommend something you like to your partner and give the reason(s) you like it. Choose from the topics below and describe your recommendation in detail.

> **Possible topics**　映画　　ゲーム　　アニメ　　本　　人　　バンド (band)
> 　　　　　　　　　　えいが　　　　　　　　　　　　ほん

Ex.　A:『七人の侍』という映画はおもしろいですから、おすすめです。
　　　　　しちにん　さむらい　　えいが
　　　　B:『七人の侍』ですか。どんな映画ですか。(← Follow-up question)
　　　　　しちにん　さむらい　　　　　えいが
　　　　A: 日本の映画です。古いですが、いい映画ですよ。<Continue>
　　　　　にほん　えいが　　　ふる　　　　　　えいが

1　Suppose you traveled in Japan recently. Describe some activities you did and did not do in Japan.

Step 1　Talk about what you **did** in Japan.

●))L5-14

Ex. 写真をとる／○ お寺　○ 神社

→ お寺で写真をとりました。それから、神社でもとりました。

1) 食べる／○ すし　○ ラーメン

2) 行く／○ 秋葉原　○ 渋谷

3) 買い物する／○ 秋葉原　○ 渋谷　　4) 日本語で話す／○ 友達　○ 町の人

Step 2　Talk about what you **did not do** in Japan.

Ex. 行く／× 山　× 海

→ 山に行きませんでした。それから、海にも行きませんでした。

1) 見る／× すもう　× サッカーの試合　　2) 泳ぐ／× 海　× プール

3) 乗る／× 自転車　× タクシー　　　　　4) 会う／× 田中さん　× 山田さん

Step 3　Talk about what you **did** and what you **did not do** in Japan.

Ex. コーヒーを飲む／○ ホテルのカフェ　× 美術館のカフェ

→ ホテルのカフェで（は）コーヒーを飲みました。でも、美術館のカフェでは

飲みませんでした。

1) 飲む／○ 日本のお茶　× 日本のビール　　2) 観光する／○ 東京と大阪　× 京都

3) 行く／○ お寺　× 神社　　　　　　　　4) 電話で話す／○ 家族　× 友達

5) Ｔシャツを買う／○ 秋葉原　× 渋谷　　6) 写真をとる／○ お寺の前　× お寺の中

2　Talk with your partner about a memorable trip each of you has taken.

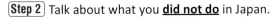

| Useful vocabulary | 行く | 食べる | 飲む | 乗る | 観光する |

Ex. A: 私は去年、韓国に行きました。

B: へえ、韓国ですか。どこに行きましたか。

A: プサン (Busan) に行きました。

でも、ソウル (Seoul) には行きませんでした。

B: そうですか。プサンでは何をしましたか。

A: えっと、屋台 (food stand) でおいしい魚を食べました。

それから、「ムン」という有名なレストランでも魚を食べました。＜Continue＞

173

3 Let's talk about places in detail.

Step 1 Suppose you work for the tourist bureau of your city. Describe what is in the following places and what people do there to appeal to Japanese tourists.

Ex.1 私の町に「トビー」というレストランがあります。トビーにはおいしいピザがたくさんあります。

Ex.2 私の町に「トビー」というレストランがあります。トビーではみんなおいしいピザを食べます。

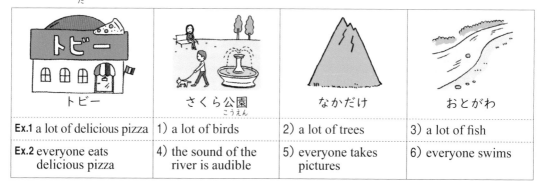

トビー	さくら公園	なかだけ	おとがわ
Ex.1 a lot of delicious pizza	1) a lot of birds	2) a lot of trees	3) a lot of fish
Ex.2 everyone eats delicious pizza	4) the sound of the river is audible	5) everyone takes pictures	6) everyone swims

Step 2 Talk about a place you would recommend using the sentence patterns from Step 1.

Group Work

4 Suppose your group represents a development company and you are making a presentation about a high-rise condominium for a competition. Which group will win by designing the most creative condo?

マンション：condominium　宇宙：space

Opening • name	**Ex.** これは「ベンリー」というマンションです。このマンションには有名なレストランがたくさんあります。だから、みんな家ではご飯を食べません。
Features • details • reason(s)	それから、建物の中には学校もあります。学校には学生がいますが、先生はいません。ロボットがたくさんいますから、学生はロボットといっしょに勉強します。マンションの上にはロケットがあります。ときどき、ロケットで宇宙を観光します。
Closing	とても楽しいマンションです。

できる III Ask and answer questions about the locations of things and people.

できる III-A　Whereabouts　XはY (Place) にあります・います

1　How much do you know about the world? Describe where each of the following is located or found.　●L5-15

Ex.1 <u>自由の女神</u>は<u>ニューヨーク</u>にあります。
じ ゆう　め がみ

Ex.2 <u>パンダ</u>は<u>中国</u>にたくさんいます。
ちゅうごく

Ex.1 自由の女神　　Ex.2 パンダ　　1) ビッグベン　　2) 富士山　　3) カンガルー
じ ゆう　め がみ　　　　　　　　　　　　　　　　　　　　ふ じ さん

4) ピラミッド　　5) キーウィ　　6) ライオン　　7) マーライオン　　8) your own

2　You are currently at a large commercial complex. Ask the information desk attendant where things are based on the cues provided.　●L5-16

Ex. A: すみません、ホテルはどこにありますか。

　　B: ホテルは７階と８階にあります。
　　　　　　　かい　　かい

　　A: ７階と８階ですね。
　　　　かい　　かい
　　　ありがとうございます。

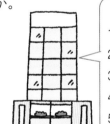

Ex. ホテル：7-8F
1) 映画館：5-6F
　えい が かん
2) レストラン：4F
3) 本屋：3F
　ほん や
4) トイレ：2F
5) ATM：1F
6) ケーキ屋：地下
　　　　や　　ち か

3　Talk about your hometown in detail.

Ex. A: ○○さんの出身はどこですか。
しゅっしん

not well-known city	well-known city
B: タイの「ラノーン」という町です。 まち	B: ニューヨークです。
A: へえ、ラノーンはどこにありますか。	
B: ミャンマーの近くにあります。 ちか	
A: ラノーンには何がありますか。 なに	A: ニューヨークには何がありますか。 なに
B: えっと、大きい公園があります。それ から、温泉 (hot springs) もありますから、 おんせん 楽しいですよ。 たの	B: 高い建物がたくさんあります。それから、 たか　たてもの 有名な美術館もありますから、おもしろ ゆうめい　び じゅつかん いですよ。
<Continue>	<Continue>

1 You have just arrived in Japan to study abroad, and the coordinator of your program is showing you around your dorm. Ask her where the following rooms are.

L5-17

Ex. A: <u>私の部屋</u>はどこですか。
　　　　　 へ や

　　 B: <u>ここ</u>です。

2 Ai is looking for the missing items below. Help her find them.

Ex. めがね (glasses)

アイ　　：あれ？　私のめがねがありません。

マーク：（アイさんのめがねは）そこにありますよ。(← demonstrative pronoun)

アイ　　：え、どこですか。

マーク：アイさんの頭 (head) の上にあります。(← location)
　　　　　　　　 あたま　　 うえ

　　　　　or アイさんの頭の上です。
　　　　　　　　　　　　 あたま うえ

アイ　　：ありがとうございます。

1) 時計
　 と けい
2) にゃんた
3) 映画のチケット
　 えい が
4) T シャツ
5) ペン

はこ (box)

3 Let's practice how to show people around a city.

Role A You are a member of a Japanese student group visiting your partner's city. Ask questions about where things are and talk about what you see.

Role B You work at your city's international affairs office. A group of university students from Japan is visiting your city. Show them around and answer their questions.

Ex. A: あのう、この近くに何がありますか。

B: 大きい郵便局や新しい美術館がありますよ。

A: へえ、そうですか。郵便局はどこにありますか。

B: ここです。

A: あ、郵便局の上にきれいな鳥がいますね。

B: そうですね。

Lesson 5

 Ask and answer questions about possessions and events.

できるIV-A **Possession X は Y があります・います**

1 Let's practice talking about what people have.

Step 1 Talk about what Aminah has based on the cues provided below. 🔊 L5-18

Ex. アミーナさんは 弟さん がいます。

アミーナ

Ex. ○ younger brother   1) ○ cat   2) ○ nice bicycle   3) ○ new watch
4) ✕ younger sister   5) ✕ dog   6) ✕ TV

Step 2 Talk about what Rich-san and Yamada-san have based on the cues below, making sure to include the quantity as provided. 🔊 L5-19

Ex.1 リッチさんはお金がたくさんあります。

Ex.2 山田さんは 弟さんが一人います。

リッチ

Ex.1 a lot of money   1) a lot of big houses   2) a lot of new cars

山田

Ex.2 one younger brother   3) two older sisters   4) three cats
5) two movie tickets   6) ten T-shirts
7) one younger brother and two older sisters

2 Talk about the members of your family with your partner. (You may talk about a famous family if you prefer.) Feel free to mention pets, as well.

Ex. A: ○○さんはご兄弟がいますか。
きょうだい

B: はい、弟が一人と妹が一人います。
おとうと　　　いもうと

A: そうですか。弟さんは学生ですか。(← Follow-up question)
おとうと

<Continue>

3 Talk with your partner about your life at university.

Step 1 First, mark ○ for each of the following that you have right now and × for each that you don't.

(　　)宿題　(　　)友達　(　　)時間　(　　)趣味　(　　)お金　(　　)クラス
しゅくだい　　ともだち　　じかん　　しゅみ

Step 2 Next, ask each other how life at university is. Answer the question using your answers from Step 1 as reasons.

Ex. A: 大学の生活 (life) はどうですか。
せいかつ

B: 毎日宿題がたくさんありますから、大変です。
まいにちしゅくだい　　　　　　　　　　たいへん

でも、友達がいますから、楽しいです。○○さんは？
ともだち　　　　　　　たの

A: 私は… <Continue>

できるIV-B **X (place) で Y (event) があります**

1 Let's practice saying dates and years in Japanese.

Step 1 Ask the dates of the following Japanese holidays and festivals.

Ex. 山の日 (Mountain Day)　8/11
やま　ひ

A: 山の日は何月何日ですか。
やま　ひ　なんがつなんにち

B: 8月11日です。

1) 元日 (New Years Day)　1/1　　2) 昭和の日 (Showa Day)　4/29　　3) 子どもの日 (Children's Day)　5/5
がんじつ　　　　　　　　　　　　　しょうわ　ひ　　　　　　　　　　　　　　　ひ

4) 七夕 (Star Festival)　7/7　　5) 文化の日 (Culture Day)　11/3
たなばた　　　　　　　　　　　ぶんか　ひ

Step 2 Ask what year the following companies were founded in.

Ex. アップル　1976

A: アップルは何年からありますか。
なんねん

B: 1976年からあります。

1) レゴ 1932　　2) コカ・コーラ 1892　　3) YouTube 2005　　4) 任天堂 1889
にんてんどう

2 (Information gap) Ask for the birthday or date of first release for each of the following famous characters using the word 誕生日.

Ex. ミッキーマウス　1928.11.18

A: ミッキーマウスの誕生日はいつですか。

B: 1928年11月18日です。

Student A

1) ハリー・ポッター _____	2) ピカチュウ _____	3) ゴジラ _____
4) スーパーマリオ 1985.9.13	5) スーパーマン 1938.4.18	6) シャーロック・ホームズ 1892.10.14

Student B ➡p.180

Lesson
5

Group Work

3 Make a group of five. Ask your groupmates' birthdays using 「誕生日は何月何日ですか。」and line up in order from the earliest birthday in January to the latest in December. Which team can form their line the fastest?

4 You have a two-week break next month. You've searched for events around you during the break and picked out some interesting ones.

Step 1 Describe the events you found.　　🔊L5-20

Ex. <u>2日</u>に<u>美術館の2階</u>で<u>コンサート</u>があります。

秋祭り: Autumn Festival

10月　イベントカレンダー

日	月	火	水	木	金	土
1	2 Ex. コンサート @ 美術館の2F	3	4 剣道の試合 @ ポートセンター の3F	5	6 秋祭り @ 公園	7
8	9 ゲームのイベント @ ホテルの地下	10 your own	11	12	13	14

Step 2 Decide which of the above events you want to go to and invite your partner to come with you.

Ex. A: あのう、来月の2日に時間がありますか。

B: はい、あります。

A: じゃ、いっしょにコンサートに行きませんか。

B: いいですね。えっと、コンサートはどこでありますか。

A: 美術館の2階であります。

B: そうですか。じゃ、2日に美術館の前で会いましょう。

5 Make a short presentation about an event at your university or in a city of your choice.

Place
• location

Event
• what/when/where
• additional
  information

Ex. 私の好きな町は日本の「函館」という町です。
　　　函館は北海道にあります。
　　　毎年８月１日に海の近くで「港祭り」という祭り (festival)
　　　があります。楽しいですから、毎年みんな港祭りに
　　　行きます。

Review

Now you can ask and answer questions about an activity's venue and its location. Imagine you have two tickets for an event. Invite your partner to come with you and answer their questions about the event.

落語: traditional Japanese comedic storytelling

Ask if your partner is available

Invite

Talk about details:
• venue
• location
• other activities

Ex. A: ○○さん、来週の土曜日に時間がありますか。

B: はい、あります。

A: そうですか。あの、私は落語のチケットが２枚あ
　　ります。よかったら、いっしょに行きませんか。

B: え、落語ですか。いいですね。どこでありますか。

A:「ポートセンター」という所であります。

B: そうですか。ポートセンターはどこにありますか。

A: 美術館のとなりにありますよ。

B: そうですか。

A: ポートセンターの中にはレストランもありますから、
　　いっしょに昼ご飯を食べませんか。

B: ええ、そうしましょう。じゃ、土曜日に。

できるⅣ-B **2**

Ex. ミッキーマウス　1928.11.18

A: ミッキーマウスの誕生日はいつですか。

B: 1928年11月18日です。

Student B

| 1) ハリー・ポッター 1980.7.31 | 2) ピカチュウ 1996.2.27 | 3) ゴジラ 1954.11.3 |
| 4) スーパーマリオ _____ | 5) スーパーマン _____ | 6) シャーロック・ホームズ _____ |

よみましょう

Getting information from photos posted on a website

1 The following is a tourist information web page for the city of Kamakura in Japan.

鎌倉は古い町です。お寺や神社がたくさんあります。東京から鎌倉まで、電車や
バスで一時間ぐらいです。人気がありますから、観光客 (tourist) がたくさんいます。

1) ( )

2) ( )

写真提供：鶴岡八幡宮

3) ( )

4) ( )

写真提供：鎌倉 長谷寺

写真提供：鎌倉市観光協会

a. **長谷寺**（はせでら）

このお寺には、あじさいという花がたくさんあります。とてもきれいなお寺です。

b. **小町通り**（こまちどおり）

小さいおみやげ (souvenir) 屋が250ぐらいあります。おいしい食べ物もたくさんあります。

c. **鎌倉の大仏**（かまくら　だいぶつ）

有名な仏像 (Buddha statue) です。外にあります。仏像は12メートルです。大きいです。

d. **鶴岡八幡宮**（つるがおかはちまんぐう）

とても大きい神社です。大きい石の階段 (stone stairs) が有名です。白いハト (white dove) が
たくさんいます。

Step 1 Match each of the photos 1)-4) with the appropriate name and caption from a.-d. above
and insert the corresponding letter into ( ).

Step 2 Answer the questions in Japanese based on the information above.

1) 鎌倉に何がありますか。　2) 東京から鎌倉までどのぐらいかかりますか。

3) 鶴岡八幡宮という神社には、何がたくさんいますか。

Are you interested in the Japan House and the people living there? Read the composition that Ai wrote about the Japan House for her Japanese class and answer the questions that follow.

シェアハウス: shared house　住んでいます: to live in　桜の木: cherry tree　だれも: nobody

1　私は去年の九月から「ジャパンハウス」(JH) というシェアハウスに住んでいます。今、JH には全部でメンバーが四人います。マークさんとタオさんとリーマンさんと私です。JH はちょっと古いですが、いい家です。JH の外に日本の桜の木があります。近くには小さい川もあります。四月にはリビングの窓からきれいな桜の花が見

5　えます。ときどきかわいい鳥の声も聞こえます。

　　JH にはベッドルームが五つあります。一階には、ベッドルームが二つとリビングとキッチンとバスルームがあります。リビングとバスルームの間にキッチンがあります。バスルームの中におふろとトイレがあります。リビングのとなりの部屋はマークさんの部屋です。バスルームの左の部屋にはだれもいません。

10　二階にはベッドルームが三つとトイレがあります。私の部屋は二階にあります。タオさんとリーマンさんの部屋も二階にあります。タオさんの部屋はリビングの上にあります。タオさんの部屋の右にリーマンさんの部屋があります。リーマンさんの部屋には漢字の本がたくさんあります。私の部屋にはよくにゃんたがいます。にゃんたはJHのペットのネコです。ベッドの下ににゃんたの小さいベッドがありますが、

15　にゃんたはたいてい私といっしょに寝ます。

　　リビングには大きいテーブルがありますから、よくみんなでリビングでいっしょにご飯を食べます。それから、JH ではときどき週末に「すし＆アニメナイト」というイベントがあります。友達やクラスメートがたくさん来ます。そして、日本語で話します。とても楽しいイベントです。

20　JH から大学まで歩いて二十分ぐらいかかりますから、みんなバスや自転車で大学に行きます。バス停まで歩いて三分です。

　　JH はとても楽しい所です。私は JH が大好きです。

Visualizing

1）Insert the letters a.-g. into the appropriate blue boxes in the drawing of the Japan House on the next page.

　a. アイの部屋　　　b. タオの部屋　　　c. リーマンの部屋　　　d. マークの部屋
　e. リビング　　　　f. トイレ　　　　　g. だれもいない (unoccupied)

2）Add simple pictures of the following things or write in the numbers ①-⑤ corresponding to them in the appropriate locations in the drawing on the next page.

　①漢字の本　　②小さいベッド　　③大きいテーブル　　④にゃんた　　⑤小さい川

Clarifying

3） Insert ○ into (　) for each statement that accurately reflects the information about the Japan House.

a. (　　　) 新しい家です。
あたら　　いえ

b. (　　　) 窓から桜の木が見えます。
まど　さくら　　み

c. (　　　) 近くに鳥がいます。
ちか　　とり

d. (　　　) 近くに小さい山があります。
ちか

e. (　　　) トイレが三つあります。

f. (　　　) 近くにバス停があります。
ちか　　　てい

g. (　　　) JHから大学まで自転車で二十分ぐらいです。
じてんしゃ　にじゅっぷん

Comprehension check

4） Mark ○ if the statement is true and × if it is false.

(　　　) JHにはメンバーが五人いますから、部屋が五つあります。
へや

(　　　) JHのメンバーはあまりリビングにいません。

(　　　) にゃんたはよく小さいベッドで寝ます。
ね

(　　　) JHでは楽しいイベントがあります。
たの

(　　　) JHのメンバーはたいてい歩いて大学に行きます。
ある　　　　い

5） Would you like to live in the Japan House? Choose an option from {　} and write the reason for your choice in ____ to complete the sentence below.

_____から、{住みたいです／住みたくないです}。
　　　　　　　　　　　　　　　す　　　　　　　　　す
　　　　　　　　　　　　　(want to live)　　(don't want to live)

・・

かくれんしゅう　*Writing Practice*

Draw or take a picture of your room (or your dream room) and then describe it in Japanese.

・・

ききましょう

Predicting: Context clues

When speaking in our native language, we always predict what we are likely to hear in a given context. We also predict what will come next in the conversation. You can improve your listening skills if you use the same strategies when learning a foreign language.

1 **Pre-listening activity:** Suppose you are studying abroad in Japan and you have been looking on the internet for a room in a shared house. Today you have found a promising advertisement online and have decided to call to find out more information. Predict the words you think you would hear in such a phone conversation and write down as many as you can on a sheet of paper. You can write in either Japanese or your native language.

2 **Listening:** L5-21

1) Now, listen to the phone conversation between Sato-san, a person also interested in the shared house, and Tanaka-san, the owner of the house.

[Step 1] List all the words and phrases that you hear on a sheet of paper. You can write in either Japanese or your native language.

[Step 2] Compare your list from the Pre-listening activity with the list you made in Step 1 and circle the words that you find on both lists. The number of the words the two lists have in common indicates how successful you were in prediction. How did you do?

2) Listen to the conversation again to pick up more details so that you can understand the conversation better. Choose the most appropriate drawing for each question below.

a. What is the inside of the house like?

(1) 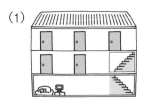   (2)    (3)

b. What are the surroundings of the house like?

(1)    (2)    (3)

Exit Check ☑

Now it's time to go back to the DEKIRU List for this chapter (p.151) and do the exit check to see what new things you can do now that you've completed the lesson.

「は」と「が」

The particles は and が are often found in similar positions within sentences. The two must be clearly distinguished, however, because their functions are fundamentally different.

"Xは" indicates that X is the topic of the sentence; i.e., X is what the rest of the sentence is about. "Xが," on the other hand, indicates that X is the subject of the sentence. (See Grammar in Depth (vol.2): E-1. は vs. が.)

Lesson
5

To see how は and が are used, let's first consider the pair of sentences in (1).

(1) a. リサは {私のルームメートです／毎日泳ぎます}。 *Lisa {is my roommate / swims every day}.*
　　　　　　　　　focus information

　　 b. リサが {私のルームメートです／毎日泳ぎます}。 *Lisa {is my roommate / swims every day}.*
　　　 focus information

Here, the objective of sentences with リサは like (1)-a is to tell the listener what Lisa is, does, etc. In other words, "what Lisa is, does, etc." is the information that the speaker most wants to convey to the listener. (Let's call this kind of information "focus information.") In (1)-a, "is my roommate" and "swims every day" are the focus information. On the other hand, the objective of sentences with リサが like (1)-b is to tell the listener who the speaker's roommate is, who swims every day, etc. In other words, the subject "Lisa" is the focus information. As seen in these sentences, when Xは is used, what comes afterward conveys the focus information, whereas when Xが is used, the focus information is conveyed by Xが itself.

It is important to know that in (1)-a, リサ is presented as the topic, but it is also the subject of the sentence. The reason that は is present but が is not in this sentence is that が cannot occur next to は (i.e., ×リサがは; ×リサはが). In other words, when the subject is presented as the topic, が is superseded by は.

Next, let's consider a sentence that involves a question word.

(2) 黒田先生の本はどれですか。 *Which one is Prof. Kuroda's book?*
　　　　　　　　　 Q-word　　　　 *(lit. Prof. Kuroda's book is which one?)*

(2) is a sentence about Prof. Kuroda's book, as 黒田先生の本 is marked by は. The structure of (2) is the same as that of 黒田先生の本はこれです (Prof. Kuroda's book is this one.), i.e., the structure "XはYです" that you learned in Lesson 1. In (2), the speaker wants to know the information in Y (in this case, "which one"), so the question word どれ is used in Y. Compare (2) with (3) below, which asks the same thing as (2) does.

(3) どれが黒田先生の本ですか。 *Which one is Prof. Kuroda's book?*
　　 Q-word

In (3), the question word どれ is marked by が. This is because an unknown thing cannot be the topic of a sentence.

Finally, let's consider two types of sentences involving あります／います. In (4) below, にゃんた is marked by は. Therefore, the topic of the sentence (i.e., what the sentence is about) is にゃんた, and the focus information is what follows にゃんたは (i.e., where Nyanta is).

(4) にゃんたは<u>テーブルの下にいます</u>。 *Nyanta is under the table*.
   した
   focus information

This type of sentence (i.e., [Person/Thing] は [Place] にあります／います) is called a "whereabouts sentence" (L5 #6).

On the other hand, the objective of (5) below is to tell the listener that "there is something (X) under the table." In other words, this sentence is not about X's whereabouts but about what is under the table. Thus, ネコ is not marked by は.

(5) テーブルの下にネコがいます。 *There is a cat under the table*.
   した

This type of sentence (i.e., [Place] に [Person/Thing] があります／います) is called an "existence sentence" (L5 #1).

As seen in (5), Xが is used not only when X is under focus, as in (1)-b, but also when X is not the topic. (See Grammar in Depth (vol.1) H. Important sentence patterns 1. ある／いる sentences.)

今みんなで探しています。
さが
We are all looking for him now.

Instructional Video
Lesson 6

DEKIRU List

できるCheck ☑

できる I
Talk about your daily life by connecting multiple actions.
日常生活で何をするか、したかについて、動作をつなげて話すことができる。

Entry ☐　Exit ☐

できる II
Ask and answer questions about what you are/were doing.
今していることや前にしていたことについて、尋ねたり答えたりすることができる。

Entry ☐　Exit ☐

できる III
Talk about a person's physical characteristics, occupation, place of residence, etc.
人物の身体的特徴、職業、住んでいる所などについて、話すことができる。

Entry ☐　Exit ☐

できる IV
Talk about what you have already done and what you have not done yet.
もうしたこと、まだしていないことについて、話すことができる。

Entry ☐　Exit ☐

できる V
Ask and answer questions about what you do on a regular basis and with what frequency.
習慣的にしていることとその頻度について、尋ねたり答えたりすることができる。

Entry ☐　Exit ☐

STRATEGIES

Conversation Tips .... • Usage of ちょっと

Reading .... • Getting information from signs
　　　　　　　　　　　　• Understanding Japanese sentence structure: XはYがZ
　　　　　　　　　　　　• Sorting information

Listening .... • Predicting: Visual clues

GRAMMAR

1 *Te*-forms of verbs 　できる I

2 ～てください [Polite command] 　できる I

3 V₁てV₂ [Actions in sequence] 　できる I

4 ～ています
　4-1 ～ています [Action in progress] 　できる II
　4-2 ～ています [Resultant state] 　できる III
　4-3 ～ています [Habitual action] 　できる III

5 XはYがZ [X's physical characteristics] 　できる III

6 もう "already" and まだ "(not) yet" 　できる IV

7 X (period of time) にY (number of times / duration)
　[Frequency / duration] 　できる V

かいわ

1 できる I,II Ai and Keita are talking on the phone after Keita has left the Japan House. 🔊 L6-1

心配です：I am worried.
しんぱい

けいた　：もしもし、アイさん？　けいたです。今日はありがとうございました。

アイ　　：あ、もしもし、けいたさん、大変です。にゃんたがいません。
　　　　　　　　　　　　　　　　　　　　たいへん

けいた　：え？　にゃんた？　ああ、ネコ？

アイ　　：ええ、今、探しています。とても心配です…
　　　　　　　　　さが　　　　　　　　　　しんぱい

けいた　：ぼくも今からジャパンハウスに行って、いっしょに探しますよ。
　　　　　　　　　　　　　　　　　　い　　　　　　　　　　さが

アイ　　：本当ですか。ありがとうございます。
　　　　　ほんとう

けいた　：ちょっと待っていてください。たぶん10分ぐらいかかります。
　　　　　　　　　　ま　　　　　　　　　　　　　ぶん

2 できる III,IV Keita has arrived at the Japan House. 🔊 L6-2

何か：something
なに

けいた　：アイさん、にゃんたの写真を見せてください。
　　　　　　　　　　　　　　しゃしん　み

アイ　　：これです。にゃんたは体が茶色いです。
　　　　　　　　　　　　　　からだ　ちゃいろ

　　　　　それから、おなかが白いです。ちょっと太っています。
　　　　　　　　　　　　　　しろ　　　　　　　　　ふと

けいた　：このネコは今日の午後、テーブルの下で寝ていましたね。
　　　　　　　　　　　　　ごご　　　　　　　　　　ね

アイ　　：ええ。

けいた　：もう家の中を探しましたか。
　　　　　　　いえ　さが

アイ　　：はい、もう全部見ました。でも、いませんでした。
　　　　　　　　　ぜんぶみ

けいた　：家の外は？
　　　　　いえ

アイ　　：あ、まだ見ていません。
　　　　　　　　み

けいた　：じゃ、外に行って探しましょう。
　　　　　　　　い　さが

<They go outside.>

アイ　　：にゃんた！　どこ？　にゃんた～！

にゃんた：ニャー！

けいた　：あ、ネコの声が聞こえますよ。
　　　　　　　　こえ　き

アイ　　：あ、あそこににゃんたがいます！

けいた　：何か持っていますよ。
　　　　　なに　も

アイ　　：あ、私のチケット！

3 できる V Ai and Keita are talking inside the Japan House.

けいた ：にゃんたはたくさん食べますね。一日に何回ご飯を食べますか。

アイ ：一日に四回食べます。

けいた ：へえ、四回！

アイ ：ええ、毎日たくさん食べますから、とても元気です。

けいたさんはいつもどこでご飯を食べていますか。

けいた ：ぼくは今、寮に住んでいますから、寮の食堂で食べています。

アイ ：そうですか。寮はどうですか。

けいた ：そうですね、部屋が小さいですから、ちょっと…

アイ ：じゃ、けいたさん、よかったら、いっしょにジャパンハウスに住みませんか。

一階にいい部屋がありますよ。

けいた ：え、本当ですか。

アイ ：はい、ここはとても楽しいですよ。みんないい友達です。

いつも日本語だけで話しています。

Lesson
6

C O N V E R S A T I O N TIPS ワンポイント L6-4

Usage of ちょっと**:** ちょっと is a very convenient expression that is often used in Japanese conversation.

1. To mean "a little (bit)":

Ａ：今日のテストはちょっと難しかったですね。

Ｂ：そうですね。それから、ちょっと長かったですね。

2. To soften your tone: When you would like to express a negative opinion or emotion, or otherwise say something with the potential to be socially difficult, you can soften your tone by using ちょっと… to replace the negative part at the end of a sentence. We first practiced using ちょっと in this way when we learned it as an expression in Lessons 2 and 3.

１）Ａ：今晩、いっしょに映画に行きませんか。

Ｂ：今晩はちょっと… ← 忙しいです is omitted here.

２）Ａ：コンサートはどうでしたか。

Ｂ：そうですね… ちょっと… ← よくなかったです is omitted here.

たんご

▶ The words written in gray are supplemental vocabulary.

● まいにちのせいかつ　Daily life

| いう (to say) | [question に] こたえる (to answer) こたえ (answer) | [person に] しつもんする (to ask a question) | [thing を] だす (to submit; to turn in) | [place に] すわる ↔ たつ (to sit down) (to stand (up)) |

| [thing を] おぼえる (to memorize) | [thing を] れんしゅうする (to practice) | [person を] てつだう (to help) [(person の) task を] てつだう (to help with) | [person に thing を] みせる (to show) | [thing/person を] さがす (to look for) | [thing/person を] まつ (to wait (for)) |

| あるく (to walk) | [place を／で] さんぽする (to take a walk) | はをみがく (to brush one's teeth) | しぬ (to die) | はなし (story) | パソコン (personal computer; PC) |

● ひとのびょうしゃ　Description of people

| [place に] すむ (to take up residence (in)) | [person と] けっこんする (to get married) | [place で] はたらく (to work) | [person に thing を] おしえる (to teach) |

| [thing/person を] しる (to get to know; to learn of) [thing/person を] しっています ↔ しりません (to know) (not to know) | ふとる (to gain weight) ふとっています (to be on the heavy side; to be fat) | やせる (to lose weight) やせています (to be skinny) |

| ながい ↔ みじかい (long) [length] (short) [length] | せがたかい ↔ せがひくい (tall) [stature] (short) [stature] | あたまがいい (smart; intelligent) |

● からだ (Body)

かみ (hair)
みみ (ear)
め (eye)
かお (face)
あたま (head)
はな (nose)
くち (mouth)
からだ (body)
おなか (stomach)
て
あし (foot; leg)

● みにつけるもの (Clothes and belongings)

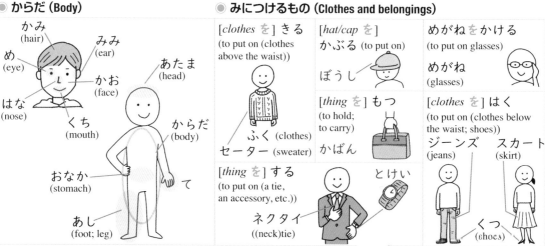

[clothes を] きる (to put on (clothes above the waist))
ふく (clothes)
セーター (sweater)

[hat/cap を] かぶる (to put on)
ぼうし

[thing を] もつ (to hold; to carry)
かばん

[thing を] する (to put on (a tie, an accessory, etc.))
ネクタイ ((neck)tie)
とけい

めがねをかける (to put on glasses)
めがね (glasses)

[clothes を] はく (to put on (clothes below the waist; shoes))
ジーンズ (jeans)　スカート (skirt)
くつ (shoes)

● かぞえる　Counting

◎ 〜かい (... times)

1	2	3	4	5	6
いっかい	にかい	さんかい	よんかい	ごかい	ろっかい
7	**8**	**9**	**10**	**11**	**?**
ななかい	はちかい／はっかい	きゅうかい	じ（ゅ）っかい	じゅういっかい	なんかい

◎ 〜にち（かん）(... days)

1	2	3	4	5	6
いちにち	ふつか（かん）	みっか（かん）	よっか（かん）	いつか（かん）	むいか（かん）
7	**8**	**9**	**10**	**11**	**?**
なのか（かん）	ようか（かん）	ここのか（かん）	とおか（かん）	じゅういちにち（かん）	なんにち（かん）

◎ 〜しゅうかん (... weeks)

1	2	3	4	5	6
いっしゅうかん	にしゅうかん	さんしゅうかん	よんしゅうかん	ごしゅうかん	ろくしゅうかん
7	**8**	**9**	**10**	**11**	**?**
ななしゅうかん	はっしゅうかん	きゅうしゅうかん	じ（ゅ）っしゅうかん	じゅういっしゅうかん	なんしゅうかん

◎ 〜かげつ（かん）(... months)

1	2	3	4	5	6
いっかげつ（かん）	にかげつ（かん）	さんかげつ（かん）	よんかげつ（かん）	ごかげつ（かん）	ろっかげつ（かん）
7	**8**	**9**	**10**	**11**	**?**
ななかげつ（かん）	はち／はっかげつ（かん）	きゅうかげつ（かん）	じ（ゅ）っかげつ（かん）	じゅういっかげつ（かん）	なんかげつ（かん）

◎ 〜ねん（かん）(... years)

1	2	3	4	5	6
いちねん（かん）	にねん（かん）	さんねん（かん）	よねん（かん）	ごねん（かん）	ろくねん（かん）
7	**8**	**9**	**10**	**11**	**?**
ななねん（かん）	はちねん（かん）	きゅうねん（かん）	じゅうねん（かん）	じゅういちねん（かん）	なんねん（かん）

● いろ　Color

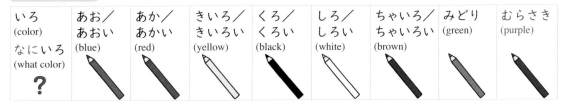

いろ (color) なにいろ (what color) **?**	あお／ あおい (blue)	あか／ あかい (red)	きいろ／ きいろい (yellow)	くろ／ くろい (black)	しろ／ しろい (white)	ちゃいろ／ ちゃいろい (brown)	みどり (green)	むらさき (purple)

● そのほかのひょうげん　Other expressions

たぶん (maybe; probably)	いつも (always)

もしもし
(Hello.
[used to begin
a phone
conversation])

〜だけ (only ...)

Exs. にほんごだけ (only Japanese)
いっかいだけ (only once)
ひとりだけ (only one person)

もうしゅくだいをしましたか。
(Have you done your homework **yet**?)

はい、もうしました。
(Yes, I have **already** done (it).)
いいえ、まだしていません。
(No, I have **not** done (it) **yet**.)

たんごリスト

🔊 **L6-5**

RU-VERBS / RU-VERB PHRASES

1	おしえる	教える	to teach; to tell [*person* に *thing* を]
2	こたえる	答える	to answer [*question* に]
3	みせる	見せる	to show [*person* に *thing* を]
4	おぼえる	覚える	to memorize [*thing* を]
	おぼえています	覚えています	to remember [*thing* を] [It means "to have not forgotten," not "to recall."]
5	きる	着る	to put on (clothes above the waist) [*clothes* を]
	きています	着ています	to be wearing [*clothes* を]
6	めがねをかける		to put on glasses
	めがねをかけています		to be wearing glasses
7	やせる		to lose weight
	やせています		to be skinny

U-VERBS / U-VERB PHRASES

8	あるく	歩く	to walk
9	いう	言う	to say
10	さがす	探す	to look for [*thing/person* を]
11	しぬ	死ぬ	to die
12	すわる	座る	to sit down [*place* に]
13	たつ	立つ	to stand (up)
14	だす	出す	to submit; to turn in; to take out [*thing* を]
15	てつだう	手伝う	to help [*person* を]; to help with [(*person* の) *task* を]
16	はたらく	働く	to work [*place* で]
17	はをみがく	歯をみがく	to brush one's teeth

18	まつ	待つ	to wait (for) [*thing/person* を]
19	かぶる		to put on [*hat/cap* を]
	かぶっています		to be wearing [*hat/cap* を]
20	しる	知る	to get to know; to learn of [*thing/person* を]
	しっています	知っています	to know [*thing/person* を]
	しりません	知りません	not to know [*thing/person* を]
21	すむ	住む	to take up residence (in) [*place* に]
	すんでいます	住んでいます	to live (in) [*place* に]
22	はく		to put on (clothes below the waist; shoes) [*clothes* を]
	はいています		to be wearing [*clothes* を]
23	もつ	持つ	to hold; to carry [*thing* を]
	もっています	持っています	to be holding; to have; to own [*thing* を]
24	ふとる	太る	to gain weight
	ふとっています	太っています	to be on the heavy side; to be fat

IRREGULAR VERB

25	する		to put on (a tie, an accessory, etc.) [*thing* を]
	しています		to be wearing (a tie, an accessory, etc.) [*thing* を]

SURU-VERBS

26	さんぽする	散歩する	to take a walk [*place* を／で]
27	しつもんする	質問する	to ask a question [*person* に]
28	れんしゅうする	練習する	to practice [*thing* を]

| 29 | けっこんする | 結婚する | to get married [*person* と] |
| | けっこんしています | 結婚しています | to be married [*person* と] |

I-ADJECTIVES / I-ADJECTIVE PHRASES

30	あおい	青い	blue
31	あかい	赤い	red
32	きいろい	黄色い	yellow
33	くろい	黒い	black
34	しろい	白い	white
35	ちゃいろい	茶色い	brown
36	ながい	長い	long [length]
37	みじかい	短い	short [length]
38	あたまがいい	頭がいい	smart; intelligent
39	せがたかい	背が高い	tall [stature]
40	せがひくい	背が低い	short [stature]

NOUNS

41	あたま	頭	head
42	かみ	髪	hair
43	かお	顔	face
44	め	目	eye
45	はな	鼻	nose
46	くち	口	mouth
47	みみ	耳	ear
48	からだ	体	body
49	おなか		stomach
50	あし	足	foot; leg
51	めがね		glasses
52	ふく	服	clothes
53	くつ		shoes
54	いろ	色	color
	なにいろ	何色	what color
55	あお	青	blue
56	あか	赤	red

57	きいろ	黄色	yellow
58	くろ	黒	black
59	しろ	白	white
60	ちゃいろ	茶色	brown
61	みどり	緑	green
62	こたえ	答え	answer
63	はなし	話	story
64	ネクタイ		(neck)tie
65	セーター		sweater
66	ジーンズ		jeans
67	スカート		skirt
68	パソコン		personal computer; PC

COUNTERS

69	～かい	～回	... times
70	～にち（かん）	～日（間）	... days
71	～しゅうかん	～週間	... weeks
72	～かげつ（かん）	～か月（間）	... months
73	～ねん（かん）	～年（間）	... years

ADVERBS

74	いつも		always
75	たぶん	多分	maybe; probably
76	まだ [＋negative]		not yet
77	もう [＋affirmative]		already
	もう [＋question]		yet; already

OTHER WORDS AND PHRASES

| 78 | ～だけ | | only ...
 Ex.1 にほんごだけ only Japanese
 Ex.2 いっかいだけ only once
 Ex.3 ひとりだけ only one person |
| 79 | もしもし | | Hello. [used to begin a phone conversation] |

かんじ

▶ **The highlighted words** below are the vocabulary you will need to learn to read and write in kanji in this chapter.
▶ ***Special reading:** A special reading is assigned to a kanji compound word as a whole; in this case, it is impossible to assign each kanji in the compound a particular part of the reading.

50 食 食 食	ショク	食事する to have a meal しょくじ	朝食 breakfast ちょうしょく
	た(べる)	食べる to eat た	食べ物 food た もの
to eat	ノ 入 A 今 今 今 食 食 食		

51 飲 飲 飲	イン	飲食店 a place serving food and drink いんしょくてん	飲料 beverage いんりょう
	の(む)	飲む to drink の	飲み物 drink の もの
to drink	ノ 入 A 今 今 今 食 食 飮 飮 飲 飲		

52 言 言 言	ゲン	言語 language げんご	言語学 linguistics げんごがく	方言 dialect ほうげん
	い(う) こと	言う to say い	言葉 word; phrase; language ことば	
to say	丶 亠 亠 言 言 言 言			

53 話 話 話	ワ	会話 conversation かいわ	世話 care せわ	電話 telephone でんわ
	はなし はな(す)	話 story はなし 話す to speak はな	話し合う to discuss はな あ	
to speak	丶 亠 亠 言 言 言 言 訂 訂 話 話 話			

54 行 行 行	コウ ギョウ	銀行 bank ぎんこう	旅行する to travel りょこう	一行目 the first line いちぎょうめ
	い(く)	行く to go い		
to go	ノ ク イ 行 行 行			

55 来 来 来	ライ	来週 next week らいしゅう	来月 next month らいげつ	来年 next year らいねん
		来学期 next semester らいがっき	将来 future しょうらい	
	く(る) き(ます) こ(ない)	来る to come く 来ない not to come [plain non-past negative form of 来る] こ く	来ます to come [polite form of 来る] き く	
to come	一 ┌ ┌ 口 平 来 来			

56 見 見 見	ケン	意見 opinion いけん	見学する to observe; to visit/tour (a place) [study by observation] けんがく	
	み(る) み(える) み(せる)	見る to see; to watch み 見える to be visible み	（お）花見 cherry-blossom viewing はなみ 見せる to show み	
to see; to watch	丨 冂 冂 月 目 貝 見			

57 持	ジ	支持する to support　持続する to last; to maintain　持病 chronic disease しじ　　　　　　　じぞく　　　　　　　　じびょう
持 持	も(つ)	持つ to hold　持っていく to take to (a different location) も　　　　　も 持ってくる to bring to (speaker's location) も お金持ち rich person　気持ち feeling　持ち物 belongings かね も　　　　　　　き も　　　　　　も もの
to hold		一 十 扌 扌 打 扗 拝 拝 持 持

58 本	ホン ボン ポン	本 book　日本 Japan　日本語 Japanese [language]　日本人 Japanese [people] ほん　　にほん　　にほんご　　　　　　　　にほんじん 本田さん Honda-san [last name]　絵本 picture book　本当 truth ほんだ　　　　　　　　え ほん　　　　　ほんとう
本 本		〜本 [counter for long, cylindrical objects]（**Exs.** 一本 one long object, ほん　　　　　　　　　　　　　　　　　　　いっぽん 二本 two long objects, 三本 three long objects, etc.） にほん　　　　　　　さんぼん
basis; book		一 十 オ 木 本

59 語	ゴ	〜語 [... language]（**Exs.** 日本語 Japanese, 英語 English, 中国語 Chinese, ご　　　　　　　　　にほんご　　　　　えいご　　　　ちゅうごくご フランス語 French, etc.）　外国語 foreign language ご　　　　　　　　　がいこくご 言語 language　語学 language learning　単語 word; vocabulary げんご　　　　　ごがく　　　　　　　　たんご
語 語	かた(る)	物語 tale; story ものがたり
word; language		丶 亠 亖 訁 語 語 語 訂 訂 語 語 語 語 語

60 体	タイ	全体 whole　体育 physical education　体験する to experience; to try ぜんたい　　たいいく　　　　　　　　たいけん 体重 body weight　体調 physical condition　体力 (physical) strength たいじゅう　　　　たいちょう　　　　　　　たいりょく
体 体	からだ	体 body からだ
body		ノ 亻 仁 什 付 休 体

61 口	コウ	人口 population じんこう
口 口	くち ぐち	口 mouth　入口／入り口 entrance　出口 exit くち　　　いりぐち　　い ぐち　　　　　でぐち 北口 north entrance/exit　西口 west entrance/exit　東口 east entrance/exit きたぐち　　　　　　　にしぐち　　　　　　　ひがしぐち 南口 south entrance/exit　中央口 central entrance/exit みなみぐち　　　　　　ちゅうおうぐち
mouth		丨 冂 口

62 目	モク	科目 subject　目次 table of contents　目的 purpose　目標 goal かもく　　　　もくじ　　　　　　　もくてき　　　　もくひょう
目 目	め	目 eye　〜目 [suffix for ordinal numbers]（**Exs.** 一日目 the first day, め　　　め　　　　　　　　　　　　　　　　　　いちにちめ 二番目 the second [in order]）　目上の人 one's (social) superior にばんめ　　　　　　　　　　めうえ ひと
eye		丨 冂 月 月 目

63 耳	ジ	耳鼻科 ENT (ear, nose, and throat) medicine; otorhinolaryngology じびか
耳 耳	みみ	耳 ear みみ
ear		丁 丌 厈 盰 耳 耳

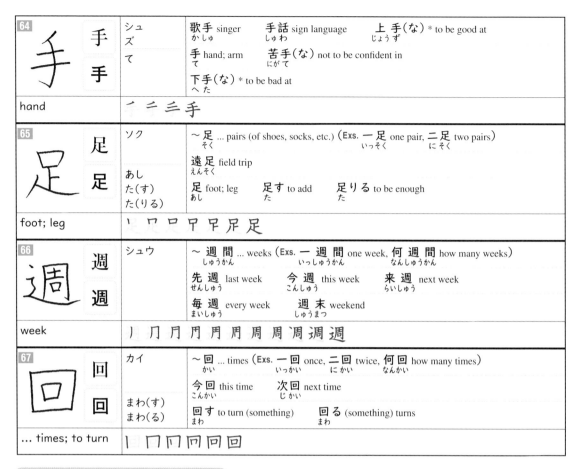

64 手	手 手	シュ ズ て	歌手 singer かしゅ　　　　手話 sign language しゅわ　　　　上手(な) * to be good at じょうず　　手 hand; arm て　　　　苦手(な) not to be confident in にがて　　下手(な) * to be bad at へた
hand			｜　二　三　手
65 足	足 足	ソク そく　　あし た(す) た(りる)	〜足 ... pairs (of shoes, socks, etc.) (Exs. 一足 one pair, 二足 two pairs) そく　　　　　　　　　　　　　　　　　　　いっそく　　　　にそく　　遠足 field trip えんそく　　足 foot; leg　足す to add　足りる to be enough あし　　　　た　　　　　た
foot; leg			｜　ロ　ワ　ア　尸　ア　足
66 週	週 週	シュウ	〜週間 ... weeks (Exs. 一週間 one week, 何週間 how many weeks) しゅうかん　　　　　　　　　　いっしゅうかん　　　　なんしゅうかん　　先週 last week　今週 this week　来週 next week せんしゅう　　　　こんしゅう　　　　　らいしゅう　　毎週 every week　週末 weekend まいしゅう　　　　しゅうまつ
week			｜　刀　月　円　円　冃　周　周　`周　凋　週
67 回	回 回	カイ まわ(す) まわ(る)	〜回 ... times (Exs. 一回 once, 二回 twice, 何回 how many times) かい　　　　　　　いっかい　　　にかい　　　なんかい　　今回 this time　次回 next time こんかい　　　　じかい　　回す to turn (something)　回る (something) turns まわ　　　　　　　　　　　　　まわ
... times; to turn			｜　冂　冂　回　回　回

● あたらしいよみかた　New reading

The following is new reading for kanji that you have already learned. Read the word aloud.

1) 日本
　　に ほん

● れんしゅう　Practice

1 Can you guess the origin of each kanji below? Match each symbol a.-e. with the kanji 1)-5) with the same meaning.

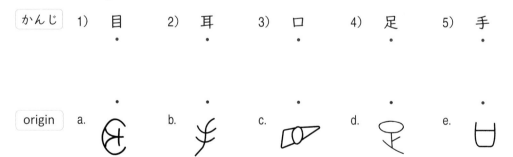

かんじ　1) 目　　2) 耳　　3) 口　　4) 足　　5) 手

origin　a.　　　b.　　　c.　　　d.　　　e.

2 Below is a passage Yamada-san has written about her pet. Read the passage aloud, then write the readings for the underlined words and choose which pet is hers from the photos a.-d. below.

私のペットはウサギ (rabbit) です。名前はミミです。ミミは体がグレーです。口と目がちょっ
と大きいです。耳はとても長いですが、足は短いです。ミミは一日に四回ご飯を食べま
すから、ちょっと太っていますが、とてもかわいいです。私はいつもミミの写真を持っ
ています。これはミミの写真です。見てください。

a.

b.

c.

d.

3 Tanaka-san has made a post on social media inviting you and a group of friends to an event. Read the post aloud, then write the readings for the underlined words.

S N S [🔍]

 Tanaka

カナダ人の友達のスミスさんが先週トロントから日本に来ました。二週間日本
にいます。明日スミスさんといっしょに大学の近くの「ラ・ポルタ」という
レストランに行って、晩ご飯を食べませんか。ラ・ポルタにはとてもおいしい
イタリア料理がたくさんあります。ピザを食べて、ワインを飲んで、たくさん
話しませんか。スミスさんは大学で日本語を勉強していますから、日本語で
話しましょう。よかったら、来てください。七時に私の名前で予約 (reservation)
をしましたから、レストランで私の名前を言ってください。

Lesson
6

197

■ 漢字とひらがな（When to use kanji and hiragana）

You have now become familiar with Japanese sentences written in a mix of hiragana, katakana, and kanji. As you have already learned, kanji express an idea or a concept, so you need to think about the meaning of the kanji you use when you write in Japanese. Suppose you want to write "Please say (it)." Which of the two sentences below should you use?

（1）行ってください。　　（2）言ってください。

In this example, the two sentences are phonetically identical（いってください）, but the kanji you select determines the meaning of the sentence. In (1), the kanji 行 means "to go" while in (2), the kanji 言 means "to say." Selecting the wrong kanji changes the meaning of the sentence entirely. Because Japanese has a comparatively small number of consonants and vowels, it has many homophones, and kanji can be key in distinguishing them in writing.

In Japanese, it is important to use kanji only when they add meaning. For example, (3) illustrates a common mistake made by learners:

（3）× 私は昨日ピザを食べま下。

Here, the sentence ends phonetically with した, and the hiragana した serves as an indicator of past tense. Substituting these hiragana with the kanji 下 fits phonetically but is inappropriate in two ways. First, the meaning of 下 ("under") has nothing to do with the meaning of the sentence. Second, by replacing the hiragana, the sentence loses its indicator of past tense.

While kanji express the core meanings of words, they do not by themselves tell us anything about tense, politeness, or whether a word is affirmative or negative. Because of this, kanji alone are not enough to write adjectives and verbs.

For example, the kanji 飲 has the meaning "to drink" in (4) below, but you cannot tell whether the sentence is about the past or present, or whether the sentence ending is affirmative or negative.

（4）× 私はジュースを飲。

The conjugating part written in hiragana for adjectives and verbs is called *okurigana* and is necessary to complete these words.

The chart below shows how *okurigana* are used to complete polite verb conjugations. The *okurigana* are written in blue.

飲む "to drink"		affirmative	negative
	non-past	飲みます	飲みません
	past	飲みました	飲みませんでした

れんしゅう Practice

Choose the most appropriate option to complete each of the sentences below.

1）明日テレビを　　　　　a. 見ます　　　b. 見す

2）昨日九時に大学に　　　a. 行きます　　　b. 行きました

3）私の町は　　　　　　　a. 大きいです　　b. 大いです　　c. 大です

4）毎日日本語を　　　　　a. 話なします　　b. 話します　　c. 話ます

5）先週友達が　　　　　　a. 来ました　　　b. 来ま四田　　c. 来まし田

ぶんぽう

1 Te-forms of verbs

In this lesson, you will be learning what are called the "te-forms" of verbs. They are so called because most of them end with the sound /te/. The way a verb's te-form is derived varies depending on the type of the verb, as seen in the following table:

Category		Dictionary form	Te-form
(a) Ru-verbs		たべる (to eat)	たべて
(b) U-verbs	Ending sound		
	う	かう (to buy)	かって
	つ	たつ (to stand up)	たって
	る	かえる (to return)	かえって
	む	よむ (to read)	よんで
	ぶ	あそぶ (to play)	あそんで
	ぬ	しぬ (to die)	しんで
	す	はなす (to talk)	はなして
	く	かく (to write)	かいて
		いく (to go)	いって (exception)
	ぐ	およぐ (to swim)	およいで
(c) Irregular verbs		する (to do)	して
		くる (to come)	きて

You can make the te-form from the dictionary form of a verb as follows:

(a) Ru-verbs: Change る to て.

(b) U-verbs:

    ・う／つ／る ending: Change う／つ／る to って.

    ・む／ぶ／ぬ ending: Change む／ぶ／ぬ to んで.

    ・す ending: Change す to して.

    ・く ending: Change く to いて. (Exception: いく → いって (× いいて))

    ・ぐ ending: Change ぐ to いで.

(c) Irregular verbs: する → して；くる → きて

(See the te-form song on p.204.)

Because verb te-forms are used in many important grammatical expressions (see #2-4, for example), you should work to make sure that you can always produce them correctly and automatically.

2 ～てください **[Polite command]** "Please V."

[2]

	V-*te*	
これを	読んで	ください。
Please read this.		

You can tell someone to do something politely and rather formally using V-*te* ください.

This expression is commonly used when a speaker of higher status than the listener tells the listener to do something (e.g., from a teacher to a student, from a manager to a subordinate, etc.), but it can also be used when the listener has the same status as the speaker does.

Exs. (1) 漢字で書い<u>てください</u>。*Please write in kanji.*

(2) ちょっと待っ<u>てください</u>。*Wait a moment, please.*

(3) もう一度言っ<u>てください</u>。*Say it again, please.*

3 V₁てV₂ **[Actions in sequence]** "V₁ and V₂"

[3]

	V₁-*te*	V₂
今からジムに	行って	運動します。
I'm going to go to the gym now and exercise.		

When you describe two or more sequential actions by one person, you use *te*-forms. Note that と can connect only nouns; therefore, you cannot use it to describe situations like [3] above. (✕ 今からジムに行きますと運動します。)

Exs. (1) 毎日6時に起き<u>て</u>ジョギングします。*I get up at six every day and jog.*

(2) 昨日は映画を見<u>て</u>11時に寝ました。
Yesterday, I watched a movie and then went to bed at eleven o'clock.

(3) 今晩いっしょに晩ご飯を作っ<u>て</u>食べませんか。
Would you like to make dinner and eat together tonight?

Note that *te*-forms carry no information about tense or politeness. Instead, that information is expressed by main verbs. For example, in (1), the tense and the politeness level are indicated by ジョギングします.

V₁-*te* V₂ is used in various situations. One situation is when two actions are an inseparable set of related actions (e.g., the first action sets up for the second action), as in [3] and (3) above, and another situation is when two actions are performed back to back, as in (1) and (2).

☞ **GID** (vol.1): G. Connecting verbs, adjectives, and sentences using *te*-forms

In the following situation, the two actions are neither an inseparable set of related actions nor performed back to back. In this case, V₁-*te* V₂ is unnatural.

✕ 私は昨日図書館で勉強し<u>て</u>ジムで運動しました。

→ 私は昨日図書館で勉強しました。それから、ジムで運動しました。
I studied in the library yesterday. Then, I exercised at the gym.

4 ～ています

4-1 ～ています [Action in progress] "be V-ing"

[4-a]

	V-*te* (continual verb)	
私 は今、晩ご飯を <small>わたし いま ばん はん</small>	作って <small>つく</small>	います。
I am fixing dinner now.		

The meaning of V-*te* います varies depending on what kind of verb V-*te* is. By using V-*te* います with continual verbs (i.e., verbs that indicate an action with a duration), you can express an action in progress.

Exs. (1) にゃんたはリーマンさんと遊んでいます。*Nyanta is playing with Riemann.*
<small>あそ</small>

(2) アイさんは今、ダイエットしています。だから、ハンバーガーを食べません。
<small>いま</small> <small>た</small>

Ai is on a diet now, so she doesn't eat hamburgers.

(3) けいたさんは昨日の夜9時ごろに剣道を練習していました。
<small>きのう よる じ けんどう れんしゅう</small>

Keita was practicing kendo around 9 o'clock last night.

4-2 ～ています [Resultant state] "be V-ed; be V-ing; be Adj; V"

[4-b]

	V-*te* (momentary verb)	
今日、リサさんはかわいいセーターを <small>きょう</small>	着て <small>き</small>	います。
Lisa is wearing (lit. has put on) a cute sweater today.		

When a verb represents an action that signifies an instantaneous change and has no duration (e.g., to marry, to die, to learn of), V-*te* います expresses the state that remains after the action of V-*te* has completed.

Exs. (1) A: 田中さんはどこですか。*Where is Tanaka-san?*
<small>たなか</small>

B: リビングのソファに座っていますよ。
<small>すわ</small>

He's sitting on the sofa in the living room.

(2) 今日、山田さんは黒いシャツを着て（いて）、赤いネクタイをしています。
<small>きょう やまだ くろ き あか</small>

Yamada-san is wearing a black shirt and a red tie today.

(3) A: ジャンという人を知っていますか。*Do you know a person named Jean?*
<small>ひと し</small>

B1: はい、知っています。*Yes, I do.*
<small>し</small>

B2: いいえ、知りません。*No, I don't.*
<small>し</small>

⚠ 知る means "to learn of," so to express the idea of "to know," which represents the resultant state of
<small>し</small>
learning of something, you use 知っています. However, the equivalent form of "not to know" is not
知っていません but 知りません, as in (3)-B2. For the meanings of 行っています, 持っています, and 住
<small>し し い も</small>
んでいます, see **GID** (vol.1): E. Auxiliaries 2. (V-*te*) いる.
<small>す</small>

4-3 〜ています [Habitual action] "V" でき る III

[4-c]

		V-te	
私 はいつも6時に <ruby>私<rt>わたし</rt></ruby> <ruby>時<rt>じ</rt></ruby>		起きて <ruby>起<rt>お</rt></ruby>	います。
I always get up at six.			

You can also use V-te います to describe someone's habitual actions.

Exs. (1) テストの<ruby>前<rt>まえ</rt></ruby>にいつも<ruby>友達<rt>ともだち</rt></ruby>といっしょに<ruby>勉強<rt>べんきょう</rt></ruby>し<u>ています</u>。

I always study with my friends before a test.

(2) <ruby>私<rt>わたし</rt></ruby> は<ruby>去年<rt>きょねん</rt></ruby>、<ruby>毎週日曜日<rt>まいしゅうにちよう び</rt></ruby>にカフェでアルバイトを<u>していました</u>。

I worked part-time at a café every Sunday last year.

(3) <ruby>私<rt>わたし</rt></ruby> はたいていスマホで<ruby>音楽<rt>おんがく</rt></ruby>を<ruby>聞<rt>き</rt></ruby>い<u>ています</u>。

I usually listen to music on my smartphone.

In Lesson 2, you learned that the non-past forms of verbs can also be used for habitual actions, as in (4). (See L2 #1.)

Ex. (4) <ruby>私<rt>わたし</rt></ruby> は<ruby>毎日朝<rt>まいにちあさ</rt></ruby>6<ruby>時<rt>じ</rt></ruby>に<u><ruby>起<rt>お</rt></ruby>きます</u>。 *I get up at six in the morning every day.*

For the difference between V-te います and V-non-past for habitual actions, see **GID** (vol.1): E. Auxiliaries 2-3. Habitual action.

---

5 XはYがZ [X's physical characteristics] "X has Y that is Z; X's Y is Z" でき る III

[5]

X (whole)		Y (part)		Z (Adj)
トムさん	は	目 <ruby>目<rt>め</rt></ruby>	が	大きいです。 <ruby>大<rt>おお</rt></ruby>
Tom has big eyes.				

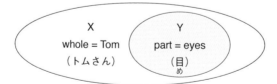

You can describe the physical characteristics of someone or something by presenting that person or thing (=X) as a topic first and then adding a description of a specific part of it (=Y) using an adjective (=Z).

Exs. (1) にゃんた<u>は</u><ruby>足<rt>あし</rt></ruby><u>が</u><ruby>短<rt>みじか</rt></ruby>いです。 *Nyanta has short legs.*

(2) <ruby>私<rt>わたし</rt></ruby> <u>は</u>あまり<ruby>背<rt>せ</rt></ruby><u>が</u><ruby>高<rt>たか</rt></ruby>くないです。 *I am not very tall (lit. As for me, [my] stature is not very high).*

(3) <ruby>私<rt>わたし</rt></ruby> <u>は</u><ruby>子<rt>こ</rt></ruby>どもの<ruby>時<rt>とき</rt></ruby>、かみ<u>が</u><ruby>長<rt>なが</rt></ruby>かったですが、<ruby>今<rt>いま</rt></ruby>は<ruby>短<rt>みじか</rt></ruby>いです。

I had long hair when I was a child, but it's short now.

6 もう "already" **and** まだ "(not) yet"

[6-a]

		V-past (affirmative)
もう	昼ご飯を ひる はん	食べました。 た
	I've already had my lunch.	

[6-b]

		V-*te*	
まだ	昼ご飯を ひる はん	食べて た	いません。
	I haven't had my lunch yet.		

The adverbs もう and まだ can be used in combination with verbs in specific tenses to indicate whether or not an action has been completed. With "もう V-past," you can express the idea that one has already done something, and with "まだ V-*te* いません," the idea that one hasn't done something yet. The following sentence is ungrammatical.

× <u>まだ</u>昼ご飯を<u>食べませんでした</u>。 → <u>まだ</u>昼ご飯を<u>食べていません</u>。
ひる はん た   ひる はん た

Exs. (1) A: <u>もう</u>明日の宿題を<u>しました</u>か。
          あした しゅくだい

        Have you done tomorrow's homework yet? / Have you already done tomorrow's homework?

     B: いいえ、<u>まだ</u>し<u>ていません</u>。*No, I haven't done it yet.*

  (2) A: <u>もう</u>サラダを<u>作りました</u>か。*Have you made the salad yet? / Have you already made the salad?*
           つく

     B: はい、<u>もう作りました</u>。テーブルの上にあります。*Yes, I have. It's on the table.*
          つく   うえ

☞ **GID** (vol.1): D. Aspect 2. もう and まだ

7 X (period of time) に Y (number of times / duration) [Frequency / duration]

[7-a]

	Period of time		Number of times / duration	
ここで	二日 ふつか	に	一回 いっかい	ミーティングがあります。
	There is a meeting here every other day (lit. once in two days).			

[7-b]

研さんは けん	一週間 いっしゅうかん	に	15時間 じかん	アルバイトをします。
	Ken works 15 hours a week at his part-time job.			

You can describe the frequency of an action/event or the duration of an action/event in a given period using the pattern [Period of time] に [Number of times / duration].

Exs. (1) にゃんたは一日に四回ご飯を食べます。だから、ちょっと太っています。
          いちにち よんかい はん た   ふと

       Nyanta eats four meals a day. Because of that, he is a little fat.

  (2) オリンピックは四年に一回あります。*The Olympic Games are held once every four years.*
            よねん いっかい

  (3) 私は高校の時、一日に2時間ぐらい数学を勉強しました。
     わたし こうこう とき いちにち じかん すうがく べんきょう

       When I was in high school, I studied math for about two hours a day.

はなしましょう

▶ **Words written in purple** are new words introduced in this lesson.

 できる I

Talk about your daily life by connecting multiple actions.

できる I-A Polite command ～てください

1 Below are the lyrics to "The *Te*-Form Song," which can be sung to the tune of "Santa Claus is Coming to Town." Practice this song until you can sing it without looking at the lyrics and use it to help you memorize the *te*-forms of verbs. 🔊 **L6-6**

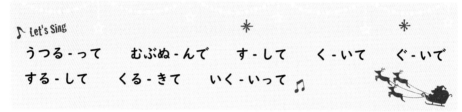

2 Let's practice *te*-form conjugations.

Step 1 Change the following verbs into their *te*-forms. 🔊 **L6-7**

Ex. たべる → たべて

1) みる 　　2) ねる 　　3) かう 　　4) かえる 　　5) よむ 　　6) あそぶ

7) はなす 　　8) きく 　　9) いく 　　10) およぐ 　　11) する 　　12) くる

Step 2 Change the following new verbs into their *te*-forms. 🔊 **L6-8**

1) こたえる 　　2) おぼえる 　　3) てつだう 　　4) いう 　　5) たつ 　　6) すわる

7) すむ 　　8) しぬ 　　9) さがす 　　10) はく 　　11) しつもんする

3 Act out the following instructions.

Step 1 What is your teacher saying? Act out what your teacher tells you to do.

Ex. 先生：この漢字を読んでください。
　　　学生：「ほん」

Step 2 Now, make some polite commands of your own and test your partner with them.

Ex. A: 窓の前に行ってください。
　　　B: はい、分かりました。

4 You are planning a party with your partner now. Ask each other to do the following things. You may accept or decline your partner's request.

Ex. A: あのう、スーパーでお酒を買ってください。

B: はい、分かりました。or うーん、お酒はちょっと…

Ex. スーパー (supermarket) でお酒を買う　　1) ケーキ屋で大きいケーキを買う

2) ６時に私の家に来る　　　　　　　　3) そうじを手伝う

4) ピザを作る　　　　　　　　　　　　5) パーティーで歌を歌う

6) パーティーでみんなにダンスを見せる　7) パーティーでみんなの写真をとる

8) パーティーでおもしろいめがねをかける　9) your own

できるⅠ-B | Actions in sequence V₁てV₂

1 Let's practice using verbs in their *te*-forms.

Step 1 Look at the pictures below and describe what Ai will do this week.

Ex. アイさんは月曜日に朝ご飯を作って、タオさんと食べます。

それから、歯をみがいて、学校に行きます。

Ex. Mon make breakfast	eat (it) with Tao	brush (her) teeth	go to school

1) Tue ask (her) teacher questions	listen to the answers	go home	practice kanji

2) Fri meet up with a friend	go to a concert together	sing at the concert	dance

3) Sat go to a park	take a walk	sit on a bench (ベンチ)	drink coffee

Step 2 Talk about your schedule for this week.

Ex. {今日／明日／〇曜日に} 友達の家に行って、いっしょにレッスン6の勉強を
します。それから、家に帰って、「ぽよぽよ」というゲームをします。

2 Take turns with your partner asking each other what you did at various periods of time in the
past.

Possible topics	先週の週末	昨日	去年の誕生日

Ex. A: 〇〇さんは先週の週末何をしましたか。

B: えっと、土曜日に友達と会って、いっしょにレストランで晩ご飯を食べました。
それから… <Continue>

3 What is your favorite part of your daily life? Is there something from it you can recommend to
your classmates? Make a short presentation about it.

Activity you do regularly Details Recommendation/ suggestion/ invitation

Ex. 私は週末よく友達と「アン」というカフェに行って、
朝ご飯を食べます。
家の近くにありますから、たいてい歩いて行きます。
とてもおいしいですから、みなさん、アンではぜひ
パンケーキを食べてください。

4 Show a picture of a trip or event you have enjoyed in the past and talk about it in detail with
your partner.

Ex. A: 〇〇さん、この写真を見てください。私の旅行の写真です。

B: おもしろい写真ですね。ここはどこですか。

A: 日本の青森の美術館です。去年、母といっしょに行って、
この大きいイヌを見ました。「あおもり犬」というイヌです。

B: へえ、そうですか。 <Continue>

Nara Yoshitomo,
Aomori-ken (Aomori Dog) 2005
Aomori Museum of Art
©Yoshitomo Nara

できる II Ask and answer questions about what you are/were doing.

できる II-A | Action in progress ～ています

1 Suppose you are at a party being held at the Japan House.

Step 1 Describe what people are doing at the party.   L6-10

Ex. アイさんは今、ケーキを食べています。

Step 2 Your partner has heard from you about the people at the Japan House but hasn't met them yet. Answer your partner's questions about who is who.   L6-11

Ex. A: アイさんはどの人ですか。

B: あの人です。今あそこでケーキを食べています。

A: ああ、あの人ですね。ありがとう。

Group Work

2 Let's play charades! Act out the action shown on a card. Your teammates will guess what you are doing. Which team will win by having the most correct guesses?

Ex. 散歩しています

3 You want to go out to dinner, a movie, etc. with someone today. Call and ask what your friends are doing now to check if they are available. (Stand or sit back to back and do not look at each other while talking to simulate an actual phone conversation.)

Ex. A: もしもし、あ、○○さん？　今、何をしていますか。

B: 今、宿題をしています。

A: そうですか。宿題は何をしていますか。

B: パソコンでリスニングの宿題をしています。

A: そうですか。あの、宿題の後でいっしょにゲームをしませんか。

B: いいですね、しましょう。or すみません、今日はちょっと…

4 Suppose you are a member of the Japan House. Describe what the other members were doing when you returned home last night.

Ex. Ai / doing homework in the living room

→ アイさんはリビングで宿題をしていました。

1) Riemann / memorizing kanji in his room　　2) Tao / practicing Japanese in her room

3) Mark / cooking in the kitchen　　4) Keita / helping Ai with her homework in the living room

5) Nyanta / waiting for Ai in Ai's room

5 Practice describing what you were doing in the past.

Step 1 Recall what you were doing from 10:00 PM to 12:00 AM last night.

	Around 10:00 PM	Around 11:00 PM
What: Where: With whom:		

ROLE PLAY

Step 2 Oh no! Your neighbor's house was broken into sometime between 10:00 PM and 12:00 AM last night.

Role A You are a police officer. Ask the neighbors what they were doing from 10:00 PM to 12:00 AM last night and pose appropriate follow-up questions (Ex. where/with whom?) as well.

Role B (two or three people) You live near the house that was broken into last night. Answer the police officer's questions honestly based on your recollections in Step 1.

Ex. A: 昨日の午後10時ごろ、何をしていましたか。

B: 10時ごろですか。えっと、テレビを見ていました。

A: そうですか。だれと見ていましたか。

B: えっと、一人で見ていました。

A: じゃ、11時ごろは？

<Continue>

A: そうですか。ありがとうございました。

　or　あやしい (suspicious) ですね。私といっしょに来てください。

Step 3 Who is the most suspicious person? State a reason to explain your thinking.

Ex. ○○さんは昨日の夜一人で家でテレビを見ていましたから、ちょっとあやしいです。

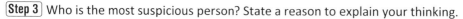

できるⅢ-A Resultant state 〜ています

1 You are uploading pictures of your new clothing on social media. Make a hashtag with a color and read it aloud. Then, make a hashtag with a verb in the form 今日〜ています and read it aloud.

Ex. ＃赤いＴシャツ　＃今日着ています

🔊 **L6-13**

Ex. 　1) 　2) 　3) 　4) 　5)

2 The following are some pictures of your friends on social media. Describe what they are wearing.

🔊 **L6-14**

Ex. 赤いセーターを着て（いて）、青いスカートをはいています。
それから、茶色いかばんを持っています。

3 Pick a classmate and describe them without saying their name. Your other classmates will try to guess who you're talking about.

Ex. A: この人は赤いぼうしをかぶって（いて）、茶色い服を着ています。
それから、青いジーンズをはいています。だれですか。

B: 答えはキムさんですか。

A: はい、そうです。or いいえ、キムさんじゃないです。

4 Practice talking about family.

Step 1 Imagine you are staying with a host family in Japan. Describe them using the information provided below.

🔊 **L6-15**

Ex. 私のホストファミリーのお父さんは病院で働いています。
東京に住んでいます。それから、山が好きです。

	Occupation	Residence	Other information
Ex. father	works at a hospital	Tokyo	likes mountains
1) mother	works at an art museum	Tokyo	a little short
2) older brother	teaches English at high school	near a famous temple	is married has a child
3) dog named ポチ	no work	older brother's house	a little fat

You are showing a picture of your host family to your partner. Your partner will ask about where they live and what they do for a living and make comments on their appearance or clothing.

Ex.　A: これはだれですか。

　　B: ホストファミリーのお父さんです。
　　　　　　　　　　とう

　　A: そうですか。仕事は何をしていますか。
　　　　　　　　　　しごと

　　B: 病院で働いています。
　　　びょういん　はたら

　　A: かっこいいネクタイをしていますね。

　　B: そうですね。

　　A: それから、この人はだれですか。 <Continue>

5　Now, talk about your own family (or your favorite fictional family) using the conversation above as a model. Show a picture of the family you're talking about. (Draw one, if necessary.)

できるⅢ-B　**X's physical characteristics　XはYがZ**

1　Describe the following animals with their characteristics.　🔊**L6-16**

Ex.　アイアイは目が大きいです。耳 {が／も} 大きいです。
　　　　　め　　　　　　　みみ

　　それから、体が黒いです。顔が茶色いです。
　　　　　　　からだ　くろ　　　かお　ちゃいろ

Ex. アイアイ	1) ダックスフンド	2) パンダ	3) ゾウ	4) ウサギ	5) your own

2　(Information Gap) You have encountered an alien!

Step 1　Describe the physical characteristics of the figure in your picture, and your partner will draw it based on your description.

Ex.　この宇宙人 (alien) は目が大きいです。耳も大きいです。でも、鼻と口が小さいです。
　　　　うちゅうじん　　　　め　　　　　　　　みみ　　　　　　　　はな　くち
　　かみが短いです。
　　　　みじか

Student A　Ex.
　1) 　2)

Student B ➡p.214

Step 2　Share your drawings and see how close they are to the originals.

Group Work

3 Conduct research on popularity.

Step 1 Think of something you know well but you don't think is popular enough among others. Ask your classmates if they know of the thing you picked.

> **Possible topics** レストラン　バンド　ゲーム　キャラクター　本　映画
> 　　　　　　　　　　　　　　　　　　　　　　　　　　　　　　　ほん　えいが

Ex. A:「ウルトラズ」というバンドを知っていますか。
　　　　　　　　　　　　　　　　　　　　し

B:{はい、知っています。／いいえ、知りません。／名前だけ知っています。}
　　　　　し　　　　　　　　　　　　し　　　　　なまえ　　し

Step 2 Report the degree to which people know about the thing you picked.

Ex. みんな「ウルトラズ」を知っています。ウルトラズは人気があります。
　　　　　　　　　　　　　し　　　　　　　　　　　　にんき

or みんな「ウルトラズ」というバンドを{あまり／全然}知りません。残念です。
　　　　　　　　　　　　　　　　　　　　　　　　ぜんぜん　し　　　　ざんねん

4 Make a brief presentation describing the clothing, physical characteristics, and other details of the following characters.　**L6-17**

Ex. これは「アーバー」というキャラクターです。知っていますか。
　　　　　　　　　　　　　　　　　　　　　　　　　　　　し

アーバーは黄色いマフラー (winter scarf) をして(いて)、青いセーターを着ています。
　　　　　きいろ　　　　　　　　　　　　　　　　　　あお　　　　　　　　き

体が茶色いです。アーバーは山に住んでいます。リサイクルが大好きです。
からだ　ちゃいろ　　　　　　　　す　　　　　　　　　　　　　だいす

Ex. アーバー
©Rose Sproat
· lives on a mountain
· loves recycling

1) ミチ
©Miranda Tucker
· studies Japanese at school
· loves Japan

2) ルル
©Lucy Liu
· lives in Hawaii
· often swims in the sea

3) トリッキー
· looking for new friends now
· your own

5 Show a picture of your family member, friend, pet, or favorite fictional character to your classmates and make a brief presentation. Afterwards, your classmates will comment and ask you questions.

Introduction

Details
· where they live
· what they do
· what they look like

Closing

Ex. 見てください。これは私の鳥です。名前はモモです。
　　　み　　　　　　　　　　とり　　　なまえ

モモは黒いケージ (cage) の中に住んでいます。モモは
　　　くろ　　　　　　　　す

体が青いです。それから、声がきれいです。
からだ　あお　　　　　　　こえ

ちょっとやせています。とても頭がいいです。
　　　　　　　　　　　　　あたま

私はモモが大好きです。
　　　　だいす

211

Talk about what you have already done and what you have not done yet.

1 Let's practice using もう with 〜ました and まだ with 〜ていません to say you have and have not done the following things.

L6-18

Ex. 漢字を全部覚える
　→ もう漢字を全部覚えました。 → まだ漢字を全部覚えていません。

1）単語を全部覚える　　　2）「よみましょう」を読む　　3）作文 (essay) を書く

4）「ききましょう」を聞く　　5）宿題を出す

2 You would like to do something with your partner.

Step 1 Ask if your partner has done each of the following activities before making an invitation.

Ex. A: もう昼ご飯を食べましたか。

B: いいえ、まだ食べていません。(← Say no)

A: じゃ、いっしょにララに行って野菜ラーメンを食べませんか。

B: いいですね。行きましょう。

Ex. 昼ご飯　　1）晩ご飯　　2）○○という映画　　3）○○の宿題　　4）your own

Step 2 Report your plan to your classmates.

Ex. 私と○○さんはまだ昼ご飯を食べていませんから、いっしょにララに行って野菜ラーメンを食べます。

Ask and answer questions about what you do on a regular basis and with what frequency.

1 Let's practice describing people's regular activities.

Step 1 Describe the things Ai does regularly.

L6-19

Ex. eat a meal / 3 times a day → アイさんは一日に三回ご飯を食べます。

1）brush teeth / 3 times a day　　　2）study Japanese / 4 hours a day

3）sleep / 7.5 hours a day　　　4）go to school / 5 days a week

5）do laundry / twice a week　　　6）practice tennis / twice a month

7）watch a movie / once a month　　　8）travel / once a year

Step 2 Now, ask your partner how often/long they do some activities of your choice.

Ex. A: 一日に何時間勉強しますか。

B: たいてい3時間ぐらい勉強します。

GroupWork

2 Suppose you are researching college students' lives.

Step 1 Choose a topic you are interested in from the box below and ask your groupmates how often they do it.

Possible topics	映画を見る	運動する	旅行する	部屋をそうじする
	えいが み	うんどう	りょこう	へ や
	スマホをチェックする		料理する	
			りょうり	

Ex. A: よく映画を見ますか。
えいが み

B: はい、私は映画が大好きですから、一週間に一回見ます。
わたし えいが だい す いっしゅうかん いっかい み

C: えっと、私は全然見ません。
わたし ぜんぜんみ

A: へえ、そうですか。私は一か月に一回見ます。
わたし いっ げつ いっかいみ

質問 しつもん	私	さん	さん
Ex. 映画を見る えいが み	2 times / month	1 time / week	0

Step 2 Report your findings to your classmates.

Ex. ○○さんはよく映画を見ます。一週間に一回見ます。
えいが み いっしゅうかん いっかい み

でも、△△さんは全然見ません。
ぜんぜんみ

GroupWork

3 Making a commercial: Collaborate with your groupmates to make a commercial for a product, restaurant, place, or food you would like to recommend. Which group can make the best commercial?

Ex. A: ○○さん、これは新しいパリングルスです。もう食べましたか。
あたら た

B: パリングルス？　何ですか。私は知りません。
し

C: えっ、知りませんか。とてもおいしいポテトチップスです。
し

A: 私は大好きです。一週間に五回パリングルスを食べますよ。
だい す いっしゅうかん ご かい た

B: じゃ、私も食べます！
た

ABC: みなさん (everyone)、ぜひパリングルスを買って、食べてください！
か た

Review

Now you can describe a person in detail. Show a picture of you when you were a child (either in a photo or a drawing) to your partner and talk about your childhood. Your partner will ask you questions and comment.

Introduction
Describe:
- where you lived
- what you looked like
- what you used to do
- how often you did it

=============

Q&A

Ex. この写真を見てください。５才の時の私です。

東京に住んでいました。

５才の時、私はかみが短かったです。

よく姉と遊びました。ときどき、日本のおかしを買っ

て、いっしょに食べました。それから、『セーラー・サン』

というアニメが大好きでした。一週間に三回ぐらい見ま

した。○○さんはセーラー・サンを知っていますか。

Q: 私もセーラー・サンをよく見ましたよ。△△さんの好

きなキャラクターはだれですか。

できるⅢ-B **2**

Ex. この宇宙人 (alien) は目が大きいです。耳も大きいです。でも、鼻と口が小さいです。
かみが短いです。

| Student B | **Ex.** | 1) | 2) |

よみましょう

Getting information from signs

1 The ability to recognize signs around stations and on transportation can be of great help when you find yourself traveling in Japan.

[Step 1] First, look at the signs below and guess what information the images are meant to convey. You can discuss with your classmates in whatever language you prefer.

[Step 2] Match the sentences a.-h. in the box below with the corresponding signs 1)-8) in Step 1.

手すり：handrail　席：seat　使う：to use
　せき　　　つか

> a. AI に日本語や英語で話してください。
> 　　　　　　　えいご
> b. IC カードをタッチしてください。
> c. ここで人と会ってください。
> 　　　　　あ
> d. 手すりを持って、エスカレーターに乗ってください。
> 　　　　　　　　　　　　　　　　　　の
> e. 右を歩いてください。
> 　　ある
> f. タクシーでは後ろの席もシートベルトをしてください。
> 　　　　　うし　せき
> g. 座って、使ってください。
> 　すわ　つか
> h. 大きいかばんは体の前で持ってください。
> 　　　　　　　まえ

2 Have you ever heard of ようかい? The passage below will give you an opportunity to learn more about these mythical Japanese creatures.

Step 1 First, let's learn some new words. Match the words 1)-5) with the corresponding pictures a.-e. below.

1）皿　　　→　ご飯の時、皿を使います (to use)。　　　　　　　（　　　）
　さら　　　　　はん　　さら　つか

2）きゅうり　→　きゅうりは 緑 の野菜です。　　　　　　　　（　　　）
　　　　　　　　　　　　　みどり　やさい

3）山伏　　　→　山伏は mountain priest です。　　　　　　　　　
　やまぶし　　　やまぶし

　　　　　　　　着物を着て、げた (Japanese wooden clogs) をはいています。　（　　　）
　　　　　　　　きもの　き

4）顔　　　　→　顔に目と鼻と口と耳があります。　　　　　　（　　　）
　かお　　　　　かお　　　はな

5）男 の子　→　男 の子は 男 の子どもです。　　　　　　　　（　　　）
　おとこ　　　　おとこ　　　　おとこ

a. 　　b. 　　c. 　　d. 　　e.

Step 2 Read the following passage about ようかい and answer the questions that follow.

1　みなさんは日本の妖怪を知っています
　　　　　　　　　　ようかい　し
か。右の写真は妖怪電車の写真です。電
　　しゃしん　ようかいてんしゃ　しゃしん　　でん
車の中におもしろい妖怪が乗っています
しゃ　　　　　　　ようかい　の
から、みんな妖怪の写真をとっています。
　　　　　　ようかい　しゃしん

写真提供：京福電気鉄道株式会社

5 この妖怪は目と口がとても大きいです。そして、顔がこわいです。
　　ようかい　　　　　　　　　　　　　　　　　　　　　　かお

日本にはたくさん妖怪の話があって、「ざしきわらし」や「かっ
　　　　　　　　ようかい
ぱ」や「てんぐ」が有名です。ざしきわらしは男 の子や女 の子
　　　　　　　　　ゆうめい　　　　　　　　　　おとこ　　　おんな
の妖怪です。子どもですから、体が小さいです。たいてい古い部
　ようかい　　　　　　　　　　　　　　　　　　　　　ふる　へ
屋に住んでいて、よくいたずらをします。
や　す

10　かっぱは川にいて、よく泳いでいます。体が緑です。 頭 の上
　　　　　　　　　　　　およ　　　　　　　みどり　あたま
に皿があって、皿の中には水があります。きゅうりが好きですか
　さら　　　　さら　　　　　　　　　　　　　　　　す
ら、よくきゅうりを食べます。町にはあまり来ません。

　　てんぐは山にいます。顔が赤いです。鼻がとても高いです。そ
　　　　　　　　　かお　あか　　　はな　　　　たか
れから、手と足のつめが長いです。山伏の着物を着て、げたをは
　　　　　　　　　　なが　　　やまぶし　きもの　き
15 いています。そして、空を飛びます。 超能力 も持っています。
　　　　　　　　　そら　と　　　ちょうのうりょく

　　みなさんはどの妖怪が好きですか。日本では妖怪のアニメや
　　　　　　　　ようかい　す　　　　　　　　　ようかい
ゲームも人気があります。色々な妖怪がいて、とてもおもしろい
　　　　にんき　　　　いろいろ　ようかい
ですから、ぜひネットで見てください。

みなさん：everyone

こわい：scary

いたずら：mischief;
trick

つめ：nail; claw

空を飛ぶ：to fly
そら　と

超能力：superpower
ちょうのうりょく

色々な：various
いろいろ

Understanding Japanese sentence structure: XはYがZ

1）Underline all instances of the XはYがZ construction in the passage where it is used to describe the characteristics of various ようかい.

▶Check Point: In Japanese, "Xは" [topic] is not repeated when a sentence has the same topic as the previous sentence.

Sorting information

2）Complete the table below in Japanese based on the information found in the passage.

Name of ようかい	Where it is found	Physical characteristics	Additional information
ざしきわらし		・	・
			・
かっぱ		・	・
		・	・
てんぐ		・	・
		・	・
		・	・

Comprehension check

3）Match each of the ようかい names below with the correct picture from a.-e.

a. 　　b. 　　c. 　　d. 　　e.

ざしきわらし（　　）　　かっぱ（　　）　　てんぐ（　　）

4）Fill in ___ below to explain which ようかい you like the most and why.

_____から、私は_____が好きです。
_す

かくれんしゅう　Writing Practice

Now, describe your favorite person, ようかい, anime/game/movie character, etc. Gather your thoughts before you begin to write.

ききましょう

Predicting: Visual clues

In everyday life, verbal communication is not your only source of information. For example, you might also be looking at photographs, illustrations, etc. when you are listening to something. These visual clues can help you make an educated guess about what you are likely to hear. In this lesson, we will practice using visual clues and prior knowledge to improve your listening skills.

1 **Pre-listening activity:** Guess where you might see the following pictures or scenes based on your own experience.

1) Choose the place (1)-(3) from the box on the right where you might see each of the following visuals a.-c. Then, guess what kind of conversation might take place in each location.

（1）美術館
　　びじゅつかん
（2）公園
　　こうえん
（3）レストラン

a. _____   b. _____   c. _____

2) Match the sentences below with the images above and insert the appropriate letter from a.-c. into each ( ).

（1）おもしろい絵ですね。「ぼうし？」というタイトルですよ。　（　　　）

（2）きれいですね。鳥の声が聞こえますね。　（　　　）
　　　　　　　　　　とり こえ き

（3）じゃ、私はこのパスタにします。　（　　　）

2 **Listening:** Your cat Yuki (see the picture to the right) is missing, so your friends have been helping you out by asking people if they have seen her. How would you describe Yuki based on her picture? L6-20

1) Write your description of Yuki below in Japanese.

2) Listen to three people a.-c. talk about the cats they have seen. Which person do you think saw Yuki?

The person who saw Yuki is (Circle your answer):　　a.　　b.　　c.

 Exit Check ☑

Now it's time to go back to the DEKIRU List for this chapter (p.187) and do the exit check to see what new things you can do now that you've completed the lesson.

DEKIRU List

できるCheck ✔

できる I

Talk in detail about things around you and things you want.
自分の身の回りのことやほしい物について、詳しく話すことができる。

Entry ☐ Exit ☐

できる II

Talk in detail about presents you have given and received.
あげたりもらったりした物について、詳しく話すことができる。

Entry ☐ Exit ☐

できる III

Talk about what you want to do.
自分がしたいことについて、話すことができる。

Entry ☐ Exit ☐

STRATEGIES

Conversation Tips .... ・うーん as a filler

Reading .... ・Getting information from a bulletin board
・Sorting information
・Understanding Japanese sentence structure: あげる, くれる, and もらう

Listening .... ・Predicting: Conjunctions as clues

---

GRAMMAR

1. *Te*-forms of *i*-adjectives and です できる I

2. ほしい and ほしがる "want" できる I

3. 何か "something; anything" and 何も〜ない "nothing; not ~ anything" できる II

4. あげる "give," くれる "give," and もらう "receive" できる II

5. V-*masu* たい and V-*masu* たがる "want to V" できる III

6. 〜てみる "V and see; try V-ing" できる III

かいわ

1 できる I　Riemann and Keita are talking together at school.　🔊 **L7-1**

刀：sword
かたな

リーマン：けいたさん、剣道の試合はどうでしたか。
　　　　　　　　　けんどう　しあい

けいた　：楽しかったですよ。子どももたくさんいました。
　　　　　たの

　　　　　みんなかわいくて元気でした。
　　　　　　　　　　　　げんき

リーマン：けいたさんも子どもの時から剣道をしていますか。
　　　　　　　　　　　　　　　　　けんどう

けいた　：ええ、６才の時から習っています。
　　　　　　　さい　　なら

　　　　　子どもの時、僕はおもちゃの刀がほしかったです。
　　　　　　　　　　ぼく　　　　かたな

　　　　　だから、剣道のクラブに入りました。
　　　　　　　　　けんどう　　　はい

リーマン：へえ、そうですか。

けいた　：リーマンさんはスポーツをしますか。

リーマン：うーん、僕はスポーツはあまり好きじゃないです。でも、漢字が好きです。
　　　　　　　ぼく　　　　　　　　す　　　　　　　　かんじ　す

けいた　：え、漢字ですか。
　　　　　　かんじ

リーマン：はい、もう漢字を850覚えました。
　　　　　　　　かんじ　　おぼ

　　　　　漢字は意味がありますから、便利でおもしろいです。
　　　　　かんじ　いみ　　　　　　べんり

　　　　　だから、もっと漢字の本やアプリがほしいです。
　　　　　　　　　　かんじ

けいた　：そうですか。リーマンさんはすごいですね。

一期一会
七転八起
日進月歩

2 できる II　The Japan House members are gathered in the living room, talking about Keita moving in.　🔊 **L7-2**

（お）弁当箱：lunch box　冗談：joke　悪い：bad
　　べんとうばこ　　　　じょうだん　　わる

アイ　：来週けいたさんがジャパンハウスに来ますね。
　　　　らいしゅう

　　　　何か引っこしのプレゼントをあげましょうか。
　　　　　　ひ

マーク　：いいですね。そうしましょう。何がいいですか。

タオ　：お弁当箱はどうですか。私は去年の誕生日にアイさんにかわいい
　　　　べんとうばこ　　　　　きょねん　たんじょうび

　　　　お弁当箱をもらいましたよ。今も使っています。
　　　　べんとうばこ　　　　　　　　つか

マーク　：うーん、けいたさんに弁当箱はちょっと…
　　　　　　　　　　　べんとうばこ

アイ　：マークさんは去年の誕生日に何かもらいましたか。
　　　　　　　　きょねん　たんじょうび

ありがとう！

マーク　：いいえ、何ももらいませんでした。

　　　　　でも、今年はみんなが何かくれますね！　ハハハ、冗談、冗談。

リーマン：僕は漢字が大好きですから、誕生日に両親が漢字の時計をくれました。

アイ　　：え、漢字の時計？　あ、ネットでかっこいい時計を売っています。

　　　　　あまり高くないですよ。

タオ　　：うーん、時計はちょっと…

　　　　　中国語では、時計のプレゼントは悪い意味がありますから…

 3 The conversation in the living room continues.　🔊 L7-3

Lesson
7

アイ　　：あ、もう11時半ですね。私は寝ます。おやすみなさい。

マーク　：僕は部屋で勉強します。じゃ、また明日。

タオとリーマン：おやすみなさい。また明日。

タオ　　：あのう、リーマンさんは今、何がほしいですか。

リーマン：え、僕ですか。僕はもっと時間がほしいです。

タオ　　：時間？

リーマン：ええ、毎日、宿題や試験が大変で…　タオさんは何がほしいですか。

タオ　　：うーん、そうですね…　私はお金！　旅行がしたいです。

　　　　　日本やオーストラリアに行ってみたいです。

リーマン：あ、僕も！　日本に行って、

　　　　　漢字ミュージアムで漢字ゲームがしてみたいです。

　　　　　それから、漢字パズルの本も買いたいです。

ワンポイント　🔊 L7-4

C O N V E R S A T I O N　T I P S

うーん **as a filler:** You can use うーん as a filler when you are hesitating to say something. It is often used together with ちょっと (see the L6 Conversation Tip). You can also use うーん when you are thinking and cannot come up with a reply immediately. In this case, it is often followed by そうですね (see the L4 Conversation Tip).

1）A：今晩、いっしょに映画を見ませんか。

　　B：うーん、今晩はちょっと…

2）A：今、何がほしいですか。

　　B：うーん、そうですね…　あ、寒いから、手ぶくろがほしいです。

たんご

● びょうしゃする　Describing people, things, and feelings

しんせつ（な）
(kind)[does good deeds]
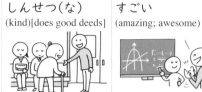

すごい
(amazing; awesome)

こわい
(scared; scary)

きたない
(dirty; messy)

へん（な）
(strange; unusual)

べんり（な）
(convenient; useful)

いろいろ（な）
(various)

うれしい
(glad; happy)

かなしい
(sad)

● ほしいもの　Things one wants

[thing が] ほしい
(to want)

もの
((physical/tangible) thing)

どうぶつ
(animal)

かれ (boyfriend; he)
かのじょ
(girlfriend; she)
きもの
(kimono)

マスク
(face mask)
マフラー
(winter scarf)
てぶくろ
(gloves)
スニーカー
(sneakers; athletic shoes)
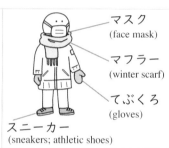

おもちゃ
(toy)

ぬいぐるみ
(stuffed animal)

けいたいでんわ／ケータイ
(mobile phone)

アプリ
(app) [software]

さいふ
(wallet)

ゆびわ
(ring)

チョコレート／チョコ
(chocolate)

● あげる・もらう　Giving and receiving

[receiver に thing を]
あげる (to give)

プレゼント
(present)
[giver に thing を]
もらう (to receive)

[receiver に thing を]
くれる
(to give (to me/
member of my family))
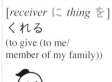

（お）みやげ
(something brought back
from a trip)

おいわい
(congratulatory gift;
celebration)

しゅうかん
(custom; habit)

（お）しょうがつ
(New Year's (holiday))

バレンタインデー
(Valentine's Day)

（〜の）ひ
(day)

Exs. ははのひ (Mother's Day)
しけんのひ (exam day)

ハロウィン
(Halloween)

クリスマス
(Christmas)

● せいかつ・りょこう　Daily life and travel

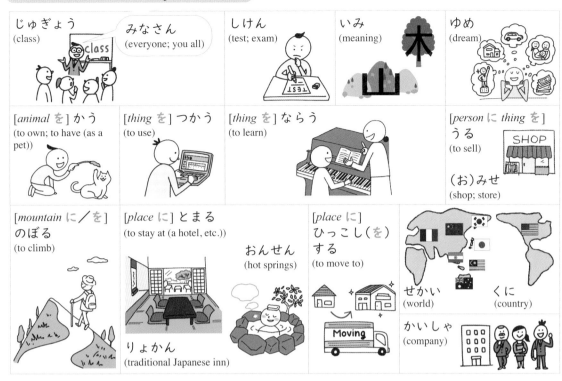

じゅぎょう
(class)

みなさん
(everyone; you all)

しけん
(test; exam)

いみ
(meaning)

ゆめ
(dream)

[animal を] かう
(to own; to have (as a pet))

[thing を] つかう
(to use)

[thing を] ならう
(to learn)

[person に thing を] うる
(to sell)

(お)みせ
(shop; store)

[mountain に／を] のぼる
(to climb)

[place に] とまる
(to stay at (a hotel, etc.))

おんせん
(hot springs)

[place に] ひっこし(を)する
(to move to)

せかい
(world)

くに
(country)

りょかん
(traditional Japanese inn)

かいしゃ
(company)

Lesson
7

● そのほかのひょうげん　Other expressions

なにか (something; anything)

だれか (someone; anyone)

どこか (somewhere; anywhere)

なにも〜ない (nothing; not ... anything)

だれも〜ない (nobody; not ... anyone)

だれとも／だれにも〜ない (not ... with/to anyone)

どこにも〜ない (not ... anywhere)

Noun のまえに
(before Noun)
Ex. じゅぎょうのまえに (before class)

もっと
(more) [number; amount; degree]

どうして
(why)

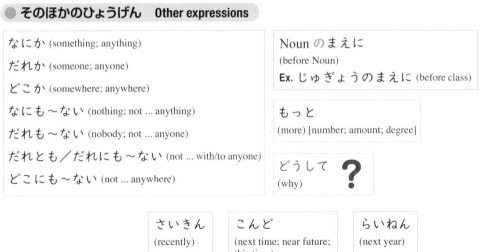

さいきん
(recently)

こんど
(next time; near future; this time)

らいねん
(next year)

またあした。
(See you tomorrow.)

またあした。

たんごリスト

RU-VERBS

1	あげる		to give [*receiver* に *thing* を]
2	くれる		to give (to me/member of my family) [*receiver* に *thing* を]

U-VERBS

3	うる	売る	to sell [*person* に *thing* を]
4	かう	飼う	to own; to have (as a pet) [*animal* を]
5	つかう	使う	to use [*thing* を]
6	とまる	泊まる	to stay at (a hotel, etc.) [*place* に]
7	ならう	習う	to learn [*thing* を]
8	のぼる	登る	to climb [*mountain* に／を]
9	もらう		to receive [*giver* に *thing* を]

SURU-VERB

10	ひっこし（を）する	引っ越し（を）する	to move to [*place* に] [changing residence]

I-ADJECTIVES

11	うれしい		glad; happy
12	かなしい	悲しい	sad
13	きたない	汚い	dirty; messy
14	こわい		scary; to be scared (of) [*1st/2nd person* は (*person/thing* が)] Ex.1 ヘビはこわい Snakes are scary. Ex.2 わたしはヘビがこわい I'm scared of snakes.
15	すごい		amazing; awesome
16	ほしい		to want [*thing* が]

NA-ADJECTIVES

17	いろいろ	色々	various
18	しんせつ	親切	kind [does good deeds]
19	へん	変	strange; unusual
20	べんり	便利	convenient; useful

NOUNS

21	かのじょ	彼女	girlfriend; she
22	かれ	彼	boyfriend; he
23	みなさん		everyone; you all [the polite counterpart of みんな; only used for people]
24	どうぶつ	動物	animal
25	おいわい	お祝い	congratulatory gift; celebration
26	みやげ／ おみやげ		something brought back from a trip [usually as a present for someone else]; present brought when visiting someone's house
27	おもちゃ		toy
28	きもの	着物	kimono [traditional Japanese clothing]
29	けいたいでんわ／ ケータイ	携帯電話	mobile phone
30	さいふ	財布	wallet
31	てぶくろ	手ぶくろ	gloves
32	ぬいぐるみ		stuffed animal
33	もの	物	(physical/tangible) thing
34	ゆびわ		ring [jewelry worn on fingers]
35	いみ	意味	meaning
36	しけん	試験	test; exam
37	しゅうかん	習慣	custom; habit
38	じゅぎょう	授業	class

39	ゆめ	夢	dream
40	おんせん	温泉	hot springs
41	かいしゃ	会社	company
42	みせ／おみせ	（お）店	shop; store; restaurant
43	りょかん	旅館	traditional Japanese inn
44	くに	国	country
45	せかい	世界	world
46	ひ	日	day
47	しょうがつ／おしょうがつ	（お）正月	New Year's (holiday)
48	クリスマス		Christmas
49	ハロウィン		Halloween
50	バレンタインデー		Valentine's Day
51	チョコレート／チョコ		chocolate
52	プレゼント		present; gift
53	マスク		face mask
54	マフラー		winter scarf
55	スニーカー		sneakers; athletic shoes
56	アプリ		app; application [software]

ADVERBIAL NOUNS

57	こんど	今度	next time; near future; this time
58	さいきん	最近	recently
59	らいねん	来年	next year

ADVERB

| 60 | もっと | | more [number; amount; degree] |

QUESTION WORD

| 61 | どうして | | why |

OTHER WORDS AND PHRASES

62	なにか	何か	something; anything [in question]
63	なにも〜ない	何も〜ない	nothing; not ... anything
64	だれか	誰か	someone; anyone [in question]
65	だれも〜ない	誰も〜ない	nobody; not ... anyone
66	だれとも〜ない／だれにも〜ない	誰とも〜ない／誰にも〜ない	not ... with/to anyone
67	どこか		somewhere; anywhere [in question]
68	どこにも〜ない		not ... anywhere
69	Noun の まえに	〜の前に	before Noun
70	またあした	また明日	See you tomorrow.

Lesson
7

かんじ

68 会 会 会 to meet	カイ	会議 meeting　かいぎ　　会社 company　かいしゃ　　会社員 company employee; office worker　かいしゃいん
		会話 conversation　かいわ　　教会 church　きょうかい
	あ(う)	会う to meet　あ
		ノ 人 人 会 会 会

69 聞 聞 聞 to listen; to hear	ブン	新聞 newspaper　しんぶん
	き(く) き(こえる)	聞く to listen; to hear; to ask　き　　聞き取り listening (comprehension)　き と
		聞こえる to be audible　き
		丨 冂 冂 冂 冂 門 門 門 門 門 門 聞 聞 聞

70 読 読 読 to read	ドク	読者 readers　どくしゃ　　読書 reading (books)　どくしょ
	よ(む)	読む to read　よ　　読み物 reading materials　よ もの
		、 亠 ニ ニ 言 言 言 言 計 計 計 詰 詰 読 読 読

71 立 立 立 to stand (up)	リツ	公立 public　こうりつ　　国立 national　こくりつ　　私立 private　しりつ
	た(つ)	立つ to stand (up)　た　　役に立つ to be useful　やく た
		、 亠 亠 立 立

72 住 住 住 to live	ジュウ	住所 address　じゅうしょ　　住人 resident　じゅうにん
	す(む)	住む to take up residence (in)　す　　住んでいる to live (in)　す
		ノ 亻 亻 仁 住 住 住

73 知 知 知 to know	チ	知事 governor　ちじ　　知人 acquaintance　ちじん
	し(る) し(らせる)	知る to get to know; to learn of　し　　知っている to know　し　　知り合い acquaintance　し あ
		知らせる to inform　し
		ノ 亠 仁 チ 矢 知 知 知

74 入 入 入 to enter	ニュウ	入院する to be hospitalized　にゅういん　　入学する to get into/start at a school　にゅうがく
	はい(る) い(れる) いり	入る to enter　はい
		入れる to put in　い　　入口／入り口 entrance　いりぐち い ぐち
		ノ 入

75 売 売 売	バイ	自動販売機 vending machine じどうはんばい き	売店 concession stand/kiosk ばいてん		
	う(る)	売る to sell う	売り場 sales area/floor/counter う ば		
to sell	一 十 土 ㄐ 声 声 売				

76 買 買 買	バイ	売買 sale and purchase ばいばい			
	か(う)	買う to buy か	買い物 shopping か もの		
to buy	買 買 買 買 買 買 買 買 買 買 買 買				

77 物 物 物	ブツ モツ	植物 plant しょくぶつ	動物 animal どうぶつ	荷物 baggage にもつ	
	もの	物 (physical/tangible) thing もの	買い物 shopping か もの	食べ物 food た もの	
		飲み物 drink の もの	読み物 reading materials よ もの	着物 kimono きもの	
		果物 * fruit くだもの	建物 building たてもの	物語 tale; story ものがたり	
thing; object	ノ 丿 匕 牛 牛 物 物 物				

Lesson 7

78 音 音 音	オン イン	音楽 music おんがく	発音 pronunciation はつおん	子音 consonant しいん	母音 vowel ぼいん
	おと ね	音 sound おと			
		音色 timbre ねいろ	本音 one's true thoughts/feelings ほんね		
sound	音 音 音 音 音 产 音 音 音				

79 楽 楽 楽	ガク ガッ ラク	音楽 music おんがく	楽器 musical instrument がっき	楽(な) easy; comfortable らく	
	たの(しい) たの(しむ)	楽しい fun たの	楽しみ(な) eagerly anticipated; looked forward to たの		
		楽しむ to enjoy たの			
pleasure	丶 冫 白 白 白 泊 泊 泊 楽 楽 楽 楽				

80 海 海 海	カイ	海外 overseas かいがい	海外旅行 trip abroad かいがいりょこう	海岸 coast; seashore かいがん	
		海軍 navy [military] かいぐん	海水浴 swimming in the ocean かいすいよく	北海道 Hokkaido ほっかいどう	
	うみ	海 sea; ocean うみ			
sea; ocean	海 海 海 海 海 汐 海 海 海				

81 国 国 国	ゴク コク	中国 China ちゅうごく	韓国 South Korea かんこく	外国 foreign country がいこく	
		外国語 foreign language がいこくご	外国人 foreigner がいこくじん	国立 national こくりつ	
	くに	国 country くに			
country	国 冂 冂 冚 国 国 国 国				

Kanji as elements

These kanji are used in many other kanji as elements, so you will encounter them frequently as you continue to study Japanese.

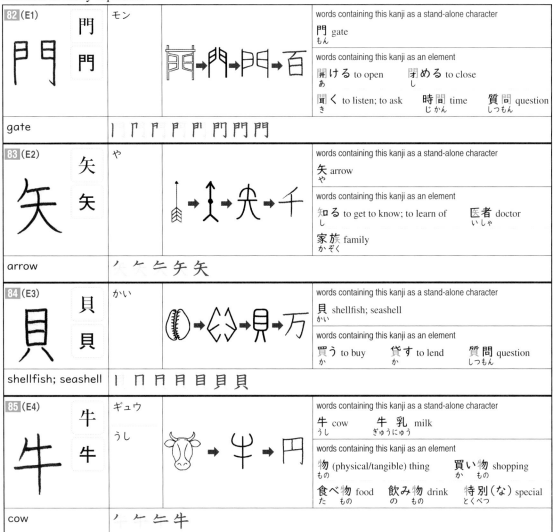

82 (E1) 門 門	モン	門 → 門 → 門 → 百	words containing this kanji as a stand-alone character 門 gate もん
			words containing this kanji as an element 開ける to open　閉める to close あ　　　　　　　し 聞く to listen; to ask　時間 time　質問 question き　　　　　　　じかん　　　しつもん
gate		丨 冂 冂 冂 門 門 門 門	
83 (E2) 矢 矢	や	→ → → 千	words containing this kanji as a stand-alone character 矢 arrow や
			words containing this kanji as an element 知る to get to know; to learn of　医者 doctor し　　　　　　　　　　　　　いしゃ 家族 family かぞく
arrow		ノ 乍 ニ チ 矢	
84 (E3) 貝 貝	かい	→ → 見 → 万	words containing this kanji as a stand-alone character 貝 shellfish; seashell かい
			words containing this kanji as an element 買う to buy　貸す to lend　質問 question か　　　　　か　　　　　しつもん
shellfish; seashell		丨 冂 冂 月 目 貝 貝	
85 (E4) 牛 牛	ギュウ うし	→ 半 → 円	words containing this kanji as a stand-alone character 牛 cow　牛乳 milk うし　　ぎゅうにゅう
			words containing this kanji as an element 物 (physical/tangible) thing　買い物 shopping もの　　　　　　　　　　　　か　もの 食べ物 food　飲み物 drink　特別(な) special た　もの　　　の　もの　　　とくべつ
cow		ノ 午 ニ 牛	

あたらしいよみかた　New readings

The following are new readings for kanji that you have already learned. Read each word aloud.

1）中国　　2）日
　ちゅうごく　　ひ

れんしゅう　Practice

1 Read the following words 1-7 aloud.

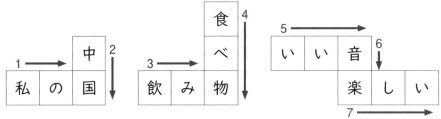

2 Below are posts your friends have made on social media. Read the posts aloud, then write the readings for the underlined words.

1)

日曜日に<u>買い物</u>に行き
ました。きれいな花を
<u>売って</u>いましたから、
<u>買いました</u>。

2)

日本の<u>音楽</u>が大好きで
すから、もっと<u>聞きたい</u>
です。いいバンドを<u>知っ</u>
<u>て</u>いますか。<u>教えて</u>くだ
さい。

3)

日本語サークル (club) に
<u>入り</u>ました。<u>色々な</u><u>国</u>
の人に<u>会って</u>、話しま
した。<u>楽しかった</u>です。

4)

<u>海</u>の近くに<u>住んで</u>いま
す。今日の<u>午後</u>は<u>友達</u>
とアイスクリームを食
べて、ビーチで本を<u>読</u>
みました。

 **The Story of Kanji**

■ **Introduction to kanji elements**

Have you noticed that some kanji actually consist of two or more parts? In this book, we call these individual parts of kanji "elements." Some elements show the meaning of the kanji, and others provide information about how the kanji is pronounced, so learning about elements can help you guess the meaning or reading of a kanji even if you have never encountered it before.

Elements that indicate a meaning typically appear in certain positions within a kanji; these positions are shown shaded below.

1) Left or right   2) Top or bottom   3) Upper left   4) Lower left   5) Enclosure

体 町   花 見   病   週   国 医 間

れんしゅう Practice

In this lesson, four elements are introduced to you: 門, 矢, 貝, and 牛. Make four kanji you have learned by combining one element each from A and B below, then write their meanings in (　) as in the example provided. Some elements may be used twice.

A	B
a 矢　b 牛	1 日　2 罒　3 目
c 門　d 貝	4 四　5 口
	6 勿　7 耳

Ex. __c__ + __7__ → 聞（く）(to listen)

1) ___ + ___ → _____ (　　)

2) ___ + ___ → _____ (　　)

3) ___ + ___ → _____ (　　)

4) ___ + ___ → _____ (　　)

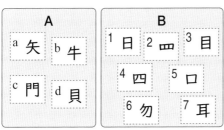

Lesson
7

229

ぶんぽう

1 *Te*-forms of *i*-adjectives and です

1-1 *Te*-forms of *i*-adjectives

[1-a]

	Adj(*i*) (*te*-form)	
このレストランは	おいし**くて**	とてもきれいです。
This restaurant is tasty and very {clean/pretty}.		
マークさんは	やさし**くて**	かっこいいです。
Mark is kind and stylish.		

As you can see in [1-a], you can combine two (or more) adjectives using *te*-form. Thus, with the *te*-forms of adjectives, you can make detailed but concise descriptions of people and things in one sentence.

As you can also see in [1-a], *te*-forms are commonly translated into "X and." In other words, *te*-forms are used when two adjectives can be combined with "and." When two adjectives represent contrastive meanings, you should use "X が、Y" (e.g., 高いですが、おいしくないです *expensive <u>but</u> not delicious*).

You can make the *te*-form of an *i*-adjective by adding **くて** to the stem (= the part that does not conjugate), as shown in the following examples. (The stems are indicated in black.)

Dictionary form	*Te*-form
大きい	大き~~い~~**くて**
おもしろい	おもしろ~~い~~**くて**
Exception: いい かっこいい	**よくて** かっこ**よくて**

(See L4 #4-1.)

Note that *te*-forms do not carry any information about tense or politeness. That information is conveyed by the verb, *i*-adjective, or です in the predicate.

Exs. (1) 日本の100円ショップは安**くて**便利です。
  Hundred-yen stores in Japan are low-priced and convenient.

 (2) 子どもの時、私の出身の町は小さ**くて**あまりにぎやかじゃなかったです。
  When I was a child, my home town was small and not very lively.

 (3) 京都は古**くて**きれいな町です。 *Kyoto is a beautiful old town (lit. old and beautiful town).*

"X は Adj-*te* いいです" ("X is nice and <Adj> (lit. <Adj> and good)"), as introduced in (4) below, is a useful sentence pattern. In this pattern, where the second adjective is いいです, the *te*-form adjective (= the first adjective) indicates why X is good, i.e., a reason that X is good. (More about this use of *te*-forms in L16 #1)

Ex. (4) タオさんの部屋は明る**くて**いいです。 *Tao's room is nice and bright (lit. bright and good).*

[1-b]

	Adj(*na*)	*Desu* (*te*-form)	
このアパートは	静か しず	で	きれいです。
This apartment is quiet and {pretty/clean}.			

[1-c]

	N	*Desu* (*te*-form)	
兄は あに	エンジニア	で	30 才です。 さい
My older brother is an engineer and is thirty years old.			

Na-adjectives and nouns do not conjugate, but the です that follows them does. (See L4 #4-2 and #4-3.) The *te*-form of です is で.

Exs. (1) リーマンさんは漢字が得意で頭がいいです。 *Riemann is good at kanji and smart.*
かん じ　とく い　あた ま

(2) 清水寺は大きいお寺でとても有名です。
きよみずでら　おお　　てら　　　　ゆうめい
Kiyomizu-dera Temple is a big temple and is very famous.

(3) 東京はにぎやかで楽しい町ですが、私の町は静かでつまらないです。
とうきょう　　　　　たの　まち　　　　わたし　まち　しず
Tokyo is a fun, lively (lit. lively and fun) town, but my town is boring and quiet (lit. quiet and boring).

---

2 **ほしい and ほしがる "want"**

[2-a]

X (first person)		Y		
私 わたし	は	新しいスマホ あたら	が	ほしいです。
I want a new smartphone.				

[2-b]

X (second person)			Y			
タオさん	は	今、 いま	何 なに	が	ほしいです	か。
Tao, what do you want right now?						

ほしい is an *i*-adjective. Using ほしい, you can say that you want something or ask the listener (i.e., second person) about what they want. Note that Y (= what X wants) is marked by が.

ほしい is not used when X is someone you want to be polite to (e.g., your teacher, superior, etc.). For example, the following sentence is not appropriate:

× 先生、飲み物は何がほしいですか。 → 先生、飲み物は何がよろしいですか。
せんせい　の　もの　なに　　　　　　　　　　せんせい　の　もの　なに

Professor, what drink would you like? (よろしい is the polite version of いい.)

Exs. (1) 誕生日に新しいくつがほしいです。 *I want a new pair of shoes for my birthday.*
たんじょう び　あたら

(2) 私は今、車はほしくないですが、自転車がほしいです。
わたし　いま　くるま　　　　　　　　　　　　　じ てんしゃ
I don't want a car right now, but I do want a bicycle.

(3) 子どもの時、弟がほしかったですが、妹はほしくなかったです。
こ　　　とき　おとうと　　　　　　　　　　　いもうと
When I was a child, I wanted a younger brother, but I didn't want a younger sister.

[2-c]

X (third person)		Y				
弟 おとうと	は	新しい自転車 あたら　じてんしゃ	を	ほし	がっています。	
My younger brother wants a new bicycle. (lit. My younger brother is showing signs of wanting a new bicycle.)						

When you want to say that a third person wants something, you have to use ほしがっています rather than ほしいです. ほしがっています consists of ほし (the stem of the *i*-adjective ほしい), がって (the *te*-form of the auxiliary verb がる "to show signs of") and います. The い of ほしい drops because がっています attaches to the stems of adjectives.

When がっています is used, Y is always marked by を. Thus, the following sentence is ungrammatical:

　　✕　弟は新しい自転車がほしがっています。
　　　　おとうと　　あたら　　じてんしゃ

Exs. (1)　にゃんたはいつもご飯を ほしがっています。*Nyanta always wants a meal.*
　　　　　　　　　　　　　　はん

　　(2)　弟は子どもの時、いつもイヌを ほしがっていました。
　　　　　おとうと　こ　　　　とき

　　　　My little brother always wanted a dog when he was a child.

☞ **GID** (vol.1): E. Auxiliaries　5. (Adj(*i*)-stem)がる

---

③ **何か** "something; anything" **and** **何も〜ない** "nothing; not ~ anything"

[3-a]

		Q-word		
A:	週末 しゅうまつ	何 なに	か	しますか。
	Are you doing {any/some}thing over the weekend?			

[3-b]

		Q-word	V (negative)
B:	いいえ、	何 なに	も	しません。
	No, I'm not doing anything.			

The question word 何 with か means "something" in a declarative sentence and either "anything" or
　　　　　　　　なに
"something" in a question sentence. The particles が and を are usually omitted after 何か.
　　　　　　　　　　　　　　　　　　　　　　　　　　　　　　　　　　　　　なに

何 with も used in combination with the negative form of a verb, an *i*-adjective, or です means "nothing; not ...
なに
anything." The particles が and を are not used with 何も. The following sentences are ungrammatical:
　　　　　　　　　　　　　　　　　　　　なに

　　✕ 何をも食べませんでした。　→ 何も食べませんでした。*I didn't eat anything.*
　　　なに　　た　　　　　　　　　　なに　　た
　　✕ この部屋には何がもありません。　→ この部屋には何もありません。
　　　　　へや　　なに　　　　　　　　　　　　へや　　なに
　　　　　　　　　　　　　　　　　There is nothing in this room.

か and も are also attached to other question words, as shown below:

Q-word	Q-word + か	Q-word (+ Prt.) + も
だれ	だれか（来ます） き someone (will come) だれかと（行きます） い (will go) with someone だれかに（会います） あ (will meet) someone	だれも（来ません） き no one (will come) だれとも（行きません） い (will not go) with anyone だれにも（会いません） あ (will not meet) anyone
どこ	どこかに（あります／行きます） い (exists/will go) somewhere	どこにも（ありません／行きません） い (does not exist/will not go) anywhere

As seen in the above table, Q-word + か functions as a single word; therefore, no particles occur between the question word and か. (The boxes around だれか and どこか indicate this point.) On the other hand, when Q-word + も is used with the particle に, へ, で, or と, the particle appears between the question word and も and forms a double particle with も, as in the above table and in (2) and (3) below. (See L5 #5.)

Exs. (1) A: 週末、セールで何か買いましたか。
しゅうまつ　　　　　なに　か
Did you buy {any/some}thing at the sale over the weekend?

B: いいえ、何も買いませんでした。*No, I didn't buy anything.*
なに　か

(2) A: 今度の休みにどこかに行きますか。
こんど　やす　　　　　　い
Are you going {any/some}where during the next break?

B: いいえ、忙しいですから、どこにも行きません。
いそが　　　　　　　　　　　　い
No, I'm busy, so I'm not going anywhere.

(3) <On the phone>

A: 今、だれかといっしょに勉強していますか。
いま　　　　　　　　　　べんきょう
Are you studying with {any/some}one right now?

B: いいえ、だれとも勉強していません。*No, I'm not studying with anyone.*
べんきょう

[3-c]

| Q-word + か | Noun phrase | | | |
	Noun modifier	N (generic)		
どこか	静かな しず	所 ところ	に	行きましょう。 い
Let's go somewhere quiet.				

Q-word + か is often used with noun phrases that consist of a noun modifier (e.g., an adjective, a noun + の, etc.) and a generic noun, as in [3-c].

Exs. (4) 何かおもしろいアニメを探しています。*I am looking for some interesting anime.*
なに　　　　　　　　　さが

(5) みかさんに何か誕生日のプレゼントを買いませんか。
なに　たんじょうび　　　　　　　　か
Would you like to buy something as a birthday present for Mika?

Lesson 7

233

4 あげる "give," くれる "give," and もらう "receive"

4-1 あげる and くれる

In Japanese, there are two verbs that mean "to give": あげる and くれる. The following figure shows how these verbs are used.

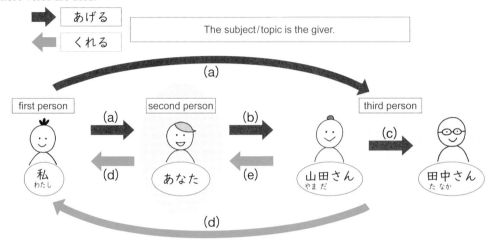

As you can see above, you use あげる:

(a) when the first person (i.e., the speaker) gives something to the second person (i.e., the listener) or a third person,

(b) when the second person gives something to a third person, and

(c) when a third person gives something to another third person.

You use くれる:

(d) when the second person or a third person gives something to the first person, and

(e) when a third person gives something to the second person.

Pay attention to the number of the person (i.e., first, second, or third) of the subject (= the giver). If the number of the person of the giver is lower than or the same as that of the receiver, you use あげる; if the number of the person of the giver is higher than that of the receiver, you use くれる.

あげる and くれる both mean "to give," but the viewpoint differs depending on which one is used. That is, when you use あげる, you are describing the giving action from the giver's viewpoint, whereas when you use くれる, you are describing the action from the receiver's viewpoint.

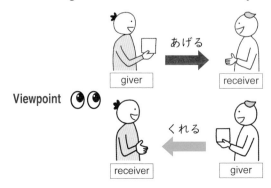

[4-a]	X (giver)		Y (receiver: not the speaker)		Z (gift)		Giving verb
	私 わたし	は	田中さん た なか	に	Tシャツ	を	あげました。
	I gave Tanaka-san a T-shirt.						

In あげる sentences, the giver is usually presented as the topic (i.e., marked by は), the receiver is marked by に, and what is given is marked by を, as in [4-a].

Exs. (1) （私は）誕生日に母に花をあげました。*I gave my mother flowers on her birthday.*
わたし　たんじょう び　はは　はな

(2) リサ：トムさんはみかさんにプレゼントをあげましたか。

　　　　Did you give a present to Mika, Tom?

　　トム：はい、本をあげました。*Yes, I gave her a book.*
　　　　　　ほん

(3) タオさんはアイさんにマレーシアのおみやげをあげました。

　　Tao gave Ai a souvenir from Malaysia.

(4) 日本では、バレンタインデーに友達や好きな人にチョコレートをあげます。
にほん　　　　　　　　　　　　　ともだち　す　　　ひと

　　In Japan, people give chocolates to their friends and people they like on Valentine's Day.

The following sentences are ungrammatical:

× 田中さんは私にプレゼントをあげました。Intended meaning: *Tanaka-san gave me a present.*
　た なか　　わたし

× ワンさん、田中さんはワンさんにプレゼントをあげましたか。
　　　　　　た なか

　　Intended meaning: *Did Tanaka-san give you a present, Wang-san?*

[4-b]	X (giver: not the speaker)		Y (receiver)		Z (gift)		Giving verb
	マークさん	は	私 わたし	に	チョコレート	を	くれました。
	Mark gave me chocolate.						

As seen in [4-b] above, in くれる sentences, the particles are used in the same way as in あげる sentences, i.e., [Giver] は [Receiver] に [Gift] をくれる.

Exs. (5) 彼は去年の私の誕生日に時計をくれました。
かれ　きょねん　わたし　たんじょう び　と けい

　　My boyfriend gave me a watch on my birthday last year.

(6) A: 研さんは誕生日に何かくれましたか。*Did Ken give you something on your birthday?*
けん　　たんじょう び　なに

　　B: いいえ、何もくれませんでした。*No, he didn't give me anything.*
　　　　　　なに

In affirmative くれる sentences, when the receiver is the speaker, it is often omitted, as in (5) and (6)-B. Likewise, in questions, when the receiver is the listener, it is often omitted, as in (6)-A.

Note that when someone gives something to a member of the speaker's family (including a pet), the situation is usually described as if the speaker were the receiver, using くれる, as in (7) and (8) below.

Exs. (7) クラスの友達はにゃんたにおもちゃをくれました。*My classmates gave Nyanta a toy.*
ともだち

(8) となりの人が弟にチョコレートをくれました。
ひと　おとうと

　　My neighbor gave my younger brother some chocolate.

4-2 もらう "receive"

You can express the idea that someone receives something from someone else using もらう. The following figure shows how this verb is used.

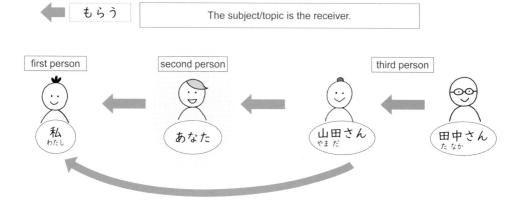

When using もらう, the number of the person (i.e., first, second, or third) of the subject (= the receiver) must be lower than or the same as that of the giver. Thus, the giver must be someone other than the speaker. The following sentence is ungrammatical:

> ✕ リサさんは私にペンをもらいました。
> わたし
>
> → 私はリサさんにペンをあげました。*I gave Lisa a pen.*
>   わたし

When you use もらう, you are describing the action from the receiver's viewpoint.

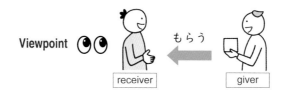

[4-c]	X (receiver)		Y (giver: not the speaker)		Z (gift)		Receiving verb
	私 わたし	は	みかさん	に	チョコレート	を	もらいました。
I received chocolate from Mika.							

In もらう sentences, the receiver is usually presented as the topic, the giver is marked by に, and what is given is marked by を, as in [4-c].

When the receiver is clear from the situation and/or context, you can omit it, as seen in (3) and (4) below. In (3) and (4)-B, the unspoken receiver is the speaker, and in (4)-A, the unspoken receiver is the listener.

Exs. (1) アイさんはけいたさんに剣道の試合のチケットをもらいました。
けんどう　しあい

Ai got a ticket for a kendo competition from Keita.

(2) 大学生の時、母は父にラブレターをもらいました。
だいがくせい　とき　はは　ちち

My mother received a love letter from my father when she was a college student.

(3) 去年の誕生日に何ももらいませんでした。
きょねん　たんじょうび　なに

I didn't receive anything for my birthday last year.

(4) A: だれにそのゲームを もらいましたか。*Who did you get that game from?*

B: リーマンさんに もらいました。*I got it from Riemann.*

The situation in (1) can also be described using あげる, as in (5).

Ex. (5) けいたさんはアイさんに剣道の試合のチケットを あげました。
けんどう　しあい

Keita gave Ai a ticket for a kendo competition.

The difference between (1) and (5) is that in (1), the subject (also the topic) is the receiver, while in (5) the subject (also the topic) is the giver. (1) describes the situation from the receiver's viewpoint while (5) describes the same situation from the giver's viewpoint.

5 **V-*masu* たい and V-*masu* たがる** "want to V"

[5-a]

X (first person)	Y (direct object)		V-*masu* *	
私 は わたし	コーヒー	が／を	飲み の	たいです。
I want to drink coffee.				

* V-*masu* is the portion of the polite non-past affirmative form that precedes ます．　Exs. 食べます, 飲みます
た　　　　の

You can tell someone that you want to do something using V-*masu* たい. たい is an auxiliary *i*-adjective. When there is a direct object, it can be marked by either が or を. When X's desire is strong, が is the best choice. The particles that mark elements other than the direct object do not change when V-*masu* たい is used. (See the underlined particles in (1) and (2) below.)

Exs. (1) 私 は週末、友達と図書館で勉強したいです。
わたし　しゅうまつ　ともだち　としょかん　べんきょう

I want to study with my friend at the library over the weekend.

(2) 私 は明日、学校に行きたくないです。家でゲームをしたいです。
わたし　あした　がっこう　い　　　　　　　いえ

I don't want to go to school tomorrow. I want to play games at home.

In general, たい is only used when the verb expresses something the speaker does. Thus, ある cannot be used with たい, even when it is being used to convey possession, because its literal meaning is that something other than the speaker exists. Thus, the following sentence is ungrammatical:

× 私 は友達がたくさんありたいです。
わたし　ともだち

→ 私 は友達がたくさんほしいです。*I want many friends.*
わたし　ともだち

When inviting someone to do something, you should not use たい. In this case, use 〜ませんか or 〜はどうですか. (See L3 #6.)

× パーティーに来たいですか。　→ パーティーに来ませんか。
き　　　　　　　　　　　　　　　　き

Would you like to come to the party?

× お茶が飲みたいですか。　→ お茶はどうですか。*How about some tea?*
ちゃ　の　　　　　　　　　　ちゃ

X (third person)	Y (direct object)		V-*masu*		
リサさんは	コーヒー	を	飲み の	た	がっています。
Lisa wants to drink coffee. (lit. Lisa is showing signs of wanting to drink coffee.)					

As in the case of ほしい, you use たがっています when X is a third person, as seen in [5-b]. If the verb has a direct object, you mark it with を. Note that が is not used here.

Ex. （3）　弟は忍者に会いたがっています。 *My younger brother wants to meet a ninja.*
おとうと　にんじゃ　あ

☞ **GID** (vol.1): E. Auxiliaries 4. (V-*masu*)たい

6　**〜てみる** "V and see; try V-ing"　

[6]

	V-*te*	
この漢字のアプリを かんじ	使って つか	みます。
I'll try using this kanji app (and see what it is like).		

You can express the idea of "to do something and see (what will happen, what it's like, etc.)" using 〜てみる. みる in this use is an auxiliary verb, and since auxiliary verbs are generally written only in hiragana, the kanji 見 is not used here, as you can see in [6].

Exs. （1）　週末、公園の近くの新しいレストランに行ってみます。
しゅうまつ　こうえん　ちか　あたら　　　　　　　　　　い

　　　　I'll go to the new restaurant near the park (and see what it is like) over the weekend.

　　（2）　日本で富士山に登ってみたいです。 *In Japan I'd like to climb Mt. Fuji.*
にほん　ふじさん　のぼ

　　（3）　A:　それは何ですか。*What's that?*
なん

　　　　　B:　たこ焼きです。おいしいですよ。食べてみてください。
や　　　　　　　　　　　　た

　　　　　　　It's takoyaki. It's good. Please try some.

〜てみる is usually used when the person hasn't experienced the activity in question before. Note that the core meaning of V-*te* みる is "V and see." In many cases, V-*te* みる serves as the equivalent of English "try," but this is not always the case. For example, (4) below is used only when the speaker actually wrote a letter, so interpreting this sentence as "I tried to write a letter in Japanese," which, without context, implies that the action was not performed, would not be appropriate.

Ex. （4）　私は日本語で手紙を書いてみました。
わたし　にほんご　てがみ　か

　　　　I wrote a letter in Japanese (to see what would happen).

はなしましょう

▶ **Words written in purple** are new words introduced in this lesson.

 Talk in detail about things around you and things you want.

できるI-A *Te*-forms of *i*-adjectives and です

1 Let's practice *te*-form conjugations for *i*-adjectives and です.　 **L7-6**

Ex.1 おいしい　　→ おいしくて

Ex.2 にぎやか　　→ にぎやかで

Ex.3 にほんじん → にほんじんで

1) おおきい　　2) おもしろい　　3) やすい　　4) いい　　5) かわいい　　6) きれい

7) ゆうめい　　8) がくせい　　9) きたない　　10) べんり　　11) へん　　12) しけん

2 Describe a school using the cues provided.

Step 1 Say two positive things or two negative things about a school. (☺ + ☺ / ☹ + ☹)　**L7-7**

Ex.　A大学／大きい／有名 → A大学は大きくて、有名です。

1) 授業 ／おもしろい／楽しい
2) 先生／親切／こわくない
3) 学生／頭 がいい／おもしろい
4) 図書館／便利／きれい
5) 食堂／高い／おいしくない
6) 寮 ／古い／きたない

Step 2 Say one negative thing and one positive thing about a school. (☹ + ☺ / ☺ + ☹)　**L7-8**

Ex.　B大学／有名じゃない／いい大学 → B大学は有名じゃないですが、いい大学です。

1) 授業 ／大変／おもしろい
2) 先生／親切／ちょっとこわい
3) 学生／元気じゃない／頭 がいい
4) 図書館／大きい／便利じゃない
5) 食堂／新しい／おいしくない
6) 寮 ／古い／きれい

3 Now, talk about positive and negative aspects of your school.

Ex.　A: この大学は有名じゃないですが、いい大学です。

でも、食堂は小さくて、あまりおいしくないですね。

B: そうですね。それから、寮 は… ＜Continue＞

A: じゃ、授業 はどうですか。

B: 数学の授業 は… ＜Continue＞

Lesson
7

4 Look at the pictures below and describe what kind of characteristics they have.

Ex. A: どんな町ですか。

B: 大きくて、便利な町です。

or 便利ですが、つまらない町です。

Ex. 町

1) 部屋

2) 授業

3) 本

4) 映画

5) 家

5 What are your favorites from the following categories? Take turns with your partner asking what each other's favorites are and expanding the conversation by asking follow-up questions.

Possible categories	本	映画	授業	町	ゲーム	有名な人

Ex. A: ○○さんの好きな本は何ですか。

B:『ハリー・ポッター』です。

A: ハリー・ポッターはどんな話ですか。（← Follow-up question）

B: ファンタジーです。おもしろくて、すごく楽しい話です。

できるI-B　ほしい

1 Let's practice using the expression ほしいです in both affirmative and negative.

Step 1 Say you want the following things.　　Ex. 　　🔊 L7-9

Ex. （私は）お金がほしいです。

1) red　　2) new　　3) cool　　4) cute　　5) various countries　　6) your own

Step 2 Say you don't want the things above.　　🔊 L7-10

Ex. （私は）お金はほしくないです。

Step 3 Now, tell your partner what you want and don't want using the cues in Step 1.

Ex. A: 私はかっこいい時計とかわいいペットがほしいです。でも、新しい携帯電話はほしくないです。○○さんは今、何がほしいですか。

B: 私は… ＜Continue＞

Group Work

2 Ask your classmates what they want right now and why. Ask as many people as possible.

Ex. A：○○さんは今、何がほしいですか。

B：うーん、私はもっとお金がほしいです。それから、試験の答えがほしいです。
<small>しけん　こた</small>

A：え、どうして試験の答えがほしいですか。
<small>しけん　こた</small>

B：来週難しい数学の試験がありますから、答えがほしいです。△△さんは？
<small>むずか　すうがく　しけん　　　　　　　　　　　　こた</small>

<Continue>

3 Did you want the following things when you were a child?

Step 1 Say you wanted the following things. L7-11

Ex. 子どもの時、（私は）本がほしかったです。

1)   2) many   3)   4)   5) (more) siblings 6) your own

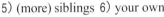 

Step 2 Say you didn't want the things above. L7-12

Ex. 子どもの時、（私は）本はほしくなかったです。

4 Talk about your childhood wishes. Ask your partner what they wanted and why.

Ex. A：○○さんは子どもの時、何がほしかったですか。

B：スマホとゲームのアプリがほしかったです。それから、私の部屋が小さかった
<small>へや</small>
ですから、大きい部屋がほしかったです。△△さんは？
<small>へや</small>

<Continue>

Group Work

5 Ask three classmates what they want for their birthday. When you answer, explain as specifically as possible.

Ex. A：○○さんは今度の誕生日に何がほしいですか。
<small>こんど　たんじょうび</small>

B：うーん、青くて、かっこいいスニーカーがほしいです。日本のスニーカーです。
<small>あお</small>
△△さんは？

<Continue>

できる II Talk in detail about presents you have given and received.

できるⅡ-A 何か and 何も〜ない

1 Let's practice using Q-word + か and Q-word + も. Ask your partner questions based on the cues provided. When asked, answer in the negative. ((◆)) **L7-13**

Ex.1 A: 何か食べますか。

B: いいえ、何も食べません。

Ex.1 何か／食べる 　　1）何か／飲む 　　　　2）何か／ある

3）何か／ほしい 　　4）だれか／来る 　　　5）だれか／待っている

Ex.2 A: だれかとご飯を食べましたか。

B: いいえ、だれとも食べませんでした。

Ex.2 だれか／ご飯を食べる 　6）だれか／話す 　　　　　7）だれか／会う

8）どこか／行く 　　　　9）どこか／こわい人がいる

2 You were really tired, so you didn't do anything over the weekend. Answer your partner's questions accordingly. Pay close attention to the particles you use. ((◆)) **L7-14**

Ex. A: 週末、どこかに行きましたか。

B: いいえ、どこにも行きませんでした。

Ex. go somewhere? 　　1）do something? 　　2）eat something?

3）meet with someone? 　4）talk with someone? 　5）your own

3 You want to do something together with your classmates. Ask your partner the questions below until they answer "no" to one, then invite them to do that activity. Once you've asked and answered, pair up with a new partner and ask a new question.

Ex. A: 授業の前に何か食べましたか。

Yes		No
B: はい、食べました。		B: いいえ、何も食べませんでした。
A: そうですか。		A: そうですか。
じゃ、また今度。(Another time.)		じゃ、いっしょに何か食べませんか。
		<Continue>

1）授業の前に何か食べましたか。 　　2）授業の後で、何かありますか。

3）今度の休みに、どこかに行きますか。 　4）今晩、だれかと〇〇ますか。

1　First, go through this rap five times to memorize the verbs for giving and receiving.

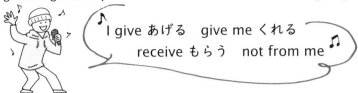

I give あげる　give me くれる
receive もらう　not from me

2　You went to Japan and brought back some souvenirs for your family and friends. Describe what you gave to each person based on the image below. 🔊 **L7-15**

Ex.1 私は 両親に 箸を あげました。
　　　　りょうしん　はし

Ex.2 私はペットのシロに何もあげませんでした。

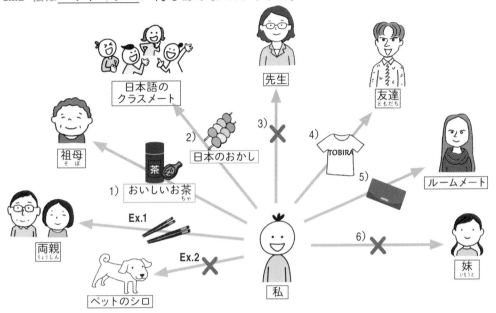

3　Describe what each of the people below gave to you or your family members last month. 🔊 **L7-16**

Ex. 先月、 両親は私にお金をくれました。
　　　　　　りょうしん

4 Look at the image in できるII-B-③ and describe what you or your family members received from each of the people pictured last month.

Ex. 先月、私は両親にお金をもらいました。
りょうしん

or 何ももらいませんでした。

5 Review how to describe giving and receiving. Describe what each of the people below gave each other during the holiday season. Describe their gifts from both the giver's and the receiver's viewpoint. Pay attention to which verb should be used. 🔊 **L7-17**

Ex. レンさんの彼女はレンさんにマフラーをあげました。
かのじょ

レンさんはレンさんの彼女にマフラーをもらいました。
かのじょ

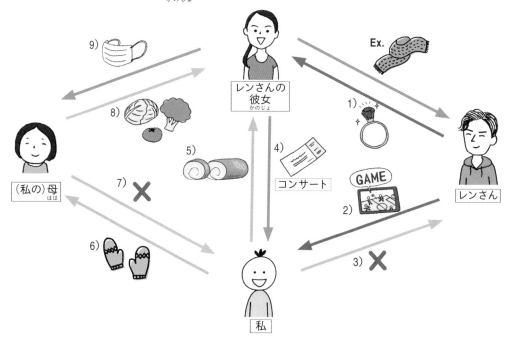

6 Talk with your partner about your experiences giving and receiving gifts. Ask follow-up questions to continue the conversation.

> **Possible topics** 誕生日 クリスマス お正月 バレンタインデー ○○のお祝い
> たんじょうび しょうがつ いわ

Ex. A: 去年の誕生日にだれかに何かもらいましたか。
きょねん たんじょうび

B: はい、もらいました。両親にお金を３万円もらいました。
りょうしん

それから… <Continue>

or いいえ、だれにも何ももらいませんでした。ちょっと悲しかったです。
かな

○○さんは… <Continue>

Group Work

7 Exchange gifts with your classmates and try your luck.

[Step 1] On a sheet of paper, draw/write something that you would be happy to receive as a gift.
Walk around and exchange your gift with a classmate, then exchange the gift you received
with another classmate, continuing until your teacher says "終わりです (time's up)."
お

Ex. A: これ、どうぞ。

B: ありがとうございます。私もプレゼントがあります。どうぞ。

A: ありがとうございます。わあ、新しいスマホですね。
あたら

ほしかったですから、うれしいです。

B: わあ、アメフト (American football) のチケットですか。すごいです！

[Step 2] Tell your partner about your series of gift exchanges and how you feel about what you
ended up with.

Ex. 私は○○さんに新しいスマホをあげて、アメフトのチケットをもらいました。そ
あたら
れから、△△さんにアメフトのチケットをあげて、世界のチーズをもらいました。
せ かい
私はチーズを食べませんから、チーズはあまりほしくなかったです。

8 Talk about the gift-giving traditions in your family, in your culture, or in the country you live in.
Choose an occasion to talk about from the box below.

Possible topics	母の日	父の日	バレンタインデー	ハロウィン	旅行の後で
	はは ひ	ちち ひ			りょこう あと

Ex. A: ○○さんの出身はトルコ (Turkey) ですね。トルコでは母の日に何をあげますか。
しゅっしん はは ひ

B: トルコでは母の日にたいてい白い花をあげます。
はは ひ しろ

A: そうですか。オーストラリアではキクの花をあげます。

B: へえ、そうですか。おもしろいですね。

キク
(chrysanthemum)

9 Have you received any gifts recently? Show a picture/drawing of a gift you've received to
your partner and tell them about it. (You can make up a story if you haven't received any gifts
recently.)

Ex. A: ○○さん、ちょっと見てください。

B: はい、何ですか。

A: 友達が漢字のTシャツをくれました。日本のおみやげです。
ともだち かんじ

B: へえ、日本のおみやげですか。おもしろくて、いいTシャツですね。

この漢字は何ですか。
かんじ

A: 「空手」という漢字ですよ。○○さんは、最近だれかに何かもらいましたか。
からて かんじ さいきん

<Continue>

Lesson 7

できる III　**Talk about what you want to do.**

できる III-A　V-*masu* たい

1 Let's practice conjugating 〜たい.

Ex. たべる

1) みる　　2) いく　　3) あう

4) かう　　5) はいる　　6) する

7) くる　　8) おしえる　　9) つかう

10) ならう　　11) のぼる

	non-past	
affirmative	たべたいです	たべたくないです
	たべたかったです	たべたくなかったです
	past	

(affirmative ← ... → negative)

🔊 L7-18

2 Are you planning a trip to Japan? Practice making some useful Japanese phrases you can use at the tourist information center.

Ex. すみません、ちょっと教えてください。
　　おいしいラーメン {が／を} 食べたいです。

Ex. 食べる

1) 行く　　2) 入る　　3) 泊まる　　4) 使う　　5) 知る　　6) your own
　　　　　　　はい　　　　　と　　　　　つか　　　　し

3 Let's play a bingo game and find out who wants to do the following things.

Step 1　Walk around and ask and answer one question with each person you speak to. If someone answers yes, write their name down in the space provided in the table below.

Ex.　A: ○○さんは今、ゲーム {が／を} したいですか。

　　　B: はい、したいです。or いいえ、したくないです。

　　　A: どんなゲーム {が／を} したいですか。(← Follow-up question, if yes.)

　　　<Continue>

Ex. ゲームをする _____さん	1) 動物を飼う _____さん	2) 日本で英語を教える _____さん
3) 引っこしをする _____さん	4) your own question _____さん	5) どこかに行く _____さん
6) 何か売る _____さん	7) 何か習う _____さん	8) だれかにプレゼントをあげる _____さん

Step 2　Did you find anything you have in common with your classmates? Report what you found out.

Ex.　○○さんと私は今、ゲームがしたいです。

4 Ask your partner if they wanted to do the following things when they were a child.

Ex. A: 子どもの時、○○さんはピアノが習いたかったですか。

B: はい、習いたかったです。or いいえ、習いたくなかったです。

△△さんはどうでしたか。 <Continue>

Ex. ピアノ／習う　　1) スポーツ／習う　　2) 友達の家／泊まる　　3) ペット／飼う
4) サンタクロース／プレゼント／もらう　　5) 一人で飛行機／乗る　　6) your own

5 Talk about what you want to give to and receive from others, and provide your reasons why.

Ex. A: ○○さんは今、だれに何をあげたいですか。

B: そうですね、母はいつも働いていますから、私は母に休みをあげたいです。
A: ○○さんはやさしいですね。じゃ、今、だれに何をもらいたいですか。

<Continue>

Lesson 7

できるⅢ-B　～てみる

1 Let's practice using the expression ～てみる。　　L7-19

Ex. たべる → たべてみます

1) みる　　2) きく　　3) よむ　　4) いく　　5) つくる　　6) つかう　　7) する

2 Take turns with your partner recommending the following things and expressing an interest in trying them, as shown in the example.　　L7-20

Ex. おかし　A: このおかしはおいしいですよ。

B: そうですか。じゃ、食べてみます。

1) ドラマ　　2) 歌　　3) 本
4) 美術館　　5) ゲーム　　6) your own

3 Suppose you are going to Japan next year. To make your travel experience special, what would you like to try there? Select from the options below and talk about it with your partner.

Ex. A: ○○さんは来年日本に行って、何がしてみたいですか。

B: きれいで有名な山ですから、富士山に登ってみたいです。
A: そうですか。時間がかかりますから、私は富士山にあまり登りたくないです。

or 私も富士山に登ってみたいです。

富士山

すもう

カプセルホテル

着物

your own

4 Is there anything you would like to recommend to your classmates (e.g., a place, a book, some music, etc.)? Give your partner your recommendation.

Possible topics	店	カフェ	所	映画	歌	ゲーム	まんが	本
	みせ		ところ	えいが	うた			

Ex. A: ○○さんは「ピース」という店を知っていますか。
みせ し

No	**Yes**
B: いいえ、知りません。 し A: おいしくて、いい店ですから、 みせ 　　ぜひ行ってみてください。 B: そうですか。じゃ、今度行ってみます。 こんど	B: はい、知っています。 し 　　サンドイッチがおいしいですね。 A: はい、全部すごくおいしいです。 ぜんぶ

Group Work

5 What would you do if you had a time machine and could use it to go anywhere and do anything you wanted?

[Step 1] First, answer brainstorming questions Q1.-Q4. below.

Useful time expressions for Q1.	～年前：～ years ago まえ ～年後：～ years in the future ご ～才の時：when I was/am ～ years old さい

Q1. {何年前に／何年後に} まえ　　　　ご 行ってみたい？	Q2. どこに行ってみたい？	Q3. だれに会ってみたい？ あ 何がしてみたい？	Q4. どうして？

[Step 2] Now, give a presentation about what you would use the time machine to do. Remember to include all the information from Q1.-Q4. in Step 1. When you are done, your group members will ask follow-up questions.

Ex. 私はショパン (Chopin) が大好きですから、180年前のフランスに行って、
だいす　　　　　　　　　　　　　　　まえ
ショパンに会ってみたいです。そして、すごいピアノを聞いてみたいです。
あ　　　　　　　　　　　　　　　　　　　　　　き
Q: ○○さんはショパンのどの曲 (piece of music) が好きですか。(← Follow-up question)
きょく　　　　　　　　　す

Review

Now you can talk about what things you want and what you want to do. Talk about your life plan with your classmate.

Step 1 First, create a simple outline for your life plan. Write things you want and things you want to do, as well as when you want to get or do them.

20代: in one's twenties
だい

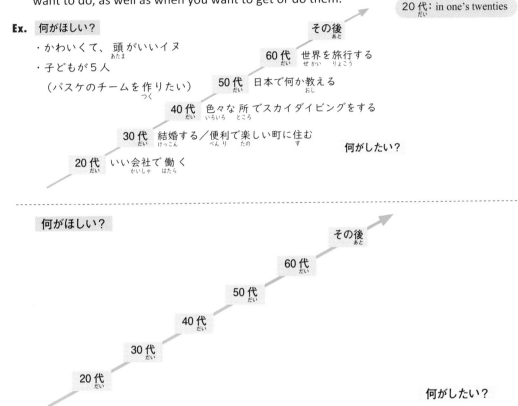

Ex. 何がほしい？

・かわいくて、頭がいいイヌ
　　　　　あたま
・子どもが５人
　（バスケのチームを作りたい）
　　　　　　　　　つく

その後
　　あと

60代　世界を旅行する
だい　せかい　りょこう

50代　日本で何か教える
だい　　　　　　おし

40代　色々な所でスカイダイビングをする
だい　いろいろ　ところ

30代　結婚する／便利で楽しい町に住む
だい　けっこん　べんり　たの　　す

何がしたい？

20代　いい会社で働く
だい　かいしゃ　はたら

何がほしい？

その後
　　あと

60代
だい

50代
だい

40代
だい

30代
だい

20代
だい

何がしたい？

Lesson
7

Step 2 Give a presentation about your plan. Your partner will ask you questions and comment.

Opening
Explain your goals for various ages in detail:
• what you want
• what you want to do
• reasons

Closing
=============
Q&A

Ex. 私の夢を聞いてください。
　　　ゆめ　き

20代はいい会社で働きたいです。それから、かわい
だい　　かいしゃ　はたら
くて、頭がいいイヌがほしいです。イヌはアニマル
あたま
シェルターでもらいたいです。30代はだれかと結婚
だい　　　　　　　けっこん
して、便利で楽しい町に住みたいです。バスケット
べんり　たの　　す
ボールのチームを作ってみたいですから、子どもが５
つく
人ほしいです。<Continue>

みなさん、私のプランはどうですか。

Q: どんな会社で働きたいですか。
かいしゃ　はたら

249

よみましょう

1 Read the conversation on the left where the Japan House members look at Japanese bulletin board postings and discuss things they want. Then, look at the postings on the right to see what people are giving away and answer the questions that follow.

1) There are two matches between the people looking to give something away and the Japan House members. Fill in the sentences below to describe those matches.

    a. _____さんは_____さんに_____をもらいます。

    b. _____さんは_____さんに_____をもらいます。

2) Choose an item you want from the bulletin board above and explain why you want it.

_____から、私は_____　_____。

2 Read the essay below about gift-giving customs in Japan and answer the questions that follow.

1　みなさんはどんな日本のプレゼントの習慣を知っていますか。日本ではお正月に子どもが家族や親せきにお年玉をもらいます。お年玉はお金です。小学校の時はたいてい三千円から五千円ぐらいもらって、高校の時は五千円から一万円ぐらい

5　a)もらいます。だから、私は子どもの時、お正月にたくさん親せきの人に会いたかったです。

　　日本のバレンタインデーは「チョコレートの日」です。前は、日本では女の人が好きな男の人や会社の男の人にチョコをあげました。でも、今はみんなが色々な人にチョコをあげます。

10　私は友達には「友チョコ」をあげて、家族には「ファミチョコ」をあげます。そして、好きな人には「本命チョコ」をb)あげます。
　　結婚の時は、結婚する人にお祝いのお金やプレゼントをあげます。私は何か物をあげたいですから、たいていほしい物を聞いて、それをあげます。

15　引っこしの時は、近所の人にあいさつの小さいプレゼントをあげます。私は今、マンションに住んでいます。先月牛田さんという人がとなりに入りました。引っこしの日、牛田さんは私の部屋に来て、あいさつのおかしをc)くれました。これは「よろしくお願いします」という意味です。

20　それから、旅行の時、日本の人は家族や友達や会社の人によくおみやげを買います。去年、私は母といっしょにイタリアを旅行しました。ミラノで音楽を聞いて、電車に乗ってシチリアの海に行きました。とても楽しくて、いい旅行でしたが、母はいつもどこかで、だれかにおみやげを買っていました。

25　日本のプレゼントの習慣はみなさんの国の習慣と同じですか。みなさんの国にはどんなプレゼントの習慣がありますか。

親せき：relatives

小学校：elementary school

前は：before

本命チョコ：chocolate you give to someone you like romantically

結婚する人：person getting married

近所の人：neighbors
あいさつ：greeting
マンション：condominium

ミラノ

シチリア

同じ：same

1) Complete the figures below illustrating who gives what to whom in Japan on the following occasions. Fill in the ☐ under the givers and receivers with the appropriate letters A.-I. from the box below, then write what is given as a gift in ( ).

A. 結婚する人	B. 家族	C. 親せき	D. 友達	E. 会社の人
けっこん	かぞく	しん	ともだち	かいしゃ
F. 男 の人	G. 女 の人	H. 子ども	I. 近所の人	
おとこ	おんな		きんじょ	

Ex. 結婚の時
けっこん

引っこしの時
ひ

旅行の時
りょこう

お正月
しょうがつ

前の
まえ
バレンタインデー

結婚おめでとう
けっこん
ございます。

となりに
引っこしました。
ひ

旅行に
りょこう
行きました。

☐　　☐

☐　　A

☐　　☐

(　　　)　(　　　)

(お金やプレゼント)

(　　　)　(　　　)

2) Who is the subject of each of the underlined verbs in the essay (reproduced below)? That is, who is the giver or receiver, depending on the verb? Write your answers in Japanese.

　a) l.5 もらいます：　　　b) l.11 あげます：　　　c) l.18 くれました：

3) Mark ◯ if the statement is true and ✕ if it is false.

（　　） この人 (= writer) は子どもの時、お金がほしかったですから、お正月に親せき
　　　　　　　　　　　　　　　　　　　　　　　　　　　　　　　しょうがつ　しん
　　　　の人に会いたかったです。

（　　） 今、日本ではバレンタインデーに 女 の人は何ももらいません。
　　　　　　　　　　　　　　　　　　　　　　おんな

（　　） この人は結婚する人にたいていお金をあげます。
　　　　　　　　　けっこん

（　　） 牛田さんの引っこしの日、この人は牛田さんに「ありがとう」の小さいプレ
　　　　　　うしだ　　　　ひ　　　　　　　　　　　うしだ
　　　　ゼントをもらいました。

（　　） 旅行の時、この人のお母さんはたくさんおみやげを買いました。
　　　　　りょこう　　　　　　　　　かあ

4) あなたは日本のどのプレゼントの 習 慣が好きですか。どうしてですか。
　　　　　　　　　　　　　　　　　　しゅうかん　す

· ·

かくれんしゅう　*Writing Practice*

Now, write a column for a Japanese website to introduce gift-giving customs in your culture or in a country you have lived in.

· ·

ききましょう

Predicting: Conjunctions as clues

Previously, we looked at how context can help us predict the content of a conversation. Conjunctions can also help us predict what someone is going to say next. Conjunctions such as それから, でも, だから, "〜が、〜," and "〜から、〜" all serve to show the relationship between the preceding sentence and the sentence that follows. By making that relationship clear, conjunctions improve the flow and cohesiveness of speech and text. Pay attention to the conjunctions you hear while listening so they can help you predict what will come next.

1 **Pre-listening activity:** Read the following sentences and predict what sentences will follow based on the conjunctions provided.

Lesson
7

1) 私は日本語を話します。それから、＿＿＿＿＿＿＿＿＿＿＿＿＿＿＿＿＿＿＿。

2) 田中さんはテニスが好きですが、＿＿＿＿＿＿＿＿＿＿＿＿＿＿＿＿＿＿＿。
　　　　　　　　　す

3) <At a restaurant>

　　今は肉を食べたくないですから、＿＿＿＿＿＿＿＿＿＿＿＿＿＿＿＿＿。
　　　にく

 L7-21

2 **Listening:** Listen to the conversations. Each conversation will be interrupted by a chime, at which point you should pause the audio and try to predict what will be said next. Then, resume playback and listen to the three choices a.-c. presented for how the conversation might continue. Circle the letter corresponding to the most appropriate continuation.

1) a.　　b.　　c.　　　2) a.　　b.　　c.　　　3) a.　　b.　　c.

4) a.　　b.　　c.　　　5) a.　　b.　　c.

Exit Check ☑

Now it's time to go back to the DEKIRU List for this chapter (p.219) and do the exit check to see what new things you can do now that you've completed the lesson.

Unit2 チャレンジ

1 Not just sushi and ramen

Japanese cuisine has so much more to offer. See if there are any Japanese restaurants near you and explore what other offerings (including drinks and sweets) they have. If you can, try a new dish and share information about it with your classmates.

#ぎゅうどん　#食べてみました　#おいしかった

2 Yuru-Chara® contest

Yuru-Chara are anime-style cartoon mascots that represent various places and organizations in Japan. Yuru-Chara are featured on posters, brochures, and websites, and are a fun and inviting symbol of the places and things they represent.

Step 1 Look into what Yuru-Chara there are in Japan and choose your favorite one to share with your classmates.

©TOKYO TOWER

Ex. これは東京タワーのふたごのゆるキャラです。
名前はノッポン兄弟です。東京タワーに住んでいます。左は弟さんで、右はお兄さんです。
ノッポンは背が高くて、顔が長いです。赤と青のオーバーオール (overalls) を着て、くつをはいています。
ノッポンはツイッター (Twitter) のアカウントを持っています。ノッポンのツイッターはとてもおもしろいです。

Step 2 Try creating a Yuru-Chara for your hometown or for your favorite city in your country! Share your character with your classmates by describing it in detail and decide who has the best one. You can find more examples on the *TOBIRA* website.

Ex.

©Center for Japanese Studies,
University of Michigan

©Emilee Meng

©Vivienne Blackburn

「ゆるキャラ®」という呼称はみうらじゅん事務所および扶桑社の所有する商標です。

は in negative sentences

You have already learned that は can be used as a topic marker and as a contrastive element marker (see L1 #1 and L3 #4). In fact, は has yet another important function: indicating the scope of negation in negative sentences. Let's consider the following examples:

（1）ユミさんは昨日テニスをしませんでした。　*Yumi didn't play tennis yesterday.*

（2）ユミさんは昨日はテニスをしませんでした。

（3）ユミさんは昨日テニスはしませんでした。

Sentences (1)-(3) are all negative sentences with ユミさん as the topic. The only difference is that another は is attached to 昨日 in (2) and to テニス in (3). This second は in (2) and (3) indicates which element of the sentence is being negated by the negative form しませんでした. In other words, は is used to indicate the scope of negation in negative sentences. (In spoken English, this is done by pronouncing the negated word with stronger stress than the other words.) Thus, (2) implies that Yumi regularly plays tennis, but she didn't play it *yesterday*. In contrast, (3) states that Yumi didn't play *tennis* yesterday, implying that she did do something else (for example, yoga). By using は in this way, you can make it clear exactly which element of a negative sentence you are negating.

Sentences (4)-(6) below provide another set of examples:

（4）雨 {は／ ?? が} 降っていません。　*It's not raining.*　Cf. 雨が降っています。　*It's raining.*

（5）スノーボード {は／ ?? が} ほしくないです。　*I don't want a snowboard.*

　　Cf. スノーボードがほしいです。　*I want a snowboard.*

（6）ゲーム {は／ ?? を／ ?? が} したくないです。　*I don't want to play games.*

　　Cf. ゲーム {を／が} したいです。　*I want to play games.*

The above examples have just one element of negation; nevertheless, は is used rather than が and を. This use of は is considered to be an extended use of は as a marker for negated elements.

Addressing and referring to people in Japanese

The way people address and refer to each other in Japanese varies depending on the situation and the relationships of the people involved. The following table summarizes some of the most common forms of address and describes the situational and relational contexts they are used in.

P=Polite　C=Casual

	Form of address	Example	Situational and relational context
P ↑	〜様 さま	ブルーノ様（アイ・ブルーノ様） さま 赤井様（赤井圭太様） あか い さま　あか い けい た さま	· from a shop keeper to a customer · from a hotel worker/server to a guest · to the addressee of a letter
	〜さん	ブルーノさん アイさん 赤井さん あか い 圭太さん けい た	· from a teacher to a student · between people of different ages/generations · among classmates, colleagues, and people of the same generation · can be used in both formal & casual situations depending on the relationship
	〜くん（君） くん	赤井くん あか い 圭太くん けい た	· usually to a boy/younger man · in close relationships such as between family members, among friends, etc.
	〜ちゃん	アイちゃん 圭太ちゃん けい た	· to children regardless of gender · in close relationships such as between family members, among friends, etc.
↓ **C**	a person's name without a suffix	アイ or ブルーノ 赤井 or 圭太 あか い　　　　けい た (first name or last name)	· from parents to children or among siblings · among close friends or in close relationships · from senior to junior students at school, in a club, etc.
	〜先生 せんせい	黒田先生 くろ だ せんせい ブラウン先生 せんせい	· from a student/parents to a teacher at school · from a patient to a medical doctor · to a specialist such as a professor, scientist, etc.

When referring to their family in formal situations, Japanese people use the terms in Table 1 below (see L3); when addressing their family members within the home, however, Japanese people generally use the terms in Table 2.

Table 1: Referring to one's family members in a formal context		Table 2: Addressing one's family members	
祖父 そ ふ	祖母 そ ぼ	（お）じい｛さん／ちゃん｝	（お）ばあさん｛さん／ちゃん｝
父 ちち	母 はは	（お）父｛さん／ちゃん｝；パパ とう	（お）母｛さん／ちゃん｝；ママ かあ
兄 あに	姉 あね	（お）兄｛さん／ちゃん｝ にい	（お）姉｛さん／ちゃん｝ ねえ
妹 いもうと	弟 おとうと	名前／名前＋ちゃん な まえ　な まえ	名前／名前＋｛ちゃん／くん｝ な まえ　な まえ

Q: Referring to the forms of address in the box below, think of how Ai and these people might address or refer to each other in Japanese and provide the reasons for your decisions. Note that there is not just one right answer.

a. 〜さん　　b. 〜くん　　c. 〜ちゃん
d. 〜先生　　e. 名前だけ
　せんせい　　　な まえ

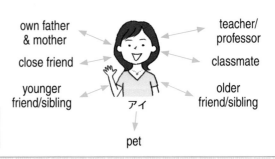

own father & mother　　teacher/professor
close friend　　classmate
younger friend/sibling　　older friend/sibling
アイ
pet

世界に目を向ける
せ　かい　　　　め　　　む
Looking out into the world

03

Unit3のまえに

The theme of this unit is "Looking out into the world." To start, let's take a brief look at some examples of traditional cultural practices in Japan.

1 The pictures below depict some traditional Japanese sports, artforms, and other cultural practices. See the *TOBIRA* website for videos briefly introducing each of them, then discuss questions Q1.-Q4. with your classmates.

a

b

c

d

e

写真：アフロ

f

Q1. ビデオはどうでしたか。何がおもしろかったですか。

Q2. 写真の [a]～[f] は下の①～⑥のどれですか。(Match [a]-[f] to ①-⑥.)

① 剣道
けんどう   ② 華道
か どう   ③ 弓道
きゅうどう   ④ 柔道
じゅうどう   ⑤ 茶道
さ どう   ⑥ 書道
しょどう

> You will notice that all of words ①-⑥ contain the kanji 道. This kanji's *on-yomi*, as shown in these words, is どう, while its *kun-yomi* is みち. The character's literal meaning in English is "way," but it means more than that in this context—in addition to being a way of polishing one's skills, each of these disciplines is thought of as a path to personal growth and a means of building mental and physical strength. It represents a cultural mindset with regard to such pursuits that is typical in Japan.

Q3. [a]～[f] の中で何がしてみたいですか。

Q4. [a]～[f] の他に (besides [a]-[f])、どんな日本の文化を知っていますか。
ほか　　　　　　　　　　　　　　　　　　　　　　　　ぶん か

2 あなたの国や他の (other) 国ではどんな文化が有名ですか。話してみましょう。
ほか　　　　　　　　ぶん か　ゆうめい
(Discuss with your classmates.)

Lesson 8

ちょっとお願いがあるんですが…
I have a favor to ask of you...

Instructional Video
Lesson 8

DEKIRU List

できるCheck ☑

できるI
Ask and answer questions about preferences, skills, and abilities.
好きなことや嫌いなこと、得意なことや苦手なことについて、尋ねたり答えたりすることができる。
Entry ☐ Exit ☐

できるII
Talk about the reason for or purpose of an activity.
することやしたことについて、理由や目的を話すことができる。
Entry ☐ Exit ☐

できるIII
Ask and answer questions about plans in casual speech.
予定などについて、くだけた話し方で尋ねたり答えたりすることができる。
Entry ☐ Exit ☐

できるIV
Request a favor or ask for permission with the appropriate level of formality.
適切なスピーチスタイルで目上の人や友達にお願いしたり、許可を求めたりすることができる。
Entry ☐ Exit ☐

STRATEGIES

Conversation Tips .... • Casual speech styles

Reading .... • How to read vertical writing
　　　　　　　　　　　 • Scanning and skimming
　　　　　　　　　　　 • Understanding the missing elements in casual expressions

Listening .... • Integration: Content prediction strategies

---

GRAMMAR

1. XはYがZ [Preference, skillfulness, ability] **できるI**

2. V-plainの [Verb nominalization] **できるI**

3. Plain non-past forms of verbs, *i*-adjectives, and です **できるII**

4. か [Alternative] "or" **できるII**

5. Place に {V-*masu* / N} にV (motion) [Purpose of motion] **できるII**

6. Casual speech **できるIII**

7. 〜ないでください [Polite prohibition] **できるIV**

8. 〜んですが [Lead-in sentence ending] **できるIV**

9. 〜てくれませんか／くださいませんか [Request] **できるIV**

10. 〜てもいい [Permission] **できるIV**

かいわ

1 できる I, II　Ai is on a video call with Jean.　🔊 L8-1

年上: older [one's age]　これから: from now on
としうえ

アイ　　：ジャンさん、久しぶりですね。
　　　　　　　　　　ひさ

ジャン：アイさん、久しぶり！　元気ですか。
　　　　　　　　　　ひさ　　　　げんき

アイ　　：はい、元気です。あのう、ジャンさん、私は日本に留学したいです。
　　　　　　げんき　　　　　　　　　　　　　　　　　　　りゅうがく

ジャン：え、留学ですか。
　　　　　りゅうがく

アイ　　：はい、私は絵を描くのが好きだから、日本の大学で美術を勉強したいです。
　　　　　　　え　か　す　　　　　　　　　びじゅつ　べんきょう

ジャン：ああ、アイさんは絵が上手だから、いいですね。大学はどこに行きたいですか。
　　　　　　　　　　え　じょうず

アイ　　：そうですね…　東京か京都の大学に行きたいです。
　　　　　　　　　　とうきょう　きょうと

ジャン：東京か京都？　じゃ、京都はどうですか。
　　　　　とうきょう　きょうと　　　きょうと

　　　　　京都には大きい美術館やまんがミュージアムがありますよ。
　　　　　きょうと　　　　びじゅつかん

アイ　　：そうですか。じゃ、京都についてもっと調べてみます。
　　　　　　　　　　　　きょうと　　　　　　しら

ジャン：がんばってください。

アイ　　：あのう、ジャンさん、私は授業でカジュアルスピーチを勉強しました。
　　　　　　　　　　　　　　　　　じゅぎょう　　　　　　　　べんきょう

　　　　　ジャンさんは年上だから、これから私にカジュアルスピーチで話してください。
　　　　　　　　　としうえ

ジャン：え、カジュアルスピーチ？　はい、あ、うん、じゃ、そうする。

2 できる II, III　Ai and Tao are talking together at the Japan House.　🔊 L8-2

おなか（が）すいた: I'm hungry.

アイ　　：タオちゃん、もう１時だよ。おなかすいたね。

　　　　　カフェに何か食べに行かない？

タオ　　：うーん、私、今、お金がないから、ちょっと…

アイ　　：じゃ、キッチンでいっしょに何か作って食べない？
　　　　　　　　　　　　　　　　　　つく

タオ　　：うん、いいね。

<In the kitchen>

タオ　　：アイちゃん、今日昼ご飯の後で、何する？
　　　　　　　　　ひる　はん　あと

アイ　　：今日は黒田先生のオフィスに行くよ。
　　　　　　　くろだ

タオ　　：え、先生のオフィス？

アイ　　：うん、来年日本に留学したいから、推薦状をお願いしに行く。
　　　　　　　　　　りゅうがく　　　すいせんじょう　ねが

260

3 できる IV Ai is visiting Prof. Kuroda's office.  L8-3

> くわしいこと：detailed information　では：polite form of じゃ

アイ　：黒田先生、失礼します。

先生　：あ、ブルーノさん。こんにちは。

アイ　：先生、ちょっとお願いがあるんですが…

先生　：はい、何ですか。

アイ　：あのう、夏休みに京都の大学に留学したいんですが、
　　　　推薦状を書いてくださいませんか。

先生　：留学ですか。京都のどの大学ですか。

アイ　：京都美術大学です。そこで日本語と日本の美術を勉強したいです。

先生　：そうですか。分かりました。いいですよ。

アイ　：どうもありがとうございます。後でくわしいことをメールで送っても
　　　　いいですか。

先生　：ええ、そうしてください。あ、でも、メールは英語で書かないでくださいね。
　　　　日本語で書いてください。

アイ　：はい、分かりました。では、よろしくお願いします。失礼します。

Lesson 8

CONVERSATION TIPS ワンポイント  L8-4

Casual speech styles: In Japanese, there are two main speech styles: "polite speech" and "casual speech." There are various factors that determine which speech style you should use. Examples of these factors include, but are not limited to, closeness, age difference, social status, and situational context.

A：ひろちゃん、おすし好き？

B：うん、好きだよ。

A：じゃ、これ、いっしょに食べない？

B：うん、食べる！　ありがとう。
　　あ、ちょっとそのしょうゆ (soy sauce)、取ってくれない？

A：うん。どうぞ。

B：ありがとう。このおすし、おいしいね。

A：うん、そうだね。

たんご

▶ The words written in gray are supplemental vocabulary.

● とくぎ　Skills

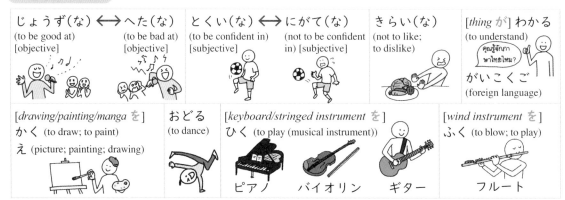

じょうず（な）←→ へた（な）
(to be good at) [objective]　(to be bad at) [objective]

とくい（な）←→ にがて（な）
(to be confident in) [subjective]　(not to be confident in) [subjective]

きらい（な）
(not to like; to dislike)

[*thing* が] わかる
(to understand)
がいこくご
(foreign language)

[*drawing/painting/manga* を]
かく (to draw; to paint)
え (picture; painting; drawing)

おどる
(to dance)

[*keyboard/stringed instrument* を]
ひく (to play (musical instrument))
ピアノ　バイオリン　ギター

[*wind instrument* を]
ふく (to blow; to play)
フルート

● せいかつ　Daily life

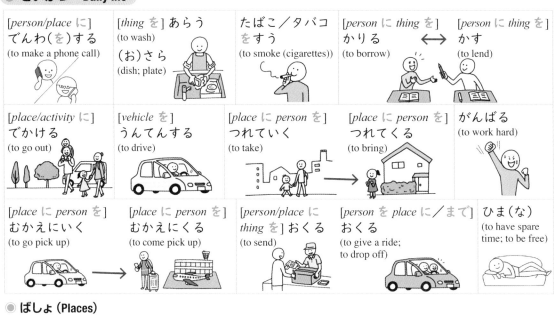

[*person/place* に]
でんわ（を）する
(to make a phone call)

[*thing* を] あらう
(to wash)
（お）さら
(dish; plate)

たばこ／タバコ
をすう
(to smoke (cigarettes))

[*person* に *thing* を]
かりる ←→
(to borrow)

[*person* に *thing* を]
かす
(to lend)

[*place/activity* に]
でかける
(to go out)

[*vehicle* を]
うんてんする
(to drive)

[*place* に *person* を]
つれていく
(to take)

[*place* に *person* を]
つれてくる
(to bring)

がんばる
(to work hard)

[*place* に *person* を]
むかえにいく
(to go pick up)

[*place* に *person* を]
むかえにくる
(to come pick up)

[*person/place* に *thing* を] おくる
(to send)

[*person* を *place* に／まで]
おくる
(to give a ride; to drop off)

ひま（な）
(to have spare time; to be free)

● ばしょ（Places）

えき
(train station)

くうこう
(airport)

きょうかい
(church)

スーパー
(supermarket)

（せんせいの）
オフィス／けんきゅうしつ
((instructor's) office)

ちかい
(near; nearby; close)

● べんきょう　Study

● ぶんか（Culture）

[*thing* に]
きょうみがある
(to be interested (in))
きょうみ (interest)

しゅうきょう
(religion)

ぶんか
(culture)

ぶんがく
(literature)

しょどう
((the Japanese art of) calligraphy)

れきし
(history)

● がっこう (School)

とる (to take)
[*thing* を] Exs. ほんをとる (to get a book)　クラスをとる (to take a class)

せんこうする (to major (in))
[*subject* を]

けんきゅうする (to research)
[*thing* を／について]

しらべる (to look up)
[*thing* を／について]

うける (to take)
[*exam/quiz* を] Ex. しけんをうける (to take an exam)

かんがえる (to think; to consider)
[*thing* について]

はじめる (to start)
[*thing* を]

おくれる (to be late)
[*class/meeting, etc.* に]

わすれる (to forget)
[*thing* を]

わすれる (to leave behind)
[*place* に *thing* を]

しょうかいする (to introduce)
[*person A* に *person B/thing* を]

きょうかしょ (textbook)

さくぶん (composition; essay)

ぶんぽう (grammar)
Grammar (ぶんぽう)

● りゅうがく (Study abroad)

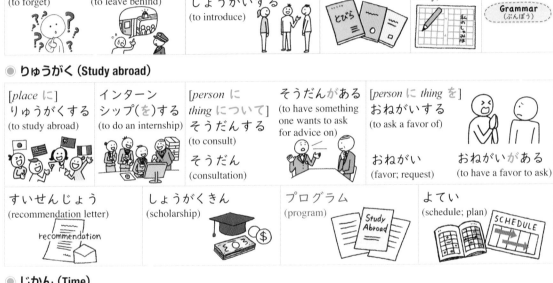

りゅうがくする (to study abroad)
[*place* に]

インターンシップ（を）する (to do an internship)

そうだんする (to consult)
[*person* に *thing* について]
そうだん (consultation)

そうだんがある (to have something one wants to ask for advice on)

おねがいする (to ask a favor of)
[*person* に *thing* を]
おねがい (favor; request)
おねがいがある (to have a favor to ask)

すいせんじょう (recommendation letter)

しょうがくきん (scholarship)

プログラム (program)

よてい (schedule; plan)

● じかん (Time)

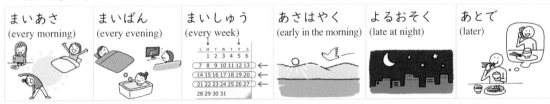

まいあさ (every morning)

まいばん (every evening)

まいしゅう (every week)

あさはやく (early in the morning)

よるおそく (late at night)

あとで (later)

● そのほかのひょうげん　Other expressions

すごく (very; really; totally)

すこし (a few; a little)

もうすこし (a little more)
もうちょっと [less formal]

Noun について (about Noun)

あなた (you)

しつれいします。
(Excuse me.)
[when entering/leaving someone's office]

ごめん！
(Sorry!) [casual]

（お）ひさしぶりです。
(Long time no see; It's been a while.)

たんごリスト

🔊 L8-5

RU-VERBS

1	うける	受ける	to take [*exam/quiz* を] **Ex.** しけんをうける to take an exam/test (not しけんをとる)
2	おくれる	遅れる	to be late [*class/meeting, etc.* に]
3	かりる	借りる	to borrow [*person* に *thing* を]
4	かんがえる	考える	to think; to consider [*thing* について]
5	しらべる	調べる	to look up; to look into [*thing* を／について]
6	でかける	出かける	to go out [*place/activity* に]
7	はじめる	始める	to start; to begin [*thing* を]
8	わすれる	忘れる	to forget [*thing* を]; to leave behind [*place* に *thing* を]

U-VERBS / U-VERB PHRASES

9	あらう	洗う	to wash [*thing* を]
10	おくる	送る	to send [*person/place* に *thing* を]; to give a ride; to drop off [*person* を *place* に／まで]
11	おどる		to dance
12	かく	描く	to draw; to paint [*drawing/painting/* *manga* を]
13	かす	貸す	to lend [*person* に *thing* を]
14	がんばる		to work hard; to persevere
15	きょうみが ある	興味が ある	to be interested (in) [*thing* に]
16	たばこ／ タバコをすう	吸う	to smoke (cigarettes)
17	とる	取る	to take [*thing* を] **Ex.1** ほんをとる to get a book **Ex.2** クラスをとる to take a class

18	つれていく	連れて いく	to take [*place* に *person* を]
19	むかえにいく	迎えに 行く	to go pick up [*place* に *person* を]
20	ひく		to play (musical instrument) [*keyboard/stringed instrument* を]
	ピアノをひく		to play the piano
	バイオリンをひく		to play the violin
	ギターをひく		to play the guitar
21	ふく		to blow; to play (musical instruments) [*wind instrument* を]
	フルートをふく		to play the flute
22	わかる	分かる	to understand [*thing* が]

IRREGULAR VERBS

23	つれてくる	連れて くる	to bring [*place* に *person* を]
24	むかえにくる	迎えに 来る	to come pick up [*place* に *person* を]

SURU-VERBS

25	うんてんする	運転する	to drive [*vehicle* を]
26	おねがいする	お願い する	to ask a favor of [*person* に *thing* を]
	おねがいが ある	お願いが ある	to have a favor to ask
27	けんきゅう する	研究する	to research [*thing* を／について]
28	しょうかい する	紹介する	to introduce [*person A* に *person* *B/thing* を]
29	せんこうする	専攻する	to major (in) [*subject* を]
30	そうだんする	相談する	to consult [*person* に *thing* に ついて]
	そうだんが ある	相談が ある	to have something one wants to ask for advice on

31	でんわ(を)する	電話(を)する	to make a phone call [*person/place* に]
32	りゅうがくする	留学する	to study abroad [*place* に]
33	インターンシップ(を)する		to do an internship

34	ちかい	近い	near; nearby; close **Ex.** ちかくのスーパー supermarket nearby (not ちかいスーパー)

35	じょうず	上手	to be good at [speaker's objective judgement; not used affirmatively to describe oneself]
36	へた	下手	to be bad at; not to be good at [speaker's objective judgement]
37	とくい	得意	to be confident in; to be good at [subjective]
38	にがて	苦手	not to be confident in; not to be good at [subjective]
39	きらい		not to like; to dislike
40	ひま		to have spare time; to be free; not busy

41	あなた		you [used generally or without a specified addressee; not usually used to address a specific listener]
42	さら／おさら	(お)皿	dish; plate
43	え	絵	picture; painting; drawing
44	がいこくご	外国語	foreign language
45	きょうかしょ	教科書	textbook
46	さくぶん	作文	composition; essay
47	しゅうきょう	宗教	religion
48	しょどう	書道	(the Japanese art of) calligraphy
49	しょうがくきん	奨学金	scholarship

50	すいせんじょう	推薦状	recommendation letter
51	ぶんか	文化	culture
52	ぶんがく	文学	literature
53	ぶんぽう	文法	grammar
54	れきし	歴史	history
55	よてい	予定	schedule; plan
56	えき	駅	train station
57	きょうかい	教会	church
58	くうこう	空港	airport
59	オフィス／けんきゅうしつ	研究室	(instructor's) office
60	スーパー		supermarket

61	まいあさ	毎朝	every morning
62	まいばん	毎晩	every evening
63	まいしゅう	毎週	every week

64	あさはやく	朝早く	early in the morning
65	よるおそく	夜遅く	late at night
66	すごく		very; really; totally
67	すこし	少し	a few; a little

68	もうすこし／もうちょっと	もう少し	a little more [もうちょっと is less formal than もう すこし.]
69	あとで	後で	later
70	Noun について		about Noun
71	ごめん		Sorry! [casual]
72	ひさしぶりです／おひさしぶりです	(お)久しぶりです	Long time no see; It's been a while.
73	しつれいします	失礼します	Excuse me. [when entering/leaving someone's office]

かんじ

86 男 男	ダン ナン	男性 male; man だんせい	男子 boy; man だんし	
		長男 first-born son ちょうなん		
	おとこ	男 male おとこ	男の人 man おとこ ひと	男の子 boy おとこ こ
male		ノ ロ 四 用 田 男 男		

87 女 女	ジョ メ	彼女 girlfriend; she かのじょ	少女 young girl しょうじょ	女子 girl; woman じょし
		女性 female; woman じょせい	長女 first-born daughter ちょうじょ	
		女神 goddess めがみ		
	おんな	女 female おんな	女の人 woman おんな ひと	女の子 girl おんな こ
female		く 女 女		

88 好 好	コウ	好物 favorite food こうぶつ		
	す(き) この(む)	好き(な) to like す	大好き(な) to like a lot; to love だい す	
		好み preference; one's taste この		
to like		く 女 女 女 好 好		

89 作 作	サク サッ	作品 work (of art, literature, etc.) さくひん	作文 composition さくぶん	名作 masterpiece めいさく
		作家 writer さっか		
	つく(る)	作る to make つく		
to make		ノ イ 仁 作 作 作 作		

90 出 出	シュツ	外出する to go out がいしゅつ	出身 one's place of origin しゅっしん	出席する to attend しゅっせき
	だ(す) で(かける) で(る)	出す to take out; to submit だ	出かける to go out で	
		出る to exit; to appear (on TV, etc.); to attend (a meeting, etc.) で		出口 exit でぐち
to go/take/put out; to turn in		一 屮 屮 出 出		

91 書 書	ショ	教科書 textbook きょうかしょ	辞書 dictionary じしょ	書道 (the Japanese art of) calligraphy しょどう
		読書 reading (books) どくしょ	図書館 library としょかん	
	か(く)	書く to write か		
to write; writing		ユ ユ ユ ヨ 亖 聿 聿 書 書 書		

92 分 分	フン プン ブン	～分 ... minute(s) (Exs. 一分 one minute, 五分 five minutes, 何分 how many minutes) ふん いっぷん ごふん なんぷん		
		気分 feeling; mood きぶん	分別する to sort ぶんべつ	分野 field (of study); specialty ぶんや
	わ(かる) わ(ける)	分かる to understand わ	分ける to share; to divide わ	
to divide; minutes		ノ 八 分 分		

93 午 午	ゴ	午前 AM 午後 PM; (in the) afternoon ごぜん　　ごご 正午 noon; midday しょうご		
noon	ノ 午 仁 午			

94 前 前	ゼン	午前 AM 前半 the first half ごぜん　　ぜんはん		
	まえ	前 before; front Noun の前 in front of Noun Noun の前に before Noun まえ　　　　　　　　　　まえ　　　　　　　　　　　　　まえ 名前 name なまえ		
before; front	前 前 前 前 前 前 前 前 前			

95 後 後	ゴ コウ	午後 PM; afternoon 最後(の) the last 後半 the second half ごご　　　　　　さいご　　　　　　こうはん		
	あと うし(ろ)	Noun の後で after Noun 後で later あと　　　　　　　あと Noun の後ろ behind Noun; the back of Noun うし		
after; back	ノ ク 彳 彳 彳 彴 後 後 後			

96 有 有	ユウ	有名(な) famous 有料 for a fee; not free ゆうめい　　　　　　ゆうりょう		
to exist; to own	ノ ナ オ 有 有 有			

97 名 名	メイ ミョウ	有名(な) famous 名所 famous place 名物 famous product ゆうめい　　　　　　めいしょ　　　　　　　めいぶつ 名字 family name みょうじ		
	な	名前 name 名札 name card; nameplate なまえ　　　　なふだ		
name; distinguished	ノ ク タ タ 名 名			

98 父 父	フ	祖父 grandfather 父母 mother and father そふ　　　　　　　　ふぼ		
	ちち とう	父 my father 父親 father [general term] 父の日 Father's Day ちち　　　　　　ちちおや　　　　　　　　　　ちち　ひ お父さん (someone else's) father とう		
father	ハ ハ グ 父			

99 母 母	ボ	祖母 grandmother 父母 mother and father 母語 mother tongue そぼ　　　　　　　　ふぼ　　　　　　　　　　ぼご		
	はは かあ	母 my mother 母親 mother [general term] 母の日 Mother's Day はは　　　　　　ははおや　　　　　　　　　　はは　ひ お母さん (someone else's) mother かあ		
mother	∟ 乚 口 口 母			

100 兄 兄	キョウ	兄弟 my sibling; siblings [general term]; brothers [general term] きょうだい		
	あに にい	兄 my older brother あに お兄さん (someone else's) older brother にい		
older brother	㇒ 口 口 尸 兄			

101 弟 弟 弟	ダイ おとうと	兄 弟 my sibling; siblings [general term]; brothers [general term] きょうだい 弟 my younger brother　　弟 さん (someone else's) younger brother おとうと　　　　　　　　おとうと
younger brother	` ソ ソ 当 肖 弟 弟	
102 姉 姉 姉	シ あね ねえ	姉妹 sisters [general term] しまい 姉 my older sister あね お姉 さん (someone else's) older sister ねえ
older sister	く 乜 女 女` 女⸍ 妒 妒 姉	
103 妹 妹 妹	マイ いもうと	姉妹都市 sister cities しまいとし 妹 my younger sister　　妹 さん (someone else's) younger sister いもうと　　　　　　　　いもうと
younger sister	く 乜 女 女⸍ 女⸗ 奸 妹 妹	

● あたらしいよみかた　**New readings**

The following are new readings for kanji that you have already learned. Read each word aloud.
(* indicates words with special readings.)

1) 外国語　　2) 来ない　　3) 上手 *　　4) 下手 *
　 がいこくご 　　　 こ 　　　　 じょうず 　　　 へ た

● れんしゅう　**Practice**

1 Find and circle five kanji compound words introduced in this lesson in the box on the left, then write their readings and meanings in the table on the right. They may appear either vertically or horizontally.

有	名	上
午	前	十
後	Ex. 五	分

Ex.	五分	ごふん	five minutes
1)			
2)			
3)			
4)			
5)			

2 Combine the kanji elements below to create four of the new kanji introduced in this lesson, then write one word containing each of the kanji on ___. Write the readings of the words you have written in ( ) below.

八　田　彡　亻　力

女　乍　亻　刀　子

[Note] Two different construction patterns
(a. left/right and b. top/bottom) are used.

a. 　　b.

Ex. ___好き___　　1) _____　　2) _____　　3) _____　　4) _____
（　すき　）　　（　　　）　　（　　　）　　（　　　）　　（　　　）

3 On-chan and Kun-chan are twins. They are talking about what they did today. Read the speech bubbles aloud, then write the readings for the underlined words and phrases.

[Hint] Many kanji have two or more readings.

Ex. 私の国では大学生がいろいろな外国語を勉強しています。
　　　くに　　　　　　　　　がいこくご　べんきょう

① 午前 11 時に友達のなおみさんと買い物に
　　　　　　ともだち
出かけました。買い物の前に郵便局で手紙
　　　　　　　　　　　ゆうびんきょく　　がみ
を出しました。

② 今日はなおみさんの誕生日ですから、
　　　　　　　　　たんじょうび
私はケーキを作りました。午後 7 時から
パーティーをしました。パーティーの後で、
パーティーについてブログを書きました。

③ ケーキを作るのは 50 分ぐらいかかりま
したが、食べるのは 5 分でした！

④ なおみさんの誕生日パーティーは
　　　　　　たんじょうび
図書館の後ろのレストランでありま
としょかん
した。レストランの名前は「マンマ」
で、おいしいパスタが有名です。私
はマンマのピザも好きです。

⑤ なおみさんのお父さんとお母さんと
お兄さんとお姉さんと妹さんと弟さん
もパーティーに来ました。なおみさん
は兄弟がたくさんいます。それから、
私の父と母と兄と姉も来ました。

269

かんじのはなし The Story of Kanji

■ Kanji elements (1)

へん	

Let's take a closer look at the elements that appear on the left side of a kanji. The kanji element appearing on the left side is called へん, and it expresses the basic meaning of the kanji. For example, the kanji 体 consists of two parts, left and right. The left-side element 亻 derives from 人, meaning "person." When 亻 is combined with 本, which means "basis," it results in 体, meaning "body." Whenever you see the left-side element 亻, the kanji will always have something to do with a person.

れんしゅう Practice

The following are examples of elements that appear on the left side of a kanji. The meaning of each element is given to you. Complete the table below by writing one kanji you have learned so far that uses each element, then providing the kanji's meaning, a word in which that kanji appears, and the reading of that word in hiragana.

Original kanji	Ex. 人 ↓	1) 食 ↓	2) 日 ↓	3) 水 ↓	4) 女 ↓	5) 手 ↓	6) 言 ↓	7) 牛 ↓
Element	亻	飠	日	氵	女	扌	言	牛
Meaning of the element	person	to eat	sun	water	woman	hand	to say	cow
Kanji	作							
Meaning of the kanji	to make							
Word using the kanji	作る							
Reading of the word in hiragana	つくる							

ぶんぽう

1 XはYがZ [Preference, skillfulness, ability]

You can express people's preferences, skill levels, and abilities using the "XはYがZ" sentence construction.

X		Y		Z
(a person who likes/dislikes s.t./s.o., is good/bad at s.t., etc.)	は	(a thing/person that X likes/dislikes, is good/bad at, etc.)	が	(an adjective/verb with the meaning of "like," "dislike," "skillful," "unskillful," etc.)

1-1 Noun が好き・きらい・上手・下手・得意・苦手・分かる
　　　 す　　　　　　じょうず　へ　た　とくい　にがて　わ
"like/dislike; be good/bad at; be confident/unconfident in; understand"

[1-a]

X		Y		Z
トムさん	は	テニス	が	{好き／きらい} です。 　す
Tom {likes/doesn't like} tennis.				
山田さん やまだ	は	歌 うた	が	{上手／下手} です。 じょうず　へ　た
Yamada-san is {good/not good} at singing. [objective]				
私 わたし	は	料理 りょうり	が	{得意／苦手} です。 とくい　にがて
I'm {good/not good} at cooking. [subjective]				
田中さん た なか	は	スペイン語 　　　　ご	が	分かります。 わ
Tanaka-san understands Spanish.				

When you want to express someone's preference, you use 好き or きらい in the "XはYがZ" construction.
　　　　　　　　　　　　　　　　　　　　　　　　　　　　す
(You already practiced "XはYが好きです" in Lesson 1.) While the English words *like* and *dislike* are verbs,
　　　　　　　　　　　　　　　す
好き and きらい are *na*-adjectives, and what one likes is marked by が rather than the direct object marker を.
す

Ex. （1）子どもの時、私は野菜がきらいでした。*I didn't like vegetables when I was a child.*
　　　　　 こ　　　 とき　わたし　や さい

上手 and 下手 are similar to 得意 and 苦手, respectively, in meaning. One difference is that 上手 and
じょうず　　へ　た　　　　　　とくい　にがて　　　　　　　　　　　　　　　　　　　　　　　　　　　　じょうず
下手 express an objective appraisal of someone's level of skill in something, whereas 得意 and 苦手
へ　た　　とくい　　にがて
convey the speaker's subjective judgment about someone's confidence (or lack of confidence) in their skill
in something. This difference in meaning naturally leads to a difference in usage. For instance, when you
want to say "I'm good at tennis," 得意 is used rather than 上手, because it sounds boastful to say that you
　　　　　　　　　　　　　　 とくい　　　　　　　　　　 じょうず
are objectively good at something.

　　　✕ 私はテニスが上手です。　→ 私はテニスが得意です。*I'm good at tennis.*
　　　　 わたし　　　 じょうず　　　　 わたし　　　　 とくい

However, when you want to say "I'm <u>not</u> good at tennis," you can use 上手じゃないです.
　　　　　　　　　　　　　　　　　　　　　　　　　　　　　　　　　 じょうず

Lesson **8**

上手 and 下手 are commonly used for things like sports and foreign languages, but not for school subjects (e.g., math, history), in which acquiring skills is not the main objective. For things like these, 得意 and 苦手 are used.

    ✕ トムさんは数学が上手／下手です。

    → トムさんは数学が得意／苦手です。 *Tom is good/poor at math.*

Exs. (2) リーマンさんは漢字と数学が得意です。 *Riemann is good at kanji and math.*

    (3) 私は料理が苦手です。そうじも得意じゃないです。
        I'm not good at cooking. I don't have much of a knack for cleaning, either.

    (4) 田中さんはダンスが上手です。 *Tanaka-san is good at dancing.*

分かる is an *u*-verb that is used in the "XはYがZ" construction rather than the "XはYをZ" construction. A variety of nouns occur in the Y position, and the corresponding English varies depending on the noun—for instance, 日本語が分かる means "understand/can comprehend Japanese," but この漢字の意味が分かる means "know the meaning of this kanji."

Ex. (5) A: あのう、日本語が分かりますか。 *Excuse me, do you understand Japanese?*

        B: はい、少し分かります。 *Yes, a little.*

☞ **GID** (vol.1): A. Basic sentence structures 3. XはYがZ

1-2 **V-plain のが好き・きらい・上手・下手・得意・苦手**

"like/dislike V-ing; be good/bad at V-ing; be confident/unconfident in V-ing"

[1-b]

	Noun phrase				
	Verb phrase				
		V-plain.non-past			
私は	まんがを	読む	の	が	好きです。
I like reading manga.					

You can use a verb or a verb phrase (e.g., まんがを読む) in the Y position of the "XはYがZ" construction. In this case, you have to change the verb or verb phrase into a noun equivalent by adding の to the plain non-past form of the verb. (For more about this use of の and the plain non-past forms of verbs, see #2 and #3-1 below.)

Exs. (1) アイさんは絵を描くのが上手です。 *Ai is good at drawing pictures.*

    (2) リーマンさんは漢字を覚えるのが得意です。 *Riemann is good at memorizing kanji.*

    (3) 私はゲームをするのがあまり好きじゃないです。 *I don't like playing games very much.*

2 V-plainの [Verb nominalization] "V-ing; to V"

[2]

Noun phrase					
Verb phrase					
	V-plain.non-past				
歌を うた	歌う うた	の	は	楽しいです。 たの	
Singing (lit. Singing songs) is fun.					

You can make noun equivalents out of verbs or verb phrases by affixing の to the plain non-past forms of the verbs. This の is called a "nominalizer." Nominalized verbs and verb phrases can be used in the same way as any other noun or noun phrase. V-plain.non-past の is equivalent to "V-ing" or "to V" in English.

Exs. (1) 「曜」という漢字を書くのは大変です。*It is difficult to write the kanji* 曜.
よう　　　　　かんじ　か　　　　たいへん　　　　　　　　　　　　　　　　　　　　　　よう

(2) 晩ご飯を作るのを手伝ってください。*Please help me make dinner.*
ばん　はん　つく　　　てつだ

☞ **GID** (vol.1): F. Nominalizers 1. の

Lesson
8

3 Plain non-past forms of verbs, *i*-adjectives, and です

In this lesson, we will learn the plain non-past forms of verbs, *i*-adjectives, and です. Plain forms are used in many grammatical expressions as well as in casual speech and formal writing:

(a) Grammatical expressions: Ex. パーティーが<u>ある</u>んですが (See #8.)

(b) Casual speech: Exs. <u>便利だ</u>よ；<u>おいしい</u>？ (See #6.)
べん り

(c) Formal writing: Plain forms are used in newspaper/magazine articles, books for adult readers, academic papers, and many other types of writing.

3-1 Plain non-past forms of verbs

You can make the plain non-past forms of verbs as follows:

(a) *Ru*-verbs:

Non-past affirmative form: The same as the dictionary form

　　Exs. 食べる；見る
　　　　 た　　　み

Non-past negative form: Change the final る to ない.

　　Exs. 食べる → 食べ<u>ない</u>；見る → 見<u>ない</u>
　　　　 た　　　　た　　　　　　み　　　み

(b) *U*-verbs:

Non-past affirmative form: The same as the dictionary form

　　Exs. 書く；買う
　　　　 か　　か

Non-past negative form: Change the final /u/ sound of the dictionary form to /a/ and add ない.

　　Ex. 書く (/kak<u>u</u>/) → 書か (/kak<u>a</u>/) ＋ ない → 書かない
　　　　 か　　　　　　　　　　か　　　　　　　　　　　　　　か

When the final syllable of the dictionary form ends with う, change the /u/ sound to /wa/ and add ない.

　　Ex. 買う (/ka<u>u</u>/) → 買わ (/ka<u>wa</u>/) ＋ ない → 買わない
　　　　 か　　　　　　　　　　か　　　　　　　　　　　　　　か

273

More examples of *u*-verb plain non-past forms are shown in the following conjugation table, along with the *masu*-forms that use a different final vowel:

帰らない かえ	話さない はな	行かない い	言わない い	← /a/ row: Plain negative forms
帰ります かえ	話します はな	行きます い	言います い	← /i/ row: *Masu*-forms
帰る かえ	話す はな	行く い	言う い	← /u/ row: Dictionary forms (plain affirmative forms)

⚠️ One exception: The plain affirmative form of あります is ある, but the plain negative form is ない, not あらない.

(c) Irregular verbs:

Non-past affirmative form: The same as the dictionary form (i.e., する, 来る)
く

Non-past negative form: する → しない; 来る → 来ない
く   こ

(See Appendix: Conjugation Tables.)

3-2 Plain non-past forms of *i*-adjectives

To make the plain non-past forms of *i*-adjectives, you can simply drop the polite ending です.

Non-past	Affirmative	Negative
Polite	おいしいです	おいしくないです
Plain	おいしい	おいしくない

3-3 Plain non-past forms of です

Unlike verbs and *i*-adjectives, *na*-adjectives and nouns have no conjugating parts—that is, they do not change their forms. Thus, when you use them as a predicate, you indicate the tense, the politeness level, and whether the sentence is affirmative or negative by affixing conjugated forms of です. The plain non-past affirmative and negative forms of です are だ and じゃない, respectively.

	Plain affirmative	Plain negative
Non-past	*Na*-adjective ＋ だ Noun ＋ だ	*Na*-adjective ＋ じゃない Noun ＋ じゃない
Exs.	便利だ べんり 日本語だ にほんご	便利じゃない べんり 日本語じゃない にほんご

3-4 Plain non-past forms ＋ から

In the structure "S₁ から S₂," the form before から changes according to the ending form of S₂ (= the main clause). That is, if S₂ ends in the plain form, the form before から must be the plain form as well. (See L5 #4.)

× ラーメンが好きですから、よく食べる。
す   た

→ ラーメンが好きだから、よく食べる。 *Because I like ramen, I often eat it.*
す   た

If S₂ ends in the polite form, however, the form before から can be either the plain form or the polite form.

Exs. (1) 今日は {忙しい／忙しいです} から、パーティーに行きません。
　　　　　I'm busy today, so I'm not going to the party.

(2) 明日テストが {ある／あります} から、今晩よく勉強します。
　　　There is a test tomorrow, so I'm going to study a lot tonight.

Additionally, (2) above can be rephrased as in (3).

Exs. (3) 今晩よく勉強します。明日テストがあるからです。
　　　　　I'm going to study a lot tonight. It's because there is a test tomorrow.

(4) A: 今日、アルバイトを休みます。*I'm taking the day off work today.*

B: どうしてですか。*Why?*

A: 明日テストがあるからです。*Because I have a test tomorrow.*

(3) is used when you want to add a reason after you have already said the result. Note that in the "Sからです" structure in (3), S must be in the plain form.

☞ **GID** (vol.1): C. Polite forms and plain forms

---

4 **か [Alternative] "or"**

[4]

	N₁		N₂	
昼ご飯はたいてい	カレー	か	ラーメン	を食べます。
I usually eat curry or ramen for lunch.				

You can express the idea of "N₁ or N₂" using "N₁ か N₂."

Exs. (1) 来年、大阪か京都に行ってみたいです。*I'd like to go to Osaka or Kyoto next year.*

(2) この文法が分からないから、先生かけいたさんに聞いてみます。
　　I don't understand this grammar, so I'll ask my teacher or Keita.

(3) アイ：今度の土曜日か日曜日にジャパンハウスに来ませんか。
　　　Would you like to come to the Japan House this Saturday or Sunday?

田中：ありがとうございます。ぜひ。*Thank you. I'd love to.*

5 Placeに {V-*masu* / N} にV (motion) [Purpose of motion] "go/come to V; go/come for V-ing/N"

[5-a]

N (destination)			V-*masu*		V (motion)
カフェ	に	コーヒーを	飲_のみ	に	行_いきます。
I'm going to a café to drink coffee.					

You can express the purpose for going or coming somewhere using V-*masu* に. Note that only motion verbs, such as 行く, 来る, and 帰る, are used at the end of the sentence in this construction.

Nouns that represent an action can also be used in place of V-*masu*, as in [5-b] below.

[5-b]

N (destination)		N (action)		V (motion)
デパート	に	買_かい物_{もの}	に	行_いきます。
I'm going to a department store to shop.				

Exs. (1) A: 週末、私の家に遊びに来ませんか。

Would you like to come to my place for a visit over the weekend?

B: ありがとうございます。*Thank you.*

(2) 私は今、寮に住んでいるから、ときどきうちに母に会いに帰ります。

I live in a dorm now, so I go home to see my mother from time to time.

(3) 昨日、公園に散歩に行きました。*I went to the park for a walk yesterday.*

---

6 Casual speech

When you talk to your family members, friends, and close colleagues, you usually talk using casual forms rather than polite forms.

Sentence-final element	Question	Statement
Verb	行く(ね)？ 行かない(ね)？	行く(よ)。 行かない(よ)。
I-adjective	おいしい(ね)？ おいしくない(ね)？	おいしい(よ)。 おいしくない(よ)。
Na-adjective / noun + だ	大変／学生(だね)？* {大変／学生}じゃない(ね)？	大変／学生(だよ)。 {大変／学生}じゃない(よ)。

* X だ？ is not grammatical.

In casual speech, you use plain forms, often with a sentence-final particle such as よ and ね. (See Language Note:「よ」と「ね」(p.150).) In questions, instead of using か, you end the sentence with a rising intonation. (In this book, "?" is used to indicate that the sentence is a question in casual speech.) Note also that the topic marker は, the object marker を, and the だ after *na*-adjectives and nouns commonly drop in casual speech. が in the "XはYがZ" structure also tends to drop in casual speech. が in sentence structures other than "XはYがZ" (e.g., XにYがある／いる), へ, and に drop in some situations. However, で, と, から, も, and the contrastive は do not drop.

In addition, はい and いいえ change to うん and ううん, respectively.

Exs. (The sentences on the right are used in casual speech.)

(1) A: すしが好きですか。 → すし、好き？ *Do you like sushi?*

   B: はい、好きです。 → うん、好き（だよ）。*Yeah, I do.*

(2) A: このすしを食べませんか。 → このすし、食べない？ *Do you wanna eat this sushi?*

   B: はい、食べます。 → うん、食べる（よ）。*Yeah, I would.*

(3) A: おいしいですか。 → おいしい？ *Is it good?*

   B: はい、おいしいです。 → うん、おいしい（よ）。*Yeah, it's good.*

(4) A: これはすしですか。 → これ、すし？ *Is this sushi?*

   B: いいえ、すしじゃないです。 → ううん、すしじゃない（よ）。*No, it's not sushi.*

7 ～ないでください [Polite prohibition] "(Please) don't ~"

[7]

	V-plain.non-past (negative)	
クラスに	遅れない	でください。
Please don't be late for class.		

You can politely tell the listener not to do something using ～ないでください. Like ～てください, you usually do not use ～ないでください when talking to someone of higher status. (See L6 #2.)

Exs. (1) 美術館では大きい声で話さないでください。*(Please) don't talk loudly in museums.*

   (2) あ、私のピザを食べないでください。*Oh, (please) don't eat my pizza.*

   (3) さようなら。これから私に電話をしないでください。

   Goodbye! (Please) don't call me anymore (lit. from now on).

8 ～んですが [Lead-in sentence ending]

[8]

	V-plain		
黒田先生、ちょっと質問が	ある	んですが、	今いいですか。
Prof. Kuroda, I have a question. Is it all right to ask you now (lit. is now good)?			

When you ask a question, request a favor, or make an invitation, you usually start with a lead-in sentence ending in んですが. In casual speech, んだけど is used. The けど here is the casual form of が. (More about けど in L10 #6)

The connection rules are as follows:

Verbs	plain form ＋ んです	食べるんです；食べないんです <small>た</small>　　　　<small>た</small>
I-adjectives	plain form ＋ んです	高いんです；高くないんです <small>たか</small>　　　　<small>たか</small>
Na-adjectives and nouns	*Na*-adj / noun ＋ な ＋ んです *Na*-adj / noun ＋ じゃない ＋ んです	便利／学生なんです <small>べん り</small>　<small>がくせい</small> 便利／学生じゃないんです <small>べん り</small>　<small>がくせい</small>

Exs. （1） おいしいコーヒーが飲みたいんですが、どこがいいですか。
<small>の</small>

　　　　　 I'd like to drink some delicious coffee—where (= which café) is good? [asking a question]

　　　（2） この単語の意味が分からないんですが、知っていますか。
<small>たん ご　い み　わ</small>　　　　　　　　　　　<small>し</small>

　　　　　 I don't know the meaning of this word—do you know it? [asking a question]

　　　（3） 今晩ひまなんだけど、いっしょにご飯（を）食べない？
<small>こんばん</small>　　　　　　　　　　　　　<small>はん</small>　<small>た</small>

　　　　　 I'm free tonight—do you wanna eat dinner with me? [making an invitation]

In situations such as those introduced above, the sentences after んですが are often omitted when the speaker expects that what they want the listener to do is clear to the listener. (More about んです in L9 #2)

Ex. （4） 先生、ちょっと質問があるんですが… *Professor, I have a question.*
<small>せんせい</small>　　　　　<small>しつもん</small>

9　**〜てくれませんか／くださいませんか [Request] "Could you ~?; Would you ~?"**　

[9]

	V-*te*	
明日のミーティングの時間を <small>あした</small>　　　　　　　　　<small>じ かん</small>	教えて <small>おし</small>	くださいませんか。(very polite) くれませんか。 くれない？ (casual)
Could I ask you to tell me tomorrow's meeting time?	
Could you tell me tomorrow's meeting time?	
Can you tell me tomorrow's meeting time?	

You can make a request by using V-*te*くれませんか. くださいませんか is used when asking a favor of the listener very politely, e.g., when talking to your teachers, your customers, etc. くれない with rising intonation is used when asking a favor of the listener casually, e.g., when talking to your close friends, family members, younger people you know well, etc.

Note that in this sentence structure, the subject (in this case, the listener) should not be included. Therefore, the following sentence is unnatural. (Tom is the listener here.)

　　　× トムさんは英語を教えてくれませんか。
　　　　　　　　<small>えい ご　おし</small>

　　　→ トムさん、英語を教えてくれませんか。*Could you teach me English, Tom?*
　　　　　　　　　<small>えい ご　おし</small>

Exs. （1） 先生、留学したいんですが、推薦状を書いてくださいませんか。
<small>せんせい　りゅうがく</small>　　　　　　　　<small>すいせんじょう</small>　<small>か</small>

　　　　　 Professor, I'd like to study abroad. Could I ask you to write me a letter of recommendation?

　　　（2） <To your host mother>

　　　　　 この漢字の意味を教えてくれませんか。*Could you tell me what this kanji means?*
<small>かん じ　い み　おし</small>

　　　（3） タオちゃん、その写真を見せてくれない？ *Can you show me that picture, Tao?*
　　　　　　　　　　　　<small>しゃしん　み</small>

"V-*te*くれませんか" and "Nをくれませんか" should not be confused. "V-*te*くれませんか" is used to ask the listener to do something, whereas "N をくれませんか" is used to ask the listener to give something to the speaker.

N		V-*te*	
たこ焼き や	を	作って つく	くれませんか。
Could you make *takoyaki* for me?			
N			
たこ焼き や	を		くれませんか。
Could you give me some *takoyaki*?			

Note that くれてくれる is ungrammatical:

× チョコレートを<u>くれて</u>くれない？

→ チョコレートをくれない？ *Can you give me some chocolate?*

10 ～てもいい [Permission] "(You) may/can ～; It's all right if (you) ～"

[10]

		V-*te*		
名前をひらがなで な まえ		書いて か	も	いいですか。
May I write my name in hiragana?				

You can ask for permission from the listener using V-*te*もいいですか, and give your permission to the listener using V-*te*もいいです.

Exs. (1) 学生：先生、相談があるんですが、後で研究室に行って<u>もいいですか</u>。
がくせい　せんせい　そうだん　　　　　　　　あと　けんきゅうしつ　い

Professor, I'd like to ask for some advice—may I come to your office later?

先生：はい、どうぞ。*Yes, you may.*
せんせい

(2) 先生：宿題の時は教科書を見<u>てもいいですが</u>、テストの時は見ないでください。
せんせい　しゅくだい　とき　きょうかしょ　み　　　　　　　　　　　　とき　み

You may look at the textbook when doing homework, but do not do so when taking a test.

(3) A: これ、ちょっと食べて<u>もいい</u>？ *Can I taste this (lit. eat this a little)?*
た

B1:うん、いいよ。*Yeah, okay.*

B2:うーん、ちょっと…*Um, actually...*

 Activities

はなしましょう

▶ **Words written in purple** are new words introduced in this lesson.

できる I Ask and answer questions about preferences, skills, and abilities.

できる I-A Preference, skillfulness, and ability XはYがZ

1 What things do you understand or know about? Take turns with your partner asking each other about the following topics.

Ex. フランス語

A: ○○さんはフランス語が分かりますか。

B: はい、（少し）分かります。or いいえ、{あまり／全然}分かりません。

1) ○○語　　2) ○○の歴史　　3) ○○の文化　　4) your own

2 Describe people's likes and dislikes.

Step 1 Describe Tao's preferences based on the cues provided.

Ex.1 タオさんは漢字が好きです。

Ex.2 タオさんはせんたくはあまり好きじゃないです。

Ex.3 タオさんはスポーツがきらいです。

好き	Ex.1 kanji	あまり好きじゃない	Ex.2 laundry	きらい	Ex.3 sports
	1) animals 2) Japanese culture		3) cleaning 4) shopping 5) composition		6) cola 7) history 8) alcohol

Step 2 Take turns with your partner asking each other if you like the things in Step 1 above.

Ex. A: ○○さんは漢字が好きですか。

B: {はい、好きです／いいえ、あまり好きじゃないです／いいえ、きらいです}。

△△さんは？　＜Continue＞

3 Describe people's skills both objectively and subjectively.

Step 1 Describe objectively what the popular idol Nana is good and not good at.

Ex.1 ナナは歌が上手です。

Ex.2 ナナは英語はあまり上手じゃないです。

Ex.3 ナナはダンスが下手です。

上手	Ex.1 songs	あまり上手じゃない	Ex.2 English	下手	Ex.3 dance
	1) piano 2) games		3) guitar 4) foreign languages		5) speeches （スピーチ） 6) sports

Ex.1 私はピアノが得意です。それから、歌も得意です。
<small>とくい</small> <small>うた とくい</small>

Ex.2 私はサッカーが得意です。でも、テニスは得意じゃないです。
<small>とくい</small> <small>とくい</small>

4 Ask and answer questions about likes and dislikes in more detail.

Step 1 Describe Riemann's preferences based on the cues provided.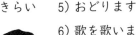

Ex. リーマンさんは音楽を聞くのが好きです。
<small>す</small>

好き <small>す</small>	Ex. 音楽を聞きます 1) 書道をします <small>しょどう</small> 2) 出かけます <small>で</small> 3) 文法について考えます <small>ぶんぽう</small> <small>かんが</small> 4) ネコと遊びます <small>あそ</small>	きらい	5) おどります 6) 歌を歌います <small>うた</small> <small>うた</small> 7) 皿を洗います <small>さら</small> <small>あら</small>

Step 2 Ask what your partner likes and dislikes doing.

Ex. A: ○○さんは何をするのが {好きですか／きらいですか}。
<small>す</small>

B: そうですね、私は歴史について考えるのが好きです。
<small>れきし</small> <small>かんが</small> <small>す</small>

だから、毎晩、歴史の本を読みます。△△さんは？ <Continue>
<small>まいばん</small> <small>れきし</small>

5 Suppose you have become a big fan of Nana, the idol mentioned in ③. You now check her social media every day and have learned a lot about her. Describe her skills objectively in more detail.

Ex. ナナは料理するのが上手です。
<small>りょうり</small> <small>じょうず</small>

上手 <small>じょうず</small>	Ex. cook 1) draw pictures 2) play the flute	あまり上手じゃない <small>じょうず</small>	3) play the violin 4) take pictures	下手 <small>へた</small>	5) drive a car 6) use chopsticks

Group Work

6 Suppose your Japanese class is holding a talent show at the end of the semester.

Step 1 Brainstorm what kind of performances you can have at the talent show.

Exs. 歌を歌います／劇 (theater play) をします／書道をします
<small>うた うた</small> <small>げき</small> <small>しょどう</small>

Lesson **8**

Step 2 Decide what you will do together as a group.

Ex. A: みなさんは何がしたいですか。

B: えっと、私は歌を歌うのが得意ですから、日本語で歌いたいです。
みなさんは歌うのが好きですか。

C: うーん、歌うのは苦手です。でも、ダンスをするのは得意です。

A: 私は… \<Continue\>

B: じゃ、歌とダンスをしましょうか。

Step 3 Report what you will do at the talent show to the class.

Ex. 私のグループは「てフォームの歌」のラップを歌います。〇〇さんは歌を歌うのが
すごく上手ですから、みんなの前で歌います。△△さんはダンスが得意ですから、
〇〇さんの後ろでおどります。それから… \<Continue\>

7 Describe your own preferences and skills so that your classmates can get to know you better. Your classmates will ask you questions after your presentation.

Ex. 私は本を読むのが大好きですから、今、文学を専攻しています。作文を書くのは
得意ですが、古い英語を読むのは苦手です。みなさんは文学が好きですか。

できる II Talk about the reason for or purpose of an activity.

できる II-A Plain non-past forms of verbs, *i*-adjectives, and です

1 Let's practice conjugating verbs into their plain non-past forms. Change the verbs below first into their plain affirmative forms and then into their plain negative forms. 🔊 **L8-10**

Ex. たべます → たべる → たべない

1) みます   2) おきます   3) かえります   4) あいます   5) はなします

6) あります   7) します   8) きます   9) はじめます   10) おくれます

11) あらいます 12) がんばります 13) つれてきます

2 Let's practice conjugating *i*-adjectives and です into their plain non-past forms. Change the following words first into their plain affirmative forms and then into their plain negative forms.

Ex.1 やすいです → やすい → やすくない   🔊 **L8-11**

Ex.2 しずかです → しずかだ → しずかじゃない

Ex.3 がくせいです → がくせいだ → がくせいじゃない

1) むずかしいです   2) こわいです   3) いいです   4) すきです

5) きれいです   6) あめです   7) げつようびです 8) ちかいです

9) にがてです   10) きらいです   11) えきです   12) きょうかしょです

1 Let's practice using the structure "plain non-past form + から" to express a reason. Give reasons for why you will or will not go out based on the cues provided. 🔊 **L8-12**

Ex. 友達に会います → 今日友達に会うから、出かけます。
ともだち　　　　　　　　　　　ともだち　　　　　　　　て

　　　　　　　　　→ 今日友達に会わないから、出かけません。
　　　　　　　　　　　ともだち　　　　　　　　　て

1) 買い物に行きます　　2) 予定があります　　3) 遊びたいです
　　　　　　　　　　　　　　よ てい　　　　　　　　　あそ

4) 天気 (weather) がいいです　5) ひまです　　6) 元気です　　7) アルバイトの日です
　　てん き　　　　　　　　　　　　　　　　　　　げん き

2 Practice giving a reason for various situations.

Step 1 Connect each sentence on the left below with the corresponding one on the right using the structure "plain non-past form + から." 🔊 **L8-13**

Ex. 明日試験を受けるから、今日たくさん勉強します。
　　　　し けん　う　　　　　　　　　　　べんきょう

Ex. 明日試験を受けます。　　•　　　　• あまり本を読みません。
　　　し けん　う

1) 友達が日本から来ます。　•　　　　• 今日たくさん勉強します。
　　ともだち　　　　　　　　　　　　　　　　べんきょう

2) 今日は寒いです。　　　　•　　　　• クラスがありません。
　　　　さむ

3) 今日は日曜日です。　　　•　　　　• 出かけます。
　　　　　　　　　　　　　　　　　　　て

4) 今日はひまです。　　　　•　　　　• 空港に友達を迎えに行きます。
　　　　　　　　　　　　　　　　　　　くうこう　ともだち　むか

5) 私はアルバイトをしていません。•　• お金がありません。

6) 文学に興味がありません。　•　　　• セーターを2枚着ています。
　　ぶんがく　きょう み　　　　　　　　　　　まい き

Step 2 Using the cues in Step 1, explain the situation first and then follow up with the reason for it using the structure "plain non-past form + からです."

Ex. 今日たくさん勉強します。明日試験を受けるからです。
　　　　　　　　べんきょう　　　　し けん　う

3 Talk with your classmates to get to know them better. Ask the reasons for their various choices and preferences.

| **Possible topics** | 専攻 | 趣味 | 好きな／きらいな○○ |
| | せんこう | しゅ み | す |

Ex. A: ○○さんの専攻は何ですか。
　　　　　　　　せんこう

B: 日本語です。

A: そうですか。どうして日本語を専攻していますか。
　　　　　　　　　　　　　　　せんこう

B: えっと、日本の文化に興味があるからです。
　　　　　　　ぶん か　きょう み

　　or 日本の文化に興味があるから、専攻しています。△△さんの専攻は？
　　　　　　ぶん か　きょう み　　　　　　せんこう　　　　　　　　　　せんこう

<Continue>

1 Suppose you are preparing to study abroad. Looking at the list of possible options below, pick two choices you like, and answer the advisor's questions.

Ex. A: どこに留学したいですか。
りゅうがく

B: 東京 **か** 京都に留学したいです。
とうきょう　きょうと　りゅうがく

1) どこで勉強したいですか。
べんきょう

2) どこに住みたいですか。

3) いつ留学したいですか。
りゅうがく

4) 何について研究したいですか。
けんきゅう

5) 何を習ってみたいですか。
なら

Study Abroad in Japan

Ex. 1) where to study:
Tokyo / Kyoto / Hokkaido

2) where to live:
host family's house / dorm / apartment

3) when to go:
this year / next year / summer break

4) what to study:
religion / history / literature / culture

5) what to learn:
calligraphy / karate (空手) / cooking
からて

2 Life is full of choices. You are planning to go out to a movie this Saturday with your partner.

Step 1 Take turns proposing two options for the various aspects of your meetup and decide what to do together.

Ex. A: 土曜日の何時に会いましょうか。

B: 3時 **か** 4時に会いませんか。

A: じゃ、3時に会いましょう。

B: どこで会いましょうか。　<Continue>

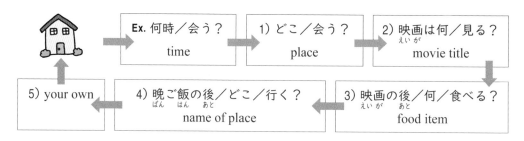

Step 2 Tell your classmates briefly about what you've planned to do together.

Ex. 私と○○さんは土曜日の3時に私の家の前で会って…　<Continue>
いえ　まえ

1 What do you go to the following places for? Match each place with an activity and make sentences.

Ex. 図書館に本を借りに行きます。
　　　としょかん　　か

Ex. 図書館　　　　　　　• ・イヌの散歩
　　　としょかん　　　　　　　　　　さんぽ
1) スーパー　　　　•　　　　・本を借りる
　　　　　　　　　　　　　　　　　　か
2) 海　　　　　　　•　　　　・買い物
　　　　　　　　　　　　　　　　か　もの
3) 美術館　　　　　•　　　　・絵を見る
　　びじゅつかん　　　　　　　　え　み
4) 大学院　　　　　•　　　　・泳ぐ
　　だいがくいん　　　　　　　　およ
5) 公園　　　　　　•　　　　・相談する
　　こうえん　　　　　　　　　　そうだん
6) 先生のオフィス　•　　　　・日本の文学を研究する
　　せんせい　　　　　　　　　　にほん　ぶんがく　けんきゅう

Group Work

2 Let's play a guessing game! One person picks a place and explains what people go there for. The other group members guess what place is being described.

Ex. A: そこに何をしに行きますか。

B: えっと、毎晩、晩ご飯を食べに行きます。でも、あまりおいしくないです。
　　まいばん　ばん　はん
　　それから… <Continue>

C: えっと、答えは寮の食堂ですか。
　　　　　こた　　りょう　しょくどう
B: はい、そうです。or いいえ、もう少し考えてください。
　　　　　　　　　　　　　　　すこ　かんが

3 Talk with your partner about a place you are going to over the weekend or on a vacation and what you are going there for.

Ex. A: 夏休みにどこかに行きますか。
　　　なつやす
B: はい、今、一人で寮に住んでいるから、うちに家族とネコに会いに帰ります。
　　　　　　　　　りょう　　　　　　　　　　　　　　かぞく　　　　　　あ　　かえ
A: そうですか。どんなネコを飼っていますか。 <Continue>
　　　　　　　　　　　　　　か

4 Make a brief presentation about a custom (e.g., an annual event) practiced by your family or in your country and mention where you/people visit as a part of this custom. Your partner or groupmates will ask you questions after your presentation.

Custom	**Ex.** 私は毎年１月１日に家族といっしょに祖母に会いに
• place/date	かぞく　　　　　　　　　そぼ
• purpose	行きます。
Activities in detail	１月１日はお正月だから、祖母のうちでいっしょに
	しょうがつ　　　　そぼ
	ご飯を食べます。「おせち料理」というお正月の料理
	はん　　　　　　　　　　　りょうり　　　　　しょうがつ　りょうり
	を食べます。それから、たいていおすしかすき焼きも
	や
	食べます。すごくおいしいです。
Closing	私はみんなでお正月の料理を食べるのが大好きです。
	しょうがつ　りょうり　　　　　　だいす

Lesson **8**

Ask and answer questions about plans in casual speech.

Casual speech

1 Talk casually about what you will or will not do today.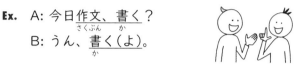

> **Step 1** Suppose you feel like doing everything today. Take turns asking the questions below and answering them in the affirmative. 🔊 **L8-15**

> **Ex.**　A: 今日作文、書く？
> 　　　　　　　さくぶん　か
> 　　　　B: うん、書く（よ）。
> 　　　　　　　か

Ex. 作文を書きますか 　　さくぶん　か	1) 教会に行きますか 　　きょうかい	2) 図書館で本を借りますか 　　としょかん　　　　か
3) 家族に電話をしますか 　　かぞく　でんわ	4) 出かけますか 　　で	5) 来週の宿題を始めますか 　　らいしゅう　しゅくだい　はじ
6) 勉強をがんばりますか 　　べんきょう	7) 予定がありますか 　　よてい	8) your own

> **Step 2** Suppose you don't feel like doing anything today. This time, answer the questions in Step 1 in the negative. 🔊 **L8-16**

> **Ex.**　A: 今日作文、書く？
> 　　　　　　　さくぶん　か
> 　　　　B: ううん、書かない（よ）。
> 　　　　　　　　　か

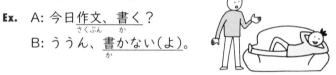

> **Step 3** What do you feel like doing today? Take turns asking the questions in Step 1 and answering them based on how you're feeling and what you're planning.

2 Talk casually about your current situation, preferences, and skills.

> **Step 1** Take turns asking the questions below and answering them in the affirmative. 🔊 **L8-17**

> **Ex.**　A: 元気？
> 　　　　　　　げんき
> 　　　　B: うん、元気（だよ）。
> 　　　　　　　　　げんき
> 　　　　A: いいね。（← Comment)

Ex. 元気ですか 　　げんき	1) 最近、忙しいですか 　　さいきん　いそが	2) 文法が好きですか 　　ぶんぽう　す
3) 外国語が得意ですか 　　がいこくご　とくい	4) 明日はひまですか 　　あした	5) 今、1年生ですか 　　いま　　ねんせい

> **Step 2** This time, answer the questions in Step 1 in the negative. 🔊 **L8-18**

> **Ex.**　A: 元気？
> 　　　　　　　げんき
> 　　　　B: ううん、元気じゃない（よ）。
> 　　　　　　　　　　げんき
> 　　　　A: 大変だね。（← Comment)
> 　　　　　たいへん

> **Step 3** Finally, take turns asking the questions in Step 1 and answering them based on your own situation, preferences, and skills.

3 Take turns asking and answering the following questions in casual speech and expand the conversation as appropriate.

Ex. 専攻は何ですか。
せんこう
A: 専攻、何？
　　せんこう
B: 歴史（だよ）。
　　れきし
A: へえ、そう。　　＜Continue＞

1）専攻は何ですか　　　2）趣味は何ですか　　　3）何人兄弟ですか
　せんこう　　　　　　　　　　しゅみ　　　　　　　　　　なんにんきょうだい
4）出身はどこですか　　5）どんな〇〇が好きですか　　6）your own
　しゅっしん　　　　　　　　　　　　　　　　す

4 Use casual speech to invite your friend to do something with you.

Step 1 Practice making invitations in casual speech.

L8-19

Ex. somewhere to eat dinner → どこかに晩ご飯（を）食べに行かない？
　　　　　　　　　　　　　　　　　　　　ばん　はん

1）a supermarket for shopping　　　　　　2）a park for a walk every morning

3）the Japan House to meet Nyanta　　　　4）a night club（クラブ）to dance

5）a museum to see Picasso's（ピカソ）paintings

6）(come to) my house to do homework　　7）your own

Step 2 Your friend will invite you to do something together. Expand the conversation and decide on the details of what you will be doing together. The particles in（　）in the model below can be omitted.

Ex. A: 〇〇さん、今度の金曜日にどこかに晩ご飯（を）食べに行かない？
　　　　　　　　こんど　　　　　　　　　　　　　ばん　はん
B: ごめん、アルバイトがあるから、金曜日はちょっと…
A: じゃ、土曜日の晩は？
　　　　　　　ばん
B: うん、いいよ。何（を）食べる？
A: うーん、トンカツ（が）食べたい。　　＜Continue＞

できる
IV
Request a favor or ask for permission with the appropriate level of formality.

できるIV-A　**Polite prohibition ～ないでください**

1 Practice forming polite prohibitions using ～ないでください.

L8-20

Ex. たべる → たべない → たべないでください

1）みる　　　2）ねる　　　3）はなす　　　4）かう　　　5）かえる

6）する　　　7）くる　　　8）はじめる　　9）でかける　　10）おくれる

11）とる　　12）うんてんする　13）つれてくる

2 Make requests not to do the following things.

Ex. 写真をとらないでください。
しゃしん

| **Ex.** take pictures | 1) drink beer in my room | 2) call me early in the morning | 3) return home late at night | 4) smoke in my room |

| 5) bring friends to my room | 6) take me to a party every week | 7) be late for a date | 8) forget my birthday | 9) your own |

3 Suppose you are working at the following places in your city and are now giving a tour to a group of Japanese visitors. Work with your partner to make instructions telling them what to do and what not to do there.

> **Possible locations** 図書館 病院 映画館 大学の寮 教会 お寺
> としょかん びょういん えいがかん りょう きょうかい

Ex. ここは大学の図書館です。ここでは大きい声で話さないでください。
だいがく としょかん こえ

小さい声で話してください。それから、電話をしないでください。
こえ でんわ

電話は外でしてください。
でんわ

できるⅣ-B **Lead-in sentence ending 〜んですが**

1 The weekend is coming soon.

Step 1 Practice creating lead-in sentence endings before making an invitation.

Ex. 今晩、時間があります → 今晩、時間があるんですが
こんばん こんばん

1) 映画のチケットが2枚あります　2) 金曜日は宿題がありません
えいが まい しゅくだい

3) 週末、出かけたいです　4) 今日の午後、何も予定がありません
しゅうまつ で ご ご よてい

5) 土曜日はひまです　6) 明日は休みです
やす

Step 2 Invite your partner to watch a movie together using the lead-in sentence endings you made in Step 1.

Ex. A: 今晩、時間があるんですが、いっしょに映画に行きませんか。
こんばん えいが

B: ええ、ぜひ。

2 Invite your classmate to join you in an activity you like doing.

A: Lead-in sentence + invitation	**Ex.** A: 週末ひまなんですが、日曜日にいっしょに出かけませんか。
	しゅうまつ て
B: Decline	B: すみません、日曜日はちょっと…
A: Suggest alternatives	A: じゃ、金曜日か土曜日はどうですか。
A & B: Decide on details	B: じゃ、金曜日にしましょう。どこに行きましょうか。
	A: 公園か美術館はどうですか。
	こうえん びじゅつかん
	<Continue>
B: Confirmation	B: じゃ、金曜日の1時に美術館の前で。
	びじゅつかん まえ

3 You want to go out to do something with your close friend. Invite them out in casual speech. 👕

Ex. A: 週末ひまなんだけど、日曜日にいっしょに出かけない？
しゅうまつ　　　　　　　　　　　　　　　　て
B: ごめん、日曜日はちょっと…　<Continue>

4 Suppose you are new to your city. Ask your partner for useful information about places you are looking for in your neighborhood.

Ex. go to watch a movie / movie theater

A: あのう、映画を見に行きたいんですが、映画館はどこがいいですか。
えいが　　　　　　　　　　　　　　　えいがかん
B: そうですね、あさひシネマかサマーシアターはどうですか。

近いから、いいですよ。
ちか
A: そうですか。じゃ、行ってみます。ありがとうございます。

1) go to drink delicious coffee / café   2) go to eat something / restaurant

3) go to buy cheap meat / supermarket   4) your own

できるⅣ-C　**Making a request 〜てくれませんか／くださいませんか**

1 Ask the following people for a favor using the appropriate level of formality.

Step 1 Ask your host mother for a favor based on the cues provided.

Ex. お母さん、作文の日本語をチェックしてくれませんか。
かあ　　　　さくぶん

Ex. 作文の日本語をチェックする　1) この文法を教える　2) 宿題を手伝う
さくぶん　　　　　　　　　　　　ぶんぽう　おし　　　　しゅくだい　てつだ
3) 歴史の本を貸す　4) 私の作文を読んでみる　5) your own
れきし　　か　　　　　さくぶん

Step 2 Now, ask your teacher for a favor politely using the cues in Step 1.

Ex. 先生、作文の日本語をチェックしてくださいませんか。
さくぶん

Step 3 Finally, ask your friend for a favor casually, again using the cues in Step 1. 👕

Ex. 作文の日本語をチェックしてくれない？
さくぶん

2 Ask your host mother for a favor.

[Step 1] Make lead-in sentences to open a conversation based on the cues provided and ask if now is a good time. 🔊 L8-24

Ex. お願いがあります → ちょっと<u>お願いがある</u>んですが、今いいですか。

1) 質問があります　2) 聞きたいです　3) 相談したいです　4) 日本語について知りたいです

[Step 2] Ask your host mother for a favor with a lead-in sentence. 🔊 L8-25

Ex. 明日東京に行く／朝、駅まで送る
　　→ <u>明日東京に行く</u>んですが、<u>朝、駅まで送って</u>くれませんか。

1) 明日電車で帰る／6時に駅に迎えに来る　　2) 買い物に行きたい／自転車を貸す
3) 今スピーチの練習をしている／聞く　　4) この漢字が分からない／教える
5) your own

3 Put together Steps 1 and 2 to have a conversation in which you ask your host mother for a favor.

Ex. あなた　：お母さん、あのう、ちょっとお願いがあるんですが、今いいですか。
　　お母さん：ええ。
　　あなた　：あのう、明日東京に行くんですが、朝、駅まで送ってくれませんか。
　　お母さん：はい、いいですよ。or　うーん、明日の朝はちょっと…

4 Ask your teacher for a favor politely.

[Step 1] Ask your teacher for a letter of recommendation, using the lead-in sentences provided in the cues below.

Ex. <u>日本に留学したい</u>んですが、<u>推薦状を書いて</u>くださいませんか。

Ex. want to study abroad in Japan　　　　1) want to do an internship

2) want to go to (lit. enter) graduate school　　3) want to study religion in Japan

4) want a scholarship　　　　　　　　　5) your own

[Step 2] Practice a full conversation in which you ask your teacher for a favor.

Opening with a lead-in sentence	Ex. 学生：先生、あのう、ちょっとお願いがあるんですが、今いいですか。
	先生：はい、何ですか。
Lead-in sentence + request	学生：私は日本の文学に興味があるんですが、いい本を紹介してくださいませんか。
	先生：はい、いいですよ。
Closing	学生：ありがとうございます。
	よろしくお願いします。

1 Practice using ～てもいい to talk about things you are allowed to do in your Japanese class.

Ex. ペンで書く → ペンで書いて → ペンで書いてもいいです

1) 友達に 教 科書を借りる
2) ネットで調べる
3) オンラインで試験を受ける
4) 水を飲む　　5) トイレに行く
6) 英語で質問する
7) イヌ (service dog) を連れてくる

2 You are showing your house to someone new. Explain what is allowed in the house.

Ex. 部屋でお酒を飲んでもいいです。

Ex. in the rooms　　1) in the rooms　　2) early morning　　3) in the rooms

4) bring friends　　5) return home late at night　　6) go out at night　　7) your own

3 Suppose you have just moved into the Japan House. Ask Mark for permission to do the following things in the living room.

Ex. drink alcohol →(○)(×)

あなた：あのう、リビングでお酒を飲んでもいいですか。

マーク：はい、飲んでもいいですよ。

　　　　or すみません、リビングでは飲まないでください。

1) smoke →(×)　　2) eat a meal →(○)　　3) sleep →(×)　　4) dance →(○)

5) make a phone call →(○)　　6) have a party →(×)　　7) your own

4 You are asking your teacher for a favor or for permission to do something, but your teacher declines your request.

Useful vocabulary for permission	出す	受ける	英語で話す／書く

Ex. 学生：先生、あのう、{質問／お願い}があるんですが…

先生：はい。

学生：あのう、明日宿題を出してもいいですか。

先生：いいえ、今日、出してください。明日出さないでください。

学生：分かりました。今からがんばります。

Lesson **8**

291

5 You are talking with your friend. Using casual speech, make and respond to a request for permission to do something. 👕

Useful vocabulary for permission	食べる	行く	乗る _の	使う _{つか}	見る	借りる _か

Ex. A: ○○さんのパソコン、後で使ってもいい？
_{あと　つか}

　　　B: うん、いいよ。or　ごめん、後で私も宿題をするから、ちょっと… <Continue>
_{あと　　　　しゅくだい}

Review

Now you can make requests and ask for permission.

ROLE PLAY　　A student has come to their instructor's office for a consultation.

[Student] Think of a situation in which you might visit your instructor's office to make a request. Make that request, then ask additional relevant questions.

[Instructor] Respond to the student's requests and questions.

Opening: 　Lead-in sentence 　to open the 　conversation Lead-in sentence + request Details ・reason   Request for permission   Closing

Ex.　学生：あのう、{お願い／相談}があるんですが…
_{ねが　　そうだん}

　　　先生：はい、何ですか。

　　　学生：夏休みに日本に宗教を勉強しに行きたいんで
_{なつやす　　　　しゅうきょう　べんきょう}
　　　　　　すが、推薦状を書いてくださいませんか。
_{すいせんじょう　か}

　　　先生：はい、いいですよ。どの大学に行きますか。

　　　学生：とびら大学に行きたいです。とびら大学には
　　　　　　有名な宗教の先生がたくさんいるからです。
_{ゆうめい　しゅうきょう}

　　　先生：そうですか。分かりました。いいですよ。
_わ

　　　学生：あのう、後で、メールでフォームを送っても
_{あと　　　　　　　　　　　おく}
　　　　　　いいですか。

　　　先生：はい、そうしてください。

　　　学生：ありがとうございます。どうぞよろしくお願い
_{ねが}
　　　　　　します。失礼します。
_{しつれい}

よみましょう

How to read vertical writing

1 Let's learn the rules for vertical writing in Japanese. Compare box A and box B, then answer the questions below about the format of each.

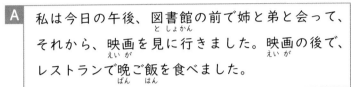

A　私は今日の午後、図書館の前で姉と弟と会って、それから、映画を見に行きました。映画の後で、レストランで晩ご飯を食べました。

■ Enter **A** or **B** in the correct ( ).

1）Writing format

　　a. Horizontal（　　　）　　　b. Vertical（　　　）

2）Start of the text

　　a. Top right（　　　）　　　b. Top left（　　　）

3）Writing direction

　　a. Left to right, top to bottom（　　　）

　　b. Top to bottom, right to left（　　　）

4）Punctuation marks

　　a. Below the bottom right corner of the preceding character（　　　）

　　b. To the right of the bottom right corner of the preceding character（　　　）

B　私は今日の午後、図書館の前で姉と弟と会って、それから、映画を見に行きました。映画の後で、レストランで晩ご飯を食べました。

Lesson 8

Japanese can be written both horizontally and vertically:

たて書き (vertical writing) is written from top to bottom, right to left.

　Exs. novels, newspapers, magazines, manga, calligraphy, traditional banners, etc.

よこ書き (horizontal writing) is written from left to right, top to bottom.

　Exs. emails, websites, movie subtitles, games, visual novels, scientific and mathematical writings, etc.

Usually a text is written in the same direction throughout, but some texts, such as newspapers, magazines, and manga, may contain a mixture of vertical writing and horizontal writing.

ニャーニャーニャーニャーニャーニャー

アイちゃん、ぼくのばんごはん、わすれないでください！

アイちゃんにでんわ

Mixed Text (vertical & horizontal writing)

文化

Vertical Writing

2. Try reading the four-panel manga (1) and (2) below. For manga (2), choose the appropriate expression from a.-d. to insert into each speech bubble.

(1)
- ぼくの名前は、にゃんた
- ちょっと有名　とても頭がいいネコです。
- この人はぼくの大好きなアイちゃん
- アイちゃん、ありがとう。でも、いたいよ～　にゃんたかわいい～

(2)

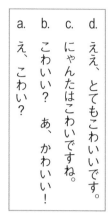

a. え、こわい？
b. にゃんたはこわいですね。
c. こわいい？　あ、かわいい！
d. ええ、とてもこわいいです。

いたいよ～：That hurts!

Scanning and skimming

Step 1 Scan and skim the vertical text of the newspaper article below and circle the katakana words.

Step 2 Draw a square around the kanji and kanji words that you know.

Step 3 Guess what the article is about using the words you picked out in Step 1 and Step 2 as clues, and think about what word should replace ??? as part of the title of the ranking on the left.

Step 4 Finally, look at the ranking and talk about the foods you like. (Ignore the name of any food that you cannot read the kanji for.)

??? ランキング

順位	食べ物	人数
1位	すし	62人
2位	カレー	52人
3位	ラーメン	33人
4位	焼肉	21人
5位	鶏の唐揚げ	20人
6位	餃子	12人
6位	チョコレート	12人
8位	アイスクリーム	11人
8位	うどん	11人
8位	ステーキ	11人
8位	パスタ	11人
8位	パン	11人

（回答総数587人）

livedoor NEWS「日本人が一番好きな食べ物が決定‼1位は日本が誇るあのソウルフード…⁉」より改変
©フルタイム

日本人の好物、「すし」が一位　カレー、ラーメンも人気

日本人の一番好きな食べ物についてアンケートをしたら、左の表のような結果が出た。どの食べ物も日本人の食生活に根付いているものばかりだ。

第二位はカレー。子供の好きな食べ物の代表格、母の味の定番のカレーが入った。そして、第一位は日本人のソウルフードのすしが輝いた。「すし」と答えた人の理由としては、「ご飯と合わせて色々な食材が食べられるし、日本人のアイデンティティを感じるから」「色々な海の幸が楽しめるから、日本人に生まれてよかった」などの意見があった。

四位以下は「焼肉」や「鶏の唐揚げ」から、女性に人気が高い「チョコレート」や「アイスクリーム」まで、様々な食べ物がランクインしている。

第三位にはしょうゆ、みそ、とんこつと色々な味が楽しめるラーメンがランクイン。

あなたの好きな食べ物はランクインしただろうか。

3 Read the email below and answer the questions that follow.

Sender:	Tao Huang <taoh@goble.edu>
Subject:	げんき？

メイちゃん、

Ex. げんき？　私は毎日すごくいそがしい！　でも、げんきだよ。メイちゃんの ¹⁾しゃしん、見たよ。²⁾メイちゃん、³⁾しゃしん ⁴⁾とるの、上手だね。シンガポール大学は ⁵⁾どう？日本語の ⁶⁾クラス、⁷⁾楽しい？　⁸⁾私、やすみにメイちゃんに会いに行っても ⁹⁾いい？メイちゃんの ¹⁰⁾よてい、おしえてくれない？　また ¹¹⁾メール書くね。

タオ

Understanding the missing elements in casual expressions

1) Insert the appropriate letter from a.-d. after each of the underlined words 1)-11) to indicate the elements that would accompany those words in the polite writing style.

Ex. げんき？　　　a. を　　b. は　　c. が　　d. ですか

Comprehension check

2) Answer the following questions in Japanese.

a. タオさんはこのメールをだれに出しましたか。

b. その人 (that person) は、今どこにいますか。何をしていますか。

---

4 Below is an email Ai sent to Prof. Kuroda after their meeting in L8 かいわ3 (p.261). Complete the email by filling in each ☐ with the appropriate expression from the box below.

しめきり：deadline

くろだ先生、　Addressee
こんばんは。　Greeting　　一年生の日本語のクラスのアイ・ブルーノです。　Self-identification
今日は ¹⁾☐。　きょうとびじゅつ大学のすいせんじょうなんですが、　Lead-in sentence
フォームをおくります。　しめきりは2月15日です。　Explanation of the situation
²⁾☐、大学のウェブサイトにアップロード ³⁾☐。　Request
どうぞ ⁴⁾☐。　Closing remark
アイ・ブルーノ　Your name

> a. よろしくおねがいします　　b. してくださいませんか
> c. すみませんが　　　　　　　d. どうもありがとうございました

- -

かくれんしゅう ～ *Writing Practice*

Write an email to your instructor with your own request. Refer to the format (see the yellow arrows) in Ai's email above when writing your message.

- -

ききましょう

Integration: Content prediction strategies
You have learned and practiced a variety of content prediction strategies in Lessons 5-7, such as using context, visual clues, and conjunctions to aid your comprehension while listening. In this lesson, try to listen and use all the prediction strategies you have learned so far.

1 **Pre-listening activity:** Look at the picture below. Guess where you might see the scene in the picture, then guess what kind of conversation might take place given this visual context. Write your educated guess in the box below in either your language or in Japanese.

りゅうがくフェア
Study abroad
ホームステイを
しませんか？

L8-28

2 **Listening:** Now, listen to the conversation taking place in the scene above. You will be asked questions while listening to the conversation. Take notes and write the answers in either your language or in Japanese.

プログラム：program

Listen to the first half of the conversation and answer questions 1)-3). Note that all questions about this conversation will be read aloud and interspersed in the dialogue.

1) _____   2) _____   3) Yes / No

Listen to the next part and answer question 4): _____

Listen to the next part and answer question 5):   5 (very close)   4   3   2   1 (not at all)

Listen to the next part and answer question 6): _____

Listen to the next part and answer question 7): _____

Exit Check ☑

Now it's time to go back to the DEKIRU List for this chapter (p.259) and do the exit check to see what new things you can do now that you've completed the lesson.

すごくこわかった！
It was so scary!

できるCheck ✓

できる I
Talk about past events in casual speech.
過去の出来事について、くだけた話し方で話すことができる。

Entry ☐　Exit ☐

できる II
Talk about a situation in detail by providing more explanation.
説明を加えて、状況を詳しく話すことができる。

Entry ☐　Exit ☐

できる III
Give impressions and opinions on a familiar topic.
身近な話題について、印象や意見を簡単に言うことができる。

Entry ☐　Exit ☐

できる IV
Report on things you have heard people say.
誰かが言っていたことについて、伝えることができる。

Entry ☐　Exit ☐

できる V
Talk about experiences.
経験について話すことができる。

Entry ☐　Exit ☐

STRATEGIES

Conversation Tips .... • Providing explanations with 実は〜んです

Reading .... • Getting information from a weather map
　　　　　　　　　　　 • Visualizing
　　　　　　　　　　　 • Sorting information

Listening .... • Listening in noisy environments (1)

GRAMMAR

1 Plain past forms of verbs, *i*-adjectives, and です　**できる I**

2 〜んです [Asking for and providing explanations]　**できる II**

3 Adjective / Verb そう [Impressions]　**できる III**

4 〜と思う [Assumptions and opinions] "think that ~; feel that ~"　**できる III**

5 〜と言う [Quotations] "say that ~"　**できる IV**

6 〜たり〜たりする [Non-exhaustive listing of actions]　**できる V**

7 〜たことがある [Experiences]　**できる V**

かいわ

1 できる I, II　At the Japan House in the morning before Japanese class.　🔊 **L9-1**

アイ　　：タオちゃん、おはよう。今朝はちょっと寒いね。

タオ　　：おはよう、アイちゃん。うん、寒いね。

　　　　　ふわぁ、すごくねむい。

アイ　　：え？　どうしたの？

タオ　　：実は昨日、夜遅く日本の古い映画を見ていたんだ…

アイ　　：えっ、どんな映画？

タオ　　：『リング』！　すごくこわかった！

アイ　　：『リング』？　ああ、とてもこわい映画だね。私も子どもの時に見たよ。

\<Riemann joins them.\>

アイ　　：あ、リーマンさん、おはよう。どうしたの？　元気がないね。

リーマン：ええ、実は頭が痛いんです…　僕、今日はクラスを休みます。

アイ　　：え？　だいじょうぶ？

2 できる III, IV　In Japanese class.　🔊 **L9-2**

CM：(TV) commercial

先生　　：おはようございます。今日は寒いですね。雪が降りそうですよ。

　　　　　みなさん、かぜをひかないでくださいね。

学生　　：はい！

先生　　：あ、ゴルドさんがいませんね。

アイ　　：黒田先生、ゴルドさんは今日クラスに来ません。

先生　　：え、どうしたんですか。

タオ　　：たぶんかぜをひいたんだと思います。

　　　　　頭が痛いから、今日は休むと言っていました。

アイ　　：後で先生にメールを書くと言っていました。

先生　　：分かりました。

　　　　　ゴルドさんに「お大事に」と言ってください。

先生　　：じゃ、みなさん、今日は日本の温泉のCMを見ましょう。

　　　　　温泉を知っていますか。

アイ　　：はい、テレビで見ました。おふろが大きくてちょっと熱そうでした。

　　　　　でも、みんな気分がよさそうでした。

先生　　：ええ、そうですね。じゃ、見てみましょう。

3 できるⅤ **At the Japan House after Japanese class.** L9-3

銭湯：public bath　コーヒー牛乳：coffee-flavored milk

アイ　　：けいたさん、今日、日本語のクラスで温泉のCMを見ました。

　　　　　けいたさんは温泉に行ったことがありますか。

スーパー銭湯

けいた　：うん、実は、僕、温泉に入るの、大好きなんだ。

　　　　　よく家の近くのスーパー銭湯に行っていたよ。

アイ　　：え？　スーパー銭湯？

けいた　：うん、スーパー銭湯には色々なおふろやサウナが

　　　　　あるんだよ。それから、おふろの後でゆっくり休んだり、

永山健康ランド 竹取の湯

　　　　　レストランでおいしい物を食べたりするんだ。

アイ　　：へえ、楽しそうな所ですね。

けいた　：うん、すごく楽しいよ。

　　　　　僕はおふろの後で、いつも同じ飲み物を飲んでいたんだ。

コーヒー牛乳

アイ　　：え、どんな飲み物ですか。

けいた　：コーヒー牛乳！　冷たくて甘いから、すごくおいしいよ。

　　　　　おすすめ！

アイ　　：へえ、私もスーパー銭湯に行って、コーヒー牛乳を

　　　　　飲んでみたいです。

ワンポイント　L9-4

CONVERSATION TIPS

Providing explanations with 実は〜んです: You can ask for or provide an explanation about a shared situation or shared information using 〜んです. The phrase 実は is often used with 〜んです to reveal a secret, provide a reason, etc.

　　A：あ、うれしそうですね。どうしたんですか。

　　B：実は今からデートなんです。

　　A：え！？　だれとデートするんですか。

たんご

▶ **The words written in gray** are supplemental vocabulary.

● せいかつ Daily life

せいかつ
(daily life; lifestyle)

[*thing* を] すてる
(to throw away)

ごみ／ゴミ
(trash; garbage)

[*place* を] かたづける
(to tidy up)

[*thing* を] かたづける
(to put away)

[*person* と] わかれる
(to break up; to part ways)

[*person* と] けんかする
(to fight; to quarrel)

[*sentence* と] おもう
(to think)

なく ⟷ わらう
(to cry)   (to laugh; to smile)

[*job/class* を] やすむ
(to be absent (from))

やすむ
(to (take a) rest)

つかれる
(to get tired)

のどがかわく
(to get thirsty)

おなかがすく
(to get hungry)

ねむい
(sleepy)

しんぶん
(newspaper)

カラオケ
(karaoke)

がいこく
(foreign country)

ゆっくり (slowly; in a relaxed fashion)

Ex.1 ゆっくりあるく
(to walk slowly)

Ex.2 ゆっくりおふろにはいる
(to have a relaxing time in the bath)

● からだのちょうし Physical well-being

げんき（な） ⟷ びょうき
(sick(ness); ill(ness))

Ex. びょうきのひと
(sick person)

かぜをひく
(to catch a cold)

かぜ
(cold) [illness]

ねつがある
(to have a fever)

ねつ
(fever)

[*body part* が]
いたい (painful; sore)

は
(tooth)

きぶんがいい ⟷ きぶんがわるい
(to feel well)   (to feel ill)

きぶん
(feeling; mood)
[physical, mental, or
emotional]

げんきがない
(out of sorts; lacking energy)

だいじょうぶ（な）
(all right; okay; safe)

どうしたんですか。
(**What's wrong?**)

じつは、おなかがいたいんです。
(**To tell the truth**, I have a stomachache.)

そうですか。**おだいじに。**
(I see. **Get well soon; Take care of yourself.**)

● びょうしゃする　Describing people, things, and feelings

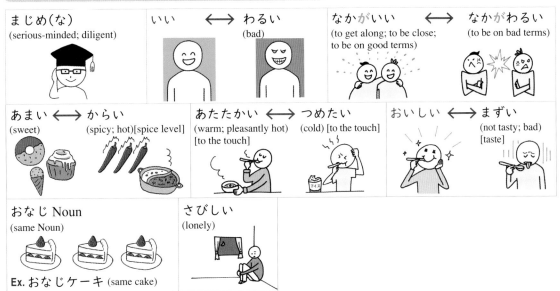

まじめ（な）
(serious-minded; diligent)

いい　⟷　わるい
　　　　　　　(bad)

なかがいい　⟷　なかがわるい
(to get along; to be close;　　(to be on bad terms)
to be on good terms)

あまい　⟷　からい
(sweet)　　　(spicy; hot)[spice level]

あたたかい　⟷　つめたい
(warm; pleasantly hot)　(cold) [to the touch]
[to the touch]

おいしい　⟷　まずい
　　　　　　　(not tasty; bad)
　　　　　　　[taste]

おなじ Noun
(same Noun)

Ex. おなじケーキ (same cake)

さびしい
(lonely)

● てんき／きせつ　Weather and seasons

てんき
(weather)

てんきよほう
(weather forecast)

はれる
(to clear up; to become
sunny (weather))

はれ
(sunny (weather))

くもる
(to cloud up)

くもり
(cloudy (weather))

あめ
(rain)

ゆき
(snow)

あめがふる　⟷　あめがやむ
(It rains.)　　　　　(It stops raining.)

ゆきがふる　⟷　ゆきがやむ
(It snows.)　　　　　(It stops snowing.)

きおん
(air temperature)

１０ど
(10 degrees)

マイナス２ど
(minus 2 degrees)

たいふう
(typhoon)

あたたかい　⟷　すずしい
(warm) [air temperature]　(cool) [air temperature]

はる
(spring)

ふゆ
(winter)

なつ
(summer)

あき
(fall; autumn)

● ～ど (... degrees [temperature])

0℃ = 32°F

-10 degrees (℃/°F)	-5 degrees (℃/°F)	0 degrees (℃/°F)	5 degrees (℃/°F)	10 degrees (℃/°F)	?
マイナスじゅうど	マイナスごど	れいど	ごど	じゅうど	なんど

● ～がっき (... semester)

last semester	this semester	next semester	spring semester	summer semester	fall semester	winter semester
せんがっき	こんがっき	らいがっき	はるがっき	なつがっき	あきがっき	ふゆがっき

たんごリスト

🔊 L9-5

RU-VERBS

1	か<u>たづける</u>		to tidy up; to put in order [*place* を]; to put away [*thing* を]
2	す<u>てる</u>	捨てる	to throw away [*thing* を]
3	つ<u>かれる</u>		to get tired
4	は<u>れる</u>	晴れる	to clear up; to become sunny (weather)
5	わ<u>かれる</u>	別れる	to break up; to part ways [*person* と]

U-VERBS / U-VERB PHRASES

6	<u>あ</u>め／<u>ゆ</u>きが ふる	雨／雪が 降る	It rains/snows.
7	<u>あ</u>め／<u>ゆ</u>きが やむ	雨／雪が やむ	It stops raining/ snowing.
8	く<u>もる</u>		to cloud up [weather]
9	おなかがす<u>く</u>		to get hungry
10	<u>のどがか</u>わ<u>く</u>		to get thirsty
11	か<u>ぜをひく</u>		to catch a cold
12	ね<u>つがある</u>	熱がある	to have a fever
13	や<u>すむ</u>	休む	to be absent (from) [*job/class* を]; to (take a) rest
14	お<u>もう</u>	思う	to think [*sentence* と]
15	な<u>く</u>	泣く	to cry
16	わ<u>らう</u>	笑う	to laugh; to smile

SURU-VERB

17	け<u>んかする</u>		to fight; to quarrel [*person* と]

I-ADJECTIVES / I-ADJECTIVE PHRASES

18	あ<u>まい</u>	甘い	sweet
19	か<u>らい</u>		spicy; hot [spice level]
20	あ<u>たたかい</u>	温かい／ 暖かい	warm; pleasantly hot [to the touch]; warm [air temperature]

21	つ<u>めたい</u>	冷たい	cold [to the touch; person]
22	す<u>ずし</u>い		cool [air temperature]
23	な<u>かがい</u>い	仲がいい	to get along; to be close; to be on good terms
24	な<u>かがわ</u>るい	仲が悪い	to be on bad terms
25	い<u>たい</u>	痛い	painful; sore; to hurt; to ache [*body part* が]
26	さ<u>びし</u>い		lonely
27	ね<u>むい</u>		sleepy
28	ま<u>ずい</u>		not tasty; bad [taste]
29	わ<u>るい</u>	悪い	bad

NA-ADJECTIVES

30	だ<u>いじょうぶ</u>		all right; okay; safe
31	ま<u>じめ</u>		serious-minded; diligent

NOUNS

32	て<u>んき</u>	天気	weather
33	て<u>んきよほう</u>	天気予報	weather forecast
34	<u>あ</u>め	雨	rain
35	く<u>もり</u>		cloudy (weather)
36	き<u>おん</u>	気温	air temperature
37	た<u>いふう</u>	台風	typhoon
38	は<u>れ</u>	晴れ	sunny (weather)
39	ゆ<u>き</u>	雪	snow
40	は<u>る</u>	春	spring
41	な<u>つ</u>	夏	summer
42	<u>あ</u>き	秋	fall; autumn
43	ふ<u>ゆ</u>	冬	winter
44	き<u>ぶん</u>	気分	feeling; mood [physical, mental, or emotional]
	き<u>ぶんが</u> いい	気分が いい	to feel well; to be in a good mood

	きぶんが わるい	気分が 悪い	to feel ill; to feel down
45	は	歯	tooth
46	びょうき	病気	sick(ness); ill(ness); disease **Ex.** びょうきのひと sick person
47	ごみ／ゴミ		trash; garbage
48	しんぶん	新聞	newspaper
49	せいかつ	生活	daily life; lifestyle
50	がいこく	外国	foreign country
51	カラオケ		karaoke
52	マイナス		minus

COUNTER

53	～ど	～度	... degrees [temperature]
	れいど	０度	zero degrees
	じゅうど	十度	ten degrees
	マイナスごど	マイナス 五度	minus five degrees; five degrees below zero
	なんど	何度	what temperature; how many degrees

SUFFIX

54	～がっき	～学期	... semester
	せんがっき	先学期	last semester
	こんがっき	今学期	this semester
	らいがっき	来学期	next semester

OTHER WORDS AND PHRASES

55	おなじ Noun	同じ～	same Noun **Ex.** おなじクラス same class
56	じつは	実は	to tell the truth; actually
57	ゆっくり		slowly; in a relaxed fashion **Ex.1** ゆっくりあるく to walk slowly/in a relaxed fashion **Ex.2** ゆっくりおふろ にはいる to have a relaxing time in the bath

58	おだいじに	お大事に	Get well soon; Take care of yourself.
59	げんきがない	元気が ない	out of sorts; lacking energy
60	どうしたんですか		What happened?; What's wrong?; What's going on?

Lesson
9

かんじ

▶ ＊Special reading

104 思	思思	シ	意思 intention い し	思考 thought し こう	不思議（な）mysterious ふ し ぎ
		おも（う）	思う to think おも	思い出す to recall おも だ	思い出 memory おも で
to think		丨 冂 冂 田 田 甲 思 思 思			

105 休	休休	キュウ	休業 する to be closed [shops, businesses, etc.] きゅうぎょう		休日 day off; holiday きゅうじつ
		やす（み） やす（む）	休み break やす	春休み spring break はるやす	夏休み summer break なつやす
			秋休み fall break あきやす	冬休み winter break ふゆやす	
			休む to be absent (from); to (take a) rest やす		
to rest		ノ イ 仁 什 休 休			

106 悪	悪悪	アク	悪人 villain; bad person あくにん	最悪 the worst さいあく	
		わる（い）	悪い bad わる	気分が悪い to feel ill/down きぶん わる	仲が悪い to be on bad terms なか わる
			意地悪（な）mean(-spirited) い じわる	悪口を言う to speak ill of わるぐち い	
bad		一 一 戸 戸 亜 亜 悪 悪 悪 悪			

107 新	新新	シン	新聞 newspaper しんぶん	新学期 new semester しんがっき	新人 new member しんじん	新入生 new student しんにゅうせい
			新幹線 (Japanese) bullet train しんかんせん	新鮮（な）fresh しんせん	新年 new year しんねん	
		あたら（しい）	新しい new; fresh あたら			
new		丶 亠 亠 立 立 辛 辛 亲 新 新 新 新				

108 古	古古	コ	考古学 archeology こうこがく	古文 classic literature こぶん	中古 secondhand; used ちゅうこ
		ふる（い）	古い old [thing] ふる	古着 used clothes ふるぎ	古本 used book ふるほん
old		一 十 古 古 古			

109 高	高高	コウ	高校 high school こうこう	高校生 high school student こうこうせい	
			最高 the highest; the best さいこう		
		たか（い）	高い high; expensive たか	背が高い tall [stature] せ たか	
high		亠 亠 亡 古 古 古 高 高 高 高			

110 校	校校	コウ	学校 school がっこう	高校 high school こうこう	高校生 high school student こうこうせい
			小学校 elementary school しょうがっこう	中学校 middle school ちゅうがっこう	
			校長 principal こうちょう		
school		一 十 才 木 木 杧 栌 校 校 校			

| 111 雨
rain | 雨
雨 | ウ | 雨天 rain; rainy weather
うてん | 梅雨 * ／ 梅雨 rainy season in East Asia
つゆ　　ばいう |
| | | あめ | 雨 rain　雨が降る It rains.　大雨 heavy rain
あめ　　あめ　ふ　　　　おおあめ | |

ー ſ ŕ 币 币 雨 雨 雨

112 雪 snow	雪 雪	セツ	新雪 fresh snow しんせつ	
		ゆき	雪 snow　雪が降る It snows.　大雪 heavy snowfall ゆき　　ゆき　ふ　　　　おおゆき	
			雪だるま snowman ゆき	

ー ſ ŕ 币 币 乕 雪 雪 雪 雪 雪

| 113 晴
sunny | 晴
晴 | セイ | 晴天 fair sky
せいてん | |
| | | は(れる) | 晴れ sunny weather　晴れる to clear up; to become sunny
は　　　　　　は | |

丨 冂 日 日 日一 日十 日丰 時 晴 晴 晴

114 度 degrees; ... times	度 度	ド	～度 ... degrees [temperature] (Exs. 十度 ten degrees, 何度 what temperature) ど　　　　　　　　じゅうど　　　　なんど		
			～度 ... times (Exs. 一度 once, 二度 twice, 三度 three times) ど　　　　　いちど　　にど　　　さんど		
			今度 next time　温度 temperature　湿度 level of humidity こんど　　　おんど　　　　しつど		
		たび	度々 frequently たびたび		

丶 亠 广 广 产 产 库 庻 度

115 天 heaven	天 天	テン	天気 weather　天気予報 weather forecast　天国 heaven てんき　　てんきよほう　　　　てんごく		
			天ぷら *tempura* [deep-fried seafood and vegetables] てん		
		あま	天の川 Milky Way あま　がわ		

ー 二 チ 天

116 気 spirit	気 気	キ ケ	気分 feeling; mood　元気(な) well [health]; energetic　天気 weather きぶん　　　　　　げんき　　　　　　　　てんき		
			人気がある to be popular　病気 sick(ness); ill(ness); disease　気温 air temperature にんき　　　　　　　びょうき　　　　　　　　　きおん		
			気持ち feelings　電気 light; electricity　湿気 humidity きも　　　　でんき　　　　　　しっけ		

ノ 乞 气 气 気 気

117 元 origin; former	元 元	ゲン ガン	元気(な) well [health]; energetic　元気がない out of sorts; lacking energy げんき　　　　　　　　げんき		
			元日 New Year's Day がんじつ		
		もと	親元 parents' home　手元 close by　元彼 ex-boyfriend　元カノ ex-girlfriend おやもと　　　　てもと　　　　もとかれ　　　　　もと		

ー 二 テ 元

| 118 病
illness; sickness | 病
病 | ビョウ | 病気 sick(ness); ill(ness); disease　病院 hospital　病人 sick people
びょうき　　　　　　　　　びょういん　　　　　びょうにん | | |

丶 亠 广 疒 疒 疗 疗 病 病 病

305

119 英	英 英	エイ	英語 English [language] えいご	英会話 English conversation えいかいわ
			英国 UK えいこく	英文学 English literature えいぶんがく
			英雄 hero; heroine えいゆう	
England; excellent	一 ナ 艹 芍 芮 芑 英 英			

120 家	家 家	カ ケ	～家 [suffix indicating an occupation] (Exs. 作家 writer, 音楽家 musician) か　　　　　　　　　　　　　　　さっか　　　　おんがくか	
			家族 family かぞく	～家 [suffix indicating house/family] (Ex. 山田家 the Yamada family) け　　　　　　　　　　　　　　　やまだけ
		いえ うち や	家／家 house いえ　うち	
			大家 landlord おおや	家賃 rent [money] やちん
house; home	丶 宀 宀 宀 宀 宇 宇 家 家 家			

Kanji as elements

This kanji is used in many other kanji as an element, so you will encounter it frequently as you continue to study Japanese.

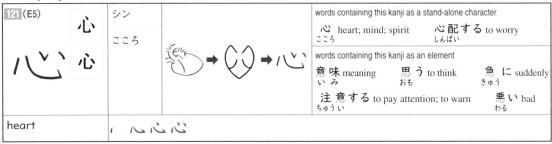

121 (E5) 心	心 心	シン こころ	words containing this kanji as a stand-alone character
			心 heart; mind; spirit こころ　　　　　心配する to worry　しんぱい
			words containing this kanji as an element
			意味 meaning　　思う to think　　急に suddenly いみ　　　　　　おも　　　　　　きゅう
			注意する to pay attention; to warn　　悪い bad ちゅうい　　　　　　　　　　　　　　わる
heart	丶 心 心 心		

あたらしいよみかた　New readings

The following are new readings for kanji that you have already learned. Read each word aloud.

1) 学校　　2) 気分　　3) 新聞
　　がっこう　　　きぶん　　　しんぶん

れんしゅう　Practice

1 Find and circle 11 words that contain kanji you have learned so far, then write the words and their readings in the spaces provided. The words may appear either vertically or horizontally.

英	語	悪	新	聞
今	高	い	元	く
度	校	病	気	分
休	む	会	Ex. 古	い

Ex. 　古い　（　ふるい　）　　1) ＿＿＿（　　　　　）

2) ＿＿＿（　　　　　）　3) ＿＿＿（　　　　　）

4) ＿＿＿（　　　　　）　5) ＿＿＿（　　　　　）

6) ＿＿＿（　　　　　）　7) ＿＿＿（　　　　　）

8) ＿＿＿（　　　　　）　9) ＿＿＿（　　　　　）

10) ＿＿＿（　　　　　）　11) ＿＿＿（　　　　　）

2 Below on the right is a weather app showing the weather and the daily high temperatures（最高気温）and low temperatures（最低気温）for Nagano. First, write the readings for the kanji a.-h. in the box below. Then, insert the appropriate letter into each ___ in sentences 1)-3) to accurately complete the weather forecast for Nagano based on the information in the graphic.

[Note] Japan uses Celsius (°C) for temperatures: 0°C = 32°F, 10°C = 50°F.

---

a. 晴れ _____ b. 雨 _____ c. 雪 _____ d. 四度 _____ e. 七度 _____

f. 十度 _____ g. マイナス三度 _____ h. マイナス八度 _____

1）金曜日の天気は_____です。最高気温は_____です。
　　　　　　　　　　　　　　　　　さいこう き おん

2）土曜日の天気は_____です。最低気温は_____です。
　　　　　　　　　　　　　　　　　さいてい き おん

3）日曜日の天気は_____です。最高気温は_____です。
　　　　　　　　　　　　　　　　　さいこう き おん

長野の天気		
なが の		
2/15（金）	2/16（土）	2/17（日）
High　4°	7°	10°
Low　-8°	-3°	5°

Lesson
9

3 Haruka wants to go to a concert with Yumi. Read Haruka and Yumi's text messages aloud, then write the readings for the underlined words.

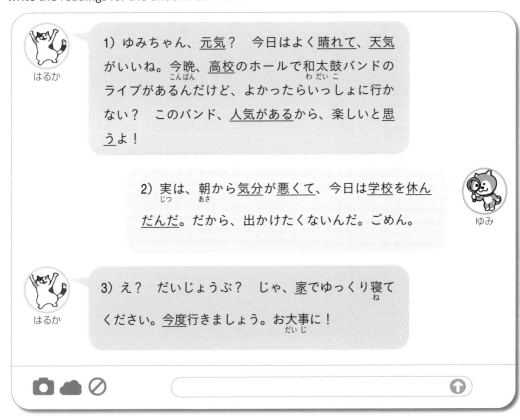

1）ゆみちゃん、元気？　今日はよく晴れて、天気がいいね。今晩、高校のホールで和太鼓バンドの
こんばん　　　　わ だい こ
ライブがあるんだけど、よかったらいっしょに行かない？　このバンド、人気があるから、楽しいと思うよ！

2）実は、朝から気分が悪くて、今日は学校を休ん
じつ　あさ
だんだ。だから、出かけたくないんだ。ごめん。

ゆみ

3）え？　だいじょうぶ？　じゃ、家でゆっくり寝て
ね
ください。今度行きましょう。お大事に！
だい じ

はるか

■ Kanji elements (2)

In Lesson 8, you learned about the elements that appear on the left side of a kanji and relate to the kanji's meaning. In addition to these, there are other meaning-related elements that appear in different positions within a kanji.

You are learning one such element in this lesson, in fact: 心 "heart," which appears at the bottom of a kanji. (You can find it, for instance, in 思 and 悪 in this lesson.) Meaning-related elements can appear on the top or bottom of a kanji, or they can frame its top and left or bottom and left sides. You will often encounter the following elements as you continue your study of kanji. Try to remember them, as they can be useful when you need to guess the meanings of kanji you do not know.

Elements				意味 い み		
	top	雨	rain		⇒	雨
		宀	roof; house	⇒	⇒	宀
		艹	grass	⇒	⇒	艹
	bottom	儿	foot; leg	⇒	⇒	儿
	top and left sides	广	roof	⇒	⇒	广
		疒	sickness	⇒	⇒	疒
	bottom and left sides	辶	to walk	⇒	⇒	辶

れんしゅう Practice

Complete the table below by writing one kanji you have learned so far that uses each element, then providing the kanji's meaning, a word in which the kanji appears, and the reading of that word in hiragana.

Elements	Ex. 雨	1) 宀	2) 儿	3) 心	4) 广	5) 疒	6) 辶
Kanji	雪						
Meaning of the kanji	snow						
Word using the kanji	雪 (がふる)						
Reading of the word in hiragana	ゆき (がふる)						

ぶんぽう

1 Plain past forms of verbs, *i*-adjectives, and です

Here you will learn the plain past forms of verbs, *i*-adjectives, and です. Using these forms, you can casually tell others what you did in the past, how something was in the past, etc. Plain past forms are also used in certain grammatical constructions.

1-1 Plain past forms of verbs

You can make the plain past forms of verbs as follows:
(a) Past affirmative form: Change the て at the end of the *te*-form to た or the で to だ.
(b) Past negative form: Change the い at the end of the non-past negative form to かった.

Affirmative			Negative	
Non-past	*Te*-form	Past	Non-past	Past
食べる た	食べて た	食べた た	食べない た	食べなかった た
話す はな	話して はな	話した はな	話さない はな	話さなかった はな
泳ぐ およ	泳いで およ	泳いだ およ	泳がない およ	泳がなかった およ
ある	あって	あった	Exception: ない （× あらない）	なかった
する	して	した	しない	しなかった
来る く	来て き	来た き	来ない こ	来なかった こ

Ex. (1) A: 昨日、クラスに行った？ *Did you go to class yesterday?*
きのう　　　　　い

B: ううん、行かなかった。*No, I didn't.*
　　　　　い

1-2 Plain past forms of *i*-adjectives

You can make the plain past forms of *i*-adjectives by changing the final い in the non-past forms to かった, as shown below:

Affirmative		Negative	
Non-past	Past	Non-past	Past
（高）い たか	（高）かった たか	（高）くない たか	（高）くなかった たか
いい	よかった	よくない	よくなかった

As seen in the conjugation table above, in the case of *i*-adjectives, the only difference between the plain forms and the polite forms is the existence of the polite ending です. (See L4 #4-1 and L8 #3-2.)

Exs. (1) A: 土曜日のパーティー、楽しかった？ *Was Saturday's party fun?*
どようび　　　　　たの

B: ううん、あまり楽しくなかった。*No, it wasn't very fun.*
　　　　　　　　たの

(2) 去年の寮の部屋は小さくて、きたなかった。
きょねん　りょう　へや　ちい

The dorm room I lived in last year was small and dirty.

You learned the plain non-past forms of です in Lesson 8 #3-3. The plain past forms of です are conjugated as follows:

(a) Past affirmative form: Change the non-past form だ to だった.

(b) Past negative form: Change the final い in the non-past negative form to かった.

	Affirmative		Negative	
	Non-past	Past	Non-past	Past
Na-adjective	（静か）だ しず	（静か）だった しず	（静か）じゃない しず	（静か）じゃなかった しず
Noun	（学生）だ がくせい	（学生）だった がくせい	（学生）じゃない がくせい	（学生）じゃなかった がくせい

Ex. （1） A: 旅行、どう<u>だった</u>？ *How was your trip?*
りょこう

　　　　B: 海がすごくきれい<u>だった</u>。でも、ホテルはあまり静か<u>じゃなかった</u>。
うみ　　　　　　　　　　　　　　　　　　　　　　　しず

　　　　The ocean was really beautiful, but the hotel wasn't very quiet.

---

2 **～んです [Asking for and providing explanations]**

[2-a]

	S-plain	
A:	何を作っている なに　つく	んですか。
	What are you making?	
B:	パスタを作っている つく	んです。
	I'm making pasta.	

You can ask for an explanation for something you have realized or learned and also provide a requested explanation using んです. For example, in [2-a], Speaker A has noticed Speaker B making something in the kitchen. In this situation, A asks B for an explanation of what B is making using んです, as in [2-a]-A, and B also responds using んです, as in [2-a]-B. In this situation, the sentences without んです (i.e., 何を 作っていますか and パスタを作っています) sound odd.
つく　　　　　　　　　　つく

Similarly, in (1) below, Speaker A has learned (either from someone else or by being in class) that Speaker B was absent from class and asks for an explanation, and B is providing that explanation. In this situation, too, the sentences without んです do not sound natural.

Ex. （1） A: どうしてクラスを休ん<u>だんです</u>か。*Why did you not come to class?*
やす

　　　　B: 熱があっ<u>たんです</u>。*Because I had a fever.*
ねつ

[2-b]

S₁	S₂	
	S-plain	
今日は休みます。 きょう　やす	頭が痛い あたま　いた	んです。
I'm going to take today off. I have a headache.		

[2-b] presents a slightly different situation in which んです is used. Here, the speaker says S₁ first and provides an explanation (in this case, a reason) for it in S₂. Similarly, in (2) and (3) on the next page, Speaker B provides an explanation for declining Speaker A's invitation or request in S₂.

Exs. (2) A: 今晩、映画に行きませんか。 *Would you like to go to a movie tonight?*
こんばん　えいが　い

B: すみません。明日テストがある**んです**。 *I'm sorry. I have a test tomorrow.*
あした

(3) A: 駅まで送ってくれませんか。 *Could you take me to the station?*
えき　おく

B: すみません。ちょっと… 予定がある**んです**。 *I'm sorry. I have plans.*
よてい

んです and its variations are also used in situations other than the above, but the fundamental condition for the use of んです is that a situation or information is shared between the speaker and the listener, and the んです sentence refers to that situation or information. For example, in [2-a], when Speaker A sees Speaker B making something, what A sees has become the shared situation, and A asks for an explanation referring to that situation. Thus, a more precise meaning of 何を作っているんですか in [2-a] would be
なに　つく
"Regarding what I see, what are you making?" In responding to this question, B answers referring to the same situation; thus, B also uses んです.

In [2-b], no visual information is shared between the speaker and the listener. In this case, however, once the speaker has uttered S₁, the information conveyed by this sentence is shared, and because the speaker is referring to this information when saying S₂, the speaker uses んです. Thus, a more precise meaning of 頭
あたま
が痛いんです would be "Regarding what I just said, I have a headache."
いた

As seen in [2-b], one of the functions of んです is to make a link to the preceding sentence if there is no other shared information to make a link to. To put this from the listener's point of view, when the listener hears んです, it indicates that the sentence with んです is in regard to the information in the preceding sentence if there is no non-verbal shared information (e.g., situational information) to make a link to.

The explanation provided in S₂ regarding what is said in S₁ is often the reason for S₁. The following sentence is not grammatical because there is no sentence or situation that the んです sentence can make a link to. (Compare this with [2-b], in which S₂, the んです sentence, can make a link to S₁.)

✕ 頭が痛い**んです**から、今日は休みます。 → 頭が痛いですから、今日は休みます。
あたま　いた　　　　　きょう　やす　　　　　あたま　いた　　　　きょう　やす
I have a headache, so I'll take today off.

When んです is used, there is generally a situation or information shared between the speaker and the listener. As a result, the use of this construction places the speaker psychologically closer to the listener and often expresses the speaker's emotion with regard to the listener or the situation (e.g., sympathy, surprise, etc.).

The forms before んです are as follows:

Verbs	plain form + んです	食べる**んです** た 食べた**んです** た	食べない**んです** た 食べなかった**んです** た
I-adjectives	plain form + んです	高い**んです** たか 高かった**んです** たか	高くない**んです** たか 高くなかった**んです** たか
Na-adjectives / nouns + だ	*Na*-adjective / noun + な／だった + んです *Na*-adjective / noun + じゃない／じゃなかった + んです	便利／学生な**んです** べんり　がくせい 便利／学生だった**んです** べんり　がくせい 便利／学生じゃない**んです** べんり　がくせい 便利／学生じゃなかった**んです** べんり　がくせい	

Note that the ん in んです is a contracted form of の. In formal speech and formal writing, のです is used rather than んです.

In casual speech, んです becomes んだ. Note that the だ in んだ is not omitted even in casual speech. (4) and (5) are casual ways of saying [2-a]-B and [2-b], respectively.

Exs. (4)　パスタを作_{つく}っている<u>んだ</u>。*I'm making pasta.*

(5)　今日_{きょう}は休_{やす}む（よ）。頭_{あたま}が痛_{いた}い<u>んだ</u>。*I'll take today off. I've got a headache.*

The casual form of んですか is の with rising intonation (indicated as の？). (6) and (7) are casual ways to say [2-a]-A and (1)-A, respectively.

Exs. (6)　何_{なに}を作_{つく}っている<u>の</u>？ *What are you making?*

(7)　どうしてクラスを休_{やす}んだ<u>の</u>？ *How come you skipped class?*

☞ **GID** (vol.1): H. Important sentence patterns　3.んです sentences

---

3 **Adjective / Verb そう [Impressions]** "look; sound; It looks like; It sounds like"

[3-a]	Adj(*i*)-stem	
にゃんたは	うれし	そうです。
Nyanta looks happy.		

[3-b]	Adj(*na*)	
このアルバイトは	大変_{たいへん}	そうです。
This part-time job looks tough.		

[3-c]	V-*masu*	
雨_{あめ}が	降_ふり	そうです。
It looks like it's going to rain.		

[3-d]	Negative	
この映画_{えいが}はあまり	おもしろくなさ	そうです。
This movie doesn't look very interesting. / It doesn't sound like this movie is very interesting. (lit. It sounds like this movie is not very interesting.)		

By adding そう to adjectives and verbs, you can express your impression when you see something/ someone or after you have heard or read about something/someone. When used with adjectives, the impression is about the state of something or someone. When used with action verbs (e.g., 降_ふる, 晴_はれる, 泣_なく, etc.), the impression is about something that is likely to happen or about someone who is likely to do something.

The forms before そう are as follows:

	Form before そう	Examples		Sentence patterns
I-adjectives	Stem (dictionary form minus the final い)	おもしろい ＋ そう	→ おもしろそう	[3-a]
		Exception: いい ＋ そう	→ よさそう	
Na-adjectives	Dictionary form	大変 ＋ そう	→ 大変そう	[3-b]
Verbs	V-*masu* (the *masu*-form of the verb minus ます)	泣きます ＋ そう	→ 泣きそう	[3-c]
〜ない (negative endings of *i*-adjectives and だ)	〜なさ	おいしくない ＋ そう	→ おいしくなさそう	[3-d]
		好きじゃない ＋ そう	→ 好きじゃなさそう	
		大学生じゃない ＋ そう	→ 大学生じゃなさそう	

Note that nouns cannot be used before そう. (× あの人は先生そうだ。)

Exs. (1) リサ：みかさん、うれしそうですね。*You look happy, Mika.*

みか：ええ、明日は天気がよさそうだから、友達とバーベキューをするんです。
Yes, since it looks like it'll be nice weather tomorrow, I'm going to have a BBQ with my friends.

(2) 研さんは最近大変そうですね。*It looks like Ken has been having a hard time recently.*

(3) A：最近、あの二人は楽しくなさそうですね。*Those two look unhappy recently.*

B：そうですね。別れそうですね。*They do, don't they? It looks like they're going to break up.*

そう is used only when you are not certain that your impression about something or someone is actually the case. The following sentence is not grammatical because in this situation there is no discrepancy between the speaker's impression and the reality.

× この部屋はきれいそうですね。 → この部屋はきれいですね。

Other adjectives that are not used with そう include かわいい, 大きい, かっこいい, and adjectives that represent colors such as 赤い and 青い.

[3-e]

Adj(*i*)-stem / Adj(*na*)		N	
おいし	そうな	ケーキ	をもらいました。

I got a delicious-looking cake.

[3-f]

	Adj(*i*)-stem / Adj(*na*)			V
みかさんは	おいし	そうに	ケーキを	食べています。

Mika is eating a cake with relish (lit. in such a way that it looks delicious).

そう is an auxiliary *na*-adjective. Thus, when it modifies nouns, it changes to そうな, as in [3-e]. When it modifies verbs, it changes to そうに, as in [3-f]. (More about this in L10 #1, where we learn the adverbial forms of *na*-adjectives.)

Exs. (4) 便利そうな時計ですね。
You have a handy-looking watch. (lit. That's a handy-looking watch, isn't it?)

(5) みんな楽しそうに歌を歌っています。

    It looks like everybody is singing songs happily (lit. Everybody is singing songs in such a way that they look happy).

☞ GID (vol.1): E. Auxiliaries 6.そう

---

4   ～と思う **[Assumptions and opinions]** "think that ~; feel that ~"

[4-a]

X (first person)	S-plain (what X thinks)		
（私は、）	田中さんは今日クラスに {来る／来ない}	と	思います。
I {think / don't think} Tanaka-san will come to class today.			

You can express your assumption or opinion about something using と思います. (と here is a quotative particle.) As seen in [4-a], when you want to say "I don't think S" in Japanese, you negate S rather than 思います. The following sentence is not appropriate:

    ×（私は、）田中さんは今日クラスに来ると思いません。

    →（私は、）田中さんは今日クラスに来ないと思います。

        I don't think Tanaka-san will come to class today.

S (i.e., the sentence that represents what is thought) can take any tense as long as it is in plain form, as in (1) and (2) below.

Exs. (1) （私は、）トムさんはパーティーに {行く／行った} と思います。

        I think Tom {will go / went} to the party.

    (2) （私は、）ワンさんはスミスさんに電話 {しない／しなかった} と思います。

        I don't think Wang-san {will call / called} Smith-san.

思います is also used in questions when the thinker (=X) is the second person, as in Tom's line in (3). In this case, X is usually omitted.

Ex. (3) トム：みかさんは研さんが好きだと思いますか。*Do you think Mika likes Ken?*

        リサ：はい、好きだと思います。*Yes, I do (lit. I think she likes him).*

[4-b]

X (third person)	S-plain (what X thinks)		
リーマンさんは、	漢字はとてもおもしろい	と	思っています。
Riemann thinks that kanji are very interesting.			

When the thinker (=X) is a third person, you use 思っています instead of 思います, as in [4-b]. (See Language Note (p.317).)

Ex. (4) リサさんは、みかさんは研さんが好きだと思っています。*Lisa thinks Mika likes Ken.*

The equivalent sentence of "What do you think?" is どう思いますか (lit. How do you think?), not 何と思いますか。

Ex. (5) 日本の政治についてどう 思いますか。*What do you think about Japanese politics?*
にほん　せいじ　　　　　　　　　おも

☞ **GID** (vol.1): B. Particles 1-6. と

---

5 〜と言う [Quotations] "say that 〜"
　　　　い

[5-a]

X (third person)	S (what X actually said)		
アイさんは	「黒田先生はスポーツが好きですよ」 くろだせんせい　　　　　　　　　す	と	言っていました。 い
Ai said, "Prof. Kuroda likes sports."			

[5-b]

X (third person)	S-plain (the content of what X said)		
アイさんは、	黒田先生はスポーツが好きだ くろだせんせい　　　　　　　　す	と	言っていました。 い
Ai said that Prof. Kuroda likes sports.			

You can tell the listener what you heard from someone (=X) using と言っていました. There are basically
　　い
two ways to convey someone's speech to someone else. One way is to repeat exactly what the person said,
as in [5-a]. This is called a direct quotation. The other way is to summarize the essential content of what the
person said, as in [5-b]. This is called an indirect quotation.

As seen in [5-a] and [5-b], in a direct quotation, what X actually said is put in quotation marks, while in
an indirect quotation, what X said is presented in the plain form with no quotation marks. The sentence
particle よ also drops. Note that the quotation marker と is necessary in both quotation forms, while in the
English equivalent *that* is used only in indirect quotations.

Exs. (1) 妹 は日本に 留学したいと 言っています。
　　　　　いもうと　にほん　りゅうがく　　　　い
　　　　　My younger sister says that she wants to study abroad in Japan.

(2) タオさんは明日テストがあると 言っていましたが、リーマンさんはないと 言っ
　　　　　　　あした　　　　　　　　い　　　　　　　　　　　　　　　　　　　　　い
ていました。*Tao said that there's a test tomorrow, but Riemann said that there isn't.*

(3) A: けいたさんは昨日の映画について何と 言っていましたか。
　　　　　　　きのう　えいが　　　　なん　い
　　　　　What did Keita say about yesterday's movie?

B: とてもおもしろかったと 言っていました。*He said that it was very interesting.*
　　　　　　　　　　　　　　　　い

[5-c]

X (word / phrase / object)	Y (language)		Z (word / phrase in Y)		
Peace	は	日本語 にほんご	で	「平和」 へいわ	と	言います。 い
"Peace" is *heiwa* in Japanese. (lit. We call "peace" *heiwa* in Japanese.)						

You can ask or tell what the Japanese for a certain word or phrase in another language is or what a certain
object is called in Japanese using the sentence pattern in [5-c].

Exs. (4) 「ごちそうさま」は英語で何と 言いますか。*How do you say "Gochisoosama" in English?*
　　　　　　　　　　　えいご　なん　い

(5) A: この 魚 は日本語で何と 言いますか。*What do you call this fish in Japanese?*
　　　　　　さかな　にほんご　なん　い

B: 「タイ」と 言います。*We call it "tai."*
　　　　　　　　　い

☞ **GID** (vol.1): H. Important sentence patterns 5. Reporting sentences

6 〜たり〜たりする [Non-exhaustive listing of actions] "do things like V₁-ing and V₂-ing"

[6]

		V₁-plain.past		V₂-plain.past		
京都で _{きょうと}	お寺を _{てら}	見た _み	り、	買い物した _{か もの}	り	しました。
In Kyoto, I did things like visiting temples and shopping.						

You can list up multiple actions using the structure 〜たり〜たりする. This structure implies that the subject also did or will do other things than the stated actions. For example, [6] implies that the speaker did other things in Kyoto in addition to visiting temples and shopping. (See L3 #5.)

Exs. (1) 休みの日には本を読んだり、音楽を聞いたりします。
_{やす ひ ほん よ おんがく き}
On my days off, I do things like reading books and listening to music.

(2) 図書館では大きい声で話したり、食べ物を食べたりしないでください。
_{としょかん おお こえ はな た もの た}
Please don't do things like speaking loudly or eating food in the library.

(3) 日本に行って、ホームステイをしたり、剣道を習ったりしたいです。
_{にほん い けんどう なら}
I want to go to Japan and do a homestay and learn kendo *(among other things) (while I'm there).*

Note that in the 〜たり〜たりする structure, the tense, the politeness level, and whether the sentence is affirmative or negative are indicated by the final する.

☞ **GID** (vol.1)：H. Important sentence patterns 4. 〜たり〜たりする

7 〜たことがある [Experiences] "have V-ed (before)"

[7-a]

	V-plain.past		
京都に _{きょうと}	行った _い	ことが	あります。
I've been to Kyoto.			

[7-b]

		V-plain.past		
A:	たこ焼きを _や	食べた _た	ことが	ありますか。
	Have you ever had *takoyaki*?			
B1:	はい、			あります。
	Yes, I have.			
B2:	いいえ、			ありません。
	No, I haven't.			

You can talk about your experiences using 〜たことがある.

When you respond to a question like A's in [7-b] with はい or いいえ, you do not have to repeat the verb and ことが, as you can see in B's responses (B1 and B2).

Exs. (1) アイ：私はタオさんとけんかしたことがありません。すごく仲がいいんですよ。
_{わたし なか}
I've never had a fight with Tao. We get along really well.

(2)　A:　北海道に行ったことがありますか。*Have you ever been to Hokkaido?*
　　　ほっかいどう　い

　　　B1:　はい、あります。*Yes, I have.*

　　　B2:　いいえ、ありません。*No, I haven't.*

(3)　マークさんは泣いたことがないと言っていました。*Mark said that he's never cried.*
　　　　　　　　な　　　　　　　　　　　　　　い

Note that while ことがある is usually translated into "have V-ed" in English, it means "have (ever) V-ed (before)" and not "have V-ed (yet)." Thus, when you ask if someone has had breakfast yet on a certain day, for example, you would use the sentence on the right below rather than the one on the left:

× 朝ご飯を食べたことがありますか。　→　もう朝ご飯を食べましたか。
　 あさ　はん　た　　　　　　　　　　　　　　　　　あさ　はん　た

Have you eaten breakfast yet? (See L6 #6.)

げんごノート　Language Note　思っている・ほしがっている・〜たがっている
　　　　　　　　　　　　　　　　おも

In Japanese, a third person's assumption, opinion, desire, etc. cannot be expressed using the same verb or adjective forms as those used for the first person (e.g., 思います, ほしいです, 〜たいです). This is because a third person's opinion, desire, etc. is not directly observable. For this reason, a third person's thought, for example, is expressed as the resultant state of the person's act in the past that revealed what the person thought, using 思っています, as in (1).
　　　　　　　　　　　　　　　おも

(1) ワンさんは、山田さんは今晩のパーティーに来ないと思っています。
　　　　　　　　やまだ　　　こんばん　　　　　　　こ　　　　おも
Wang-san thinks Yamada-san won't come to tonight's party.

In the case of ほしい and 〜たい, the third person's desire is expressed using the auxiliary verb がる ("to show signs of ~"), as in (2) and (3), or using と言っています, as in (4) and (5).
　　　　　　　　　　　　　　　　　　　　　　　　　　　　　　　　　　　い

(2) みかさんは新しい時計をほしがっています。
　　　　　　　あたら　とけい
Mika wants a new watch. (lit. Mika is showing signs of wanting a new watch.)

(3) トムさんはアフリカに行きたがっています。
　　　　　　　　　　　　い
Tom wants to go to Africa. (lit. Tom is showing signs of wanting to go to Africa.)

(4) みかさんは新しい時計がほしいと言っています。
　　　　　　　あたら　とけい　　　　　　い
Mika says she wants a new watch.

(5) トムさんはアフリカに行きたいと言っています。
　　　　　　　　　　　　い　　　　い
Tom says he wants to go to Africa.

はなしましょう

▸ **Words written in purple** are new words introduced in this lesson.

 Talk about past events in casual speech.

できるI-A **Plain past forms of verbs, *i*-adjectives, and です**

1 Let's practice conjugating verbs in their plain past forms.

Step 1 Below, "The *Te*-Form Song" you learned in Lesson 6 has been modified to reflect the conjugation patterns for the plain past affirmative forms of verbs. Sing it a few times to help you memorize these patterns.

♪ Let's Sing

うつる - った　むぶぬ - んだ　す - した　く - いた　ぐ - いだ
する - した　くる - きた　いく - いった ♫

Step 2 Now practice conjugating the following verbs into their plain past affirmative forms.

Ex. たべる → たべた

1) みる　　　2) おきる　　3) かえる　　4) かく　　　5) ならう　　6) さがす

7) あそぶ　　8) いく　　　9) くる　　　10) する　　11) している　12) かたづける

13) わらう　14) やすむ　15) かぜをひく

Step 3 This time, practice conjugating all of the verbs from Step 2 into all of their plain forms, as shown below. **L9-7**

Ex.

	non-past	
affirmative	たべる	たべない
	たべた	たべなかった
	past	

2 Let's practice conjugating *i*-adjectives and *na*-adjectives/nouns＋です into all of their plain forms. **L9-8**

Ex.1

	non-past	
affirmative	おいしい	おいしくない
	おいしかった	おいしくなかった
	past	

Ex.2

	non-past	
affirmative	しずかだ / がくせいだ	しずかじゃない / がくせいじゃない
	しずかだった / がくせいだった	しずかじゃなかった / がくせいじゃなかった
	past	

1) いそがしい　2) たのしい　　3) おもしろい　4) きれい　　　5) ざんねん

6) ひま　　　7) せんせい　　8) いたい　　　9) あたたかい　10) すずしい

11) わるい　　12) はれ　　　13) あめ

1 What would you say to a friend in the following situations? Check the new vocabulary you need for each situation first, then make a sentence using a plain past form. 👕 L9-9

Ex. A: 雨がやんだね。
あめ
B: うん、そうだね。

Ex. stopped raining　1) hungry　　　2) thirsty　　　3) tired　　　4) a little late

2 Find out what your friend did yesterday. 👕

Step 1 Change the verb phrases below first into their plain past affirmative forms and then into their plain past negative forms. L9-10

Ex. 朝ご飯を食べる → 朝ご飯を食べた → 朝ご飯を食べなかった
あさ　はん　　　　あさ　はん　　　　　あさ　はん

1) 友達と出かける　　2) お皿を洗う　　　　3) ジムに行く　　4) 晩ご飯を作る
ともだち　　　　　　　さら　あら　　　　　　　　　　　　　　ばん　はん
5) 宿題がある　　　　6) 日本語を勉強 する　7) 友達が来る　　8) your own
しゅくだい　　　　　　　　べんきょう　　　　　ともだち

Step 2 Ask your friend questions about what they did yesterday using the phrases from Step 1 as cues.

Ex. A: 昨日、朝ご飯食べた？
きのう　あさ　はん
B: うん、食べた(よ)。 or ううん、食べなかった(よ)。

A: そう(か)。

3 Find out how your friend's day was yesterday. 👕

Step 1 Change the *i*-adjectives and *na*-adjectives/nouns+です below first into their plain past affirmative forms and then into their plain past negative forms. L9-11

Ex. 忙しい → 忙しかった → 忙しくなかった
いそが　　　いそが　　　　　いそが

1) 楽しい　　2) 天気が悪い　　3) ひま　　4) 晴れ　　5) 休み　　6) your own
たの　　　　　　　わる　　　　　　　　　　　は　　　　　やす

Step 2 Suppose you are talking online with your friend living abroad. Find out how their day was yesterday using the phrases from Step 1 as cues.

Ex. A: 昨日、忙しかった？
きのう　いそが
B: うん、忙しかった(よ)。 or ううん、忙しくなかった(よ)。
いそが　　　　　　　　　　　　いそが
A: そう(か)。

Lesson
9

4 Talk casually about what you did in the following past time frames. Expand the conversation and improvise as appropriate.

Ex. 昨日
きのう

A: 昨日何した？
きのう

B: 友達とレストランに晩ご飯食べに行った（よ）。
ともだち　　　　　　　　　　ばん　はん

A: いいね。レストランで何食べた？

B: おすし（食べた）。
た

A: どうだった？

B: すごくおいしかった（よ）。　　<Continue>

1) 昨日　　　　2)（先週の）週末　　　3)（去年の）夏休み
きのう　　　　　　　　　しゅうまつ　　　　　きょねん　なつやす

できる
Ⅱ
Talk about a situation in detail by providing more explanation.

できるⅡ-A　**Asking for and providing explanations 〜んです**

1 Your classmate looks off. Take turns asking and explaining what is wrong using 〜んです. 🔊 **L9-12**

Ex. 熱があります
ねつ

A: どうした**ん**ですか。

B: 熱がある**ん**です。
ねつ

A: そうですか。だいじょうぶですか。（← Comment）

1) 歯が痛いです　　　　　2) すごくねむいです　　　3) 気分がよくないです
は　いた　　　　　　　　　　　　　　　　　　　　　　きぶん
4) 勉強が大変です　　　　5) ネコが病気です　　　　6) デートが楽しくなかったです
べんきょう　たいへん　　　　　　　びょうき
7) 宿題を忘れました　　　8) かぜをひきました　　　9) 友達とけんかしました
しゅくだい　わす　　　　　　　　　　　　　　　　　　ともだち
10) your own

2 Use the same cues as in the previous exercise, but this time have your conversation in casual speech.

Ex. 熱があります
ねつ

A: どうした**の**？

B: 熱がある**んだ**。
ねつ

A: え、だいじょうぶ？（← Comment）

3 Imagine that something unexpected has happened to you. Choose the most appropriate facial expression for this event from among the pictures below and point to it. Your partner will then ask you what has happened.

Ex. A: どうしたんですか。

B: 実は {彼／彼女／パートナー} と別れたんです。
じつ　　かれ　かのじょ　　　　　　　　　　　わか

A: え、本当ですか。どうして別れたんですか。（← Follow-up question）　＜Continue＞
ほんとう　　　　　　　　　　わか

4 Take turns making invitations 1)-4) and requests 5)-8) with your partner. The person receiving the invitation or request should decline and provide a reasonable explanation.

Ex.1 今晩パーティーをする
こんばん

A: ○○さん、今晩、いっしょにパーティーをしませんか。
こんばん

B: うーん、今晩はちょっと…　宿題がたくさんあるんです。
こんばん　　　　　　　　しゅくだい

1) 明日美術館に行く　2) 週末近くの山に登る　3) 今晩こわい映画を見る　4) your own
びじゅつかん　　　　しゅうまつちか　のぼ　　こんばん　　えいが

Ex.2 宿題を手伝う
しゅくだい　てつだ

A: ○○さん、宿題を手伝ってくれませんか。
しゅくだい　てつだ

B: すみません、今、ちょっと気分が悪いんです。
きぶん　わる

5) リビングをかたづける　6) 部屋のごみを捨てる　7) お皿を洗う　8) your own
へや　　す　　　　さら　あら

できる III　**Give impressions and opinions on a familiar topic.**

できるIII-A　**Impressions ～そう**

1 Look at the pictures below and say what your impression of each is using ～そう。　

Ex.1 おいしい

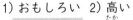 → このケーキはおいしそうです。

Ex.2 おいしくない

→ このケーキはおいしくなさそうです。

1) おもしろい　2) 高い　3) 暖かい　4) まずい　5) 頭がいい　6) 便利
たか　　あたた　　　　　　　あたま　　べんり

7) まじめじゃない 8) 甘くない　9) からくない 10) 元気がない 11) 泣く 12) 今日／雨が降る
あま　　　　　　　　　げんき　　な　　　　あめ　ふ

2 Rephrase your impressions from 1)-6) in the previous exercise as in the example below.

Ex. <u>おいし</u>そうな<u>ケーキ</u>ですね。

3 Look at the pictures below and describe them using 〜そうに+verb. 🔊L9-15

Ex. 泣いています
な
悲しそうに泣いています。
かな　　　な

1) 働いています
はたら

2) 遊んでいます
あそ

3) コーヒーを飲んでいます

4) 笑っています
わら

4 Practice commenting on photos.

Step 1 Your classmate has posted the photo below on social media. Give your impressions of the photo as in the examples.

Ex.1 このおすしはおいしそうですね。or おいしそうなおすしですね。

Ex.2 リーさんはさびしそうに立っています。

Step 2 Suppose you and your friend are looking at the picture above. Give your impressions in casual speech. 👕

Ex. A: このおすし、おいしそうだね。

B: うん、そうだね。

5 Share a photo of a trip you took, an event you attended, food you enjoyed, etc. with your groupmates. Expand your conversation by responding to their comments on the photo.

できるⅢ-B　**Assumptions and opinions 〜と思う**

1 Let's review plain forms and practice using them with 〜と思います.　(L9-16)

Ex.　たべる

	non-past	
affirmative　たべると思います	たべないと思います　negative	
たべたと思います	たべなかったと思います	
	past	

1) わかれる　　　2) すてる　　　　3) あめがやむ　　4) かぜをひく

5) けんかする　　6) つかれている　7) あたたかい　　8) なかがわるい

9) なかがいい　　10) まじめ　　　11) びょうき

2 Let's play charades! One student will perform charades while the others guess what action they are performing.

Ex.　A: (performs charade)

B: 顔を洗っていると思います。

A: はい、そうです。or いいえ、もう少し考えてください。

3 Choose one of the Japan House members and make some guesses about them regarding the information provided. (If necessary, refer to the "Main Characters" section on p.30.)

Ex.　やさしい人です

→（私は）マークさんはやさしい人だと思います。

or やさしい人じゃないと思います。

1) たばこを吸います　　2) よく笑います　　3) カラオケが得意です

4) 部屋がきたないです　5) まんがをたくさん持っています　6) 高校の時、人気がありました

7) 高校の時、まじめでした　　8) 子どもの時、かわいかったです　　9) your own

4 Pick a person that both you and your partner would know (e.g., a teacher, a singer, a politician) and guess various things about that person in response to the questions that follow.

Ex. 今晩何をしますか
こんばん

A: ○○先生は今晩何をすると思いますか。
こんばん　　　　　　おも

B: うーん、そうですね、(私は)先生は今晩たくさん仕事すると思います。
こんばん　　　　　しごと　　　　おも

A: どうしてそう思いますか。
おも

B: 先生はいつも忙しそうだからです。
いそが

A: 私もそう思います。
おも

　　　　or そうですか。私は先生は今晩だれかとデートをすると思います。　<Continue>
こんばん　　　　　　　　　おも

1) 今週の週末何をしますか　　2) 何をするのが得意ですか
しゅうまつ　　　　　　　　　　　　　　とくい

3) だれと仲がいいですか　　　4) 子どもの時、よく何をしましたか　　5) your own
なか

5 What color do you associate with the following words? If necessary, refer to the L6 vocabulary list on p.191 for color words.

Ex. A: 冬は何色だと思いますか。
ふゆ　なにいろ　　おも

B: 白だと思います。
しろ　　おも

A: どうしてそう思いますか。
おも

B: 冬はたくさん雪が降るからです。
ふゆ　　　　　ゆき　ふ

A: 私もそう思います。or そうですか。私は… <Continue>
おも

Ex. 冬　　　　1) 春　　　　2) 夏　　　　3) 先学期　　　　4) 太陽 (sun)
ふゆ　　　　　はる　　　　　なつ　　　　　せんがっき　　　　たいよう

5) 月曜日　　6) 日本語　　7) your own

6 Let's exchange opinions!

Step 1 Choose some topics from the options below and ask your partner's opinion about them.

日本の○○ Exs. 料理, 文化 りょうり　ぶんか	日本語のクラス	仮想通貨 (virtual currency) か そうつうか
SNS Exs. ツイッター, インスタグラム	AI (Artificial Intelligence)	your own

Ex. A: ○○さんは日本の料理についてどう思いますか。
りょうり　　　　おも

B: (私は)ヘルシー (healthy) で、おいしいと思います。△△さんはどう思いますか。
おも　　　　　　　　　　　おも

<Continue>

Step 2 Report to the class what you and your partner think about the topics you discussed.

Ex.1 ○○さんは日本の料理はおいしいと思っていますが、私は… <Continue>
りょうり　　　　　おも

Ex.2 ○○さんは日本の料理はおいしいと思っています。私もそう思います。
りょうり　　　　　おも　　　　　　　　　　おも

できる IV　Report on things you have heard people say.

できる IV-A　Quotations　〜と言う

1　Report what you have heard from the following sources.　🔊L9-17

Ex.　A: 天気予報は何と言っていましたか。
　　　てんきよほう
　　　B: (天気予報は) 今日は晴れると言っていました。
　　　　てんきよほう　　　　は

Ex. 今日は晴れます。
　　　　　は

1) 来週、東京に台風が来ます。
　　　とうきょう　たいふう
2) 午後からくもります。
3) 午後はすずしいです。
4) 明日はくもりです。

天気予報
てんきよほう

けいた

5) 今、ジャパンハウスに住んでいます。
6) 昨日みんなでカラオケに行きました。
　　きのう
7) カラオケでたくさん歌いました。
　　　　　　　　　　　うた
8) 昨日はあまり寝ませんでした。
　　きのう　　　　ね

9) 昨日の晩は楽しかったです。
　　きのう　ばん
10) 昨日、クラスは休みでした。
　　きのう　　　　やす
11) 今学期は毎日忙しいから、もっと休みがほしいです。
　　こんがっき　　いそ　　　　　　　　やす
12) 新しいアニメはおもしろそうです。
　　あたら

タオ

2　How do your classmates spend their free time?

Step 1　Ask your partner what they have done over recent breaks and what they will do during the next one. Make sure to ask follow-up questions as well.

1) 最近、休みに何をしましたか。　　2) 今度の休みに何をしますか。
　　さいきん　やす　　　　　　　　　　こんど　やす

Step 2　Report how your partner has spent recent breaks/will spend the next break.

Ex.　○○さんは最近、休みに友達 10 人と近くのビーチに行って、泳いだと言ってい
　　　　　　　さいきん　やす　ともだち　　　ちか　　　　　　　　　　およ
　　　ました。それから、今度の休みには友達の誕生日のパーティーに行くと言ってい
　　　　　　　　　　こんど　やす　　　ともだち　たんじょうび
　　　ました。だから、○○さんの生活は楽しそうです。
　　　　　　　　　　　　　　せいかつ

3　Have you heard anything newsworthy recently? Report what you heard to your partner.

Ex.　A: 今朝、天気予報は明日台風が来ると言っていましたよ。聞きましたか。
　　　けさ　てんきよほう　　たいふう
　　　B: へえ、知りませんでした。or　はい、聞きました。　<Continue>

Lesson 9

4 (Information Gap) Let's learn some Japanese computer jargon! Ask each other how to say the words 1)-6) in the table below in Japanese and fill in the table.

Ex. A: "to charge" は日本語で何と言いますか。

B:「充電する」と言います。
じゅうでん

Student A

英語	日本語	英語	日本語
Ex. to charge	充電する じゅうでん		
1) to copy & paste		2) selfie	
3) programming		4)	添付する てんぷ
5)	返信する へんしん	6)	検索する けんさく

Student B ➡p.330

 Talk about experiences.

できるV-A **Non-exhaustive listing of actions ～たり～たりする**

1 Let's practice using ～たり～たりする to talk about weekend activities. 🔊 L9-18

Ex. コーヒーを飲む／映画を見る
えいが

→ 週末にコーヒーを飲んだり、映画を見たりします。
しゅうまつ　　　　　　　　　　えいが

1) 音楽を聞く／新聞を読む
しんぶん

2) パーティーに行く／友達と遊ぶ
ともだち　あそ

3) ゆっくりおふろに入る／たくさん寝る
ね

4) 車を洗う／部屋をかたづける
くるま　あら　　へや

5) 散歩する／絵を描く
さんぽ　え　か

6) 山に登る／ジョギングをする
のぼ

Group Work

2 Let's play a guessing game! One person chooses a place from the box below and gives a few examples of things people do there. The other group members guess which place is being described.

Ex. 図書館
としょかん

A: ここで本を読んだり、勉強したりします。
べんきょう

B: そこは図書館ですか。
としょかん

A: はい、そうです。or いいえ、もう少し考えてください。
すこ　かんが

C: じゃ、そこはカフェですか。(← Another guess, if no.)　<Continue>

Ex.	図書館 としょかん	会社 かいしゃ	飛行機の中 ひこうき
	カフェ	うち	海
	クラブ (night club)	先生のオフィス	公園 こうえん

3 Ask each other what you do/did during the following time frames.

Ex. 今週の週末
しゅうまつ

A: 〇〇さんは今週の週末、何をしますか。
しゅうまつ

B: そうですね、ジムで運動したり、仲がいい友達と遊んだりします。
うんどう　　　　なか　　ともだち　あそ

A: そうですか。友達と何をしますか。(← Follow-up question)
ともだち

1) 今週の週末　　2) 雨の日　　3) 先週の週末　　4) 去年の夏休み　　5) your own
しゅうまつ　　　　あめ　　　　せんしゅう しゅうまつ　　きょねん なつやす

4 You have decided to go to Tokyo with your classmates over the next break.

Step 1 Suppose your friend who has visited Tokyo before told you the following things about some popular tourist areas in the city. Report what your friend said.

Ex. （友達は）浅草で大きくて、きれいなお寺を見たと言っていました。
ともだち　あさくさ

Ex.

浅草
あさくさ
saw big, beautiful temples

写真提供：浅草寺

1)

両国
りょうごく
watched sumo

写真提供：日本相撲協会

2)

お台場
だいば
went into (lit. entered)
the hot springs

3)

多摩
たま
climbed beautiful mountains

4)

秋葉原
あきはばら
went to anime and manga shops

5)

原宿
はらじゅく
bought a lot of cute things

Step 2 Based on the information in Step 1 and your own knowledge and experiences, decide what you would like to do in Tokyo.

Ex. A: 〇〇さんは、東京で何がしたいですか。
とうきょう

B: 私は秋葉原でアニメの店に行ったり、原宿で買い物をしたりしたいです。
あきはばら　　　　みせ　　　　　はらじゅく
△△さんは？ <Continue>

Step 3 Report your trip plan to your classmates.

Ex. 私と〇〇さんは秋葉原のアニメの店に行ったり、お台場で温泉に入ったりしたい
あきはばら　　　みせ　　　　　だいば おんせん
です。温泉はとても気分がよさそうだと思います。それから… <Continue>
おんせん　　　　きぶん　　　　　おも

1 Let's practice using 〜たことがある in both the affirmative and the negative.　🔊**L9-19**

Ex. たこ焼きを食べる → <u>たこ焼きを食べた</u>ことがあります。

　　　　　　　　　 → <u>たこ焼きを食べた</u>ことがありません。

1）宿題を忘れる
2）冷たいピザを食べる
3）日本語の授業を休む
4）日本料理を作る
5）日本の新聞を読む
6）先生のオフィスに質問をしに行く
7）バイオリンを習う
8）留学する　　　　　　9) your own

2 Let's play a bingo game in order to help you get to know your classmates a little better.

[Step 1] Ask if your classmates have had the following experiences.

Ex. A: 納豆を食べたことがありますか。

　　 B: はい、あります。or いいえ、ありません。

納豆 (fermented soy beans)

Ex. 納豆を食べる Yes ・ No _____さん	1）温泉に入る Yes ・ No _____さん	2）高い山に登る Yes ・ No _____さん
3）友達とけんかする Yes ・ No _____さん	4) your own Yes ・ No _____さん	5）映画を見て、泣く Yes ・ No _____さん
6）好きな人に花をあげる Yes ・ No _____さん	7）外国で生活する Yes ・ No _____さん	8）試験に遅れる Yes ・ No _____さん

[Step 2] Pick one piece of information you learned about your classmates and report it to the class. Add your own information as well.

Ex. ○○さんは納豆を食べたことがあると言っていました。

　　 私もあります。or 私はありません。

3 Do you have any unique experiences?

[Step 1] Ask your partner if they have done any of the following activities. Ask follow-up questions as well.

Ex. 日本／行く → A: ○○さんは日本に行ったことがありますか。

Yes	No
B: はい、あります。	B: いいえ、ありません。
A: そうですか。どこに行きましたか。	でも、行ってみたいです。
B: 東京や京都に行きました。	A: じゃ、どこに行ってみたいですか。
とうきょう　きょうと	B: 大阪や東京に行ってみたいです。
<Continue>	おおさか　とうきょう
	<Continue>

1) 外国／行く　　2) 有名な人／会う　　3) めずらしい (rare; unusual) 物／食べる　　4) your own

[Step 2] Report your partner's experiences to the class.

Ex.1 ○○さんは東京でカラオケをしたり、京都を観光したりしたことがあると
　　　　　　とうきょう　　　　　　　　きょうと　かんこう
言っていました。

Ex.2 ○○さんは日本に行ったことがありませんが、大阪や東京に行ってみたいと
　　　　　　　　　　　　　　　　　　　　おおさか　とうきょう
言っていました。

4 Talk with your friend about your travel experiences. 👕

Ex. A: ○○さん、エジプトに行ったこと(が)ある？

　　B: ううん、ない。△△さんは？

　　A: あるよ。

　　B: そう、いいね。エジプトで何した？

　　A: ピラミッドを見たり、ラクダ (camel) に乗ったりした(よ)。
　　　　　　　　　　　　　　　　　　　　　　の
　　<Continue>

Review

Now you can share things you have heard from your friends, on TV, or on the radio with your classmates. Share something interesting you've heard and show a picture if you have one.

Possible topics おかし　ゲーム　ミュージックビデオ　映画　ロボット

Share what you have heard	
Ex.	A: テレビで、日本では今「ピザポテト」というおかしが人気があると言っていました。とてもおいしいと言っていましたよ。食べたことがありますか。
	B: いいえ、ありません。どんなおかしなんですか。
Ask if your partner has any experience with it	A: これです。
	B: へえ、おいしそうなおかしですね。
Exchange opinions	A: ○○さん、このおかしはアメリカでもヒットする (to be a hit) と思いますか。
	B: そうですね。アメリカでもピザとポテトチップスは人気があるから、ヒットすると思います。
	A: 私もそう思います。

できるIV-A　4

Ex.　A: "to charge" は日本語で何と言いますか。

　　　B:「充電する」と言います。
　　　　　じゅうでん

Student B

英語	日本語	英語	日本語
Ex. to charge	充電する じゅうでん		
1)	コピペする	2)	自撮り じ　ど
3)	プログラミング	4) to attach	
5) to reply		6) to search	

よみましょう

Getting information from a weather map

1 Look at the world weather map below and answer the quesions about it, using your background knowledge and context clues to guess the meanings of any words you don't know.

Step 1 Read aloud the names of the cities on the map below and discuss the weather and temperature in them, going through as many cities as possible.

Ex. シドニーの天気は晴れです。気温は21度です。
き おん

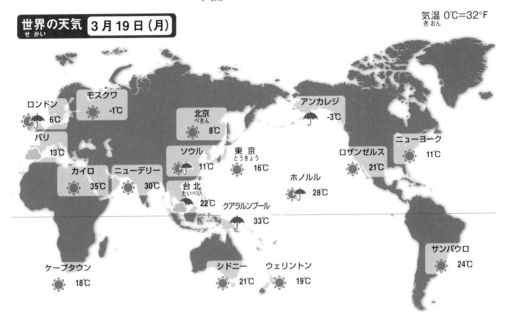

世界の天気 3月19日（月）
せ かい

気温 0℃=32°F
き おん

ロンドン 6℃
パリ 13℃
モスクワ -1℃
北京 8℃
べきん
カイロ 35℃
ニューデリー 30℃
ソウル 11℃
東京 16℃
とうきょう
台北 22℃
たいぺい
クアラルンプール 33℃
アンカレジ -3℃
ロザンゼルス 21℃
ニューヨーク 11℃
ホノルル 28℃
ケープタウン 18℃
シドニー 21℃
ウェリントン 19℃
サンパウロ 24℃

Lesson
9

Step 2 Answer the questions below. For questions 3) and 4), give your answer in comparison to the temperature of the place you live now.

1) これはいつの天気ですか。

2) この日のモスクワは、どんな天気ですか。

3) どこが暑そうだと思いますか。
あつ

4) どこが寒そうだと思いますか。
さむ

2 Look at the map presenting tomorrow's weather forecast for Japan and answer the questions below.

1) 明日の東京の天気はどうですか。
とうきょう

2) 明日、広島はどんな天気ですか。
ひろしま

3) 暑そうな所はどこですか。
あつ　　　ところ

4) 晴れの所はどこですか。
ところ

5) 朝から晩まで雨の所はどこですか。
あさ　　ばん　　　　ところ

6) 午後に雨が降りそうな所はどこですか。
ふ　　　　　ところ

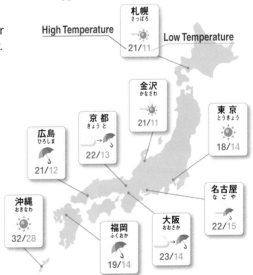

札幌 さっぽろ 21/11
High Temperature
Low Temperature
金沢 かなざわ 21/11
東京 とうきょう 18/14
京都 きょうと 22/13
広島 ひろしま 21/12
名古屋 なごや 22/15
沖縄 おきなわ 32/28
福岡 ふくおか 19/14
大阪 おおさか 23/14

3 Read the article below and answer the questions that follow.

火山：volcano　昔から：since long ago　ゆかた：casual cotton kimono
畳：*tatami* [traditional Japanese straw mat]　布団：*futon* [traditional Japanese bedding]　石：stone
自然：nature　ニホンザル：Japanese snow monkey　サル：monkey　その他：in addition
カピバラ：capybara　クマ：bear　日本に行ったら：if you go to Japan

日本の温泉

みなさんは日本の温泉に行ったことがありますか。日本は 1
火山の国だから、色々な所に温泉があります。日本人は昔か
らおふろに入るのが大好きで、温泉はとても人気があります。
温泉では旅館に泊まって、大きいおふろに入ったり、ゆかた
を着たりします。そして、おいしい日本料理を食べて、畳の 5
部屋で布団で寝ます。
　温泉の旅館にはたいてい露天風呂というおふろがありま
す。露天風呂は石や木のおふろで、建物の外にあります。自
然の中で温かいおふろに入るのはとても気分がいいです。
　実は日本では動物も温泉に入るんです。寒い日にはニホン 10
ザルが山から温泉に入りに来ます。子どものサルはとても元
気で、木の上からジャンプして温泉に入ったり、温泉の中で
泳いだりします。そして、冬には雪でボールを作ったりして
遊びます。ネットにビデオがたくさんあるから、見てみてく
ださい。みんな楽しそうで、とてもかわいいです。 15
　その他、カピバラやクマも温泉に入りま
す。みんな気分がよさそうです。でも、人
と動物は同じ温泉には入りません。
　みなさんも日本に行ったら、ぜひ温泉に
行ってみてください。日本のおふろの文化 20
が少し分かると思います。

Visualizing

1) Suppose you are the writer of this article and are reviewing photos to be published along with it. Arrange photos a.-h. below in the order that the content within them appears in the article.

写真：(　　　) → (　　　) → (　　　) → (　　　) → (　　　) → (　　　) → (　　　) → (　　　)

a.

b.

c.

d.

e.

f.

g.

h.

Sorting information

2） Mark ◯ for the things you can do at a Japanese *onsen* and ✕ for the things you cannot.

（　　　） 旅館に泊まって、畳の部屋で寝る。
りょかん　と　　　　　たたみ　へや　ね

（　　　） 露天風呂に入る。
ろてんぶろ

（　　　） ゆかたを着て、おいしい料理を食べる。
き　　　　　　　　　　りょうり

（　　　） 木の上からジャンプして、温泉に入る。
き　　　　　　　　　　　　　　おんせん

（　　　） カピバラといっしょに温泉に入る。
おんせん

（　　　） 日本のおふろの文化を知る。
ぶんか

Comprehension check

3） Mark ◯ if the statement is true and ✕ if it is false.

（　　　） 日本には火山がある。
かざん

（　　　） 温泉の旅館にはたいてい外におふろがある。
おんせん　りょかん

（　　　） 子どものサルは、寒い日には温泉に入りに来ない。
さむ　　　　おんせん

（　　　） 色々な動物も温泉に入るのが好きだ。
いろいろ　どうぶつ　おんせん

（　　　） 温泉は新しい日本の文化だ。
おんせん　　　　　　ぶんか

4） Choose the most appropriate subtitle for this article from the box below.

a. 火山と温泉　　b. おいしい日本料理！　　c. 動物も温泉が大好き！　　d. 温泉の歴史
かざん　おんせん　　　　　　　　りょうり　　　　どうぶつ　おんせん　　　　　おんせん　れきし

5） Answer the following questions based on what you have read in the article.

（1） 記事 (article) の中で、何がおもしろかったですか。
きじ

（2） 温泉で何をしてみたいと思いましたか。どうしてですか。
おんせん

＿＿＿＿＿＿＿＿＿＿＿＿＿＿＿＿＿＿＿＿＿＿＿＿＿＿＿と思いました。

＿＿＿＿＿＿＿＿＿＿＿＿＿＿＿＿＿＿＿＿＿＿＿＿＿＿＿からです。

かくれんしゅう *Writing Practice*

Write your own article about a place where you can see the culture of a country or community you are familiar with. Use the vertical writing format.

Possible topics	スポーツスタジアム (stadium)	美術館	古い建物	自然 (nature)
		びじゅつかん	たてもの	しぜん

ききましょう

>>>> リスニング・ストラテジー : Listening strategy <<<<

Listening in noisy environments (1)
You will sometimes need to participate in conversations in noisy surroundings. To communicate successfully, you will need to ignore the noise and concentrate on listening for necessary information.

 L9-20

1 **Pre-listening activity:** Listen to each question and choose the most appropriate answer from a.-c. Can you figure out the questions despite the noise?

1) a. あ、いえ、山下だと思います。　　b. あ、はい、本田です。

　c. いいえ、どういたしまして。

2) a. えっと、火曜日だよ。　　b. えっと、メールを書くよ。　　c. えっと、3時半だよ。

3) a. うーん、図書館に行く。　　　　b. うーん、コーヒーにする。

　c. ううん、飲んだことない。

 L9-21

2 **Listening:** Listen to conversations 1)-3) between two friends and choose the most appropriate answer from a.-c. for each of the questions based on what you hear.

1) なおみさんは週末、何をすると思いますか。

　a. 公園でテニスをします。　　b. 家でネコと遊びます。　　c. 友達と山に登ります。

2) ゆみさんとたか子さんはこれから何をすると思いますか。

　a. 温泉に行って、何か食べます。　　b. たか子さんの家で晩ご飯を食べます。

　c.「ナポリ」というレストランでパスタを食べます。

3) 上田さんは電話の後で、まずはじめに (first of all) 何をしますか。

　a. 花を買いに行きます。　　　　b. アイスクリームを買いに行きます。

　c. 先生に電話をします。

 Exit Check ☑

Now it's time to go back to the DEKIRU List for this chapter (p.297) and do the exit check to see what new things you can do now that you've completed the lesson.

二人で花火を見に
はなび
行きたかったけど…
I wanted to go to watch the fireworks together, just the two of us, but...

Instructional Video
Lesson 10

DEKIRU List

できるCheck ✔

できる I
Ask and answer questions about changes in yourself and things around you.
自分自身や身近な物事の変化について、尋ねたり答えたりすることができる。
Entry ☐ Exit ☐

できる II
Compare three or more things and talk about which you think is at the top of a certain category.
物事を比べて、一番だと思うことについて話すことができる。
Entry ☐ Exit ☐

できる III
Compare two things and talk about differences and similarities.
二つのことを比べて、違う点や同じ点について話すことができる。
Entry ☐ Exit ☐

できる IV
Contrast two things to express your opinion about something.
二つのことを比べて、自分の意見を言うことができる。
Entry ☐ Exit ☐

STRATEGIES

Conversation Tips .... • Showing your hesitation with 〜が and 〜けど
Reading .... • Getting information from a chart
• Understanding demonstratives (そ-words)
• Recognizing sequence
Listening .... • Listening in noisy environments (2)

GRAMMAR

1 Adverbial forms of adjectives できる I

2 {Adj(*i*)-stem く / Adj(*na*) に}なる・する；Nになる・する "become Adj / N; make ~ Adj; make ~ into N" できる I

3 Superlative sentences できる II

   3-1 XはYの中で一番Adj
　　　　いちばん

   3-2 Xの中でYが一番Adj
　　　　いちばん

   3-3 Xの中でY Prt 一番よく Verb
　　　　いちばん

4 XもYも "both X and Y; neither X nor Y" できる III

5 Comparative sentences できる III

   5-1 XはYより Adj

   5-2 XとYと {どちら／どっち}のほう Prt {Adj /よく Verb}

6 〜けれど／けど "but; however; although" できる IV

7 〜ことができる "can V; be able to V" できる IV

335

かいわ

1 できる Ⅰ　**Ai and Jean are on a video call.**　🔊 **L10-1**

ボリューム：volume

アイ　　：ジャンさん、お元気ですか。

ジャン　：あ、アイちゃん？　ごめん、声がよく聞こえないんだけど…

　　　　　ボリューム大きくするから、ちょっと待って。

アイ　　：あ、はい…　今、だいじょうぶですか。

ジャン　：うん、オッケー。よくなった。

アイ　　：三月になって暖かくなりましたが、東京はどうですか。

ジャン　：うん、東京も暖かくなったよ。

2 できる Ⅱ,Ⅲ　**Ai and Jean continue their conversation.**　🔊 **L10-2**

キュレーター：curator　例えば：for example　現代アート：contemporary art　ユニーク（な）：unique

ジャン　：アイちゃん、留学のプログラム、もう決めた？

アイ　　：はい、決めました。今年の夏、京都に美術を勉強しに行きます。

ジャン　：へえ、そうか。アイちゃんは美術を勉強して、将来、何がしたいの？

アイ　　：あのう、実は将来、日本の美術のキュレーターになりたいんです。

ジャン　：日本の美術？　例えば、浮世絵？

アイ　　：ええ、浮世絵もいいんですが、私は日本の美術の中で現代アートが

　　　　　一番好きです。日本の現代アートは浮世絵よりおもしろいと思います。

ジャン　：へえ、そう。アーティストの中でだれが一番好き？

アイ　　：草間彌生が一番好きです。草間は世界で一番ユニークなアーティストだと

　　　　　思います。

ジャン　：ああ、彼女はフランスでも有名だよ。

Ukiyoe: woodblock prints
"The Great Wave" by Hokusai
The Metropolitan Museum of Art.

Yayoi Kusama "Pumpkin"（1994）
Photo: Shigeo Anzai

3 Ai is visiting Prof. Kuroda during her office hours. 🔊 L10-3

アイ　　：黒田先生、あの、ちょっと相談があるんですが…
　　　　　くろ　だ　　　　　　　　　　そうだん

先生　　：あ、ブルーノさん。何ですか。

アイ　　：実は、今留学の準備をしているんですが、先生は大学の寮と
　　　　　じつ　　　　りゅうがく　じゅん び　　　　　　　　　　　　　　　　　　りょう
　　　　　ホームステイとどちらのほうがいいと思いますか。

先生　　：寮もホームステイもどちらもいいですが…　うーん、寮よりホームステイの
　　　　　りょう　　　　　　　　　　　　　　　　　　　　　　　　　　　りょう
　　　　　ほうがいいと思いますよ。日本の文化をよく知ることができますから。
　　　　　　　　　　　　　　　　　　　　　ぶん か

アイ　　：そうですか。

先生　　：あ、でも、ホームステイより寮のほうがたくさん友達を作ることが
　　　　　　　　　　　　　　　　　　　りょう　　　　　　　　ともだち
　　　　　できますよ。

アイ　　：そうですか。日本の文化をよく知りたいけれど、友達もほしいです。うーん、
　　　　　　　　　　　　　　ぶん か　　　　　　　　　　　ともだち
　　　　　もう少し調べて考えてみます。先生、どうもありがとうございました。
　　　　　　　すこ　しら　　かんが

4 Mark and Keita are talking about Ai at the Japan House. 🔊 L10-4

けいた　　：アイちゃん、夏に京都に留学するね。
　　　　　　　　　　　　　なつ　きょうと　りゅうがく

マーク　　：そうだね。今年の夏はさびしくなるね。
　　　　　　　　　　　　　　　なつ

にゃんた：ニャー…

けいた　　：僕、夏はアイちゃんと二人で花火を見に行きたかったけど…
　　　　　　ぼく　なつ　　　　　　　　　　　　はな び

マーク　　：え？　二人で？

けいた　　：うん。でも、アイちゃん、いないから…

マーク　　：え？

けいた　　：あ、実は、僕…
　　　　　　　　じつ　ぼく

にゃんた：ニャニ、ニャニ？　　<To be continued...>

C O N V E R S A T I O N　TIPS　ワンポイント　🔊 L10-5

Showing your hesitation with ～が and ～けど: You can show hesitation by adding ～が or ～けど at the
end of a sentence. Expressing hesitation like this can keep you from sounding too harsh, bossy, or direct.

　　　A：あのう、ちょっとお願いがあるんですが…
　　　　　　　　　　　　ねが

　　　B：え、何？　ごめん、今、ちょっと出かけるんだけど…

　　　A：すみません。えっと、ちょっと自転車を借りたいんですが…
　　　　　　　　　　　　　　　　　じてんしゃ　か

　　　B：あ、自転車？　うん。どうぞ、使ってもいいよ。
　　　　　　じてんしゃ　　　　　　　　つか

たんご

▶ The words written in gray are supplemental vocabulary.

びょうしゃする　Describing people, things, and feelings

あかるい ⟷ くらい
(bright) [space]　(dark) [space]
(cheerful) [person]　(gloomy) [person]

おおい ⟷ すくない
(a lot; numerous;　(not much; little; few)
plentiful)

はやい ⟷ おそい
(fast; quick)　(slow)

9:00

(early)　(late)

つよい ⟷ よわい
(strong)　(weak)

ひろい ⟷ せまい
(wide; spacious;　(narrow; small
roomy)　[space]; cramped)

かるい ⟷ おもい
(light) [weight]　(heavy) [weight]

あんぜん(な) ⟷ あぶない
(safe; secure)　(dangerous)

おとしより
(elderly)

わかい
(young)

たいせつ(な)
(important;
precious)

しあわせ(な)
(happy)

だめ(な)
(no good)

いちばん
(the first (place);
the best; the most)

かわる　Changing

むかし
(the past; old times)

いま

しょうらい
((one's) future)

[*thing/person* が] かわる
(to change)

いなか
(countryside; rural area)

とかい
(city; urban area)

みち
(road)

せいせき
(grade (on a test, etc.))

しょうらい　One's future

[*thing* に] なる
(to become)

いしゃ
(doctor)
[medical]

べんごし
(lawyer;
attorney)

しゃちょう
(company
president)

さっか
(novelist;
writer)

かしゅ
(singer)

はいゆう
(actor)

スポーツせんしゅ (athlete)

Exs. やきゅうせんしゅ (baseball player)
やきゅう (baseball)

すいえいせんしゅ (swimmer)
すいえい (swimming)

～せんしゅ (... player; athlete who does ...)

おかねもち
(rich person)

[*person* を] たすける
(to save; to help)

● せいかつ　Daily life

ふね (boat; ship)	バイク (motorcycle)	せき (seat)	やちん (rent)	じゅぎょうりょう (tuition)
じしん (earthquake)	かじ (fire) [destructive (forest, building, etc.)]	はなび (fireworks)	じ (character; letter) **と　ら** 　**び**	かみ (paper)

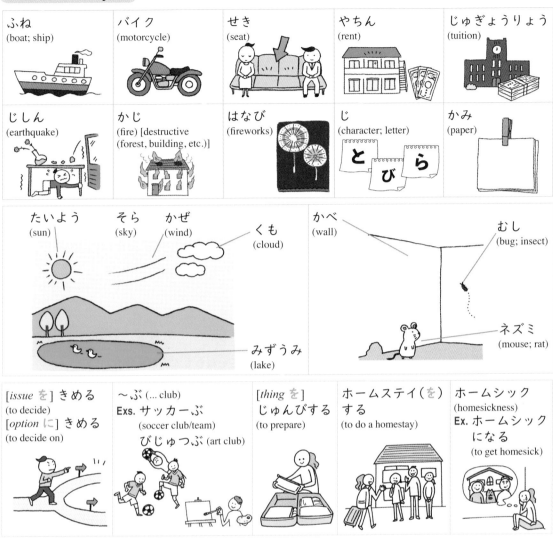

たいよう (sun)　そら (sky)　かぜ (wind)　くも (cloud)　みずうみ (lake)
かべ (wall)　むし (bug; insect)　ネズミ (mouse; rat)

[issue を] きめる (to decide) [option に] きめる (to decide on)	〜ぶ (... club) **Exs.** サッカーぶ (soccer club/team) びじゅつぶ (art club)	[thing を] じゅんびする (to prepare)	ホームステイ（を） する (to do a homestay)	ホームシック (homesickness) **Ex.** ホームシック になる (to get homesick)

● そのほかのひょうげん　Other expressions

どちら／どっち [casual] (which (of two))	すぐ(に) (at once; immediately)
どちらも／どっちも [casual] (both)	ほんとうに (really; actually)

よく
(well)

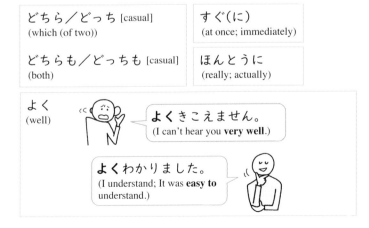

よくきこえません。
(I can't hear you **very well**.)

よくわかりました。
(I understand; It was **easy to** understand.)

たんごリスト

🔊 **L10-6**

RU-VERBS

1	きめる	決める	to decide [*issue* を]; to decide on [*option* に]
2	たすける	助ける	to save (from a tough situation); to help (out of a tough situation) [*person* を]

U-VERBS

3	かわる	変わる	to change [*thing/person* が]
4	なる		to become [*thing* に]

SURU-VERBS

5	じゅんびする	準備する	to prepare [*thing* を]
6	ホームステイ （を）する		to do a homestay

I-ADJECTIVES

7	あかるい	明るい	bright [space]; cheerful [person]
8	くらい	暗い	dark [space]; gloomy [person]
9	おおい	多い	(there are/one has) a lot; numerous; plentiful **Ex.1** ひとがおおい There are many people. **Ex.2** たくさんのひと (not おおいひと) many people
10	すくない	少ない	(there are/one has) not much; little; few **Ex.1** ひとがすくない There are few people. **Ex.2** すこしのひと (not すくないひと) a few people
11	はやい	速い 早い	fast; quick; early
12	おそい	遅い	slow; late
13	つよい	強い	strong
14	よわい	弱い	weak
15	ひろい	広い	wide; spacious; roomy

16	せまい		narrow; small [space]; cramped
17	かるい	軽い	light [weight]
18	おもい	重い	heavy [weight]
19	わかい	若い	young
20	あぶない	危ない	dangerous

NA-ADJECTIVES

21	あんぜん	安全	safe; secure
22	しあわせ	幸せ	happy
23	たいせつ	大切	important; precious
24	だめ		no good

NOUNS

25	いしゃ	医者	doctor [medical]
26	おかねもち	お金持ち	rich person
27	かしゅ	歌手	singer
28	さっか	作家	novelist; writer (of a book, playwright, etc.)
29	しゃちょう	社長	company president; CEO
30	スポーツ せんしゅ	スポーツ 選手	athlete
	〜せんしゅ	〜選手	... player; athlete who does ... **Ex.1** やきゅうせんしゅ baseball player **Ex.2** すいえいせんしゅ swimmer
31	すいえい	水泳	swimming
32	やきゅう	野球	baseball
33	はいゆう	俳優	actor
34	べんごし	弁護士	lawyer; attorney
35	かじ	火事	fire [destructive (forest, building, etc.)]
36	かぜ	風	wind
37	かべ		wall
38	かみ	紙	paper

39	く\overline{も}	雲	cloud
40	\overline{じ}	字	character; letter
41	じし\overline{ん}	地震	earthquake
42	せ\overline{き}	席	seat
43	そ\overline{ら}	空	sky
44	た\overline{いよう}	太陽	sun
45	は\overline{なび}	花火	fireworks
46	ふ\overline{ね}	船	boat; ship
47	む\overline{し}	虫	bug; insect
48	せ\overline{いせき}	成績	grade (on a test, etc.)
49	じゅぎ\overline{ょう}りょう	授業料	tuition
50	や\overline{ちん}	家賃	rent [money for rented living space]
51	い\overline{なか}		countryside; rural area
52	と\overline{かい}	都会	city; urban area
53	み\overline{ち}	道	road
54	みず\overline{うみ}	湖	lake
55	ネ\overline{ズミ}		mouse; rat
56	バ\overline{イク}		motorcycle
57	ホ\overline{ームシック}		homesickness **Ex.** ホームシックになる to get homesick

ADVERBIAL NOUNS

58	い\overline{ちばん}	一番	the first (place); the best; the most
59	\overline{しょうらい}	将来	(one's) future
60	む\overline{かし}	昔	the past; old times

ADVERBS

61	す\overline{ぐ}(に)		at once; immediately
62	ほ\overline{んとうに}	本当に	really; actually
63	よ\overline{く}		well **Ex.1** よくきこえません。 I can't hear you very well. **Ex.2** よくわかりました。 I understand; It was easy to understand.

QUESTION WORDS

64	ど\overline{ちら}		which (of two)
65	ど\overline{っち}		which (of two) [casual]

SUFFIX

66	～\overline{ぶ}	～部	... club **Exs.** サッカーぶ soccer club/team びじゅつぶ art club

OTHER WORDS AND PHRASES

67	ど\overline{ちらも}		both
68	ど\overline{っちも}		both [casual]

Lesson **10**

かんじ

122 帰 帰 帰	キ	帰国 する to return to one's home country きこく	
	かえ（る）	帰 る to return (to one's home base); to go home かえ	
		帰り道 the way back; the way home かえ みち	日帰り day... (trip, etc.); non-overnight ひがえ
homecoming	１ リ リ´ リ⌐ リヨ ⺻ ⺻ 帰 帰 帰		

123 使 使 使	シ	使用 する to use; to make use of しよう	大使館 embassy たいしかん
		天使 angel てんし	
	つか（う）	使 う to use つか	使い方 how to use つか かた
to use	ノ イ イ´ イ⌐ 佢 佢 使 使		

124 暗 暗 暗	アン	暗記 する to memorize あんき	暗証番号 PIN あんしょうばんごう
	くら（い）	暗 い dark [space]; gloomy [person] くら	真っ暗（な）pitch-dark ま くら
darkness	１ ⺆ ⺆ 日 日´ 旷 旷 旷 晬 晬 暗 暗 暗		

125 早 早 早	サッ ソウ	早速 immediately; right away さっそく	早朝 early morning そうちょう
	はや（い）	早 い early [i-adjective] はや	早口 fast-talking はやくち
		早 く early [adverbial form of 早い] はや はや	朝早 く early in the morning あさはや
early	１ ⼝ 口 早 早 旦 早		

126 広 広 広	コウ	広告 advertisement こうこく	
	ひろ（い）	広 い wide; spacious; roomy ひろ	広島県 Hiroshima [prefecture in Japan] ひろしまけん
		広場 open space; public square ひろば	
wide	広 広 広 広 広		

127 安 安 安	アン	安心 する to feel relief あんしん	安全（な）safe 不安（な）uneasy あんぜん ふあん
		平安時代 the Heian period [period between 794-1185 in Japan] へいあんじだい	
	やす（い）	安 い inexpensive やす	安田さん Yasuda-san [last name] やすだ
to relax; inexpensive	安 安 安 安 安 安		

128 親 親 親	シン	親切（な）kind [does good deeds] しんせつ	親戚 relatives しんせき
		親友 best friend 両親 parents しんゆう りょうしん	
	おや した（しい）	親 parent 父親 father 母親 mother 親しい close; (intimately) familiar おや ちちおや ははおや した	
parent; intimate	親 親 親 親 立 立 立 辛 亲 亲 亲 新 新 新 親 親 親		

129 切 切 切	セツ	親切（な）kind [does good deeds] しんせつ	大切（な）important たいせつ
	き（る） きっ	切る to cut き	しめ切り deadline き
		切手 stamp きって	切符 ticket きっぷ
to cut	一 七 切 切		

130 番 番 番	バン	一番 the first (place); the best; the most いちばん	二番 second にばん
		交番 police box　順番 order こうばん　じゅんばん	テレビ番組 TV program ばんぐみ
		番号 number　留守番電話 voicemail; answering machine ばんごう　るすばんでんわ	
turn [in order]; (ordinal) number	一 � 平 平 平 釆 釆 番 番 番		

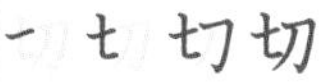

131 社 社 社	シャ ジャ	会社 company かいしゃ	会社員 company employee; office worker かいしゃいん
		社長 company president しゃちょう	社会 society　社会学 sociology しゃかい　しゃかいがく
		神社 (Shinto) shrine じんじゃ	
company	丶 ラ オ ネ ネ 社 社		

132 長 長 長	チョウ	社長 company president しゃちょう	学長 university president がくちょう
		市長 city mayor　部長 section head; club president しちょう　ぶちょう	身長 height [person] しんちょう
	なが（い）	長い long　長崎県 Nagasaki [prefecture in Japan] なが　ながさきけん	
long; head [organization]	一 丆 乕 乕 巨 長 長 長		

133 道 道 道	ドウ トウ	書道 (the Japanese art of) calligraphy しょどう	剣道 kendo　茶道 tea ceremony けんどう　さどう
		柔道 judo　水道 tap; water supply じゅうどう　すいどう	北海道 Hokkaido [prefecture in Japan] ほっかいどう
	みち	神道 Shinto [religion] しんとう	道 road みち
road; way	丶 丷 丷 首 首 首 首 首 道 道		

134 昔 昔 昔	むかし	昔 the past; old times むかし	昔々 once upon a time　昔話 old tale むかしむかし　むかしばなし
old days; long ago	一 一 一 共 昔 昔 昔 昔		

135 友 友 友	ユウ	親友 best friend しんゆう	友人 friend [more formal than 友達] ゆうじん　ともだち
	とも	友達 friend ともだち	
friend	一 ナ 方 友		

136 達 達 達	ダチ タチ タツ	友達 friend ともだち	
		〜達 [plural marker for people] (Ex. 学生達 students, 私達 we) たち　がくせいたち　わたしたち	
		配達する to deliver はいたつ	発達する to develop はったつ
accomplished	一 十 达 达 达 幸 幸 幸 達 達 達 達		

#	Kanji	Forms	Readings	Compounds	Meaning
137	文	文 / 文	ブン / モン / モ	作文 composition（さくぶん）　文化 culture（ぶんか）　文学 literature（ぶんがく）　文 sentence（ぶん）　文法 grammar（ぶんぽう）　文句 complaint; grumbling（もんく）　文字 character; letter（もじ）	sentence

Stroke order: 丶 一 ナ 文

#	Kanji	Forms	Readings	Compounds	Meaning
138	化	化 / 化	カ / ケ / ば(ける)	文化 culture（ぶんか）　化学 chemistry（かがく）　化石 fossil（かせき）　国際化 globalization（こくさいか）　変化する to change（へんか）　化粧する to put on makeup（けしょう）　お化け ghost（ばけ）	to change

Stroke order: ノ イ イ 化

#	Kanji	Forms	Readings	Compounds	Meaning
139	末	末 / 末	マツ / すえ	週末 weekend（しゅうまつ）　～末 end of ...（まつ）（Exs. 月末 end of the month（げつまつ）, 年末 end of the year（ねんまつ）, 今週末 this weekend（こんしゅうまつ）, 先週末 last weekend（せんしゅうまつ)) 期末試験 final exam（きまつしけん）　末っ子 the youngest child in the family（すえこ）	extremity

Stroke order: 一 二 キ 末 末

● あたらしいよみかた　New readings

The following are new readings for kanji that you have already learned. Read each word aloud.

1) 明るい（あか）　　2) 作文（さくぶん）　　3) 作家（さっか）　　4) 書道（しょどう）　　5) 大切(な)（たいせつ）　　6) 花火（はなび）

● れんしゅう　Practice

1 Provide *okurigana* for each kanji 1)-7) to make an adjective, then write the reading for each adjective in (　) to its right. Finally, match each adjective with the corresponding picture from a.-h.

Ex.　古〔い｜ふるい〕

1) 長〔　〕
2) 広〔　〕
3) 暗〔　〕
4) 安〔　〕
5) 早〔　〕
6) 新〔　〕
7) 高〔　〕

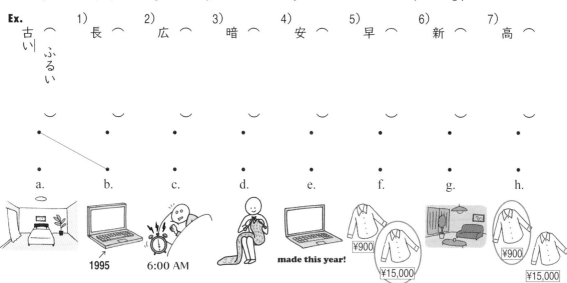

a.　b.　c.　d.　e.　f.　g.　h.

1995　6:00 AM　made this year!　¥900　¥15,000　¥900　¥15,000

2 Write the reading for each word 1)-5) in (   ), then match each word with the phrase a.-f. on the right that explains its meaning.

Ex. 会社 （　かいしゃ　） •

1）週末 （　　　　　） •

2）友達 （　　　　　） •

3）文化 （　　　　　） •

4）社長 （　　　　　） •

5）昔 （　　　　　） •

• a. 土曜日と日曜日です。

• b. ここで仕事をして、給料 (salary) をもらいます。
　　　　し ごと　　　　　　　きゅうりょう

• c. 会社で一番上の人です。

• d. 日本には書道や剣道があります。
　　　　　　　　　　けんどう

• e. おじいさんの子どもの時です。

• f. 仲がいい人です。
　　なか

3 Below is a post Kim-san made on social media about a trip he took to Hokkaido. Read the post aloud, then write the readings for the underlined words.

キム

私の友達の田中さんが夏に北海道の家に帰りました。だから、私は七月に田中
　　　　　　　　なつ　ほっかいどう

さんに会いに北海道に行きました。そして、田中さんの家族といっしょに北海
　　　　　ほっかいどう　　　　　　　　　　　　　　　　かぞく　　　　　　　ほっかい

道を観光しました。田中さんの家族はとても親切でした。
どう　かんこう　　　　　　　　　　かぞく

北海道は道がとても長くて広かったです。有名なラベンダーファームに行きま
ほっかいどう

した。ファームでラベンダーの写真をとったり、ラベンダーのアイスクリーム
　　　　　　　　　　　　しゃしん

を食べたりしました。右のラベンダーの写真は、新しいスマホのアプリを使っ
　　　　　　　　　　　　　　　　しゃしん

てとりました。

この旅行は今年の一番大切な思い出 (memory)
　　りょこう　　　　　　　　おも　で

になりました。

Lesson
10

345

■ Creating your own kanji stories

As you have learned, each kanji has one or more meanings. The elements that make up a kanji, too, often have meanings that relate to that of the kanji, and you can put together the meanings of these elements into a story to help you remember the meaning of the kanji as a whole. For example, the kanji 明 "bright" consists of 日 "sun" and 月 "moon." How can you use the meanings of these two elements to create your story? How about "It is very bright when the sun and moon are in the sky

Ex.1 明

It is very **bright** when the "sun" and "moon" are in the sky together.

together?" Another example of a kanji story is shown on the left for 楽 (Ex.2). Don't you

Ex.2 楽

think the shape of 楽 looks like birds getting together, singing happily in a tree and having fun? You can create your own kanji stories based on the shapes and meanings of kanji and their elements, just like in these examples. Now it's your turn–what stories can you come up with?

れんしゅう Practice

1 Before creating your story for each kanji from 1)-3), write down the meanings of the elements you've learned so far, and then try to think up a mnemonic device for each of the remaining elements based on their appearance.

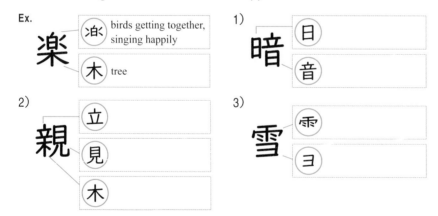

Ex. 楽
- 冫八: birds getting together, singing happily
- 木: tree

1) 暗
- 日:
- 音:

2) 親
- 立:
- 見:
- 木:

3) 雪
- ⻗:
- ヨ:

2 Now, create your own kanji stories using the kanji element meanings you wrote down above. Be creative! Share your favorite stories with your classmates.

Kanji	Ex. 楽	1) 暗	2) 親	3) 雪	4) your own
Kanji story	Watching birds singing in a tree is fun!				
Meaning of kanji	fun, pleasure				

ぶんぽう

1 **Adverbial forms of adjectives**

You can change an adjective into an adverb as follows:

(a) *I*-adjectives: Change the final い of the dictionary form to く.

(b) *Na*-adjectives: Add に.

	Dictionary form	Adverbial form	Noun-modifying form (See L4 #3.)
I-adjective	（高）い たか	（高）く たか	（高）い たか
	いい（よい*）	よく	いい
Na-adjective	（静か） しず	（静か）に しず	（静か）な しず

* よい is the original form of いい.

The adverbial forms of adjectives are used to explain how one does something.

Exs. (1) 先生：この漢字を練習しましょう。ノートに大きく書いてください。
せんせい　　　　　かんじ　れんしゅう　　　　　　　　　　　　　　おお　か
Let's practice this kanji. Write it big in your notebook.

(2) 田中さんはいつも静かに話します。*Tanaka-san always talks quietly.*
たなか　　　　　　しず　　はな

(3) タオさんは楽しそうに歌を歌っています。
たの　　　　　うた　うた

Tao seems to be having fun singing songs. (lit. Tao is singing songs in a way that makes it look like she is having fun.)

そう in (3) is an auxiliary *na*-adjective. (See L9 #3.)

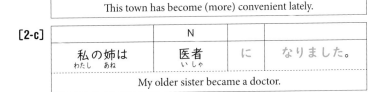

2 **{Adj(*i*)-stem く / Adj(*na*) に} なる・する; N になる・する** "become Adj/N; make ~ Adj; make ~ into N"

[2-a]		Adj(*i*)-stem		
	私の成績は わたし せいせき	よ	く	なりました。
	My grades have gotten better.			

[2-b]		Adj(*na*)		
	この町は最近 まち さいきん	便利 べんり	に	なりました。
	This town has become (more) convenient lately.			

[2-c]		N		
	私の姉は わたし あね	医者 いしゃ	に	なりました。
	My older sister became a doctor.			

Lesson **10**

You can express changes (e.g., something/someone becomes <Adjective>; something/someone becomes <Noun>) using "Adj(*i*)-stem くなる," "Adj(*na*)になる," and "Nになる."

Exs. (1) 私の弟は高校生になって背が高くなりました。
   My younger brother got taller once he became a high school student.

(2) ワンさんは日本語が上手になりました。
   Wang-san's Japanese has improved. (lit. Wang-san has become good at Japanese.)

(3) 子ども：将来、忍者になりたい！ *I want to be a ninja in the future!*

[2-d]

	Noun phrase			Adj(*i*)-stem		
		N				
私は	テレビの	音	を	小さ	く	しました。

I turned down the volume on the TV.
(lit. I made the sound of the TV smaller.)

[2-e]

	N		Adj(*na*)		
トムさんは	テーブル	を	きれい	に	しました。

Tom cleaned the table. (lit. Tom made the table clean.)

[2-f]

	Noun phrase		N₂		
	N₁				
この	まんが	を	アニメ	に	しましょう。

Let's make an anime from this manga.
(lit. Let's change this manga into an anime.)

You can express the idea that someone changes the state of something or someone using "Adj(*i*)-stem くする," "Adj(*na*)にする," or "(Adj) Nにする."

Exs. (4) <At a workshop>
   すみません。聞こえませんから、マイクの音を大きくしてくださいませんか。
   I'm sorry, I can't hear you—could you turn up the volume on your microphone?

(5) あなたを幸せにします。結婚してください。 *I'll make you happy. Please marry me.*

(6) 私は政治家になってこの町をよくしたいと思います。
   I think I would like to become a politician and make this town better.

(7) <On New Year's Day>
   今年をいい年にしたいです。 *I want to make this year a good year.*

3 Superlative sentences

You can express ideas such as "X is the most <Adjective>," "X is the most <Adjective> <Noun>," and "X <Verb> the most <Adverb>" with superlative sentences. You can make superlative sentences using the following sentence patterns:

3-1 X は Y の中で一番 Adj "X is the most Adj in/among Y"

[3-a]	X (topic)		Y					Adj
	山田さん	は	私 の友達	の中で	一番		背が	高いです。
	Yamada-san is the tallest among my friends.							

You can describe someone/something as the tallest, the most delicious, etc. in a certain group of people/objects using the sentence pattern [3-a].

Exs. (1) 「マンマ」はこの町のイタリアンレストランの中で一番おいしいと思います。

I think Mamma is the most delicious among the Italian restaurants in this town.

(2) タオさんはジャパンハウスのメンバーの中で一番料理が上手です。

Tao is the best cook among the member of the Japan House.

の中 cannot be used after place nouns such as that in (3) below.

Ex. (3) 私のサッカーチームはこの町で一番弱いです。*My soccer team is the weakest in this town.*

Thus, the following sentence is ungrammatical:

× 東京は日本の中で一番人が多いです。 → 東京は日本で一番人が多いです。

Tokyo has the largest population in Japan.

3-2 X の中で Y が一番 Adj "Y is the most Adj among X"

[3-b]		X		Y (Q-word)			Adj	
A:		この町のピザ屋	の中で	どこ	が	一番	おいしいです	か。
		Whose pizza is the most delicious (lit. What place is the most delicious) among the pizza restaurants in this town?						
				Y			Adj	
B:				「トニオ」	が	一番	おいしいです。	
		Tonio's is the most delicious.						

You can ask and answer superlative questions using the sentence pattern in [3-b]. Note that どこ is used rather than 何 or だれ when you ask about restaurants, schools, companies, sports teams, etc. (See L1 #4-2.)

Exs. (1) けいた：日本の食べ物の中で何が一番好きですか。

What do you like the most among Japanese foods?

アイ ：たこ焼きが一番好きです。*I like takoyaki the most.*

(2) A: このクラスの中でだれが一番歌が上手だと思いますか。

Who do you think is the best singer (lit. the best at singing) in this class?

B: 山田さんが一番上手だと思います。*I think Yamada-san is the best singer.*

Lesson
10

	X (a list of three or more items)		Y (Q-word)			Adj	
A:	トムさんと ジョンさんと 研さん	の中で なか	だれ	が	一番 いちばん	まじめです	か。
	Among Tom, John, and Ken, who is the most diligent?						
			Y			Adj	
B:			研さん けん	が	一番 いちばん	まじめです。	
	Ken is the most diligent.						

A list of nouns can also be used in the X position, as in [3-c]. In this case, の中 is mandatory.
なか

Note that だれ is used in the Y position, as in [3-c], when the nouns in the X position refer to people, and どこ is used, as in (3), when they refer to places, restaurants, schools, companies, and teams. In other cases, どれ is commonly used rather than 何, as in (4).
なに

Exs. (3) A: ８月に日本に行くんですが、東京と大阪と北海道の中でどこが一番いいですか。
がつ　にほん　い　　　　　　とうきょう　おおさか　ほっかいどう　なか　　　　　　いちばん

I'm going to Japan in August. Which place (lit. where) is the best [to go] among Tokyo, Osaka, and Hokkaido?

B: すずしいから、北海道が一番いいと思いますよ。
ほっかいどう　いちばん　　　おも

I think Hokkaido is the best because the temperature is cool.

(4) A: 日本語と韓国語と中国語の中でどれが一番難しいと思いますか。
にほんご　かんこくご　ちゅうごくご　なか　　　　　いちばんむずか　　　おも

Which do you think is the most difficult among Japanese, Korean, and Chinese?

B: 漢字がたくさんあるから、中国語が一番難しいと思います。
かんじ　　　　　　　　　　ちゅうごくご　いちばんむずか　　　おも

I think Chinese is the most difficult because there are a lot of kanji.

Note that in the Adj position, nouns containing an adjectival meaning can also be used, as in (5). Examples of nouns with an adjectival meaning include 都会, いなか, and お金持ち.
とかい　　　　　　　　　かねも

Ex. (5) A: 沖縄でどこが一番都会ですか。 *Where is the most urban area in Okinawa?*
おきなわ　　　　いちばん　とかい

B: 那覇です。 *Naha is.*
なは

Nouns modified by an adjective can also be used in the Adj position of superlative sentences, as in (6).

Ex. (6) A: 世界でだれが一番有名な作家だと思いますか。
せかい　　　　　いちばん　ゆうめい　さっか　　　おも

Who do you think is the most famous writer in the world?

B: えっと、私はシェークスピアだと思います。 *Hmm. I think Shakespeare is.*
わたし　　　　　　　　　　　　　おも

X の中で Y Prt 一番よく Verb "V (to/with, etc.) Y the most (often) among X"

[3-d]	X		Y (Q-word)	Prt			V	
A:	スポーツ	の中で	何 なに	を	一番 いちばん	よく	見ます み	か。
A:	What sport do you watch the most often? (lit. What do you watch the most often among sports?)							
			Y	Prt			V	
B:			サッカー	を	一番 いちばん	よく	見ます。 み	
B:	I watch soccer the most often.							

You can express the idea that someone does something the most often among a certain group using the sentence pattern in [3-d]. The particle in the Prt position changes according to the role of Y in the sentence (e.g., を if it is the direct object, に if it is the direction, etc.).

Exs. (1) A: この町のレストランの中でどこに一番よく行きますか。
まち　　　　　　なか　　　　　　いちばん　　　い

Which restaurant do you go to the most often among those in this town?

B: 安くておいしいから、「きく」というレストランに一番よく行きます。
やす　　　　　　　　　　　　　　　　　　　　　いちばん　　　い

I go to a restaurant called Kiku the most often because it's cheap and delicious.

(2) A: 兄弟の中でだれと一番よく話しますか。
きょうだい　なか　　　　　いちばん　　　はな

Who do you talk with the most often among your siblings?

B: 兄と一番よく話します。
あに　いちばん　　　はな

I talk with my older brother the most often.

(3) A: この町のカフェの中でどこで一番よくコーヒーを買いますか。
まち　　　　　　なか　　　　　いちばん　　　　　　　　か

Where do you buy coffee the most often among the cafés in this town?

B: 「ピース」で一番よく買います。*I buy coffee at Peace the most often.*
いちばん　　か

---

4 X も Y も "both X and Y; neither X nor Y"

[4-a]		X		Y		
私は わたし		イヌ	も	ネコ	も	（どちらも）好きです。 す
	I like both dogs and cats.					
		スミスさん	も	山田さん やまだ	も	（どちらも）大学生じゃないです。 だいがくせい
	Neither Smith-san nor Yamada-san is a college student.					

Using X も Y も, you can express the idea of "both X and Y" or "neither X nor Y." どちらも is optional. When particles such as に, で, と, and から are in use, も is attached to them, yielding double particles, as in (2) and (3). (See L5 #5.)

Exs. (1) 東京には古い文化も新しい文化も（どちらも）あります。
とうきょう　　ふる　ぶんか　あたら　ぶんか

Tokyo has both old culture and new culture.

(2)　京都にも奈良にも（どちらにも）行ってみたいです。
　　　　きょうと　　なら　　　　　　　　　　　　　　　い

　　　I'd like to go to both Kyoto and Nara.

(3)　『となりのトトロ』という映画は日本語でも英語でも（どちらでも）見たことがあ
　　　　　　　　　　　　　　えいが　　にほんご　　　えいご　　　　　　　　　　　　　み

りません。*I have never watched "My Neighbor Totoro" in either Japanese nor English.*

5　Comparative sentences

You can compare two people or things and express ideas like "X is more <Adjective> than Y" and "X <Verb> more <Adverb> than Y" with comparative sentences. You can make comparative sentences using the following sentence patterns:

5-1　X は Y より Adj "X is more Adj than Y"

[5-a]

X (topic)		Y			Adj
田中さんは た なか	は	私 わたし	より	背が せ	高いです。 たか
Tanaka-san is taller than I am.					

You use the above sentence pattern when you talk about someone/something (=X), comparing it with someone/something else (=Y).

Exs. (1)　私 は 弟 がいます。弟 は 私 よりまじめです。
　　　　　　わたし　おとうと　　　　おとうと　わたし

　　　　I have a younger brother. He is more serious than I am.

(2)　今日は昨日より 宿 題が多かったから、ちょっと大変でした。
　　　きょう　きのう　　しゅくだい　おお　　　　　　　　　　　たいへん

　　　We had more homework today than yesterday, so it was a little hard.

(3)　田中さんは「私 の町はこの町より都会だよ」と言っていました。
　　　た なか　　　わたし　まち　　まち　　とかい　　　い

　　　Tanaka-san said, "My town is a more urban area than this town."

As in (3), nouns with an adjectival meaning can also be used in the Adj position in [5-a].

5-2　X と Y と {どちら／どっち} のほう Prt {Adj／よく Verb}

You can ask questions like "Which one do you like more, X or Y?" and "Which person knows more kanji, X or Y?" using X と Y と {どちら／どっち}のほう. どっち is more casual than どちら.

5-2-1　X と Y とどちらのほうが Adj "Which is more Adj, X or Y?"
　　　　X より Y のほうが Adj "Y is more Adj than X"

[5-b]

	X		Y				Adj	
A:	ラーメン	と	うどん	と	どちら	のほうが		好きです す	か。
	Which do you like more, ramen or *udon* noodles?							

	X			Y		Adj	
B:	（ラーメン	より）		うどん	のほうが	好きです。 す	
	I like *udon* more (than ramen).						

You can ask a comparison question using the sentence pattern [5-b]-A. In this sentence pattern, you compare two things or people with adjectives.

Exs. (1) A: 時間とお金と どちらのほうが大切ですか。*Which is more important, time or money?*

B: 私は今とても忙しいから、（お金より）時間のほうが大切です。
I'm very busy now, so time is more important (than money).

(2) A: ここから美術館までタクシーと地下鉄と どちらのほうが早いですか。
Which will get us to the museum faster from here, a taxi or the subway?

B: そうですね、（タクシーより）地下鉄のほうが早いと思います。
Let me think. I think the subway would be faster (than a taxi).

(3) A: サッカーとバスケットボールと どっちのほうが好き？
Which do you like better, soccer or basketball?

B: サッカーもバスケットボールも（どっちも）好き。*I like both soccer and basketball.*

5-2-2 **X と Y とどちらのほう Prt よく Verb** "Which one ~ V (to/in, etc.) more (often), X or Y?"

X より Y のほう Prt よく Verb "V (to/in, etc.) Y more (often) than X"

[5-c]

	X		Y				Prt		V	
A:	コーヒー	と	お茶	と	どちら	のほう	を	よく	飲みます	か。
A:	Which one do you drink more, coffee or tea?									
	X			Y		Prt		V		
B:	（お茶	より）	コーヒー	のほう	を	よく	飲みます。			
B:	I drink coffee more (than tea).									

You can ask a different kind of comparison question using the sentence pattern in [5-c]-A. With this sentence pattern, you compare two things or people with verbs.

The particle in the Prt position changes according to the role of X and Y. (See #3-3 in this lesson.)

Exs. (1) A: 映画はアクションとアニメと どちらのほうをよく見ますか。
Which type of movie do you watch more often, action or animation?

B: 私は日本のアニメが好きだから、（アクションより）アニメのほうをよく見ます。*Because I like Japanese anime, I watch animation more often (than action films).*

(2) A: スーパーは「トミー」と「パロー」と どちらのほうによく行きますか。
Which supermarket do you go to more often, Tommy or Parrow?

B: 安くて近いから、（「パロー」より）「トミー」のほうによく行きます。
I go to Tommy more often (than to Parrow), because things are cheap there and it's close.

(3) A: 図書館とカフェと どっちのほうでよく宿題する？
Where do you do homework more often, the library or a café?

B: （カフェより）図書館のほうが静かだから、図書館のほうでよくするよ。
The library is quieter (than a café), so I do my homework there (lit. at the library) more often.

6 **～けれど／けど** "but; however; although"

[6]

S₁	けれど／けど、	S₂
日本語は 難しい(です)		授業 は楽しいです。

Japanese is difficult, but the class is fun. / Although Japanese is difficult, the class is fun.

You can express the idea of "but; however; although" using けれど or けど. In terms of meaning, けれど and けど are equivalent to が. (See L3 #4.) Between けれど and けど, けど is more casual.

Note that these conjunctions are affixed to the end of a sentence. If S₂ is in the polite form, S₁ can be either in the plain form or the polite form, as in [6]. If S₂ is in the plain form, S₁ must be in the plain form, too, as in (3) below.

Exs. (1) このレストランは安くない(です)けれど、人気があります。

This restaurant isn't cheap, but it is popular.

(2) 今日ケーキを作ってみたけれど、すごくまずかったです。

I made a cake today, but it tasted horrible.

(3) にゃんたはネコだけど、日本語がよく分かる。

Nyanta is a cat, but he understands Japanese well.

7 **～ことができる** "can V; be able to V"

[7]

		V-plain.non-past	
日本のコンビニでは	おいしいスイーツを	買う	ことができます。

You can buy tasty sweets at convenience stores in Japan.

Using the sentence pattern in [7], you can express the idea that a person (or people in general) can do something (=X) because:

(a) the person has the ability to do X, or

(b) something is available that allows people to do X. (See (2) and (3).)

(More about "can V" expressions in *TOBIRA II* L12 #1 Potential forms)

Exs. (1) A: 日本の歌を歌うことができますか。*Can you sing a Japanese song?*

B: はい、「てフォームの歌」を歌うことができます！

Yes, I can sing "The Te-Form Song!"

(2) このアプリで色々な絵を描くことができます。*You can draw various pictures with this app.*

(3) 私の町の美術館では、ピカソの絵を見ることができるけれど、草間彌生の絵を見ることはできません。

At the museum in my town, you can see Picasso's paintings, but you cannot see Yayoi Kusama's paintings.

はなしましょう

Activities

できる
I
Ask and answer questions about changes in yourself and things around you.

できるI-A　Adverbial forms of adjectives

1 Let's practice changing adjectives into their adverbial forms.　 L10-7

Ex.1 おおきい → おおき<u>く</u>

Ex.2 しずか　→ しずか<u>に</u>

1) おもしろい　　2) むずかしい　　3) いい　　　4) かっこいい　　5) きれい

6) じょうず　　　7) べんり　　　　8) おいしそう　　9) はやい　　　10) おそい

2 Describe the manner in which you and Ren do things using the cues provided.　 L10-8

Ex.1 起きる（朝早い）→ 私は<u>朝早く</u>起きます。

Ex.2 働く（まじめ）　→ レンさんは<u>まじめに</u>働きます。

1) クラスに行く（早い）　2) 授業を聞く（静か）　3) 勉強する（楽しい）

4) 字を書く（大きい）　　5) 手を洗う（きれい）　6) 子どもに話す（やさしい）

7) 歌う（元気）　　　　　8) 寝る（夜遅い）

私

- -

9) 日本語を話す（上手）　　　　10) おどる（かっこいい）

11) 友達と話す（楽しそう）　　　12) コーヒーを飲む（おいしそう）

13) 彼女の話を聞く（つまらなそう）

レン

できるI-B　{Adj(*i*)-stem く/Adj(*na*)に} なる; Nになる

1 Let's talk about how people change over time.

Step 1 Talk about the following changes in Mark's life.　 L10-9

Ex.1 マークさんは高校に入って、背が高くなりました。

Ex.2 （マークさんは）大学に入って、料理が得意になりました。

Ex.3 （マークさんは）留学して、少しホームシックになりました。

高校に入る	大学に入る	留学する
Ex.1 背が高い	Ex.2 料理が得意	Ex.3 少しホームシック
1) 日本の文化が好き	3) 勉強が忙しい	5) 日本語が上手
2) 写真部のメンバー	4) 色々な人と友達	6) もっと明るい

Lesson
10

Step 2 Now, choose a time in your life and talk about the changes that happened during that time.

> **Possible topics**　〜に入る（高校／大学／クラブ）　〜に留学する　〜を始める
> りゅうがく　　　　　　はじ

Ex.　A: 私は大学に入って、友達が多くなりました。〇〇さんはどうですか。
　　　　　　　　　　ともだち　おお

　　B: 私は大学に入って、毎日がもっと楽しくなりました。

　　A: へえ、そうですか。いいですね。

　　B: あの、△△さんは日本語の勉強を始めて、何か変わりましたか。　　＜Continue＞
　　　　　　　　　　　　　べんきょう　はじ　　　　か

2 Compare cities and places in the past and present.

Step 1 Look at the then-and-now pictures of Tokyo below and talk about the changes you see and can think of with your partner. Use the cues provided to start and expand your conversation.

Ex.　A: 東京は昔と比べて (compared to the past)、人が多くなりましたね。
　　　　とうきょう　むかし　くら　　　　　　　　　　　　おお

　　B: そうですね。それから、高い建物が・・・　＜Continue＞
　　　　　　　　　　　　　　　たてもの

Ex. people / more

1) tall buildings / more

2) trees / fewer

3) city / cleaner（きれい）

4) daily lives /
　probably more convenient

5) daily lives /
　probably more interesting

6) your own

50 年前 (ago)

今

Step 2 Now, talk about another place. Pick a place you are familiar with and tell your partner how it has changed over time.

Ex.　A: 私の出身は〇〇なんですが、〇〇はちょっと変わりました。
　　　　　しゅっしん　　　　　　　　　　　　　　　　か

　　　最近、ちょっと危なくなりました。
　　　さいきん　　　あぶ

　　B: そうですか。どうしてですか。（← Follow-up question）＜Continue＞

3 Talk with your partner about what you wanted to be when you were a child.

Ex.　A: 〇〇さんは子どもの時、何になりたかったですか。

　　B: 私はパン屋になりたかったです。
　　　　　　　や

　　A: へえ、そうですか。どうしてパン屋になりたかったんですか。
　　　　　　　　　　　　　　　　　や

　　B: パンが大好きで、毎日おいしいパンが食べたかったからです。

　　　△△さんは？

　　＜Continue＞

1 Photo editing apps allow you to manipulate images in a variety of interesting ways.

[Step 1] Describe how you edited each of the photos below and what the result was.

Ex. ［Your edit］空が暗いから、空を明るくしました。
　　　　　　　　　　そら くら　　　　そら　あか
　→ ［The resulting change］空が明るくなりました。
　　　　　　　　　　　　　　そら　あか

Ex. 空が暗い 😞
　　　そら くら

1）人が多い 😞
　　　　おお

2）色がきれいじゃない 😞
　　いろ

3）青が好きじゃない 😞
　　あお

4）天気がくもり 😞　　　　　晴れ！

5）つまらない写真 😞
　　　　　　　しゃしん

[Step 2] Your partner is a web designer. Ask them to edit the photos in Step 1 or your own photos.

Ex. A: すみません、この写真の空を明るくしてくれませんか。
　　　　　　　　　　しゃしん そら　あか
　　　B: はい、今、明るくします。ちょっと待ってください。
　　　　　　　　　　あか　　　　　　　　　　　　　ま
　　　　明るくなりましたよ。
　　　　あか
　　　A: わあ、すごくよくなりましたね。(← Comment)

[Step 3] Now, talk about the app(s) you use to make your photos, videos, etc. look more attractive.

Ex. A: 私は「ピクスアート」というアプリを使って、色をきれいにしたり、
　　　　　　　　　　　　　　　　　　　つか　　　いろ
　　　　写真をかっこよくしたりします。○○さんはどんなアプリで何をしますか。
　　　　しゃしん
　　　B: 私は‥‥ <Continue>

2 If you encountered the situations below in a Japanese restaurant, what would you ask the person working there to do? Make an appropriate request for each of the situations provided.

Ex. あなた：あの、ちょっとすみません。

店<small>みせ</small>の中が暑<small>あつ</small>いんですが、<u>すずしくしてくれませんか</u>。

店<small>みせ</small>の人：はい、すぐ<u>すずしく</u>します。（← Response）

Ex. inside / hot 😓
1) table / dirty
2) soup（スープ）/ cold
3) music / loud

4) curry（カレー）/ not spicy 😠
5) don't have much time → quick
6) bug in salad → new salad
7) your own

𝒢roup 𝒲ork

3 Give a presentation about your professional future. Share three things you would or would not want to do while working in the profession of your choice.

Step 1 Brainstorm about what job you would want to do in the future, why, and what you would do in it.

Future job	
Reason, would/wouldn't want to do, etc.	①
	②
	③

Step 2 Share your thoughts with your classmates.

Ex. 私は将来<small>しょうらい</small>、弁護士<small>べんごし</small>になりたいです。

① 弁護士<small>べんごし</small>になって、弱<small>よわ</small>い人や会社<small>かいしゃ</small>を助<small>たす</small>けたいからです。

② みんなを幸<small>しあわ</small>せにして、世界<small>せかい</small>をよくしたいです。

③ 悪い人は助<small>たす</small>けません。

みなさん、何か質問<small>しつもん</small>がありますか。

Compare three or more things and talk about which you think is at the top of a certain category.

できるⅡ-A Superlative sentences

1 Did you know the following fun facts? Make sentences based on the information provided.

Ex. 琵琶湖は日本の 湖 の中で一番大きいです。
びわこ　　　　　　みずうみ　　　　　いちばん　　おお L10-11

Ex.

| 1 | 琵琶湖
びわこ |
| 2 | 霞ヶ浦
かすみがうら |
| 3 | サロマ湖
こ |

日本の湖
みずうみ
（大きい）
おお

1)

| 1 | 信濃川
しなのがわ |
| 2 | 利根川
とねがわ |
| 3 | 石狩川
いしかりがわ |

日本の川

（長い）
なが

2)

| 1 | 東京大学
とうきょう |
| 2 | 京都大学
きょうと |
| 3 | 東北大学
とうほく |

日本の大学

（古い）
ふる

3)

| 1 | 佐藤
さとう |
| 2 | 鈴木
すずき |
| 3 | 高橋
たかはし |

日本人の名前

（多い）
おお

4)

| 1 | 香川
かがわ |
| 2 | 大阪
おおさか |
| 3 | 東京
とうきょう |

県 (prefecture)
けん
（せまい）

2 Practice asking interesting questions to each other using superlatives.

Step 1 Make superlative questions using the cues provided and the correct question words.

Ex.1 大学の授 業（楽しい）→ 大学の授 業 の中で何が一番 楽しいですか。
じゅぎょう　　　　　　じゅぎょう　　　　なに　いちばん

Ex.2 そうじ／せんたく／料 理（好き）
りょうり

→ そうじとせんたくと 料 理の中でどれが一番 好きですか。
りょうり　　　　　　　いちばん

1) 大学の授 業（難 しい）　　2) 家族や友達（おもしろい）　　3) この町のカフェ（いい）
だいがく　じゅぎょう　むずか　　　かぞく　ともだち

4) 地震／火事／病気（こわい）　5) 歌／スポーツ／外国語（得意）　6) your own（好き）
じしん　かじ　びょうき　　　　うた　　　　　がいこくご　とくい

Step 2 Ask your partner any questions you like from Step 1.

Ex. A: 〇〇さんはそうじとせんたくと 料 理の中でどれが一番 好きですか。
りょうり　　　　いちばん

B: 料 理するのが楽しいから、 料 理が一番 好きです。△△さんは？
りょうり　　　　　　　　　　りょうり　いちばん

A: 私も 料 理が一番 好きです。 or 私は… ＜Continue＞
わたし　りょうり　いちばん

3 In the country you live in, what people/things are at the top in the following categories?
Exchange opinions with your partner.

Ex. ファストフード（人気がある）

A: アメリカ（← country）のファストフードの中で何が一番 人気があると思いますか。
いちばん

B: 私はハンバーガーが一番 人気があると思います。
いちばん

A: そうですか。私はピザが一番 人気があると思います。
いちばん

or 私もハンバーガーが一番 人気があると思います。
いちばん

1) 食べ物（おいしい）　　2) 町（都会）　　　　　3) 若い俳優（人気がある）
た　もの　　　　　　　　とかい　　　　　　　　わか　はいゆう

4) 会社（有名）　　　　　5) スポーツ選手（お金持ち）　6) your own
かいしゃ　　　　　　　　　　せんしゅ

Lesson 10

Group Work

4 Find out about what things your classmates do the most often.

[Step 1] First, make question sentences based on the cues provided in the table below. Then, pair up and ask one of those questions to your partner. Move on to a new partner after asking one question.

Ex. A: ○○さんはスポーツの中で何を一番よくしますか。

B: 私は今は水泳を一番よくします。

A: そうですか。たいていどこで泳ぎますか。(← Follow-up question or comment)

＜Continue＞

Question	Answer 1	Answer 2
Ex. スポーツ／一番よくする	水泳 （フェルプスさん）	テニス （ なおみ さん）
1) SNS／一番よく見る	（　　　　さん）	（　　　　さん）
2) カフェ／一番よく行く	（　　　　さん）	（　　　　さん）
3) クラスメート／一番よく話す	（　　　　さん）	（　　　　さん）
4) your own	（　　　　さん）	（　　　　さん）

[Step 2] Report what you have learned about your classmates to the class.

Ex. フェルプスさんはスポーツの中で水泳を一番よくすると言っていました。

それから、なおみさんは… ＜Continue＞

できる III Compare two things and talk about differences and similarities.

できるIII-A XもYも

1 Brain exercises! Say what each pair of words has in common.

Ex. ネズミ／ネコ

→ ネズミもネコも（どちらも）｛動物です／あまり大きくないです etc.｝。

1) ニューヨーク／東京　　2) 映画館の中／夜の道　　3) 時間／お金

4) コンピュータウイルス (virus)／病気のウイルス　　5) your own

2 As you know, Ai is very enthusiastic about learning Japanese. Describe Ai's experience with Japan and Japanese language and culture so far.   🔊 **L10-14**

Ex.1 日本語／日本の文化（好き）

　　　→ アイさんは<u>日本語</u>も<u>日本の文化</u>も（どちらも）<u>好きです</u>。

Ex.2 北海道／沖縄（行ったことがない）

　　　→ アイさんは<u>北海道にも沖縄にも</u>（どちらにも）<u>行ったことがありません</u>。

1）古い文化／ポップカルチャー（好き）　　2）日本のアニメ／日本のドラマ（よく見る）

3）たこ焼き／たい焼き（食べたことがない）　4）日本人の友達／先生（日本語でメールを書く）

5）日本の美術館／カラオケ（行ったことがある）

6）クラスの中／クラスの外（日本語を話す）

7）富士山／スカイツリー（登ったことがない）

たこ焼き　　　たい焼き

3 Talk about some things you would like to try doing in Japan. If you don't know much about Japan, look things up on the internet or use the possible topics provided below. Remember to include reason(s) for your answers.

> **Possible topics**
>
> 食べてみたい（たこ焼き／たい焼き etc.）　見てみたい（富士山／お城 (castle) etc.）
>
> 行ってみたい（温泉／いなか etc.）　　　　買い物してみたい（100円ショップ／コンビニ etc.）

Ex. A: ○○さんは日本でたこ焼きやたい焼きを食べてみたいですか。

　　B: はい、私はたこ焼きもたい焼きも食べたことがないから、食べてみたいです。

　　　△△さんは？

　　A: 私はたこ焼きもたい焼きも食べたことがあるから、今度はお好み焼きを食べて

　　　みたいです。or おいしそうだから、私もたこ焼きもたい焼きも食べてみたいです。

できるⅢ-B **Comparative sentences**

1 Describe the difference between each set of people or things below based on the cues provided.

Ex. <u>ホストファミリーのお母さん</u>は<u>お父さん</u>より<u>背が高い</u>です。 🔊 **L10-15**

ホストファミリーの
お母さん　　お父さん

飛行機の
ファーストクラス　エコノミークラス

新しい
パソコン

古い
パソコン

Ex. tall

1) young　2) kind

3) expensive　4) seat / spacious

5) meals / good

6) light (weight)　7) fast

8) convenient　9) your own

2 Compare the two things presented in each question below with your partner using the cues in the blue boxes.

Ex. 日本 vs インド

> 小さい／暑い／〜が少ない etc.
> あつ　　すく

A: 日本とインドについて話しましょう。

日本はインドより小さいです。

B: そうですね。それから、たぶんインドの夏は日本の
夏より暑いと思います。　　　<Continue>
なつ　あつ

1) 高校のクラス vs 大学のクラス

2) オンラインの授業 vs 教室の授業
じゅぎょう　　　きょうしつ　じゅぎょう

> 難しい／やさしい／おもしろい／つまらない／
> むずか
> 〜が多い／〜が少ない etc.
> おお　　　　すく

3) 昔の〇〇 vs 今の〇〇　　　4) your own
むかし

3 Take turns asking and answering questions about Japan based on the cues provided.　🔊 **L10-16**

Ex.　Q: 東京 vs 大阪（都会）→ 東京と大阪とどちらのほうが都会ですか。
とうきょう　おおさか　とかい　とうきょう　おおさか　とかい

A: ★東京　　大阪 → 大阪より東京のほうが都会です。
とうきょう　おおさか　おおさか　とうきょう　とかい

東京 ＝ 大阪 → 東京も大阪も（どちらも）都会です。
とうきょう　おおさか　とうきょう　おおさか　とかい

1) Q: 東京　　vs 大阪　　（家賃が高い）　A: ★東京　　　大阪
とうきょう　　　おおさか　　やちん　　　　　とうきょう　　おおさか

2) Q: 九州　　vs 北海道　（広い）　　　A:　九州　★北海道
きゅうしゅう　　ほっかいどう　ひろ　　　　　　きゅうしゅう　ほっかいどう

3) Q: 神社　　vs お寺　　（多い）　　　A: ★神社　　　お寺
じんじゃ　　　　　　　　おお　　　　　　じんじゃ

4) Q: ペット vs 子ども　（少ない）　　A:　ペット　★子ども
すく

5) Q: 野球　　vs サッカー（人気がある）A:　野球 ＝ サッカー
やきゅう　　　　　　　　　　　　　　　やきゅう

4 Compare two things and exchange your opinions about them.

Step 1 Ask and answer questions with your partner using the cues provided.

Ex.　水 vs 雪（重い）→ A: 水と雪とどちらのほうが重いと思いますか。
おも　　　　　　　　　　　　　　　おも

B: 雪より水のほうが重いと思います。
おも

1) 地震 vs 火事（こわい）　　　2) 飛行機 vs 車（安全）
じしん　かじ　　　　　　　　　　ひこうき　くるま　あんぜん

3) 重いスイカ (watermelon) vs 軽いスイカ（甘い）　　4) E-book vs 紙の本（いい）
おも　　　　　　　　　　　　かる　　　あま　　　　　　　　　　　　かみ

5) 東京 vs your own（都会）
とうきょう　　　　　とかい

Step 2 Now, make your own comparison questions using the cues provided and ask them to
your partner.

1) 好き　　2) いいと思う　　3) 強いと思う　　4) 大切だと思う　　5) your own
つよ　　　　　　たいせつ

362

5 Find out what activities your classmate does more than others. Do you have similar patterns and preferences?

Step 1 First, make questions. Pay attention to which particle you use with each verb. 🔊 L10-17

Ex. そうじ vs 料理（する）→ そうじと料理とどちらのほうをよくしますか。

1) YouTube vs テレビ（見る）　　2) パソコン vs スマホ（使う）

3) 電車やバス vs 自転車（乗る）　　4) 山 vs 海（行く）

5) 店：○○ vs △△（買い物をする）　6) your own

Step 2 Choose two activities and ask your partner which of them they do more often. You can use some of the questions you made in Step 1.

Ex. A: ○○さんはそうじと料理とどちらのほうをよくしますか。

B: 私はそうじするのが苦手だから、そうじより料理のほうをよくします。

△△さんは？

A: 最近、すごく忙しいから、私は料理もそうじも（どちらも）あまりしません。

\<Continue\>

6 Which would you choose and why?

Step 1 Exchange your opinions about the topics provided below.

Ex. お金 vs 時間（ほしい）

A: お金と時間とどちらのほうがほしいですか。

B: うーん、毎日忙しいから、お金より時間のほうがほしいです。　\<Continue\>

1) ジブリのアニメ vs ディズニーのアニメ（好き）　　2) イヌ vs ネコ（幸せだと思う）

3) 聞くのが上手な人 vs 話すのが上手な人（なりたい）　4) your own

Group Work

Step 2 Talking casually, ask and answer the questions in Step 1 with your classmates. 👕

Ex. A: ○○さんはジブリのアニメとディズニーのアニメとどっちのほうが好き？

B: 私はジブリのアニメのほうが好き。or 私はどっちも好き。

△△さんはどっちのほうが好き？

C: うーん、私は… \<Continue\>

できる
IV
Contrast two things to express your opinion about something.

できるIV-A　**〜けれど／けど**

1 Match each sentence on the left with the appropriate contrasting one on the right and connect them using 〜けれど.　🔊 **L10-18**

Ex.　この大学の授業料は高いけれど、いいクラスがたくさんあります。
　　　　じゅぎょうりょう

Ex. この大学の授業料は高いです。　　　・　　　・ 成績はよかったです。
　　　じゅぎょうりょう　　　　　　　　　　　　　　　　せいせき

1) 友達はいい人です。　　　　　　　・　　　・ いいクラスがたくさんあります。
　ともだち

2) 寮は安全です。　　　　　　　　　・　　　・ よくクラスに遅れます。
　りょう　あんぜん　　　　　　　　　　　　　　　　　おく

3) 試験の前にあまり勉強しませんでした。・　　　・ もうきたなくなりました。
　しけん　　　　　べんきょう

4) 人と話すのが得意じゃないです。　　・　　　・ 部屋がせまいです。
　　　　　　　　とくい　　　　　　　　　　　　へや

5) 昨日部屋をそうじしました。　　　　・　　　・ 料理が上手になりません。
　きのうへや　　　　　　　　　　　　　　　　りょうり

6) 毎日ご飯を作っています。　　　　　・　　　・ がんばって、みんなと話しています。
　　　　はん

2 Ai is talking about the Japan House. Combine each pair of sentences below into one sentence using either 〜けれど or 〜て.　🔊 **L10-19**

Ex.1 家は古いです ☹。きれいです ☺。　→ 家は古いけれど、きれいです。

Ex.2 部屋は明るいです ☺。広いです ☺。 → 部屋は明るくて、広いです。
　　　　へや　あか　　　　　ひろ　　　　　　　　　　　へや　あか　　　　　ひろ

1) ジャパンハウスの生活はおもしろいです。楽しいです。
　　　　　　　　せいかつ

2) 初めは (in the beginning) ネコがちょっと苦手でした。今は大好きになりました。
　はじ　　　　　　　　　　　　　　にがて

3) タオさんはかたづけるのが得意です。いつも部屋をきれいにしています。
　　　　　　　　　　　とくい　　　　　へや

4) リーマンさんはすごくまじめです。ときどき授業に行きません。
　　　　　　　　　　　　　　　　じゅぎょう

5) ときどきけんかします。みんな仲がいいです。
　　　　　　　　　　なか

6) 今年ジャパンハウスは家賃がちょっと高くなりました。今も住んでいます。
　　　　　　　　　やちん

3 Choose a topic you are interested in and ask your partner's opinion about it. When you answer, contrast the topic's good and bad points.

Possible topics	○○の生活　　　歌手／俳優／スポーツ選手の○○
	せいかつ　　かしゅ　はいゆう　　せんしゅ
	大学の○○ (place)／(city) の○○

Ex.　A: 今の大学の生活についてどう思いますか。
　　　　　　　　　せいかつ

　　　B: 楽しいと思うけれど、ときどきちょっとさびしくなります。ホームシックにな

　　　　るからです。でも、高校より大学のほうがおもしろいと思います。○○さんは

　　　　どう思いますか。

　　　A: そうですね… ＜Continue＞

1 Practice using 〜ことができる to say what you can do at a university. L10-20

Ex. 外国語を習います → 大学で外国語を習うことができます。

1) 好きな研究をします　　2) 本をたくさん借ります　　3) 有名な先生の話を聞きます

4) 新しい友達を作ります　5) 色々な国の文化を知ります　6) your own

2 Describe what you can and cannot do in the places or with the devices below. L10-21

Ex. ネコカフェではネコと遊ぶことができるけれど、勉強することはできません。

Ex. ネコカフェ	1) スマホ	2) 公園	3) ネット	4) your own
○ ネコと遊ぶ	○ 人と話す	○ 散歩する	○ 授業を受ける	○ ＿＿＿＿
× 勉強する	× 本当に会う	× 泳ぐ	× ホームステイする	× ＿＿＿＿

3 Talk about what you can do in your hometown.

Ex. A: ○○さんの出身はどこですか。

B: ドイツ (Germany) のフランクフルトです。

A: フランクフルトですか。フランクフルトでは何をすることができますか。

B: そうですね、ゲーテ (Goethe) の家に行ったり、船に乗って川から町を見たり

することができます。

A: そうですか。楽しそうな所ですね。

Lesson
10

4 Talk about the legal age for various activities in Japan and the country you live in. First, talk about the legal ages in Japan shown in the pictures below, and then compare and contrast them with those in the other country you are talking about.

Ex. A: 日本では何才からバイクに乗ることができますか。

B: 16才からバイクに乗ることができますよ。

A: そうですか。アメリカのアラスカでは14才からバイクに乗ることができます。

Ex. 16　　1) 18　　2) 20　　3) 20　　4) 18　　5) 18

選挙で投票する
(to vote in an election)

Review

Now you can express your opinions and talk about your preferences. Exchange opinions with your partner about which of two places you would rather live in.

> **Possible topics** 都会 vs いなか　　シェアハウス (shared residence) vs アパート
> ディズニーの世界 vs ジブリの世界

A: Choose a topic and ask a question

B: Present your opinion
- reason(s)
- what you can/can't do

B: Ask your partner's opinion

A: Respond
- opinion
- reason(s)
- what you can/can't do

Ex.

A: ○○さんは都会といなかとどちらのほうに住みたいですか。

B: そうですね、いなかより都会のほうに住みたいです。

A: へえ、そうですか。どうしてですか。

B: 便利だからです。それから、都会はおもしろいイベントに行ったり、色々な所で遊んだりすることができます。

A: ああ、分かります。

B: いなかは静かでいいけれど、ちょっとつまらないと思います。△△さんはどう思いますか。

A: うーん、私はいなかのほうに住みたいです。都会は楽しそうだけれど、人や車が多くて木や花が少ないからです。だから、あまりリラックスする (to relax) ことができないと思います。

B: そうですね…　＜Continue＞

よみましょう

Getting information from a chart

1 Food prices have a big impact on your budget when you travel. Compare the prices of a hamburger and a caffe latte between six popular travel destinations and answer the questions in Japanese.

	390 円	415 円	485 円	245 円	500 円	290 円
旅行で 人気がある国	日本	タイ	イギリス	トルコ	スペイン	メキシコ
	380 円	375 円	360 円	180 円	320 円	215 円

1) ハンバーガーは、6つの国の中でどこが一番高いですか。

2) ハンバーガーは、日本とタイとどちらのほうが安いですか。

3) カフェラテは、6つの国の中でどこが一番安いですか。

4) カフェラテは、イギリスとスペインとどちらのほうが高いですか。

5) ハンバーガーを食べて、カフェラテを飲みます。日本とスペインとメキシコの中で、

どこが一番高いですか。どこが一番安いですか。

Understanding demonstratives (そ-words)

Demonstratives are used in writing to avoid repetition and wordiness and also to create cohesion within and between sentences. そ-words (e.g., それ, そこ, その時, その+Noun) refer to what has been mentioned earlier. Consider the following examples:

週末、私は友達の部屋に遊びに行きました。①そこにネコがいました。②そのネコは私を見てニャーニャーと言って、私の近くに来ました。③その時、私は④そのネコの顔を見て、「目がとてもきれいだね」と言いました。⑤それを聞いて、友達は「私は顔がかわいいと思う」と言いました。

The arrows indicate the words and phrases that each そ-word refers to. ①そこ refers to 友達の部屋, which was mentioned in the preceding sentence. そのネコ in ② is used to refer to the cat previously mentioned, and ③その時 refers to the time when the event described in the preceding sentence occurred. ④そのネコ refers to the cat which was mentioned in the first line, and ⑤それ refers to what 私 (the author) said to 友達 in the preceding sentence.

Lesson
10

367

2 『ネズミの結婚』という 昔 話 (old tale) を読んで、質問に答えましょう。

※ネズミは「チュー」となきます (to squeak)。

ネ ズ ミ の 結 婚　[お父さんネズミ]　[チュー子]

1　昔、ある 所 にお金持ちのネズミの家族がいました。お父さんネズミ

　とお母さんネズミと一人娘のチュー子です。チュー子はかわいくて親切

　だったから、町で一番人気がありました。色々なネズミがチュー子の家に

　「チュー子さん、私と結婚してください。」とお願いに来ました。でも、お

5　父さんネズミは「だめです。チュー子は世界で一番強い相手と結婚するん

　です。」と言って、①そのお願いを全部 断 りました。そして、世界で一番

　強い相手を探しに出かけました。

　　お父さんネズミは広い空を見て、世界を明るくするから、太陽が世界で

　一番強いと思いました。だから、まず太陽に話しに行きました。「太陽さん、

10　私はあなたが世界で一番強いと思います。私の 娘 と結婚してくださいま

　せんか。」とお願いしました。でも、太陽は「私よりもっと強い男がいま

　すよ。②それは雲さんです。雲さんは私をかくすことができるんです。」と

　言いました。

　　③その時、雲が太陽の前に来て、空が暗くなりました。お父さんネズミ

15　は今度は雲に「雲さん、あなたは太陽さんより強いですね。娘のチュー

　子と結婚してくれませんか。」と聞きましたが、雲は「僕より風さんのほ

　うがもっと強いですよ。」と答えました。④その時、風がふいてきて、雲を

　飛ばしました。

　　お父さんネズミは⑤それを見て、今度は風に「風さん、娘のチュー子と

20　結婚してください。」と言いました。でも、風は「僕よりかべさんのほう

　が強いですよ。かべさんは僕を止めることができますから。」と言いました。

　　お父さんネズミは家に帰って少し 考 えて、今度はかべに会いに行きま

　した。そして、「かべさん、私はあなたが世界で一番強いと思います。娘

　のチュー子と結婚してくれませんか。」とお願いしました。でも、かべは

25　言いました。「僕は一番強くないですよ。僕はネズミさんより弱いです。」

　「え、どうしてですか。」「ネズミさんは　　　　　　からです。」

　　⑥その答えを聞いて、お父さんネズミは「そうですか。ネズミが世界で

　一番強いんですね。分かりました！」と言いました。

　　しばらくして、チュー子は若くて 頭 がいいネズミと結婚しました。そ

30　して、幸せになりました。めでたし、めでたし。

昔、ある 所 に：
once upon a time
(lit. long ago, in a
certain place)

一人娘：
only daughter

相手：partner
断 る：to refuse

まず：first

男：male

かくす：to hide

ふいてくる：
to blow toward
(the cloud)

飛ばす：
to blow away

止める：to block

しばらくして：
after a while
めでたしめでたし：
[set phrase for the
happy ending of a
story]

1) What do the そ-words（①〜⑥）in the passage refer to? Underline the words or sentences and draw arrows to connect them with the そ-words which refer to them.

2) Put the story in proper chronological order. Indicate the order by writing numbers in ( ) below each picture.

a. (　　)

b. (　　)

c. (　　)

d. (　　)

e. (　　)

f. (　　)

3) Answer the following questions in Japanese.

（1）チュー子はどんなネズミですか。

（2）お父さんネズミはどうして太陽が世界で一番強いと思いましたか。

（3）チュー子はどうしてネズミと結婚しましたか。

4) What do you think かべ said to お父さんネズミ in l.26 to answer his question? Write your own answer that fits in ☐ in the space provided below.

かべは「ネズミさんは_____からです。」と答えました。

- -

かくれんしゅう　*Writing Practice*

Write your own story answering the question: ○○の中で、だれが一番○○ですか.

- -

ききましょう

Listening in noisy environments (2)

As you practiced in the previous lesson, you will sometimes need to participate in conversations in noisy surroundings. In this lesson, you will get more practice listening in noisy environments, so try to use the strategies you've learned so far (predicting, listening for keywords, etc.).

1 **Pre-listening activity:**

1) Look at the picture on the right. It is 6PM on Saturday, and Miyata-san and Sakamoto-san have just finished watching a movie together and are talking in front of the movie theater. Given that context, guess what they might do next and what they might talk about.

🔊 L10-22

2) Listen to the conversation between Miyata-san and Sakamoto-san in front of the movie theater. How close was your prediction to what the two of them actually said? What was the same as your prediction? What was different?

🔊 L10-23

2 **Listening:** Listen to the conversation between Miyata-san and Sakamoto-san and answer questions 1)-5). Take notes and respond to each of the questions by writing your answer in either your language or in Japanese, or by choosing the appropriate answer from the options provided below. Note that all questions about this conversation (and answer options, if applicable) will be read aloud and interspersed in the dialogue.

スパイス：spice

1) a.　　　b.　　　c.

2) Answer: _____; My prediction was: correct / incorrect.

3) Sakamoto-san will. / Sakamoto-san will not.

4) Yes / No; My prediction was: correct / incorrect.

5) a.　　　b.　　　c.

Exit Check ☑

Now it's time to go back to the **DEKIRU List** for this chapter (p.335) and do the exit check to see what new things you can do now that you've completed the lesson.

Unit3 チャレンジ

1 Show your talent

Do you have any talents other people don't know about (e.g., playing a musical instrument, singing, speaking another foreign language, dancing)? Share a video of your hidden talent online with your classmates and comment on each other's videos in Japanese as well.

Ex. とても上手だね！

この歌、私にも教えてくれない？

私もおどってみたい！

すごく楽しそう！

Lesson
10

2 TV shows

Now you may be able to understand some of what is said in Japanese TV shows, movies, etc. Search for a show or movie that is currently popular in Japan to watch online and see if there are any phrases/words/sentences that you can understand.

日本　人気がある　ドラマ

3 What is your level of Japanese?

Since this is the last chapter of *TOBIRA I*, let's see how much your Japanese skills have improved.

Step 1 First, take a look back through the exit checks for each of the lessons we've completed so far and see what you have learned to do with your Japanese skills.

Step 2 There are some international standards by which you can measure your language proficiency. Check some of these standards to see what proficiency level you would be placed at based on your current language ability, then think about what you need to do in order to move up to the next level.

* Some standards are available on the *TOBIRA* website.

Vocabulary Index

373

おぼえる [ru]	覚える	to memorize [thing を]	L6	かのじょ	彼女	girlfriend; she	L7
おもい	重い	heavy [weight]	L10	かばん		bag	L4
おもう [u]	思う	to think [sentence と]	L9	カフェ		café	L2
おもしろい		interesting; funny	L4	かぶる [u]		to put on [hat/cap を]	L6
おもちゃ		toy	L7	かべ		wall	L10
およぐ [u]	泳ぐ	to swim [place で]	L3	かみ	髪	hair	L6
おんがく	音楽	music	L1	かみ	紙	paper	L10
おんせん	温泉	hot springs	L7	かようび	火曜日	Tuesday	L2
～かい	～階	[counter for floors]	L5	からい		spicy; hot [spice level]	L9
～かい	～回	... times	L6	カラオケ		karaoke	L9
がいこく	外国	foreign country	L9	からだ	体	body	L6
がいこくご	外国語	foreign language	L8	かりる [ru]	借りる	to borrow [person に thing を]	L8
かいしゃ	会社	company	L7				
かいしゃいん	会社員	company employee; office worker	L1	かるい	軽い	light [weight]	L10
				かれ	彼	boyfriend; he	L7
かいもの	買い物	shopping	L2	かわ	川	river	L5
かう [u]	買う	to buy [thing を]	L2	かわいい		cute	L4
かう [u]	飼う	to own; to have (as a pet) [animal を]	L7	かわる [u]	変わる	to change [thing/person が]	L10
かえる [u]	帰る	to return [one's home base に]; to go home	L2	かんがえる [ru]	考える	to think; to consider [thing について]	L8
かお	顔	face	L6	かんこうする	観光する	to sightsee [place を]	L5
かかる [u]		to take [time が]; to cost [money が]	L4	かんこく	韓国	South Korea	L1
				かんじ	漢字	kanji; Chinese character	L3
かく [u]	書く	to write [thing を]	L3	がんばる [u]		to work hard; to persevere	L8
かく [u]	描く	to draw; to paint [drawing/painting/manga を]	L8	き	木	tree	L5
がくせい	学生	student	L1	きいろ	黄色	yellow [noun]	L6
～かげつ(かん)	～か月(間)	... month(s)	L6	きいろい	黄色い	yellow	L6
				きおん	気温	air temperature	L9
かじ	火事	fire [destructive (forest, building, etc.)]	L10	きく [u]	聞く	to listen to; to hear [thing を]; to ask [person に]	L2
かしゅ	歌手	singer	L10	きこえる [ru]	聞こえる	to be audible [sound/voice が]	L5
かす [u]	貸す	to lend [person に thing を]	L8				
かぜ	風	wind	L10	ギターをひく [u]		to play the guitar	L8
かぜをひく [u]		to catch a cold	L9	きたない	汚い	dirty; messy	L7
かぞく	家族	my family; family [general term]	L3	キッチン		kitchen	L5
				きっぷ		ticket	L4
かたづける [ru]		to tidy up; to put in order [place を]; to put away [thing を]	L9	きのう	昨日	yesterday	L3
				きぶん	気分	feeling; mood [physical, mental, or emotional]	L9
～がつ	～月	... month	L3	きぶんがいい	気分がいい	to feel well; to be in a good mood	L9
～がっき	～学期	... semester	L9				
かっこいい		cool; good-looking [appearance]	L4	きぶんがわるい	気分が悪い	to feel ill; to feel down	L9
がっこう	学校	school	L2	きめる [ru]	決める	to decide [issue を]; to decide on [option に]	L10
かなしい	悲しい	sad	L7				
(お)かね	(お)金	money	L4	きもの	着物	kimono [traditional Japanese clothing]	L7

Vocabulary Index

375

さかな	魚	fish	L3
さくぶん	作文	composition; essay	L8
（お）さけ	（お）酒	alcohol; Japanese sake	L3
さっか	作家	novelist; writer (of a book, playwright, etc.)	L10
さびしい		lonely	L9
さむい	寒い	cold [air temperature]	L4
（お）さら	（お）皿	dish; plate	L8
サラダ		salad	L3
さん	三	three	L1
さんがつ	三月	March	L3
ざんねん（な）	残念	unfortunate; regrettable; disappointing	L5
さんねんせい	三年生	third-year student; junior	L1
さんぽする	散歩する	to take a walk [place を]	L6
じ	字	character; letter	L10
～じ	～時	... o'clock	L2
しあい	試合	game; match [competition]	L5
しあわせ（な）	幸せ	happy	L10
ジーンズ		jeans	L6
しがつ	四月	April	L3
じかん	時間	time	L5
～じかん	～時間	... hour(s)	L4
しけん	試験	test; exam	L7
しごと	仕事	job; work	L1
じしょ	辞書	dictionary	L4
じしん	地震	earthquake	L10
しずか（な）	静か	quiet	L4
した	下	under; below [thing の]	L5
しちがつ	七月	July	L3
じつは	実は	to tell the truth; actually	L9
しつもんする	質問する	to ask a question [person に]	L6
しつれいします	失礼します	Excuse me. [when entering/ leaving someone's office]	L8
じてんしゃ	自転車	bicycle; bike	L3
しぬ [u]	死ぬ	to die	L6
ジム		gym	L2
じゃ		well; if that's the case	L2
しゃしんをとる [u]	写真をとる	to take a picture	L3
しゃちょう	社長	company president; CEO	L10
シャワーをあびる [ru]	シャワーを浴びる	to take a shower	L3
じゅう	十	ten	L1
じゅういちがつ	十一月	November	L3
じゅうがつ	十月	October	L3
しゅうかん	習慣	custom; habit	L7
～しゅう（かん）	～週間	... week(s)	L6
しゅうきょう	宗教	religion	L8
じゅうにがつ	十二月	December	L3
しゅうまつ	週末	weekend	L2
じゅぎょう	授業	class	L7
じゅぎょうりょう	授業料	tuition	L10
しゅくだい	宿題	homework	L1
しゅっしん	出身	one's place of origin (hometown, home country, etc.)	L1
しゅみ	趣味	hobby	L1
じゅんびする	準備する	to prepare [thing を]	L10
しょうかいする	紹介する	to introduce [person A に person B/thing を]	L8
しょうがくきん	奨学金	scholarship	L8
（お）しょうがつ	（お）正月	New Year's (holiday)	L7
じょうず（な）	上手	to be good at [speaker's objective judgement]	L8
しょうらい	将来	(one's) future	L10
ジョギング		jogging	L1
しょくどう	食堂	cafeteria; dinining hall	L2
しょどう	書道	(the Japanese art of) calligraphy	L8
しらべる [ru]	調べる	to look up; to look into [thing を/について]	L8
しる [u]	知る	to get to know; to learn of [thing/person を]	L6
しろ	白	white [noun]	L6
しろい	白い	white	L6
～じん	～人	... person/people [nationality]	L1
じんじゃ	神社	(Shinto) shrine	L5
しんせつ（な）	親切	kind [does good deeds]	L7
しんぶん	新聞	newspaper	L9
すいえい	水泳	swimming	L10
すいせんじょう	推薦状	recommendation letter	L8
すいようび	水曜日	Wednesday	L2
すうがく	数学	mathematics	L1
スーパー		supermarket	L8
スカート		skirt	L6
すき（な）	好き	to like [thing/person が]	L4
すぐ（に）		at once; immediately	L10
すくない	少ない	(there are/one has) not much; little; few	L10
すごい		amazing; awesome	L7
すごく		very; really; totally	L8
すこし	少し	a few; a little	L8

376

（お）すし		sushi	L3	そうですか		I see. [with falling intonation]	L1
すずしい		cool [air temperature]	L9	そこ		that place; there	L5
すてる [ru]	捨てる	to throw away [thing を]	L9	そして		and (then); also	L3
スニーカー		sneakers; athletic shoes	L7	そと	外	outside [thing の]	L5
スポーツ		sports	L1	その Noun		that Noun	L4
スポーツせんしゅ	スポーツ選手	athlete	L10	そふ	祖父	my grandfather	L3
スマホ		smartphone	L1	ソファ		sofa; couch	L5
すむ [u]	住む	to take up residence (in) [place に]	L6	そぼ	祖母	my grandmother	L3
する [irr.]		to do [thing を]; to put on (a tie, an accessory, etc.) [thing を]	L2, L6	そら	空	sky	L10
				それ		that (one)	L4
				それから		and (then); in addition	L2
すわる [u]	座る	to sit down [place に]	L6	**た** だいがく	大学	university; college	L1
せ せいかつ	生活	daily life; lifestyle	L9	だいがくいん	大学院	graduate school	L1
せいじ	政治	politics	L1	だいがくいんせい	大学院生	graduate student	L1
せいせき	成績	grade (on a test, etc.)	L10	だいがくせい	大学生	university student; college student	L1
セーター		sweater	L6				
せかい	世界	world	L7	だいじょうぶ（な）		all right; okay; safe	L9
せがたかい	背が高い	tall [stature]	L6	だいすき（な）	大好き	to like a lot; to love [thing/person が]	L4
せがひくい	背が低い	short [stature]	L6				
せき	席	seat	L10	たいせつ（な）	大切	important; precious	L10
ぜひ		by all means	L3	たいてい		usually; generally; almost always	L4
せまい		narrow; small [space]; cramped	L10				
				たいふう	台風	typhoon	L9
ぜろ／ゼロ		zero	L1	たいへん（な）	大変	tough [situation]	L4
せん	千	thousand	L4	たいよう	太陽	sun	L10
せんがっき	先学期	last semester	L9	たかい	高い	high; expensive	L4
せんげつ	先月	last month	L3	だから		therefore; so	L2
せんこう	専攻	major [field of study]	L1	たくさん		many; a lot	L2
せんこうする	専攻する	to major (in) [subject を]	L8	タクシー		taxi	L4
～せんしゅ	～選手	... player; athlete who does ...	L10	～だけ		only ...	L6
				だす [u]	出す	to submit; to turn in [thing を]; to take out [thing を]	L6
せんしゅう	先週	last week	L3				
せんせい	先生	teacher	L1	たすける [ru]	助ける	to save (from a tough situation); to help (out of a tough situation) [person を]	L10
ぜんぜん [+ negative]	全然	(not) ... at all; never	L2				
せんたくする		to do the laundry; to wash (in the laundry) [thing を]	L3	たつ [u]	立つ	to stand (up)	L6
				たてもの	建物	building	L5
ぜんぶ	全部	all	L5	たのしい	楽しい	fun	L4
ぜんぶで	全部で	in total; in all	L5	たばこ／タバコ をすう [u]	吸う	to smoke (cigarettes)	L8
そ そうじする		to clean [place を]	L3				
そうしましょう		Let's do that; Let's do so.	L3	たぶん	多分	maybe; probably	L6
そうだんが ある [u]	相談が ある	to have something one wants to ask for advice on	L8	たべもの	食べ物	food	L3
				たべる [ru]	食べる	to eat [thing を]	L2
そうだんする	相談する	to consult [person に thing について]	L8	だめ（な）		no good	L10
				だれ	誰	who	L1
そうです		That's right; It is so.	L1	だれか	誰か	someone; anyone [in question]	L7

だれとも／ だれにも [+ negative]	誰とも／ 誰にも	not ... with/to anyone	L7
だれの Noun	誰の	whose Noun	L4
だれも [+ negative]	誰も	nobody; not ... anyone	L7
たんご	単語	vocabulary; word	L3
たんじょうび	誕生日	birthday	L5
ダンス		dance	L1
ち ちいさい	小さい	small	L4
ちか	地下	basement; underground	L5
ちかい	近い	near; nearby; close	L8
ちかく	近く	near; nearby [thing/person の]	L5
ちかてつ	地下鉄	subway	L4
チケット		ticket	L4
ちち	父	my father	L3
ちゃいろ	茶色	brown [noun]	L6
ちゃいろい	茶色い	brown	L6
ちゅうごく	中国	China	L1
チョコレート／チョコ		chocolate	L7
ちょっと		a little	L2
つ ～つ		[general counter for things without a specific counter]	L4
ついたち	一日	the first day of the month	L5
つかう [u]	使う	to use [thing を]	L7
つかれる [ru]		to get tired	L9
つくえ	机	desk	L5
つくる [u]	作る	to make [thing を]	L3
つまらない		boring	L4
つめたい	冷たい	cold [to the touch; person]	L9
つよい	強い	strong	L10
つれていく [u]	連れて いく	to take [place に person を]	L8
つれてくる [irr.]	連れて くる	to bring [place に person を]	L8
て て	手	hand	L4
Ｔシャツ／ティーシャツ		T-shirt	L4
デートする		to go out on a date [person と]	L3
テーブル		table	L5
でかける [ru]	出かける	to go out [place/activity に]	L8
てがみ	手紙	letter [correspondence]	L3
てつだう [u]	手伝う	to help [person を]; to help with [(person の) task を]	L6
てぶくろ	手ぶくろ	gloves	L7
でも		however; but	L2
（お）てら	（お）寺	(Buddhist) temple	L5
テレビ		TV	L2
てんき	天気	weather	L9
てんきよほう	天気予報	weather forecast	L9
でんしゃ	電車	train	L4
でんわ	電話	phone	L1
でんわ（を）する	電話（を） する	to make a phone call [person/place に]	L8
でんわばんごう	電話番号	phone number	L1
と ～ど	～度	... degrees [temperature]	L9
ドア		door	L5
トイレ		bathroom; restroom; toilet	L5
どう		how; how about	L4
どうして		why	L7
どうしたんですか		What happened?; What's wrong?; What's going on?	L9
どうぶつ	動物	animal	L7
どうやって		how; in what way; by what means	L4
とおか	十日	the tenth day	L5
とかい	都会	city; urban area	L10
ときどき	時々	sometimes	L2
とくい（な）	得意	to be confident in; to be good at [subjective]	L8
とけい	時計	watch; clock	L4
どこ		where	L1
どこか		somewhere; anywhere [in question]	L7
どこにも [+ negative]		not ... anywhere	L7
ところ	所	place	L5
としょかん	図書館	library	L2
どちら		which (of two)	L10
どちらも		both	L10
どっち		which (of two) [casual]	L10
どっちも		both [casual]	L10
とても		very	L4
となり		next to [thing/person の]	L5
どの Noun		which Noun	L4
どのくらい／どのぐらい		how far [distance]; how long [time]; how many; how much	L4
とまる [u]	泊まる	to stay at (a hotel, etc.) [place に]	L7
ともだち	友達	friend	L1
どようび	土曜日	Saturday	L2
とり	鳥	bird	L5

とる [u]	取る	to take [*thing* を]	L8
～ドル		dollar	L4
どれ		which (one)	L4
どんな Noun		what kind of Noun	L4

な

なか	中	inside [*thing* の]	L5
ながい	長い	long [length]	L6
なかがいい	仲がいい	to get along; to be close; to be on good terms	L9
なかがわるい	仲が悪い	to be on bad terms	L9
なく [u]	泣く	to cry	L9
なつ	夏	summer	L9
なつやすみ	夏休み	summer vacation/break/holiday	L3
なな／しち	七	seven	L1
なに／なん	何	what	L1
なにいろ	何色	what color	L6
なにか	何か	something; anything [in question]	L7
なにで／なんで	何で	how; by what means	L4
なにも [+ negative]	何も	nothing; not ... anything	L7
なのか	七日	the seventh day	L5
（お）なまえ	（お）名前	name	L1
ならう [u]	習う	to learn [*thing* を]	L7
なる [u]		to become [*thing* に]	L10
なんかい	何階	what floor	L5
なんかい	何回	how many times	L6
なんがつ	何月	what month	L3
なんさい	何才／何歳	how old	L1
なんじ	何時	what time	L2
なんじかん	何時間	how many hours	L4
なんど	何度	what temperature; how many degrees	L9
なんにち	何日	what day of the month	L5
なんにん	何人	how many people	L3
なんねん	何年	what year	L5
なんねんせい	何年生	what year in school	L1
なんばん	何番	what number	L1
なんびき	何びき	how many (small animals)	L5
なんぷん	何分	how many minutes	L4
なんまい	何枚	how many (flat objects)	L5
なんようび	何曜日	what day of the week	L2

に

に	二	two	L1
にがつ	二月	February	L3
にがて（な）	苦手	not to be confident in; not to be good at [subjective]	L8

にぎやか（な）		lively; busy [place]; boisterous [person]	L4
にく	肉	meat	L3
Noun にする		to decide on Noun	L4
～にち	～日	[counter for days of the month]	L5
～にち（かん）	～日（間）	... day(s)	L6
にちようび	日曜日	Sunday	L2
Noun について		about Noun	L8
にねんせい	二年生	second-year student; sophomore	L1
にほん	日本	Japan	L1
にほんご	日本語	Japanese language	L1
にほんじん	日本人	Japanese person/people	L1
ニュース		news	L2
～にん	～人	[counter for people]	L3
にんきがある [u]	人気がある	to be popular	L5

ぬ

| ぬいぐるみ | | stuffed animal | L7 |

ね

ネクタイ		(neck)tie	L6
ネコ		cat	L3
ネズミ		mouse; rat	L10
ねつがある [u]	熱がある	to have a fever	L9
ねむい		sleepy	L9
ねる [ru]	寝る	to sleep; to go to bed	L2
～ねん	～年	the year...	L5
～ねん（かん）	～年（間）	... year(s)	L6
～ねんせい	～年生	...-year student [grade in school]	L1

の

Noun のあとで	～の後で	after Noun	L2
ノート		notebook	L4
のどがかわく [u]		to get thirsty	L9
Noun のとき	～の時	at the time of Noun; when (someone) was Noun	L3
のぼる [u]	登る	to climb [*mountain* に/を]	L7
Noun のまえに	～の前に	before Noun	L7
のみもの	飲み物	drink; beverage	L3
のむ [u]	飲む	to drink [*thing* を]	L2
のる [u]	乗る	to get on; to ride [*transportation/thing* に]	L3

は

は	歯	tooth	L9
パーティー		party	L2
はい		yes	L1
バイオリンをひく [u]		to play the violin	L8
バイク		motorcycle	L10
はいゆう	俳優	actor	L10
はいる [u]	入る	to enter [*place* に]	L3

はく [u]		to put on (clothes below the waist; shoes) [*clothes* を]	L6
（お）はし	（お）箸	chopsticks	L4
はじめる [ru]	始める	to start; to begin [*thing* を]	L8
バス		bus	L4
バスてい	バス停	bus stop	L4
パソコン		personal computer; PC	L6
はたち	二十才／二十歳	twenty years old	L1
はたらく [u]	働く	to work [*place* で]	L6
はち	八	eight	L1
はちがつ	八月	August	L3
はつか	二十日	the twentieth day	L5
バッグ		bag	L4
はな	花	flower	L5
はな	鼻	nose	L6
はなし	話	story	L6
はなす [u]	話す	to speak [*language* を]	L3
はなび	花火	fireworks	L10
はなや	花屋	flower shop	L5
はは	母	my mother	L3
はやい	速い／早い	fast; quick; early	L10
はる	春	spring	L9
はれ	晴れ	sunny (weather)	L9
はれる [ru]	晴れる	to clear up; to become sunny (weather)	L9
バレンタインデー		Valentine's Day	L7
ハロウィン		Halloween	L7
はをみがく [u]	歯をみがく	to brush one's teeth	L6
～はん	～半	half (past)	L2
ばん	晩	night; evening	L3
～ばん	～番	number ...	L1
パン		bread	L3
ばんごう	番号	number	L1
ばんごはん	晩ご飯	dinner; supper	L2
ひ ひ	日	day	L7
ピアノをひく [u]		to play the piano	L8
ビール		beer	L3
～ひき		[counter for small animals/insects]	L5
ひく [u]		to play (musical instruments) [*keyboard/stringed instrument* を]	L8
ひこうき	飛行機	airplane	L4
ピザ		pizza	L3

（お）ひさしぶりです	（お）久しぶりです	Long time no see; It's been a while.	L8
びじゅつ	美術	art	L1
びじゅつかん	美術館	art museum	L5
ひだり	左	left [*thing/person* の]	L5
ひっこし（を）する	引っ越し（を）する	to move to [*place* に] [changing residence]	L7
ひと	人	person	L3
ひとつ	一つ	one; one object	L4
ひとり	一人	one person	L3
ひとりっこ	一人っ子	only child	L3
ひとりで	一人で	alone; by oneself	L3
ひま（な）		to have spare time; to be free; not busy	L8
ひゃく	百	hundred	L4
びょういん	病院	hospital	L5
びょうき	病気	sick(ness); ill(ness); disease	L9
ひる	昼	daytime; midday	L2
ひるごはん	昼ご飯	lunch	L2
ひろい	広い	wide; spacious; roomy	L10
ふ ～ぶ	～部	... club	L10
ふく	服	clothes	L6
ふく [u]		to blow; to play (musical instruments) [*wind instrument* を]	L8
ふたつ	二つ	two; two objects	L4
ふたり	二人	two people	L3
ふつか	二日	the second day	L5
ふとる [u]	太る	to gain weight	L6
ふね	船	boat; ship	L10
ふゆ	冬	winter	L9
フランス		France	L1
ふるい	古い	old [thing; not used for people]	L4
フルートをふく [u]		to play the flute	L8
プレゼント		present; gift	L7
～ふん	～分	... minute(s)	L4
ぶんか	文化	culture	L8
ぶんがく	文学	literature	L8
ぶんぽう	文法	grammar	L8
へ へた（な）	下手	to be bad at; not to be good at [speaker's objective judgement]	L8
ベッド		bed	L5
ペット		pet	L3
へや	部屋	room	L2

	やすむ [u]	休む	to be absent (from) [job/class を]; to (take a) rest	L9
	やせる [ru]		to lose weight	L6
	やちん	家賃	rent [money for rented living space]	L10
	やま	山	mountain	L5
ゆ	ゆうびんきょく	郵便局	post office	L5
	ゆうめい（な）	有名	famous	L4
	ゆき	雪	snow	L9
	ゆっくり		slowly; in a relaxed fashion	L9
	ゆびわ		ring [jewelry worn on fingers]	L7
	ゆめ	夢	dream	L7
よ	ようか	八日	the eighth day	L5
	～ようび	～曜日	...day	L2
	よかったら		if you like; if possible	L5
	よく		often; well	L2, L10
	よこ	横	beside [things/person の]	L5
	よっか	四日	the fourth day	L5
	よてい	予定	schedule; plan	L8
	よねんせい	四年生	fourth-year student; senior	L1
	よむ [u]	読む	to read [thing を]	L2
	よる	夜	night; evening	L2
	よるおそく	夜遅く	late at night	L8
	よわい	弱い	weak	L10
	よん／し	四	four	L1
ら	らいがっき	来学期	next semester	L9
	らいげつ	来月	next month	L5
	らいしゅう	来週	next week	L2
	らいねん	来年	next year	L7
り	リビング		living room	L5
	りゅうがくする	留学する	to study abroad [place に]	L8
	りゅうがくせい	留学生	international student	L1
	りょう	寮	dormitory	L2
	りょうしん	両親	my parents	L3
	りょうりする	料理する	to cook [thing を]	L3
	りょかん	旅館	traditional Japanese inn	L7
	りょこうする	旅行する	to travel to [place に]; to travel in/around [place を]	L3
れ	れいど	0度	zero degrees	L9
	れきし	歴史	history	L8
	レストラン		restaurant	L2
	れんしゅうする	練習する	to practice [thing を]	L6
ろ	ろく	六	six	L1
	ろくがつ	六月	June	L3

わ	わかい	若い	young	L10
	わかる [u]	分かる	to understand [thing が]	L8
	わかれる [ru]	別れる	to break up; to part ways [person と]	L9
	わすれる [ru]	忘れる	to forget [thing を]; to leave behind [place に thing を]	L8
	わたし	私	I	L1
	わらう [u]	笑う	to laugh; to smile	L9
	わるい	悪い	bad	L9
	X は Y がすきです	～が好きです	X likes Y.	L1
	X は Y がだいすきです	～が大好きです	X likes Y a lot; X loves Y.	L1
	Noun はちょっと…		I don't particulary care for Noun; Noun isn't good for me. [indirect rejection]; Noun is a little (inconvenient for me). [used to reject a suggestion or invitation indirectly].	L2, L3
	Noun はどうですか		How about Noun?	L3
	Topic はなにがすきですか	～は何が好きですか	When it comes to [the topic], what do you like?	L2

著者紹介

※以下アルファベット順

■ 岡 まゆみ（おか まゆみ）• Mayumi Oka ［編著］

現職　ミシガン大学日本研究センター研究員
　　　ミドルベリー日本語学校日本語大学院プログラム講師
教歴　ミシガン大学アジア言語文化学科日本語学課長
　　　プリンストン大学専任講師, コロンビア大学専任講師, 上智大学講師
著書　『中上級者のための速読の日本語第2版』(2013);
　　　『マルチメディア日本語基本文法ワークブック』共著 (2018)(以上、ジャパンタイムズ出版);『上級へのとびら』(2009);『きたえよう漢字力』(2010);『中級日本語を教える教師の手引き』(2011);『これで身につく文法力』(2012);『日英共通メタファー辞典』(2017)(以上共著、くろしお出版);その他
その他　全米日本語教師学会理事(2007-2010)
　　　ミシガン大学 Matthews Underclass Teaching Award(2019)

■ 近藤 純子（こんどう じゅんこ）• Junko Kondo ［編著］

現職　ミシガン大学アジア言語文化学科専任講師
教歴　マドンナ大学講師
著書　『上級へのとびら』(2009);『きたえよう漢字力』(2010);『中級日本語を教える教師の手引き』(2011);『これで身につく文法力』(2012)(以上共著、くろしお出版)

■ 筒井 通雄（つつい みちお）• Michio Tsutsui ［文法解説］

現職　ワシントン大学人間中心設計工学科名誉教授
教歴　コロンビア大学日本語教育夏期修士プログラム講師, ワシントン大学教授, マサチューセッツ工科大学助教授, カリフォルニア大学デービス校客員助教授
著書　『日本語基本文法辞典』(1986);『日本語文法辞典〈中級編〉』(1995);『日本語文法辞典〈上級編〉』(2008);『マルチメディア日本語基本文法ワークブック』(2018)(以上共著、ジャパンタイムズ出版);『上級へのとびら』(2009);『きたえよう漢字力』(2010);『中級日本語を教える教師の手引き』(2011);『これで身につく文法力』(2012)(以上共著、くろしお出版);その他
その他　全米日本語教師学会理事 (1990-1993, 2009-2012)

■ 森 祐太（もり ゆうた）• Yuta Mori

現職　ライデン大学地域研究科講師及び、国際学科日本語プログラムコーディネーター
教歴　ミシガン大学専任講師, ハーバード大学専任講師, ミドルベリー大学夏期日本語学校講師

■ 奥野 智子（おくの ともこ）• Tomoko Okuno

現職　ミシガン大学レジデンシャルカレッジ日本語プログラムコーディネーター
教歴　ミシガン州立大学専任講師, 北海道国際交流センター日本語日本文化講座夏期セミナー講師, 金沢工業大学夏期日本語教育プログラム講師

■ 榊原 芳美（さかきばら よしみ）• Yoshimi Sakakibara

現職　ミシガン大学アジア言語文化学科専任講師
教歴　ミシガン州立大学専任講師, 北海道国際交流センター日本語日本文化講座夏期セミナー講師
著書　『マルチメディア日本語基本文法ワークブック』共著 (2018)(ジャパンタイムズ出版)

■ 曽我部 絢香（そがべ あやか）• Ayaka Sogabe

現職　ミシガン大学アジア言語文化学科専任講師
教歴　バンダービルト大学専任講師, ミドルベリー大学夏期日本語学校講師

■ 安田 昌江（やすだ まさえ）• Masae Yasuda

現職　ミシガン大学アジア言語文化学科専任講師
教歴　オークランド大学特別講師

制作協力

■ 反転授業用動画作成、英語校閲・校正・監修

クリストファー・シャード（Christopher Schad）

現職 ミシガン大学アジア言語文化学科専任講師

教歴 プリンストン大学専任講師, スワスモア大学講師,
　　　ミドルベリー大学夏期日本語学校講師

■ 校正・英語校正

平川ワイター永子（Eiko Hirakawa Weyter）

現職 フリーランス日本語教師

教歴 ミシガン大学専任講師, パデュー大学専任講師

■ イラスト

坂木浩子

村山宇希

■ 装丁・本文デザイン

鈴木章宏

■ 音声録音協力

まつむら りょう

幸

ジェニファー・クリスト

■ 編集

市川麻里子

金髙浩子

■ 写真・画像提供
青森県立美術館
アフロ
大江戸温泉物語ホテルズ＆リゾーツ株式会社
株式会社北村サンプル
株式会社 TOKYO TOWER
鎌倉市観光協会
鎌倉 長谷寺
清水寺
京福電気鉄道株式会社
公益社団法人青森観光コンベンション協会
合資会社海地獄
国営沖縄記念公園（海洋博公園）・沖縄美ら海水族館
さっぽろ観光写真ライブラリー
写真 AC
ジョイパックレジャー株式会社
浅草寺
鶴岡八幡宮
とくしまフォトギャラリー
日本相撲協会
ひろしま観光ナビ
ベネッセアートサイト直島
GAHAG
iStock
photolibrary
pixabay

■ 転載協力
一般財団法人奈良美智財団
株式会社草間彌生
株式会社扶桑社
鎌倉小町商店会
鎌倉大仏殿高徳院
京都錦市場商店街
竹浪比呂央ねぶた研究所
有限会社山川牧場自然牛乳

■ 出典
児玉幸多（編）（1978）『くずし字解読辞典 机上版』東京堂出版
株式会社フルタイム

初級日本語 **とびらⅠ**

TOBIRA Ⅰ : Beginning Japanese

2021年 7月 4日　第1刷発行
2021年11月18日　第2刷発行

著 者　岡まゆみ・近藤純子・筒井通雄・森祐太・奥野智子・榊原芳美・曽我部絢香・安田昌江

発行人　岡野秀夫

発行所　くろしお出版

〒102-0084　東京都千代田区二番町4-3

Tel: 03-6261-2867　　Fax: 03-6261-2879

URL: https://www.9640.jp　Email: kurosio@9640.jp

印 刷　シナノ印刷

© 2021 Mayumi Oka, Junko Kondo, Michio Tsutsui, Yuta Mori, Tomoko Okuno, Yoshimi Sakakibara, Ayaka Sogabe, Masae Yasuda
Printed in Japan
ISBN978-4-87424-870-6 C0081

Conjugation Tables

A-1. *U*-verbs

Plain neg.		言(い)わ 持(も)た 帰(かえ)ら¹	飲(の)ま 遊(あそ)ば 死(し)な	話(はな)さ	聞(き)か	泳(およ)が	ない
	Non-past						ない
	Past						なかった
Masu-form	Non-past Aff.	言(い)い 持(も)ち 帰(かえ)り	飲(の)み 遊(あそ)び 死(し)に	話(はな)し	聞(き)き	泳(およ)ぎ	ます
	Non-past Neg.						ません
	Past Aff.						ました
	Past Neg.						ませんでした
Plain non-past affirmative (=Dictionary form)		言(い)う 持(も)つ 帰(かえ)る	飲(の)む 遊(あそ)ぶ 死(し)ぬ	話(はな)す	聞(き)く	泳(およ)ぐ	1. The plain non-past and past negative forms of ある are ない and なかった respectively.
Te-form		言(い)って 持(も)って 帰(かえ)って	飲(の)んで 遊(あそ)んで 死(し)んで	話(はな)して	聞(き)いて²	泳(およ)いで	2. The *te*-form and plain past form of 行(い)く are 行って and 行(い)った, respectively.
Plain past affirmative		言(い)った 持(も)った 帰(かえ)った	飲(の)んだ 遊(あそ)んだ 死(し)んだ	話(はな)した	聞(き)いた²	泳(およ)いだ	

A-2. *Ru*-verbs and irregular verbs

		Ru-verbs	Irregular verbs		
Plain neg.	Non-past	見(み) 食(た)べ	来(こ)	し	ない
	Past				なかった
Masu-form	Non-past Aff.	見(み) 食(た)べ	来(き)	し	ます
	Non-past Neg.				ません
	Past Aff.				ました
	Past Neg.				ませんでした
Plain non-past affirmative (=Dictionary form)		見(み) 食(た)べ	来(く)	す	る
Te-form		見(み) 食(た)べ	来(き)	し	て
Plain past affirmative		見(み) 食(た)べ	来(き)	し	た